Christ Died for Our Sins

Christ Died for Our Sins

Representation and Substitution in Romans and Their Jewish Martyrological Background

Jarvis J. Williams

☙PICKWICK *Publications* · Eugene, Oregon

CHRIST DIED FOR OUR SINS
Representation and Substitution in Romans and Their Jewish Martyrological Background

Copyright © 2015 Jarvis J. Williams. All rights reserved. Except for brief quotations in critical publications or reviews, no part of this book may be reproduced in any manner without prior written permission from the publisher. Write: Permissions, Wipf and Stock Publishers, 199 W. 8th Ave., Suite 3, Eugene, OR 97401.

Pickwick Publications
An Imprint of Wipf and Stock Publishers
199 W. 8th Ave., Suite 3
Eugene, OR 97401

www.wipfandstock.com

ISBN 13: 978-1-60899-436-6

Cataloguing-in-Publication Data

Williams, Jarvis J.

   Christ died for our sins : representation and substitution in Romans and their Jewish martyrological background

   xxiv + 222 p. ; 23 cm. Includes bibliographical references and indices.

   ISBN 13: 978-1-60899-436-6

   1. Paul, the Apostle, Saint—Theology. 2. Jesus Christ—Crucifixion. 3. Bible. Romans—Criticism, interpretation, etc. 4. Death—Religious aspects. 5. Martyrdom. 6. Atonement—Biblical teaching. 7. Bible. Apocrypha. Maccabees. I. Title.

BS2655.A7 W555 2015

Manufactured in the U.S.A.   05/18/2015

For Tom Schreiner, my *Doctorvater*, mentor, and friend, because of his willingness to speak the truth to me in love and because of his love for the cross of Jesus Christ!

Contents

Preface | ix
Abbreviations | xvii

1 Thesis and History of Research | 1
2 Representation and Substitution in the Hebrew Cult and in Isaiah 53 | 35
3 Representation and Substitution in Second Temple Jewish Martyrologies | 74
4 Jewish Martyrology and Substitution in Romans 3:21—4:25 | 105
5 Jewish Martyrology and Substitution in Romans 5:6–11, 8:1–4, and 8:31–34 | 141
6 Jewish Martyrology and Representation in Romans 5:12—6:23 | 171
7 Conclusion | 184

Bibliography | 189
Ancient Documents Index | 199

Preface

In 2010, I published *Maccabean Martyr Traditions in Paul's Theology of Atonement: Did Martyr Theology Shape Paul's Conception of Jesus' Death?*[1] I argued that Paul's presentation of Jesus' death should be understood as an atoning sacrifice and as a saving event because Maccabean martyr theology shaped his understanding of Jesus' death.[2] The book has five chapters, but the central exegetical section is chapters 2–4. Chapter 2 investigated martyrdom in 2 and 4 Maccabees. Chapter 3 investigated martyrdom in the Hebrew Bible by analyzing selected texts that mention human sacrifice. Chapter 4 investigated martyrdom in selected letters that bear Paul's name. I focused much of my investigation on Rom 3:25 and 4 Macc 17:22 because these two texts are the only places in any extant literature where an author applies ἱλαστήριον to the deaths of Torah-observant Jews for the soteriological benefits of non-Torah-observant sinners.

Several factors, however, warrant my current and related project. First, the present monograph focuses on representation and substitution exclusively in Romans and the Jewish martyrological background behind these concepts in Romans.

Second, many years have passed since I completed and successfully defended the original doctoral thesis in 2007 at the Southern Baptist Theological Seminary and since I published it in 2010. From 2007 to the present, I have spent much time reflecting upon the origins of Paul's understanding of Jesus' death, upon the impact of his Damascus Road encounter with the risen Christ, upon his presentation of Jesus' death, and upon the available

---

1. Throughout the monograph, I will use the phrases "martyr theology," "martyr traditions," "martyrological," "Jewish martyrological narratives," or "martyr texts" to refer to 2 and 4 Maccabees and to other Second Temple Jewish texts that contain the concepts of pious, Torah-observant Jews who died for the soteriological benefits of non-Torah-observant Jews. For a working definition of Jewish martyrology, see Van Henten, *The Maccabean Martyrs as Saviours of the Jewish People*.

2. Williams, *Maccabean Martyr Traditions*, 2.

first-century cultic, economic, and social categories, concepts, and traditions from which he readily borrowed to present his understanding of the meaning and significance of Jesus' death for others.

Third, since the publication of my 2007 doctoral thesis in 2010, I have given numerous lectures in both university and seminary contexts about atonement and soteriology in Second Temple Judaism and about Jesus' death in Paul. I have also presented numerous papers at the Society of Biblical Literature (SBL) along with or in the presence of experts in Pauline theology, experts in Romans and Galatians, experts in Second Temple Judaism, and experts in early Christian origins. These diverse groups at SBL have provided me some new conversation partners regarding the origins of Paul's understanding and presentation of Jesus' death in Romans, conversation partners whose work I had only read but with whom I had not interacted face to face when I wrote the original doctoral thesis. Additionally, I have been involved in numerous conversations and debates with significant scholars in the area of early Christian origins via email and at SBL's 2010–14 national meetings in the Function of the Apocrypha and Pseudepigrapha on early Christianity study group, in the Cult, Sacrifice, and Atonement study group, in the Pauline Epistles study group, in the so-called Disputed Pauline Epistles study group, and in the African-Americans Biblical Hermeneutics group, not to mention the numerous conversations and debates on Jesus' death in Paul with Greek text open at SBL over breakfast, lunch, dinner, or at the book exhibitions with many of the scholars with whom I was in close dialogue in my previous work and with whom I have either strongly or partially disagreed in recent publications.[3] These priceless conversation partners have provided stimulating critique of my previous work, they have provided provocative dialogue about my work, they have raised new questions in my mind, and they have made me aware of both the problems with reading Paul *exclusively* through the lens of Jewish martyr theology and with forcing one theological model of Jesus' death on Paul's letters.[4]

Instead of arguing that martyr theology *primarily* or *exclusively* shaped Paul's conception of Jesus' death by analyzing every Pauline statement that mentions Jesus' death or the benefits of his death for others—which is what

---

3. I am extremely grateful to Cilliers Breytenbach, Steve Finlan, Simon Gathercole, and Mike Gorman for individually meeting with me throughout the weekend at the 2013 national SBL meeting in Baltimore, MD. Their input and pushback have tremendously helped me to think more precisely about the best way to execute my thesis in this monograph, and their different insights helped me to see the benefit of narrowing my thesis to Romans in this monograph.

4. Daniel P. Bailey has been especially helpful in presenting challenges and pointing out some weaknesses in my thesis.

I originally wanted to argue when I first conceived of this project—I think that it is more plausible to argue that martyr theology was one tradition (among other traditions) that influenced both Paul's *conception* of and *presentation* of Jesus' death and the benefits of his death for others in his letters and that the Jewish martyrological narratives have a prominent background in Paul's presentation of Jesus' death as both a substitute for and representative of Jews and Gentiles in Romans. However, these traditions neither show up in every letter that bears his name nor are they the only background in front of which we should read Paul's presentation of Jesus' death in his letters. Since Paul often used a variety of Greco-Roman and Jewish and first-century social and economic metaphors that refer to the benefits of Jesus' death for others and since he simultaneously conflates these metaphors in his letters to present the effects of Jesus' death for others, I can plausibly argue in this monograph that martyr theology was a background behind his presentation of Jesus' death as both a substitution and representation for Jews and Gentiles in Romans, although this does not need to be the case for every Pauline letter.

This above modification from my previous work allows me to take seriously the force of Paul's Damascus Road experience in his initial encounter with Jesus, the crucified and risen Christ,[5] and the numerous additional traditions from which Paul borrowed to communicate the meaning and significance of Jesus' death for others (e.g., Jewish cultic, economic, law court).[6] Moreover, this modification also prevents me from forcing one specific background or model on Paul's other letters in which he mentions or discusses Jesus' death. Once Paul encountered Jesus—the crucified, resurrected, and exalted Lord and Messiah—on the Damascus Road, virtually everything that he had believed about YHWH, Torah, Gentiles, and the crucified criminal from Nazareth radically changed. It is reasonable that Paul believed Jesus was rightly crucified as a criminal before Damascus (per his efforts to destroy the church, as narrated in Acts and as he states in his letters). But after he encountered Jesus as the resurrected and exalted Lord, he began to reconsider and reformulate his conception of Jesus' death. In addition to the OT cultic traditions and Isaiah 53, he likely looked to additional Jewish traditions that appropriated those traditions to the deaths

---

5. So Kim, *Origins of Paul's Gospel*.

6. I am especially thankful to Steve Finlan for pointing this out to me. In both his work on the background behind Paul's cultic atonement metaphors and in a personal conversation at the national meeting of SBL 2013 in Baltimore, MD, he persuaded me that it is incorrect to limit Paul's background influences to only one. For his major work on Paul's atonement metaphors, see Stephen Finlan, *The Background and Content of Paul's Cultic Atonement Metaphors*.

of Torah-observant Jews for non-Torah-observant sinners to achieve their soteriological benefits.

For example, after he encountered Jesus on the Damascus road, he argued that if Jews compelled Gentiles to conform to a Jewish way of life, the Gentiles would be placed under the Deuteronomic curse (Gal 2:14), that "everyone who is from the works of the law is under a curse" (Gal 3:10). His conduct toward Christ-followers changed radically after his vision of Christ (cf. his treatment of Christ-followers within former conduct in Judaism).[7] He now preached the gospel of Jesus Christ, and he began to identify with a multi-ethno-racial Gentile-inclusive Christian community (Gal 1:13—2:21). Paul's soteriological framework after he saw the Damascus Road vision of Jesus was entirely different from his view of YHWH, Torah, Jesus, Gentiles, and Christ-followers prior to his faith in Jesus (cf. Deut 27:1—28:62; Acts 7:58—8:4; 9:1–2; Gal 1:13–14).

Thus, shortly after his conversion, Paul more than likely thought very carefully about scriptural concepts and metaphors in the Jewish Scriptures, in other Jewish writings, and in available oral Jewish traditions to communicate to others the significance and meaning of Jesus' death for others, since his vision of the crucified, resurrected, and exalted Lord presented him with a major soteriological problem. Namely, if Jesus is in fact the crucified, resurrected, and exalted Lord, then YHWH no longer accepts people within his believing community exclusively based on Torah observance, and he no longer provides atonement for sins by means of the Hebrew cult. Instead, Jesus—the crucified, resurrected, and exalted Lord—is the one who saves Jews and Gentiles alike, by faith.[8] Contrary to Sam K. Williams, I do not think that the tragedy of Jesus' death caused early Christians to search for its significance and meaning. Instead, the jubilation and the shock of his resurrection enabled them to think carefully about the significance and meaning of his death for others. Paul likely thought that since in fact YHWH resurrected the crucified Christ, then the reality of his resurrection must mean that his death has a specific soteriological significance, both now

---

7. I am aware of the many discussions regarding the complexities of Second Temple Judaism.

8. I affirm that Paul's letters reflect that he believed at some level the human plight needed the solution of Jesus' cross, resurrection, and exaltation. However, my point above is simply that Paul's vision of Jesus on the Damascus Road caused him to rethink and maybe even un-think some of his pre-conversion and pre-calling conceptions about the non-Torah observant and Gentile inclusive nature of the gospel of Jesus Christ. For Paul's soteriological framework as solution to plight, see E. P. Sanders, *Paul and Palestinian Judaism*. For Paul's soteriological framework as plight to solution, see Frank Thielman, *From Plight to Solution*.

and eschatologically, for Jews and Gentiles, apart from Torah-observance.[9] Paul's Damascus Road encounter with the risen Christ explains in part why both his views of the crucified Jesus and of Christians dramatically changed. He persecuted Christians prior to his vision of the risen Christ (Acts 7:58—8:3; 9:1–19).

Fourth, I published my third monograph *For Whom Did Christ Die* in 2012. In this work, I spent an entire chapter (chapter 4) defending the thesis that Paul believed that Jesus' death was *exclusively* for *all* elect Jews and Gentiles whom God predestined to be united to the believing community by faith in Jesus because martyr theology shaped his understanding of Jesus' death.

Fifth, in 2012, I published an essay in a Brill Academic volume along with an international team of biblical scholars who specialize in early Judaism, early Christian origins, or both.[10] My essay is titled "Martyr Theology in Hellenistic Judaism and Paul's Conception of Jesus' Death in Romans 3:21–26." This essay borrowed material from my 2010 work, but I presented fresh insights and new evidence that support martyr theology's influence on Paul in Rom 3:21–26. For example, I offer an up-to-date history of research in the current work, and I present additional lexical, grammatical, exegetical, and conceptual arguments to support my thesis in the current monograph.

Sixth, J. W. van Henten's critical review of my 2010 monograph in the *Review of Biblical Literature* was especially helpful to me.[11] Van Henten's review was generally positive, but he helpfully pointed out weaknesses. He noted that the monograph often made assertions without substantiating its claims, and he stated ways to make the arguments stronger.[12] This current monograph seeks to rectify a few of the weaknesses in the first monograph and to build upon my previous work by focusing on representation and substitution and by focusing on Paul's Jewish martyrological background for these categories by analyzing the relevant texts in Romans.

---

9. For the significance of the resurrection of Jesus in early Judaism and in early Christianity, see N. T. Wright, *The Resurrection of the Son of God*.

10. For the complete volume, see Porter and Pitts (eds.), *Christian Origins and Hellenistic Judaism*.

11. His review is in the *Review of Biblical Literature* January 2013 at www.bookreviews.org/.../8091_8847.pdf.

12. My 2012 Brill essay offered some fresh arguments for a martyrological reading of Rom 3:25. Brill originally planned to publish the essay in 2009. However, since one of its editors became ill, there was a delay in publication until 2012. Since I submitted the essay in 2009 and since it did not appear in print until 2012, several works were published, of which I was not aware, between my original submission in 2009 and the actual publication in 2012.

To complete this book has taken nearly five years. By means of many toils and snares, I have finished it with God's help, by God's grace, and with much prayer. As with every publication, there are many people to thank.

I owe many thanks to Jim Tedrick and Robin Parry at Wipf and Stock for their eager willingness to publish this monograph. I owe a special thanks to Robin for his editorial work.

I owe thanks to many scholars and friends in the guild of NT studies for reading part or all of the manuscript and for offering helpful suggestions. In this regard, Daniel P. Bailey, Lynn Cohick, Stephen Finlan, Mike Gorman, Tom Schreiner, and Steve Wellum deserve a word of thanks. Lynn and Stephen Finlan went the extra mile in their feedback, for which I am grateful. Tom, as always, went several miles by reading the entire manuscript and by submitting to me rapid-fire emails while reading the manuscript as he spotted weaknesses. These provided me detailed responses that challenged points of weaknesses. Their comments have certainly strengthened the monograph. I am thankful to Cilliers Breytenbach, Mike Gorman, Stephen Finlan, and Simon Gathercole for individually meeting with me to discuss this project at the 2013 national meeting of the Society of Biblical Literature (SBL) in Baltimore, MD. Although they offered different suggestions and raised distinct questions and challenges, their remarks were very helpful and are represented in different places throughout this monograph. Simon deserves a special word of thanks for helping me narrow my thesis to Romans instead of focusing on the entire Pauline corpus.

I owe many thanks to my colleagues, who participated in the Function of the Apocrypha and Pseudepigrapha study group from 2010–12, at the national meetings of the SBL. I owe an additional thanks to my colleagues who participated in the Pauline Epistles group in 2012 Chicago, IL and in the Cult and Atonement study group at the 2013 national meeting of SBL in Baltimore, MD. Scholars like Dan Bailey, David DeSilva, Robert Doran, Stephen Finlan, Caroline Johnson-Hodge, Brigitte Kahl, Amy-Jill Levine, Mark Reasoner, and so many others in these groups have sharpened this current monograph with their critical engagement of my presentations related to it. I also owe many, many thanks to David DeSilva for his many helpful comments and suggestions about my work on Jewish martyrology and Paul. I am particularly thankful for his friendship and for the constant encouragement that he has given me in my scholarly work and pursuits. I am especially thankful for his gracious and kind words of encouragement during a professional difficult time in the fall of 2012 and in the spring of 2013. I owe thanks to Jan Wilhelm van Henten for his helpful critical review of my 2010 monograph on Jewish martyrology and Paul in the *Review of Biblical Literature*, and I am thankful for his critical engagement with my work in numerous emails from my days as a doctoral student in 2005–7 and for our personal interaction over coffee at SBL 2009 in New Orleans, LA.

Several PhD students in biblical studies at the Southern Baptist Theological Seminary carefully read parts of the manuscript and offered helpful suggestions. In this regard, special thanks go to Michael Graham, Jr., Jonathan Kiel, and Trey Moss. Michael carefully read chapters 1–4 and provided helpful suggestions, especially for my chapter on Romans 3. Trey also created the scripture and sacred writings index. Jonathan carefully read chapters 1–2. His remarks and corrections of my understanding of Hebrew grammar in chapter 2 saved me both from embarrassment and from severe criticism of Hebrew grammar specialists that might read the monograph. Trey formatted the entire manuscript, created the abbreviations page, fixed footnotes where necessary, and got the entire manuscript ready for my editor. I owe many thanks to Bobbie Jamieson (PhD student in NT at Cambridge University), my friend and former student at Southern Seminary, for critically reading chapter 2 and for making several helpful suggestions about cult and sacrifice.

I owe thanks to the publishers and journals that permitted me to use material from previous publications. Brill Academic, Broadman and Holman Academic, Paternoster, and Wipf and Stock allowed me to use some material from work that I published with them in 2010–2012. In addition, the *Princeton Theological Review* and the *Journal of the Evangelical Theological Society* likewise allowed me to reproduce some material that I originally published with them in 2007 and 2010.

I owe a special, special thanks to all of my colleagues at Southern Seminary and to all friends associated with this beloved institution! I especially thank Drs. R. Albert Mohler, Jr. (President), Russell Moore (former Provost and current president of the Ethics and Religious Liberties Commission of the Southern Baptist Convention), Randy Stinson (Provost), Gregory Wills (Dean of the School of Theology), and Thomas R. Schreiner (Associate Dean of Scripture and Interpretation) for their full support of me, for their confidence in me as a young scholar and minister of the gospel, and for entrusting me with the stewardship of the gospel and scholarship at our beloved institution. In addition, I offer a special thanks to my colleagues in the NT department at Southern Seminary. Drs. Bill Cook, Jonathan Pennington, Rob Plummer, Mark Seifrid, Tom Schreiner (now Professor of Biblical Theology), and Brian Vickers (now Professor of Biblical Theology) welcomed me onto the faculty in the fall of 2013 with open arms and continue to offer me much love and support in all of my scholarly pursuits. My short time at Southern as a full-time associate professor of NT has brought me back home to the place in my life where my wife and I spent our happiest days as a newly married seminary couple. I am so thankful and blessed to serve at this institution with colleagues committed to the gospel, the church, and scholarship!

Scholars have lives apart from scholarship—at least, this one does. The most important people in my life are my wife, Ana, and my beloved six-year-old son, Jaden. They have sacrificed so much time, money, and energy for me. Ana literally left her country of Costa Rica to become my wife. She has faithfully loved me for thirteen years of marriage in spite of my many, many flaws! I owe many thanks to Ana and Jaden for enduring so much to support me in the joyful and yet painful calling to the ministry of academic scholarship and in the joyful and painful calling to gospel ministry in the church. I would not have finished this book without their prayers, love, support, and sacrifices. Even as I write these words, I recall Jaden innocently praying so fervently many times for Jesus to help "daddy" finish this book so I could play with him. I am so thankful that Jesus heard and answered his prayers!

I owe a final word of thanks to Tom Schreiner, my *Doctorvater*. Anyone who spends a little time with me knows that I deeply love and respect Tom and I owe him an infinite amount of gratitude. He is my mentor, *Doctorvater*, former pastor, friend, colleague, and office neighbor in Norton Hall at Southern Seminary. He has invested many years into my life and continues to do so. In the fifteen years that I have known Tom, he has been quick either to encourage or to rebuke me when I needed one or the other. He has simultaneously been both the most critical person of my scholarship (besides me) and the biggest supporter of my scholarship (besides my wife). His criticism has never torn me down, but has always built me up. I aspire to the high standard that he so humbly sets forth with his scholarship, which is always marked by sharp acumen and Christian charity. In my pursuit of Christian obedience and in my constant search for and pursuit of what a rigorous Christian NT scholar should be, I often look to him as an example as he imitates Christ in his scholarship. It is, therefore, with much love, appreciation, and admiration that I dedicate this book to Tom Schreiner, my *Doctorvater*, mentor, and friend, because of his willingness to speak the truth to me in love and because of his love for the cross of Jesus Christ! I pray that this book would make him forever proud to be my *Doctorvater*!

Jarvis J. Williams
Louisville, KY.
August 2014

Abbreviations

AGJU	*Arbeiten zur Geschichte des Antiken Judentums und des Urchristentums*
AUSS	*Andrews University Seminary Studies*
Bib	*Biblica*
BN	*Biblische Notizen*
BZAW	Beihefte zur Zeitschrift für die Alttestamentliche Wissenschaft
BZNW	*Beihefte zur Zeitschrift für die Neutestamentliche Wissenschaft und die Kunde der Älteren Kirche*
CBQ	*Catholic Bible Quarterly*
CBET	*Contributions to Biblical Exegesis and Theology*
CD	*Church Dogmatics*. Karl Barth. Translated by G. T Thomson et. al. Edinburgh: T. & T. Clark, 1936–77.
ConBOT	Coniectanea Biblica Old Testament Series
CTJ	*Calvin Theological Journal*
EKKNT	*Evangelisch-katholischer Kommentar zum Neuen Testament*
EvQ	*Evangelical Quarterly*
FAT	*Forschungen zum Alten Testament*
FRLANT	*Forschungen zur Religion und Literatur des Alten und Neuen Testaments*
HDR	Harvard Dissertations in Religion
ICC	International Critical Commentary on the Holy Scriptures of the Old and New Testaments
IDB	*The Interpreter's Dictionary of the Bible*. 4 vols. Edited by George Arthur Buttrick. Nashville: Abingdon, 1976.
Int	*Interpretation*
JAOS	*Journal of the American Oriental Society*

JBL	*Journal of Biblical Literature*	
JETS	*Journal of the Evangelical Theological Society*	
JSJSup	*Supplements to the Journal for the Study of Judaism*	
JSNTSup	Journal for the Study of the New Testament Supplement	
JSOTSup	Journal for the Study of the Old Testament Supplement	
JTS	*Journal of Theological Studies*	
LASBF	*Liber Annuus Studii Biblici Franciscani*	
LNTS	Library of New Testament Studies	
LXX	Septuagint	
NICOT	New International Commentary on the Old Testament	
NovT	*Novum Testamentum*	
NovTSup	Supplements to Novum Testamentum	
NTS	*New Testament Studies*	
OBT	Overtures to Biblical Theology	
SBLSP	Society of Biblical Literature Seminar Papers	
Scr	Scripture	
SJLA	*Studies in Judaism in Late Antiquity*	
SNT	*Studien zum Alten und Neuen Testament*	
SNTSM	Society for New Testament Studies	
SNTSMS	Society for New Testament Studies Monograph Series	
SP	Sacra Pagina	
TrinJ	*Trinity Journal*	
TynBul	*Tyndale Bulletin*	
WMANT	Wissenschaftliche Monographien zum Alten und Neuen Testament	
WUNT	Wissenschaftliche Untersuchungen zum Neuen Testament	

BIBLICAL TEXTS

Old Testament

Gen	Genesis
Exod	Exodus
Lev	Leviticus
Num	Numbers

Deut	Deuteronomy
Josh	Joshua
Judg	Judges
Ruth	Ruth
1–2 Sam	1–2 Samuel
1–2 Kgs	1–2 Kings
1–2 Chr	1–2 Chronicles
Ezra	Ezra
Neh	Nehemiah
Job	Job
Ps	Psalm
Prov	Proverbs
Eccl	Ecclesiastes
Song	Song of Solomon
Isa	Isaiah
Jer	Jeremiah
Lam	Lamentations
Ezek	Ezekiel
Dan	Daniel
Hos	Hosea
Joel	Joel
Amos	Amos
Mic	Micah
Zeph	Zephaniah
Hag	Haggai
Zech	Zecharaiah
Mal	Malachi

New Testament

Matt	Matthew
Mark	Mark
Luke	Luke
John	John
Acts	Acts

Rom	Romans
1–2 Cor	1–2 Corinthians
Gal	Galatians
Eph	Ephesians
Phil	Philippians
Col	Colossians
1–2 Thess	1–2 Thessalonians
1–2 Tim	1–2 Timothy
Titus	Titus
Phlm	Philemon
Heb	Hebrews
Jas	James
1–2 Pet	1–2 Peter
1–2–3 John	1–2–3 John
Jude	Jude
Rev	Revelation

ANCIENT SOURCES

Jewish Sources

Apocrypha

Tob	Tobit
Jdt	Judith
Wis	Wisdom of Solomon
Sir	Sirach
Bar	Baruch
1–3 Esd	1–3 Esdras
Ep Jer	Letter of Jeremiah
Sg Three	Song of the Three Young Men
Sus	Susanna
Bel	Bel and the Dragon
1–4 Macc	1–4 Maccabees

Dead Sea Scrolls

CD	Cario Genizah copy of *Damascus Document*
1Q34bis	1Q*Festival Prayers*
1QH	*Thanksgiving Hymns*
1QIsa^a	Isaiah^a
1QIsa^b	Isaiah^b
1QM	*War Scroll*
1QpHab	*Pesher Habbakuk*
1QS	*Rule of the Community*

Josephus

Ant.	*Jewish Antiquities*
Ag. Ap.	*Against Apion*
J.W	*Jewish War*

Philo of Alexandria

Abr.	*De Abrahamo*
Cher.	*De cherubim*
Decal.	*De decalogo*
Det.	*Quod deterius potiori insidari soleat*
Ebr.	*De ebrietate*
Flacc.	*In Flaccum*
Fug.	*De fuga et inventione*
Her.	*Quis rerum divinarum heres sit*
Leg. 1,2,3	*Legum allegoriae* I,II, III
Legat.	*Legatio ad Gaium*
Migr.	*De migratione Abrahami*
Mos.	*De vita Mosis*
Mut.	*De mutatione nominum*
Opif.	*De opificio mundi*
Pream.	*De praemiis et poenis*
Somn.	*De somniis*

Spec.   *De specialibus legibus*

Pseudepigrapha

2 Bar	*2 Baruch* (Syriac Apocalypse)
1 En	*1 Enoch*
4 Ezra	*4 Ezra*
Jub	*Jubilees*
L.A.B.	*Liber antiquitatum biblicarum*
Let. Aris.	*Letter of Aristeas*
Pss. Sol.	*Psalms of Solomon*
Sib. Or.	*Sibylline Oracles*
T. Ash.	*Testament of Asher*
T. Dan	*Testament of Daniel*
T. Jos.	*Testament of Joseph*
T. Jud.	*Testament of Judah*
T. Iss.	*Testament Issachar*
T. Lev	*Testament of Levi*
T. Naph.	*Testament of Naphtali*

Greek and Latin Works

Dionysius of Halicarnassus

Ant. rom.   *Antiquitates romanae*

Euripidies

Alc.	*Alcestis*
Heracl.	*Heraclidae*
Hec.	*Hecuba*
Iph. aul.	*Iphigenia aulidensis*
Iph. taur.	*Iphigenia taurica*
Phoen.	*Phoenissae*

Horace

Carm.   *Carmina*

Plato

Menex.   *Menexenus*
Symp.   *Symposium*

Plutarch

Pel.   *Pelopidas*

Seutonius

Dom.   *Domitianus*

Papyri

P.Giss.   *Griechische Papyri*
P.Mich   *Michigan Papyri*

1

Thesis and History of Research

THESIS

What kind of death did Jesus die, according to the NT authors: representative or substitutionary? And what background influences shaped the NT authors' presentation of Jesus' death? In this monograph, I argue a twofold thesis. First, in the Epistle to the Romans, Paul presents Jesus' death as both a *representation of* and a *substitute for* Jews and Gentiles. Second, the Jewish martyrological narratives are a background behind his presentation of Jesus' death in Romans. By representation, I mean that Jesus became the sinner in that he functioned as the sinner in life and in death, although he was not an ontological sinner. By substitution, I mean that Jesus, a Torah-observant Jew, died in the place of non-Torah-observant Jewish and Gentile sinners in order to accomplish specific soteriological benefits for them.[1] By Jewish martyrological narratives, I refer to the narratives in 2 and 4 Maccabees and LXX Dan 3:1–90 that record the deaths of Torah-observant Jews for the salvation of non-Torah-observant Israel.

I endeavor to support the thesis in this book and to advance the arguments by means of grammatical-historical exegesis and by means of a conceptual, theological, and comparative analysis of all of the relevant texts in the Jewish martyrological narratives and in Romans. I develop the following arguments to support my thesis. First, the Jewish martyrological narratives appropriated Levitical cultic language and Isaianic language to

---

1. For a similar approach, see Simon J. Gathercole, *Defending Substitution*.

the deaths of the Jewish martyrs (Torah-observant Jews) to present their deaths as a representation, a substitution, and as Israel's Yom Kippur for non-Torah-observant sinners. Second, in a parallel way Paul similarly appropriated Levitical cultic language and Isaianic language to the death of Jesus (a Torah-observant Jew) to present his death as a representation, a substitution, and as the Yom Kippur for Jews and Gentiles (non-Torah-observant sinners).[2]

HISTORY OF RESEARCH[3]

Jesus' death for others is an important historical and theological motif in many of Paul's letters.[4] Discussions about the background influences behind and the origins of Paul's conception of Jesus' death have a long and prestigious history in biblical scholarship.[5] Scholarly discussion, however, as to whether martyr theology influenced Paul's conception of Jesus' death gained widespread attention in the twentieth century. The discussion focused mainly on five trajectories of thought, which I discuss in detail below.

    2. To clarify, I do not argue for a central atonement model in Romans. Instead, I simply argue that both representation and substitution are present in Romans and that the Jewish martyrological narratives are *a* background behind Paul's presentation of Jesus' death in Romans. Furthermore, my book does not attempt to engage dogmatic claims in favor of or against representation and substitution. Rather, I discuss representation and substitution as these categories appear in Paul's argument in Romans. Finally, my book does not attempt to discuss all of the related theological, philosophical, and practical implications of representation and substitution in Romans. To the contrary, my book proposes that both representation and substitution are important elements in Romans.

    3. This history of research overlaps with my 2010 book *Maccabean Martyr Traditions*, but this monograph provides an up to date survey of scholarship up to 2015.

    4. In a 1995 monograph on the death of Jesus, John T. Carroll and Joel B. Green rightly acknowledged that "Paul is widely recognized as the quintessential theologian of the cross. The aptness of the description is suggested not only by the sheer quantity of references to the cross in his correspondence but also by the multitudinous ways in which Jesus' suffering and death are woven into the fabric of Paul's letters. Indeed, the passion of Christ is related to all aspects of Paul's apostolic message—especially his soteriology, Christology, eschatology, and ethics—and is pivotal to his self-characterization as an apostle and servant of Christ." For the full quote and scriptural citations that support the statement, see Carroll and Green, *The Death of Jesus in Early Christianity*, 113. However, the authors of the preceding quote likewise contended that scholars have overemphasized substitutionary atonement in Paul's letters and in his soteriology and that Paul does not view Jesus' death as a vicarious punishment. For example, Carroll and Green, *The Death of Jesus in Early Christianity*, 113–15, 123.

    5. For a bibliography, see Finlan, *The Background and Content of Paul's Cultic Atonement Metaphors*; Williams, *Maccabean Martyr Traditions*, 6–26; Williams, *For Whom Did Christ Die?* 24–27.

The first part of the history of research focuses on scholars who have discussed the background behind Paul's understanding and presentation of Jesus' death. The second part of the history of research focuses on scholars who have argued that Paul presents Jesus' death as a substitution for or as a representation of others.

1. Jewish Martyrological Narratives Not the Background behind Paul's Presentation of Jesus' Death in Paul

Jewish Martyrological Narratives, Jesus' Death, and ἱλαστήριον

First, there are those scholars who argued that martyr theology was *not* the background behind Paul's presentation of Jesus' death. Ethelbert Stauffer was the first scholar to analyze the relevant literature and then to set martyr theology into systematic categories.[6] In 1955, Stauffer discussed martyrdom in 2 and 4 Maccabees, the New Testament, Polycarp, and in texts that post-date the New Testament. However, he does not discuss whether martyr theology is the background in front of which interpreters should read Paul.

In 1955, Leon Morris considered the background behind Paul's conception of Jesus' death.[7] His investigation was particularly concerned with the meaning of ἱλαστήριον in Rom 3:25. He argued that there is no clear meaning of ἱλαστήριον. Yet, he contended that it refers not to the mercy seat nor to the Yom Kippur ritual, but to the removal of God's wrath. Regarding martyr theology and ἱλαστήριον, Morris argued that 4 Macc 17:21–22 is parallel with Rom 3:25 since both contain ἱλαστήριον.[8] He likewise argued that a parallel between these two texts based on this one term does not necessarily mean that martyr theology (and particularly 4 Macc 17:21–22) shaped Paul's understanding of Jesus' death. Instead, Morris emphasized that the two texts have similar terms, and he forcefully argued that the OT was Paul's primary background.[9]

---

6. Stauffer, *New Testament Theology*, 185–334.

7. Morris, "The Meaning," 3–43. References are to the third edition published in 1965.

8. This is the only extant text where the author applies ἱλαστήριον to the vicarious death of a Torah-observant Jew for the Torah-disobedience for their soteriological benefit.

9. Although the following scholars interpret Rom 3:25–26 differently, see additional arguments against a martyrological background behind Paul's use of ἱλαστήριον in Rom 3:25 in Fryer, *"Hilastērion,"* 99–116, esp. 103–4; Stuhlmacher, *Romans*, 58–61; Travis, *Christ and the Judgment of God*, 190–91; Moo, *Romans*, 230–40, esp. 27–30; Jewett, *Romans*, 286; Grayston, "Atonement and Martyrdom," 250–63; Knöppler, *Sühne*, 112–17;

In his 1999 unpublished doctoral thesis at Cambridge University, Daniel P. Bailey provided the most detailed analysis of ἱλαστήριον in current English-speaking scholarship. Bailey's work is intensely lexical. He analyzed all of the relevant extant texts wherein ἱλαστήριον and related terms occur in pagan Hellenistic literature and in Hellenistic Jewish literature, and he compared those occurrences with Paul's use of the term in Rom 3:25. He argued with lexical *tour de force* that the term's occurrences in 4 Macc 17:22 and Rom 3:25 have a distinct meaning from one another. After Bailey reviewed the evidence in the relevant Hellenistic literature that he argued supports reading the term as propitiatory, he argued that various inscriptions confirm that ἱλαστήρια were offered either to appease the offended deity or to elicit a favor from it. Additionally, Bailey claims that his analysis supports that -τήριον words regularly refer to places instead of to actions. He concludes that the meaning of ἱλαστήριον in 4 Macc 17:22 as it relates to the martyrs' deaths should be sought against a non-sacrificial background. 4 Maccabees nowhere states that the martyrs died as atoning sacrifices for Israel's sin, and Paul's background behind ἱλαστήριον is the OT mercy seat instead of martyr theology.[10]

In his 2002 monograph *Christ as Devotio*, Basil S. Davis argued that Paul presents Jesus as *Devotio* in Gal 3:13.[11] In the Greco-Roman world, there were different types of *Devotio* sacrifices. One type died in order to save the people from an imminent disaster. Davis contended that the curse language in Galatians should be understood in light of the Greco-Roman culture of cursing. To defend this thesis, Davis offered evidence from the curse tablets and from Greek and Latin authors who were contemporaries of

---

Holland, *Contours*, 157–82.

10. Bailey, "Mercy Seat." The mercy seat reading has a long and prestigious history. For example, Origen, *Romans*, 216–25; Calvin, *Romans*, 75; Barth, *Romans*, 104–5; Manson, "ἱλαστήριον," 1–10; Nygren, *Romans*, 156–62; Lyonnet, "expiationis," 336–52; Lyonett, *Sin*, 157–66; Bruce, *Romans*, 104–7; Swain, "For Our Sins," 131–39; Wilckens, *Römer*, 191–92; Käsemann, *Romans*, 97; Janowski, *Sühne*, 350–54; Meyer, "The Pre-Pauline Formula," 198–8; Hultgren, *Paul's Gospel and Mission*, 59–60; Hultgren, *Paul's Letter to the Romans*, 156–57; Schreiner, *Romans*, 192 n. 24 and 192–95; Newton, *The Concept of Purity at Qumran*, 76–77; Barrett, *Romans*, 73–75; Schlatter, *Romans*, 99; Byrne, *Romans*, 132–33; Hooker, *Not Ashamed*, 43–44; Kraus, *Der Tod Jesu*; Ben Ezra, *Yom Kippur*, 198–202; Knöppler, *Sühne*, 112–17; Jewett, *Romans*, 286–87. Similarly Talbert (*Romans*, 110–15), who argues that ἱλαστήριον refers to the new mercy seat as the locus of the divine presence. Since Bailey's 1999 doctoral thesis, no scholar who defends the mercy seat interpretation of Rom 3:25 has offered any fresh arguments for this interpretation. Instead, scholars continue to recycle old arguments to support this reading.

11. Davis, *Christ as Devotio: The Argument of Galatians 3:1–14*.

Paul.¹² Basil contended that one should look beyond the Jewish background when searching for the origins of Paul's cursing language in Gal 3:10–13.¹³ According to him, if one finds similar curse language in non-Jewish texts as one finds in Gal 3:10–13, then one should include those texts in the investigation by considering the meaning of the curse language in their literary contexts as a key for interpreting the curse language in Gal 3:13.¹⁴ Davis offered an impressive analysis of ancient Greek and Latin texts with a *Devotio* theme in them with the intent of highlighting the parallels between those traditions and Gal 3:10–13.¹⁵ Davis argues since the *Devotio* curse formula was present in Paul's Greco-Roman culture and since Paul states that Jesus redeemed the "us" from the curse of the law with language similar to that of ancient *Devotio* texts, the latter likely provided Paul with the background for his description of Christ as a redeemer of those under the curse.

In a 2012 essay, Markus Tiwald assumed that the Yom Kippur ritual was the background behind Rom 3:25. He argued that the background behind Paul's use of ἱλαστήριον in Rom 3:25 is not martyrological for at least two reasons: grammar and date. That is, if Rahlfs' critical edition to the Septuagint is correct in that an article should precede ἱλαστήριον, then in 4 Macc 17:22 the latter is an adjective describing θανάτου (τοῦ ἱλαστηρίου θανάτου). The preceding construction makes a connection with Romans 3 unlikely since ἱλαστήριον is not attributive in Rom 3:25. Furthermore, if most scholars are correct, then we should date 4 Maccabees to the latter part of the first century (e.g., 90–100 CE). According to Tiwald, therefore, 4 Maccabees should no longer be seen as a reference text for Paul in Romans 3 as Eduard Lohse maintained in a monograph on martyrdom in 1955 and again in his Romans commentary in 2003.¹⁶ Contrary to Bailey's 1999 doctoral thesis, Tiwald argued that ἱλαστήριον in Rom 3:25 refers to the Yom Kippur ritual and not necessarily to the mercy seat.¹⁷ As Tiwald stated,

> Yom Kippur was the most important celebration in the second temple. And כַּפֹּרֶת was the holiest place of the temple. Even if it no longer existed in the second temple, its mythic importance continued unbroken. Therefore, by using the expression that God has displayed Christ publicly as ἱλαστήριον, Paul maintains that in Jesus' death the apex of fulfillment of all the expectations

---

12. Ibid., 12, 119–200.
13. Ibid., 139.
14. Ibid., 141.
15. Ibid., 119–220.
16. Tiwald, "Christ as *HILASTERION* (Rom 3:25)," 189–208, esp. 192.
17. Ibid., 194, 198.

of redemption has now been reached. Christ is the fulfillment of all hopes to obtain salvation and atonement. In this *pars pro toto* view two different aspects of interpretation, which sometimes have been seen as a contradiction, may also coexist: Christ now becomes the eschatological atonement for our sin . . . and he also becomes the place of the presence of God in this world.[18]

Jewish Martyrological Narratives, Jesus' Death, and Reconciliation

In his 1953 monograph on reconciliation, Jacques Dupont offered a detailed analysis of Paul's reconciliation motif and related terms. According to Dupont, martyr traditions were not Paul's background behind his reconciliation motif in Romans and 2 Corinthians.[19] In 1981, Ralph Martin's classic work on reconciliation in Paul discussed the similarities between martyr theology and Paul with regard to reconciliation.[20] Martin limited his study to Rom 5:9–11 and 2 Cor 5:18–21. He acknowledged that the presence of καταλλάσσω and of the concepts of God's wrath, judgment, and vicarious suffering for sin seem to support a connection between 2 Macc 7:32–33 and Paul. However, he suggested that the distinctions between the traditions suggest otherwise. For example, Martin first pointed out that in 2 Macc 7:33, the martyrs asked God to be reconciled to their servants (καὶ πάλιν καταλλαγήσεται τοῖς ἑαυτοῦ δούλοις). The martyrs did not ask God to reconcile them to him. Second, Martin noted that the martyrs offered themselves to God as vicarious acts of piety and merit. Third, Paul and the other apostles emphasize that God initiates reconciliation and that he is never the object of reconciliation in the New Testament.[21]

Stanley E. Porter's discussion of martyr theology and Paul focuses on the occurrence of the καταλλάσσω and καταλλαγή terminology. Porter's thesis is that Paul's reconciliation terminology is unique to him because in Paul God initiates reconciliation, because reconciliation includes the concept

---

18. Ibid., 205.

19. Dupont, *La reconciliation*.

20. Martin, *Reconciliation*, 105–6. Against a martyrological background behind Paul's reconciliation terminology, see also Beale, "Reconciliation in 2 Corinthians 5–7," 550–81.

21. For further observations about the differences between reconciliation in 2 Maccabees and Paul's letters, see Porter, καταλλάσσω, 39–77; Breytenbach, *Versöhnung*, 40–83; Breytenbach, "Versöhnung, Stellvertretung," 59–73; Breytenbach, "Christus starb für uns," 447–75; Breytenbach, "Salvation of the Reconciled," 271–86; Beale, "Reconciliation in 2 Corinthians 5–7," 550–81; Thrall, *Second Corinthians*, 429–39, esp. 429–30.

of justification, because Paul uses passive verbs when he speaks of reconciliation, because Paul grounds reconciliation in Jesus' death, and because for Paul reconciliation communicates a personal and intimate relationship between parties. Consequently, martyr theology is not the background in front of which to read reconciliation in Paul.[22]

In a series of publications dating from 1989 to 2010,[23] Cilliers Breytenbach argued that the reconciliation terminology in 2 Maccabees was not Paul's background for his use of reconciliation terminology. Instead, non-religious Hellenistic literature influenced Paul. There reconciliation terminology only appears in political or military contexts. According to Breytenbach, the reconciliation terminology in Paul is different from its occurrence in 2 Maccabees, Philo, and Josephus, each of which emphasizes the need for God to be reconciled to his people, while Paul stresses the need for sinners to be reconciled to God. He additionally argued that Paul's use of this terminology is not sacrificial.[24]

In a 2010 essay, Breytenbach argued that Paul's reconciliation metaphor should be understood as two different domains: target domain and source domain. The target domain is the audience to which the reconciliation metaphor is directed. The source domain is the place from which the metaphor emerges. Paul's target domain determined how he structured parts of the source domain to appropriate his target domain. The result was that Paul used a non-religious metaphor from one target domain and religiously applied it to a different target domain. Consequently, Breytenbach concluded that some scholars have misinterpreted Paul's use of the reconciliation metaphor in that they required "the reproduction of the source domain in the target domain. In terms of the rules and functions of mapping across semantic boundaries, it is inappropriate to demand the target to be described as a replica of the source."[25]

By means of an impressive analysis of a few secular Hellenistic and Roman texts, Breytenbach argued that Paul's usage of the reconciliation metaphor in 2 Cor 5:18–20 is similar to the usage in Hellenistic and Roman polis-diplomacy texts. For example, he cited texts in Diodor (5.75.1; 16.82.3), Cassius Dio (41.16.4; 48.11.1–2), 2 Maccabees (4:11; 5:17; 8:17), Dionysius of Halicarnassus (*Ant. Rom.* 2.45.6; 3.9.2; 3.50.4; 5.21.1; 5.31.1–2; 5.62.1; 6.67.2; 6.88.2), Josephus (*Ant.* 15.136), private letters from the CE

22. Porter, καταλλάσσω in Ancient Greek Literature.

23. Breytenbach, "Salvation of the Reconciled," 171–86.

24. Breytenbach, *Versöhnung*, 40–83; Breytenbach, "Versöhnung," Stellvertretung," 59–73; Breytenbach, "Christus starb für uns," 447–75; Breytenbach, "Salvation of the Reconciled," 271–86; Breytenbach, "Salvation of the Reconciled," 177–79.

25. Breytenbach, "Salvation of the Reconciled," 173.

era (*P.Mich.* 8.502.7–8; *P.Giss.* 17.13–14), Plutarch (*Pel.* 26.2), Chersias the poet (*Mor.* 156f), and Aelius Aristides (*Orationes* 3.344) that discuss reconciliation with similar or the same vocabulary as Paul. These texts express that ambassadors pursued reconciliation by politically negotiating peace between two parties by begging or urging the estranged party to be reconciled to the offended party.²⁶ Breytenbach, therefore, concluded that "there can be little doubt that Paul depicts his role as apostle to the Corinthians metaphorically in the language of the Hellenistic and Roman polis-diplomacy."²⁷ He based his conclusion on the use of the verbs πρεσβεύομεν, παρακαλοῦντος, and δεόμεθα, which occur in 2 Cor 5:20 and in secular texts that he discussed. The lexical parallels suggest that Paul borrowed from the domain of Greco-Roman political diplomacy to depict his mediating role to the Corinthians, not from the domain of sacrificial ritual. According to Breytenbach, the latter point explains why sacrificial language is absent in 2 Cor 5:18–20 and Rom 5:10–11. Accordingly, the language of reconciliation "has in fact no cultic background. Furthermore, it rarely transferred to relationships between gods and between gods and humans."²⁸

In a series of publications in 1981, 1996, and 2002, Seyoon Kim discussed the origins of Paul's gospel.²⁹ With regard to reconciliation, Kim argued that it is unlikely that martyr traditions influenced Paul's understanding of Jesus' death. Although he acknowledged the possibility of a martyrological reading of reconciliation in Paul, he asserted that such

26. Dio Halicarnassus *Ant. Rom.* 2.45.6; 3.9.2; 3.50.4; 5.21.1; 5.31.1–2; 5.62.1; 6.67.2; 6.88.2; 2 Macc 4:11.

27. Breytenbach, "Salvation of the Reconciled," 175.

28. Ibid., 175–76. Breytenbach argued that a few secular texts in Greco-Roman literature describe reconciliation as the actions of a deity or the relationship between the gods. But the emphasis in these texts is on human action instead of divine action. The former's actions alter the relationship between these two parties from enmity to friendship. For his discussion of these texts, see "Salvation of the Reconciled," 176–79. Breytenbach's 2010 essay further contended that Paul's Christ died ὑπὲρ πάντων language in 2 Cor 5:14 does not refer to atonement since his background is the Greek tradition of "dying for," albeit that he gives the Greek tradition an awkward twist when he uses it to describe how humanity benefits from Christ's death for all. Breytenbach offers three unconvincing reasons. First, in 2 Cor 5:14, Paul states that Christ died "for all" instead of "for our sins" as in 1 Cor 15:3. Second, ὑπὲρ in 2 Cor 5:14 communicates the benefit of Christ's death for every sinner. By this, Paul universalizes and personalizes the efficacy of Jesus' death. Third, Paul substitutes εἷς for Χριστός. See his, "Salvation of the Reconciled," 180. For his discussion of non-sacrificial vicarious suffering in Paul's letters, see his 2010 essay ("The 'For Us' Phrases in Pauline Soteriology, 59–81").

29. Kim, "2 Cor. 5:11–21 and Reconciliation," 360–84; Kim, *The Origins of Paul's Gospel*, 215–38. The latter work is a revised version of his 1977 doctoral thesis submitted at the University of Manchester and originally published in 1981 by Mohr Siebeck. My discussion from Kim primarily comes from his 2002 edition.

a reading cannot explain either the means by which Paul soteriologically applies the reconciliation terminology to the death of Jesus or the reason that Paul describes his ministry as a τὴν διακονίαν τῆς καταλλαγῆς.[30] Kim specifically defended his thesis that the Damascus-Road experience is the background behind Paul's reconciliation terminology by asserting that Paul uses the terminology to suggest that God reconciles humans to himself or to other human beings and never to declare that God is reconciled or that God reconciles himself to human beings.[31] For example, in 2 Macc 7:32–33, the seventh martyr utters: εἰ δὲ χάριν ἐπιπλήξεως καὶ παιδείας ὁ ζῶν κύριος ἡμῶν βραχέως ἐπώργισται καὶ πάλιν καταλλαγήσεται τοῖς ἑαυτοῦ δούλοις.[32]

Contrary to Paul's usage of the reconciliation terminology in 2 Cor 5:18–20[33] and Rom 5:10–11,[34] Kim asserts that the Hellenistic Jewish usage and the profane Hellenistic usage affirm that God needs to be reconciled to the people.[35] These distinctions between Paul and the Hellenistic Jewish traditions suggest that "Paul deliberately makes a fundamental correction of the Hellenistic Jewish conception of reconciliation between God and human beings: it is not God who needs to be reconciled to human beings, but it is human beings who need to be reconciled to God; and it is not by repentance, prayers, or good works on the part of the human beings that reconciliation is brought between God and human beings, but it is by his grace that God reconciles human beings to himself."[36] Kim thinks 2 Cor 5:11–21 provides the earliest and the best access to the origin of reconciliation in Paul.[37]

In his 2011 monograph on Romans, Richard N. Longenecker distinguished between the use of reconciliation language among the Jews in

---

30. Kim is reacting to I. Howard Marshall's view here (to be discussed later) in his "Reconciliaiton," 129ff.

31. Kim (*The Origin of Paul's Gospel*, 220) acknowledged that Hofius ("Erwägungen," 14) first suggested this idea but that he did not defend it.

32. Kim, *The Origins of Paul's Gospel*, 217.

33. τὰ δὲ πάντα ἐκ τοῦ θεοῦ τοῦ καταλλάξαντος ἡμᾶς ἑαυτῷ διὰ Χριστοῦ καὶ δόντος ἡμῖν τὴν διακονίαν τῆς καταλλαγῆς,ὡς ὅτι θεὸς ἦν ἐν Χριστῷ κόσμον καταλλάσσων ἑαυτῷ, μὴ λογιζόμενος αὐτοῖς τὰ παραπτώματα αὐτῶν καὶ θέμενος ἐν ἡμῖν τὸν λόγον τῆς καταλλαγῆς. Ὑπὲρ Χριστοῦ οὖν πρεσβεύομεν ὡς τοῦ θεοῦ παρακαλοῦντος δι' ἡμῶν· δεόμεθα ὑπὲρ Χριστοῦ, καταλλάγητε τῷ θεῷ.

34. εἰ γὰρ ἐχθροὶ ὄντες κατηλλάγημεν τῷ θεῷ διὰ τοῦ θανάτου τοῦ υἱοῦ αὐτοῦ, πολλῷ μᾶλλον καταλλαγέντες σωθησόμεθα ἐν τῇ ζωῇ αὐτοῦ· οὐ μόνον δέ, ἀλλὰ καὶ καυχώμενοι ἐν τῷ θεῷ διὰ τοῦ κυρίου ἡμῶν Ἰησοῦ Χριστοῦ δι' οὗ νῦν τὴν καταλλαγὴν ἐλάβομεν.

35. Kim, *Origins of Paul's Gospel*, 217.

36. Ibid.

37. Ibid., 220. On the similarities and differences between Paul's reconciliation motif and 2 Maccabees' reconciliation motif, see Barnett, *Second Corinthians*, 303 n. 10.

2 Maccabees, in Josephus, and its use in Paul. According to Longenecker, God is reconciled in the Jewish texts, whereas in Paul God reconciles sinners to God. Since Paul is the only NT author to use the reconciliation language and since the language does not appear in the earliest Christian writers, Paul probably learned this language because of its inclusion in early Christian confessional material. He came to appreciate such language as accurately expressing what he personally experienced in his relationship with God through Christ by the Spirit. Longenecker stated four reasons why Paul likely borrowed his reconciliation language from early Christian confessions, all of which he based on 2 Cor 5:18–20. First, Paul presents in 2 Cor 5:20 a certain balance structure. Second, Paul introduces the verse with the particle ὅτι, which Paul and other NT writers used to introduce a quotation from traditional material. Third, the verse formally incorporates early Christian proclamation. Fourth, 5:19 is central to 5:18 and 5:20.[38]

Jewish Martyrological Narratives, Jesus' Death, and Sacrifice

In a series of publications in the 1990s, Bradley H. McLean focused on both the background behind Paul's presentation of Jesus' death and on whether Jesus' death was an atoning sacrifice. His most detailed work on Jesus' death in Paul appeared in a monograph in 1996.[39] He specifically focused on the meaning and background behind Gal 3:13.[40] He argued that Paul's explanation of the cursed Christ is bound up with the larger question of the relationship between transgression, law, and faith, for Paul cites his image of the cursed Christ in the context of arguing against Gentile observance of the Jewish law.[41] Paul's concept of being under a curse should be understood in physical terms. That is to say, transgressors actually incur a deadly curse and are subject to its power, because Paul describes sin as not merely the sum of wrongdoings, but as a hostile power that clings to the human flesh. Consequently, Paul's "under a curse" language is synonymous with his "under sin" language.[42] Even if Christians were able to do all the law's ordinances, they would still be doomed since the law belongs to the old age.[43] McLean

---

38. For Longenecker's discussion, see *Introducing Romans*, 337–43.

39. Mclean, *The Cursed Christ*.

40. For a detailed analysis of the background behind Gal 3:13, see my forthcoming *Christ Redeemed "Us" From the Curse of the Law . . . : A Martyrological Reading of Galatians 3:13* LNTS (London: T. & T. Clark, forthcoming).

41. McLean, *The Cursed Christ*, 113.

42. Ibid. 123.

43. Ibid.

affirms substitutionary atonement.[44] "Christ offered his own life as payment for (in exchange for) the lives of Christians who were slaves to the law. This commercial exchange explains how Christians are freed from the curse at the cost of Christ's life which was given in exchange."[45] However, McLean argues that Christ's substitutionary death in Gal 3:13 should be understood as a curse instead of as an atoning sacrifice.[46] The curse of Christ originated from the law, not God.[47] McLean concluded that one cannot support a genealogical connection between martyr traditions and Paul. Instead, he contended that the best one can do is argue that Paul shared the same available paradigm as the traditions that he parallels.[48]

In his 1995 monograph on Paul's gospel, Christopher Davis agreed that Paul's presentation of Jesus' death has parallels with the martyr theology in 4 Maccabees. However, he disagreed that martyr theology could have been the background behind Paul's presentation of Jesus' death. Paul sets apart Christ's death from other humans who suffered an unjust execution when he attaches purgative significance to Jesus' death. Paul may offer faint echoes of substitution, but he does not present Jesus' death as a vicarious substitutionary atonement when he uses the Christ-died-for-us formula.[49]

In a 2005 essay, Henk S. Versnel argued that the kind of vicarious death for the soteriological benefit of another that occurs in the NT and in Paul's letters does not occur in the OT or in 2 Maccabees. Instead, he argued that Greco-Roman pagan texts provided the background for the concept of vicarious death for the soteriological benefits of others in 4 Maccabees, in the NT outside of Paul, and in the Pauline letters. Versnel analyzed several Greek and a few Roman texts. With this analysis, he differentiated between the concepts of dying for a creed, dying for or instead of someone, patriotic death, vicarious death in classical Greece and the early Roman Republic and the later Republic and early Principate, the Devotio, and the Devotio for the Principate.[50]

Based upon his analysis of the aforementioned texts, Versnel suggested the following four arguments: First, Greek elements of the "dying for" motif

44. Ibid., 126–31 and n. 66.

45. Ibid., 131.

46. McLean developed the above argument earlier in two articles in the 1990s. For example, see his "Christ as *Pharmakos* in Pauline Soteriology"; McLean, "The Absence of Atoning Sacrifice in Paul's Soteriology." For a short discussion of martyr theology and sacrifice in Paul, see Daly, *Christian Sacrifice*, 236–50.

47. McLean, *The Cursed Christ*, 137.

48. Ibid., 12–9.

49. Davis, *The Structure of Paul's Gospel*, 120–24.

50. Versnel, "Making Sense of Jesus' Death: The Pagan Contribution," 227–53.

influenced various terminological and conceptual elements of the idea of "dying for" in 2 and 4 Maccabees, Paul, and other NT letters.[51] Second, in agreement with Williams and Hengel, Versnel stated that the "dying for" formula in 2 Maccabees betrays Greek influences, but these influences should be restricted to notions of noble death, which belong to the categories of philosophical and patriotic death. The vicarious death for the soteriological benefit of another is not present in 2 Maccabees. It is only present in 4 Maccabees.[52] "There existed no explicit reference to a consciously intended vicarious soteriological death in pre-NT Jewish scriptures."[53]

Third, according to Versnel, NT authors neither directly nor exclusively developed the notion of the vicariousness of Jesus' death from 2 and 4 Maccabees. Thus, since both the Jewish Scriptures and the pre-Christian non-canonical texts are without the idea of a vicarious death for the soteriological benefit of another in the sense that Versnel defines it, such interpretations of Jesus' death in the NT were likely modeled after non-Jewish, Greco-Roman examples.[54] Fourth, the preceding points presented Versnel with an historical problem, which he asserted that many scholars had ignored prior to his work. Namely, "how are we to explain that these ideas of vicarious dying for the sake of others, so well-known from classical Greek culture, were suddenly adopted in the first century AD in both Christian and independently, or so it seems, Jewish writings, starting in the fifties (Paul) and subsequently in later writings, such as the Gospels—especially John—Hebrews, 1 Clement, and 4 Maccabees?"[55] Versnel's answer was that "in the ongoing discussion on tradition, transmission and borrowing of ideas and terminology of vicarious (atoning) death, we should pay much more attention to comparable ideas and practices current in the *contemporaneous* pagan *Umwelt* of the NT."[56] That is, both Jewish and Christian sources used Greco-Roman pagan sources, or at least the ideas of vicarious death in the sources, in order to construct their presentation of the vicarious death of a human for the soteriological benefit of another, since the idea occurs nowhere in Jewish culture.[57]

---

51. Ibid., 254.
52. Ibid., 255.
53. Ibid., 225.
54. Ibid., 255.
55. Ibid.
56. Ibid.
57. For Versnel's entire essay, see 213–94.

2. Jewish Martyrological Narratives Possibly a Background behind Paul's Presentation of Jesus' Death

Jewish Martyrological Narratives, Jesus' Death, and ἱλαστήριον

Second, some scholars cautiously argued that the Jewish martyrological narratives were possibly the background behind Paul's presentation of Jesus' death. For example, in their classic 1896 Romans commentary, W. Sanday and A. C. Headlam argued that the Yom Kippur ritual was not the background behind Paul's use of ἱλαστήριον in Rom 3:25, while they simultaneously affirmed that other textual traditions could have been the background for Paul. They argued that Paul presents Jesus' death as an atoning sacrifice and that the NT authors often use cultic language to explain the significance of his death for others. Nevertheless, their work expresses doubts as to whether the OT is the background behind Rom 3:25.[58]

In his 1925 work on atonement, Hastings Rashdall acknowledged that martyr traditions were the background behind Paul's formulation of Jesus' death in Rom 3:25. But Rashdall also argued that the OT was the most important background behind a sacrificial understanding of Jesus' death in Paul. He affirmed the presence of sacrificial ideas in 4 Macc 17:22 when the text states that the martyrs died as atoning sacrifices for Israel's sin, through whose deaths God saved Israel. He asserted that a martyrological influence on Paul's understanding of the sacrificial nature of Jesus' death in Rom 3:25 is highly probable.[59]

In his 1975 Romans commentary, C. E. B. Cranfield disagreed that Paul's identification of Jesus as ἱλαστήριον in Rom 3:25 refers to the mercy seat. He contended that the martyr traditions' impact on Paul is clear. He especially argued that Paul's presentation of Jesus' death reflects 2 Macc 7:30-38; 4 Macc 6:27-29, and 4 Macc 17:21-22. Cranfield de-emphasized God's wrath in Rom 3:25. However, he acknowledged that the Jewish martyrs died as atoning sacrifices. This martyrological idea was well known to early Judaism and to Paul. While he agreed that martyr traditions were the background for Paul, Cranfield urged that the *Akedah Hypothesis* and Isa 53:10 must also be taken seriously as possible background influences upon Paul.[60] Similar to Cranfield, James D. G. Dunn in both his 1988 Romans commentary and in his 1998 book on Pauline theology agreed that martyr traditions could have influenced Paul in Rom 3:25.[61] However, he remained

---

58. Sanday and Headlam, *Romans*, 87-88, 91-94.
59. Rashdall, *Atonement*, 130-32.
60. Cranfield, *Romans*, 1:214-18, esp. 1:217-18.
61. Dunn, *Romans* 1:170-72, 180, esp. 171, 180; Dunn, *Theology*, 207-33, esp. 215.

unconvinced that setting up martyr theology and cultic theology as diametrically opposed alternatives was helpful (on the grounds that the martyr texts are already infused with cultic theology).[62]

Jewish Martyrological Narratives, Jesus' Death, and Reconciliation

In a 1974 essay, I. Howard Marshall argued that martyr theology probably shaped Paul's understanding of Jesus' death as the means of reconciliation to God.[63] He suggested that Paul's motif of reconciliation appears most frequently in 2 Corinthians and that 2 Maccabees probably has provided the catalyst to the development of Paul's use of the category of reconciliation. Martyr theology presents the deaths of the martyrs as sacrificial offerings (2 Macc 7:32–38). Their offerings were the means by which God ended his wrath against the nation. Paul likewise presents Jesus' death as the means by which God ends his wrath against the nations (2 Cor 5:18–21). The influence of martyr theology on Paul's conception of Jesus' death cannot be categorically proven, but it can be argued and affirmed with a high degree of probability that Paul borrowed from the martyr theology of 2 and 4 Maccabees to present Jesus' death as an atoning sacrifice.

3. Jewish Martyrological Narratives as Paul's Non-Sacrificial Background behind His Presentation of Jesus' Death

Jewish Martyrological Narratives, Jesus' Death, and ἱλαστήριον

Third, some scholars argued that the Jewish martyrological narratives were Paul's background and that this tradition's non-sacrificial presentation of the martyrs' deaths shaped Paul's non-sacrificial understanding of Jesus' death. Two significant works appeared in the 1970s and in the 1990s that argued that martyr theology shaped Paul's conception and understanding of Jesus' death, but they argued that neither martyr theology nor Paul presented the death of a human for others as atoning sacrifices. In 1975, Sam K. Williams' published dissertation provided the most important work on the origins

---

62. In his 1998 commentary on Romans, Schreiner (*Romans*, 192 n. 24 and 192–95) was cautiously optimistic that martyr theology could have shaped Paul's understanding of Jesus' death in Rom 3:25. Yet, he expressed doubt about whether 4 Maccabees postdated Romans. However, in conversation after the publication of his Romans commentary, he acknowledged to me that he is now more favorable toward a martyrological reading of Rom 3:25 than he was when he originally wrote his commentary in 1998.

63. Marshall, "Reconciliation," 117–32, esp. 120–21, 129–30.

of Paul's understanding and presentation of Jesus' death.⁶⁴ Williams' work focused on the origins of early Christianity's belief that Jesus' death was a saving event. He contended that the early church interpreted Jesus' death through the lens of Greco-Roman ideas of the effective death of a righteous human. Williams argued that vicarious, expiatory suffering and death are seldom found (if ever) in the OT or in Second Temple Judaism. Instead, the effective suffering and death of a human are found in Hellenistic literature. Fourth Maccabees contains themes of effective suffering and death due to Hellenistic ideas. These ideas likewise provided a framework by which the author of 4 Maccabees interpreted the martyrs' deaths, and these Greek ideas provided new Christians with a needed interpretation of Jesus' death. Consequently, the message of Jesus' effective death spread from Antioch and was widely accepted as a central component of the gospel. According to Williams, Rom 3:21–26 is the central text regarding the influence of martyr theology on Paul's conception and presentation of Jesus' death because of the occurrence of ἱλαστήριον.⁶⁵

Williams boldly stated that no one understood the martyrs' deaths to be vicarious prior to the writing of 4 Maccabees, which Williams labeled as an early Christian document written in Antioch. Paul instead adopted a pre-Pauline Christian formula that interpreted Jesus' death as an expiation for sin. Williams argued that neither 2 Maccabees nor 4 Maccabees teaches vicarious atonement and that 4 Macc 6:28–29 and 17:21–22 were Paul's background. Thus, Williams argued that Paul does not present Jesus' death as a death *qua* death in Rom 3:25–26. Instead, early Christianity interpreted Jesus' death as a saving event in light of the Greco-Roman idea of a human's effective death. Early Christianity interpreted Jesus' death as a saving event both to provide an apologetic response to and to solve the problem of his tragic death.⁶⁶

In 1990, David Seeley investigated the historical influences behind Paul's interpretation of Jesus' death. But he specifically argued that the Greco-Roman theme of noble death influenced Paul's understanding and presentation of Jesus' death. Seeley offered five elements of noble death in

---

64. Williams, *Jesus' Death*.

65. Ibid., 39–41, 165–202, 233–54. Martin Hengel did not appear to be familiar with Williams' work when he published his 1981 monograph on atonement, but he challenged the latter's thesis. Hengel argued that Greco-Roman literature was a crucial background behind the early church's understanding of the saving significance of Jesus' death. Jesus was the first person to interpret his death as an atoning sacrifice. The OT background alone is insufficient to explain the soteriological categories that the NT authors apply to Jesus' death. Hellenistic religious ideas were very influential on Jewish writers and on Paul. See Hengel, *The Atonement*.

66. Williams, *Jesus' Death*, 39–41, 165–202, 233–54.

Paul and in 4 Maccabees: (1) obedience, (2) the overcoming of physical vulnerability, (3) military setting, (4) vicarious suffering, and (5) sacrificial metaphors. Seeley agreed that 4 Maccabees' understanding of vicarious suffering and death for others shaped Paul's understanding of Jesus' death. However, Seeley redefined vicarious suffering and death to mean exemplary death. He concluded that OT cultic language played no role in shaping Paul's conception of Jesus' death.[67] In a 2001 monograph about salvation and participation, Daniel G. Powers likewise agreed that martyr theology influenced Paul's interpretation of Jesus' death. He suggested that this martyrological influence came from 2 Maccabees, Judith, *Assumption of Moses*, and the additions of Daniel. However, he argued that 2 Maccabees does not teach vicarious, substitutionary atonement.[68]

In his major 2009 work on Paul's soteriology, Douglas A. Campbell discussed martyr theology's influence on Paul's atonement theory in Rom 3:25.[69] He argued that Paul describes Jesus' death in martyrological categories. The categories of faith, blood, execution, and the vindication of a heroic person in Rom 3:21–26 points to a martyrological reading of Rom 3:25.[70] Campbell rejected a direct relationship between Rom 3:25 and 4 Maccabees, for the similarities between the two texts lack the precision needed to support such a claim.[71] He asserted (without substantiation) that since 2 Maccabees 6 and 7 indisputably predate Paul and since these chapters contain the atoning efficacy of the martyrs' deaths, to appeal to Greco-Roman influences on Paul are unnecessary to explain Paul's atonement theory. But he contended that a martyrological reading of Genesis 22 is the background in front of which to read Rom 3:25. Campbell stated that this interpretation is supported by the following arguments. First, Paul emphasizes Jesus' faithfulness (vv. 22, 25, 26). Second, Paul utilizes the heroic death motif and the cultic term ἱλαστήριον (vv. 21–26). Third, a martyrological reading of Genesis 22 allows Paul's talk of "blood" in v. 25b to integrate more smoothly within his argument. Fourth, Paul offers multiple references to the resurrection in Romans 3–4. Fifth, this reading explains the presence of a broader discourse of cultic imagery in Romans. Christ dies as the new Isaac. Therefore, Paul recapitulates (even if implicitly) the cultus.[72]

---

67. Seeley, *The Noble Death*.
68. Powers, *Salvation through Participation*, 199–211, esp. 210.
69. Campbell, *The Deliverance of God*, 647–56.
70. Ibid., 648.
71. Ibid.
72. Entire paragraph is paraphrased from ibid., 654–55.

4. Jewish Martyrological Narratives as a Background to Sacrifice in Paul

Jewish Martyrological Narratives, Jesus' Death, and Sacrifice

Fourth, some scholars argued that the Jewish martyrological narratives were Paul's background and that the former presents the martyrs as atoning sacrifices. In 1967, David Hill argued that 4 Macc 17:21–22 was Paul's background in Rom 3:25. Hill agreed that ἱλαστήριον refers to the mercy seat in Heb 9:5 and many times in the LXX. However, although the Yom Kippur ritual is the context where ἱλαστήριον mainly occurs in the canonical LXX, it was not the source of Paul's comments in Rom 3:25. Instead, martyr theology was Paul's source for his propitiatory and sacrificial presentation of Jesus' death for the following reasons. First, both 4 Macc 17:21–22 and Rom 3:25 speak of God's wrath. Second, both textual traditions speak of the shedding of blood at the expense of one's life. Third, death for sin occurs in both texts. Fourth, both texts state that death was the means by which God's mercy and deliverance came to the transgressors. Fifth, both the death of the martyrs and Jesus' death were vicarious sacrifices in the respective texts. Sixth, God initiates atonement in both texts. Seventh, if the author of 4 Maccabees wrote prior to AD 70, Paul could have had access to the text as a source.[73]

In a 1975 essay, Joseph A. Fitzmyer argued that martyr theology shaped Paul's reconciliation motif.[74] In the Greco-Roman world, reconciliation spoke of the restoration of broken relationships. When used religiously, the concept spoke of the reconciliation between the gods/God and humans (Sophocles, *Ajax* 744; 2 Macc 1:5; 7:33; 8:29). Since Hebrew does not have a specific word for reconciliation, Fitzmyer insisted that the Greco-Roman world and its martyr theology were Paul's sources for his reconciliation motif; Paul applied martyr theology to the Christ-event, and Paul used martyr theology to fit his theological purposes.

In 1980, J. C. Becker devoted a discussion on Paul's conception of Jesus' death while he defended his thesis that Paul's theology is mainly apocalyptic. Hellenistic-Jewish Christianity applied atoning significance to Jesus' death. The concept of a human atonement for the sins of others was a foreign concept to Jews, but many Jews accepted this concept via Diaspora theology. Wisdom of Solomon suggests that the deaths of righteous sufferers benefit others, while 2 and 4 Maccabees highlight the atoning value of these deaths. Paul received the creedal formulation of martyr theology from

---

73. Hill, *Greek Words and Hebrew Meanings*, 36–48, esp. 38–48.
74. Fitzmyer, "Reconciliation in Pauline Theology," 155–77.

the Jewish-Hellenistic church (1 Cor 15:3; Rom 4:25), from which he also inherited the interpretation that Jesus' death was a sacrificial offering (Exod 12:13; 1 Cor 5:7), expiation (Rom 3:25), and a covenant sacrifice (Exod 24:4–8; 1 Cor 11:23).[75]

In 1986, John S. Pobee devoted his work to construct a Jewish theology of martyrdom. He suggested that a Jewish martyr theology existed, not a Maccabean martyr theology. He asserted that the following components are present in a Jewish martyr theology: First, the nation suffered because of its sin. Second, God poured out wrath upon the martyrs to propitiate wrath. Third, God judged the martyrs through suffering to avert his eschatological wrath away from them. Fourth, Israel's persecution validated a cosmic war. Fifth, suffering was the means by which the war was manifested. Pobee extended his discussion of martyr theology beyond the Maccabean literature, and he interacted with all Jewish writings from the fourth century BC through the rabbinic period. He affirmed that there was a late Jewish martyr theology in Second Temple Judaism and that martyr theology was the background behind Paul's conception of Jesus' death.[76]

In his 1992 monograph on Christian Origins and in his 2002 Romans commentary, N. T. Wright argued that martyr theology shaped Paul's conception of Jesus' death in Rom 3:25. The martyrs and other Jews understood the martyrs' deaths as atoning sacrifices for Israel, and they understood that the Lord would save Israel from his wrath through their deaths (4 Macc 6:28–29). The Yom Kippur ritual and Isaiah 40–55 was also a background behind Rom 3:25. According to Wright, Paul presented Jesus' death as an atoning sacrifice for sin by using cultic language from Leviticus 16, Isaiah's Servant Songs, and martyr theology.[77] However, in his commentary on Romans, Wright seems to place greater emphasis upon Isaiah 40–55 and Dan 11:35 and 12:1–12 as primary backgrounds for Paul's remarks in Rom 3:25 than upon martyr theology.

In his 2001 doctoral thesis, completed under the supervision of Wright, Stephen Anthony Cummins argued that martyr theology shaped Paul's conception of Jesus' death. However, Cummins' work was more concerned with the Antiochean Incident in Gal 2:11–14.[78] Cummins specifically argued that grasping the historical and theological significance behind the Antiochean incident in Gal 2:11–12 would add clarity to the meaning of the incident if

---

75. Becker, *Paul the Apostle*, 182–212, esp. 191, 203–5.

76. Pobee, *Persecution and Martyrdom*.

77. Wright, *The New Testament and the People of God*, 272–79; Wright, "Romans," 475.

78. Cummins, *Paul and the Crucified Christ*.

interpreters would read the incident through the lens of a Maccabean martyr model of Judaism. According to Cummins, martyr theology provided early Christians with an application for the earliest soteriological interpretation of Jesus' death.

5. Jewish Martyrological Narratives as the Primary Background for Paul

Jewish Martyrological Narratives, Jesus' Death, and Atoning Sacrifice

Fifth, some scholars have argued that Jewish martyrological traditions were Paul's primary background and that the martyrs' deaths were atoning sacrifices. In 1963, Eduard Lohse was one of the first scholars to argue that the Maccabean martyrs functioned as substitutes for Israel.[79] He argued that Jewish martyr theology was important for early Christians and to Paul's conception of Jesus' death. He excluded Hellenism and Hellenistic Judaism from being martyr theology's background for the vicarious death of a human for the benefit of others. He argued that the concept of martyrdom in 2 and 4 Maccabees was due to Palestinian Jewish thought. Palestinian Judaism, rather than Hellenistic Judaism, provided the earliest examples of martyrdom. According to Lohse, expiatory death is not explicitly stated in 2 Maccabees. Instead, he argued that 2 Maccabees emphasizes that the Jewish martyrs died as representatives for the nation, whereas 4 Maccabees teaches vicarious atonement. The latter traditions influenced Paul. In his 2003 Romans commentary, Lohse argued that the martyr theology in 4 Macc 17:21-22 was Paul's background for his presentation of Jesus' death in Rom 3:25 and that Paul conflated martyr theology with OT cultic language.[80]

In a series of publications from 1988-98, Marinus de Jonge investigated the earliest formulations of Jesus' death for others.[81] He argued that the deaths of the martyrs in 2 and 4 Maccabees should be understood as substitutionary atonement for Israel. Greek, Hellenistic, and Roman ideas influenced 2 and 4 Maccabees. The martyrs' deaths were the means by which God averted his wrath away from the nation and brought peace to Israel. The

---

79. Lohse, *Märtyrer und Gottesknecht*, 37-78, 150-52.

80. Lohse, *Römer*, 134-35.

81. De Jonge, "Jesus' Death for Others," 142-51; reprinted in *Jewish Eschatology*, 125-34; De Jonge, *Christology*; De Jonge, *Jesus, the Servant-Messiah*, 37-48; De Jonge, *God's Final Envoy*, 12-33.

efficacy of the martyrs' prayers before their deaths echoes various OT texts (Exod 32:30–34; Ps 106:16–23; Num 25; LXX Dan 3:38–40). The martyrs' deaths helped early Christians understand both Paul's presentation of Jesus' death and the presentation of his death in early confessional formulas.[82]

J. W. van Henten is the most prolific scholar of early Christian origins to have written about martyr theology's influence on the NT authors.[83] In a 1991 essay, he argued that martyr theology was Paul's primary background in Rom 3:25.[84] In 1998, his Dutch doctoral thesis on 2 and 4 Maccabees was translated and published in English. This work is a detailed investigation of the martyrological themes in both books. Van Henten argued that the Maccabean martyrs were exemplars of noble death. The deaths of Eleazar, the unknown mother, and her seven sons were idealized stories and representative of specific religious, political, and philosophical ideas. The martyrs' deaths in 2 Macc 7:32–38 are vicarious for Israel. Fourth Maccabees is a spiritualized book that highlights the deaths of the martyrs and the vicarious aspect of their deaths. The authors of both works likely borrowed the concept of vicarious atonement from Greco-Roman traditions. In a 2004 essay, van Henten confirmed this thesis.[85]

In his 2004 monograph about the cultic background behind Paul's atonement metaphors, Stephen Finlan devoted an entire chapter to martyrology.[86] He agreed with van Henten that martyrdom was the most prominent model behind Paul's conception of Jesus' death and that Paul borrowed from the OT cultic context to convey his martyrological ideas to teach substitutionary atonement. To clarify, Finlan does not pit martyrdom and sacrifice against one another. Instead, he argues that martyrdom is a model of interpretation, because it always refers to a human's death for a noble purpose. Sacrifice is a metaphor, because these kinds of death are not actually part of the sacrificial system.[87] However, Finlan argued that Paul diverged

---

82. In a 1987 unpublished dissertation ("Maccabean Martyr Theology: Its Genesis, Antecedents, and Significance for the Earliest Soteriological Interpretation of the Death of Jesus"), Warren Joel Heard provided a detailed study of the origins of Jewish martyr theology. He also argued that martyr theology shaped Paul's conception of Jesus' death. For additional argumentation in favor of a martyrological influence on Paul, see Barth, *Der Tod Jesu Christi*, 37–71.

83. Van Henten, *The Maccabean Martyrs as Saviours of the Jewish People*.

84. Van Henten, "The Tradition-Historical Background," 101–28.

85. Van Henten, "Jewish Martyrdom and Jesus' Death," 139–68. See also David A. DeSilva's 2006 4 Maccabees commentary for sacrifice and substitution in 4 Maccabees.

86. Finlan, *The Background and Content of Paul's Cultic Atonement Metaphors*, 193–224.

87. I am very thankful to Steve for clarifying to me his position in personal correspondence after reading a pre-published version of this monograph.

from martyr theology's propitiatory ideas in that he does not describe God as needing appeasement since God and Jesus initiated his death for the ungodly (Rom 5:5–6). In my 2010 monograph and in my 2012 essay, I built on Van Henten's thesis, with a lexical and conceptual analysis, that martyr theology was Paul's primary background for his conception of Jesus' death in Rom 3:25 and that those traditions teach substitutionary atonement.[88]

REPRESENTATION AND SUBSTITUTION IN PAUL?[89]

In this monograph, I will also argue that in Romans Paul presents Jesus' death both as a representation of and as a substitution for Jews and Gentiles. I support this thesis by arguing that the Jewish martyrological narratives are a background behind Paul's presentation of Jesus' death in Romans. Thus, my history of research below discusses both the major scholars who have written about the origins of Paul's understanding of Jesus' death and the scholars who have considered whether Jesus' death should be understood as a substitute for or as a representative of those for whom he died. Some scholars have discussed both the origins of and the nature of Jesus' death. When possible, I attempt below to avoid unnecessary overlap with earlier discussions. However, some overlap is unavoidable due to the contributions of certain scholars.

Representation

Representation (=inclusive place taking) was a prominent understanding of Jesus' death in twentieth-century German scholarship. I first encountered this view in 2004 as a ThM student by reading essays on the death of Jesus by Otfried Hofius. However, the major pioneer of this view (also known as the Tübingen view) was Hartmut Gese, a professor of OT at Tübingen. According to Gese and the Tübingen school, atonement occurs through identification instead of through substitution. The event of atoning sacrifice addresses a specific plight. The Israelite forfeits life, and she or he becomes symbolically willing to die. The Israelite needs to be rescued from death, not necessarily from personal transgressions. This need for deliverance from death is true both for the individual Israelite and for the entire Jewish community. The two important features for atonement on Yom Kippur is both

---

88. Williams, *Maccabean Martyr Traditions*; Williams, "Martyr Theology in Hellenistic Judaism and Paul's Conception of Jesus' Death in Romans 3:21–26."

89. For a lucid, compelling, and concise defense of substitution in Paul, see Gathercole, *Defending Substitution*.

the laying on of hands and the sacrificial ritual. The laying on of hands on the goat identifies the Israelite with the sacrifice. The animal is entrusted to the priest, who in turn makes atonement for the whole person and nation. The laying on of hands connects the individual and the nation so that when the animal dies, the individual dies with it. Through the animal's death, the Israelite and the community symbolically experience the judgment of death, but not in a substitutionary sense. Through the sacrificial blood ritual, the animal symbolically takes the people into the holy of holies through judgment and connects them with God. The animal gives up its life, but the blood manipulation provides atonement, through which the priest and the people are reconciled and connected to God.[90]

Otfried Hofius applied Gese's theory to the death of Jesus in the NT. In a collection of essays published in 1989, Hofius discussed atonement and reconciliation.[91] In an essay titled *Sühne und Versöhnung: Zum paulinischen Verständis des Kreuzestodes Jesus*, Hofius discussed Rom 5:8–10 and 2 Cor 5:18–20. He took Rom 5:8–10 as his starting point for his discussion of the death of Jesus. He began by acknowledging that Paul describes in Rom 5:8 Jesus' death as an apparent proof of God's love. After he noted that Rom 5:9 speaks of atonement and 5:10 speaks of reconciliation, Hofius asked: in what sense is the apostle Paul speaking of atonement and reconciliation? With this question, Hofius meant: according to Paul, what kind of death did Jesus die?

In Hofius' view, the death of Jesus should be understood in the following four ways in Rom 5:8–10 and in 2 Cor 5:18–21. First, the OT sin-cult was a participatory *Mitbeteiligung* atonement-action.[92] The man, who offered atonement, identified himself with the offering by placing his hands on it, and the priest would execute this act as God's representative of the blood-ritual.[93] In the occurrences of atonement by means of Jesus' crucifixion, God alone is the doer of atonement, "*Im Sühnegeschenen des Kreuzestodes Jesu ist Got allein der Handelnde.*"[94] God himself takes the initiative and gives his own Son in death, and he identifies with sinful humanity with the crucifixion and the resurrection of Christ.[95] Needy mankind receives atonement and reconciliation in a completely passive way from God through the

---

90. Entire paragraph paraphrased from Gathercole, *Defending Substitution*. For original primary citations, see Hartmut Gese, "Atonement," in *Essays in Biblical Theology*, 93–116.

91. Otfried Hofius, *Paulusstudien*, 25–49.

92. Ibid., 48.

93. Ibid.

94. Ibid.

95. Ibid.

representative or inclusive place-taking *stellvertretenden*, atoning death of Jesus. This is why Paul asserts in 2 Cor 5:18 that τὰ δὲ πάντα ἐκ τοῦ θεοῦ.[96] Second, the OT atonement cult has a certain inner logic to it.[97] Israel relies upon the repetition of the sacrificial cult.[98] The atoning offering of Jesus, however, happens once and for all.[99] His death actualizes an eternal, valid, atonement and reconciliation. In the word of the cross, the message of reconciliation is proclaimed (1 Cor 1:18; 2 Cor 5:19).[100] Third, Jesus is the sin-offering for all sins unlike the OT sin-offering.[101] In the crucifixion of Jesus Christ, God has acted to grant atonement and reconciliation for sinful men.[102] Fourth, the OT sin-offering was only for Israel and not for the heathens.[103] Jesus' representative and crucifying death is a universal action of atonement for Jews and heathens.[104]

In a 1994 book on interpretations of Jesus' death in the NT, Morna D. Hooker argued against substitution in favor of a view of representation that she called interchange.[105] Commenting on 1 Thess 5:9–10, she contended that Paul presents Jesus' death as a sharing in the experiences of those for whom he died instead of as dying as a substitute for others. She supported this by suggesting that Jesus' death does not eliminate the possibility of one's physical death and by suggesting that one still dies with Jesus. In addition, Hooker argued that Christ gives life to those who participate in his death. "He has been raised from the dead, and we share that resurrection life. It is not, then, a question of Christ and the believer exchanging places; it is rather a sharing of experiences. Christ died, and we live with him."[106] In her discussion on the death of Jesus in Galatians, Hooker clearly stated

---

96. Ibid.
97. Ibid., 48.
98. Ibid., 49
99. Ibid.
100. Ibid.
101. Ibid.
102. Ibid.
103. Ibid.
104. Ibid.

105. In his 1990 monograph on the death of Jesus in the Pauline letters, Charles B. Cousar emphasized representation, but he did not deny substitution. See *A Theology of the Cross*, 44, 74.

106. Hooker, *Not Ashamed of the Gospel*, 28–29; Hooker, "Interchange in Christ." For a recent article that discusses the importance of interchange in defining what it means to become the righteousness of God in 2 Cor 5:21, see Hooker, "On Becoming the Righteousness of God: Another Look at 2 Cor 5:21."

that Jesus' death was a representation instead of a substitution.[107] According to her, Paul believed that he participated in the death of Jesus when he was crucified with Christ (Gal 2:20).[108] In her own words, "he died as our representative, on our behalf."[109] In Hooker's view, Jesus died so that those redeemed from the curse in Gal 3:10–14 would participate in his life-giving resurrection. "Christ shared our humanity, our estrangement from God, in order that we might share his sonship, his relationship with God."[110] She argued the same point when she discussed other Pauline texts that have traditionally been interpreted to refer to substitution.[111]

In a 2007 monograph about deliverance from evil, Richard H. Bell argued that the NT teaches the defeat of Satan or redemption from Satan.[112] Bell devoted two chapters to Paul in which he discussed Jesus' death as a representation for others and the sinner's participation in his death and resurrection.[113] Bell provided a detailed analysis and critique of Hartmut Gese's understanding of the OT sin-offering, who argued that the animal represents a subjective existential inclusive-place-taking through transference symbolized by the laying of a hand on the animal. Bell instead contended that the use of the word soul (נֶפֶשׁ) best describes what the participant has in common with the animal with whom he identifies by the laying on of the hand and because sacrificial texts (e.g., Lev 17:11) use the word נֶפֶשׁ to talk about the soul's survival of death. Bell's analysis challenged both Gese and Bernd Janowski, who argued that the animal's life in Lev 17:11 is bound up with the blood and that its life is somehow abstracted from the animal's body.[114]

According to Bell, the Israelite's soul should be distinguished from its life in Lev 17:11, even though this distinction is not always clear in the OT. Bell defended this distinction with the following argument. "If one is to speak of the participation in the 'life' of the animal in 'substantial' terms, if the Israelite really does die in some sense with the animal, if he undergoes the sentence of death and thereby comes into the presence of God, is it not his 'soul' which participates in the 'soul' of the animal? The essential being

---

107. Hooker, *Not Ashamed of the Gospel*, 30.
108. Ibid.
109. Ibid.
110. Ibid., 34.
111. Ibid., 29–45.
112. Bell, *Deliver Us from Evil*.
113. Ibid., 189–291.
114. I got this sentence from Bell, *Deliver Us*, 197. For original citation, see Bernd Janowski, *Sühne als Heilsgeschehen: Studien zur Sühnetheologie der Priesterschrift und zur Wurzel KPR im Alten Orient und im Alten Testament*, 247.

of the Israelite participates in the essential being of the animal."[115] In addition, Bell argued, נֶפֶשׁ occurs in LXX Lev 17:10 to refer to a person. In LXX Lev 17:11, there is a sentence of death. However, after the animal's death, the blood, the soul-substance, enters into the presence of God. The soul survives the death (i.e., the giving up of life) of the animal.[116]

Bell applied his understanding of the OT sin-offering to Jesus' death in Paul.[117] He argued that the hand-placement of the Israelite on the animal in Leviticus suggests that the Israelite participated in the death of the animal. Agreeing with Hofius, Bell suggested that Jesus' death in Paul is an inclusive place-taking, just as the OT sin-offering.[118] Paul presents Jesus' death as an identification with sinners instead of a substitution for sinners.[119] Sinners identify with Christ by faith and baptism.[120] This identification corresponds to the OT's sin-offering.[121] By identification with Christ, we have union with Christ, and this union is celebrated in the event of the Lord's Supper.[122] "So participation in Christ may appear to be for Christians only. In one sense, this act of identification is made after the sacrifice of the victim in that one comes to faith and baptism at some point after crucifixion."[123] However, according to Bell, identification with Christ also occurs at the moment of Christ's crucifixion.[124]

Bell continued that Paul does not always mention faith and baptism in relation to participation in Christ's death. He appealed to 2 Cor 5:14–15a to support this assertion. In Bell's view, Christ's death is the death of all people, "even for those who are not in Christ," which (Bell asserted) the following text crystallizes: ἡ γὰρ ἀγάπη τοῦ Χριστοῦ συνέχει ἡμᾶς, κρίναντας τοῦτο, ὅτι εἷς ὑπὲρ πάντων ἀπέθανεν, ἄρα οἱ πάντες ἀπέθανον καὶ ὑπὲρ πάντων ἀπέθανεν, ἵνα οἱ ζῶντες μηκέτι ἑαυτοῖς ζῶσιν ἀλλὰ τῷ ὑπὲρ αὐτῶν ἀποθανόντι καὶ ἐγερθέντι.[125] The three-fold use of πάντες indicates all people, whereas οἱ ζῶντες refers to those "in Christ, who through Christ's atoning death

---

115. Bell, *Delivers Us*, 196.
116. Ibid., 196–97.
117. Ibid., 190–200.
118. Ibid., 200.
119. Ibid.
120. Ibid.
121. Ibid.
122. Ibid.
123. Ibid.
124. Ibid.
125. Ibid., 201.

have come to life and participate in Christ's resurrection" (2 Cor 5:15b).[126] However, Bell stated that these verses appear to affirm that God reconciles all people and that Paul supports his interpretation in 2 Cor 5:19 (ὡς ὅτι θεὸς ἦν ἐν Χριστῷ κόσμον καταλλάσσων ἑαυτῷ, μὴ λογιζόμενος αὐτοῖς τὰ παραπτώματα αὐτῶν καὶ θέμενος ἐν ἡμῖν τὸν λόγον τῆς καταλλαγῆς).[127]

According to Bell, another difference between participation in the OT sin-offering and in Jesus' death in Paul is resurrection. In 2 Cor 5:15b, Paul refers to the resurrection by connecting the active participle ἀποθανόντι to the passive participle ἐγερθέντι. "Humans participate in and experience the death of Jesus when the soul is transferred into the reality of the crucified Christ."[128] In Bell's view, Christ's soul (i.e., his essential person) and the sinner's soul (i.e., his/her essential person) are knitted together. Paul does not play Jesus' divinity and humanity against one another. "In Paul, Christ is man not in contrast to the fact that elsewhere He is termed the Son of God, but because he is Son of God, and expresses and demonstrates Himself as such in the fact that He is man."[129] Therefore, when we participate in Christ by means of his soul, we participate in both his divinity and humanity (i.e., his essential nature).[130] In Bell's view, the believer actually participates in Jesus' death on the cross, because 2 Cor 5:14b states εἷς ὑπὲρ πάντων ἀπέθανεν, ἄρα οἱ πάντες ἀπέθανον.[131]

Only Substitution or Both Representation and Substitution?

Leon Morris offered a classical defense of substitution in Paul. In 1965, he argued in a monograph on the cross in the NT that substitution is at the heart of the atonement in the NT. He grounds his analysis of atonement in the Pauline letters in man's plight, God's salvation, and man's response.[132] Morris argued that Paul has a serious view of man's plight.[133] According to him, Paul sees sin as pregnant with devastating consequences, and he con-

---

126. Ibid.
127. Ibid.
128. Ibid.
129. Ibid. Original quote comes from Karl Barth, *CD* 3/2:46.
130. Ibid, 209.
131. Ibid., 210–11.
132. Leon Morris, *The Cross in the New Testament*, 180–269. In addition to the scholars whom Morris cites, see the following works in agreement with his view. For a recent defense of penal substitution from Evangelical scholars, see Mike Ovey et al., *Pierced for Our Transgressions*.
133. Morris, *The Cross in the New Testament*, 180–269.

nects humanity's sin with wrath, death, and other forces opposed to man.[134] God acted on behalf of humanity by taking the initiative in choosing to redeem his people and by sending his Son, Jesus, to pay for their sins via the cross.[135] Man should, therefore, respond to God's great act of salvation in the substitutionary cross of Jesus Christ with faith to experience deliverance from God's wrath.[136]

In 1990, Charles B. Cousar argued that Jesus' death is both a representation and substitution in Romans and in 2 Corinthians. He especially noted that Paul presents Jesus as a substitute in 2 Cor 5:21 since he states that Christ was a replacement for sinful men and women. However, Cousar went on to say that Paul does not "go on to say that [God] accepts their punishment so as to appease the otherwise unsatisfied anger of God, an observation that leads many simply to avoid the use of the term substitution altogether."[137] In a co-authored work in 1995 on the death of Jesus in early Christianity, John T. Carroll, Joel Green, and contributors argued in a chapter on Paul that he does not portray God as an angry God in need of mollification, for Paul does not present God's wrath as divine retribution. Instead, when men and women resist God's saving righteousness, they experience God's righteous condemnation in that God hands them over to experience the consequences of their own sin that they choose. In their view, this suggests that "Paul does not regard the death of Jesus as a vicarious punishment." His theology of Jesus' cross "lacks a developed sense of divine retribution." Instead, according to Rom 5:6–8, Paul presents Jesus' death as the ultimate expression of God's love." For Paul, the death of Jesus proves God to be a covenant keeping God, not primarily as one who judges.[138] Carroll and Green affirm that Jesus' death effects atonement, but their view contends that the cross in Paul's letters is about God's faithfulness despite humanity's unfaithfulness.[139] However, they acknowledge that vicarious substitution and representation are two of the many Pauline metaphors of atonement and that the latter does not truncate the former.[140]

---

134. Ibid.

135. Ibid.

136. Ibid., 260–69.

137. Cousar, *A Theology of the Cross*, 79. Cousar interestingly notes "that there is nothing to suggest that Jesus' death is to be attributed to God in the sense that God killed Jesus" (*A Theology of the Cross*, 109). He suggests instead that Paul's letters persist in presenting that of Jesus theonomously and as an event of revelation.

138. Entire paragraph above comes from Carroll, Green, et al., *The Death of Jesus in Early Christianity*, 122–23.

139. Ibid., 123–24.

140. Ibid., 125–29.

In a recent 2015 monograph on substitution in Paul, Simon J. Gathercole defends substitution. Gathercole's work provides the most balanced presentation with the fewest words since Martin Hengel's classical work on the atonement.[141] Gathercole wisely resists the common either-or impulse in biblical scholarship to defend only one particular theory of the atonement in Paul over and against others or to argue for a central atonement theory in Paul. By providing an analysis of selective texts from 1 Cor 15:3 and Rom 5:6–8 and by interacting with the major retractors of substitution in Paul, Gathercole defends substitution as one of Paul's important atonement models.

Apocalyptic Readings of Jesus' Death in Paul[142]

Since the publication of J. Louis Martyn's articles and influential Galatians commentary, in which he argued for an apocalyptic soteriology in Paul, scholars have advocated an apocalyptic understanding of Jesus' death in Paul's letters. In 1995, Alexandra R. Brown devoted an entire monograph to Paul's apocalyptic word of the cross in 1 Corinthians.[143] She argued that Paul's proclamation of the cross was both an inclusive and empowering message of liberation, peace, and reconciliation. There is much conflict and division in the church in 1 Corinthians. Paul attacks the center of the schism in the church at Corinth. Contrary to the barriers of ego, ideology, and social status, all of which divided the believers at Corinth, Paul proclaims a liberating word. Brown considered the way that Paul's word about the cross in 1 Corinthians invaded its hearers' understanding. She further considered how Paul's word liberated the Corinthians from the old age with all of its enslaving powers and convictions and instead ushered the Corinthians into the world of new creation revealed by the cross.

Brown contended that Paul states early in 1 Corinthians that the word of the cross is an apocalyptic word in 1 Cor 1:18 and in 2:8. In 1:18, Paul connects the word of the cross with end-time apocalyptic judgment in that

---

141. However, Hengel's aim was not to defend substitution but to discuss the origins of the concept of atonement in the NT.

142. There are different apocalyptic understandings of Jesus' death within the apocalyptic view: cosmological apocalyptic and forensic apocalyptic. For the purpose of this section, I simply discuss the key scholars within an apocalyptic framework without distinguishing between the different apocalyptic readings. For essays on apocalyptic readings of Paul, see Davis and Harink (eds.), *Apocalyptic and the Future of Theology*; Gaventa, *Apocalyptic Paul*.

143. Alexandra R. Brown, *The Cross & Human Transformation: Paul's Apocalyptic Word in 1 Corinthians*.

he divides humanity into those who are perishing and those who are being saved. In 2:8, he attaches apocalyptic significance to the word of the cross by referring to the rulers of this age. Again, in 2:8, Paul apocalyptically speaks of the word of the cross by referring to the present age, which (Brown argued) implies another age. Consequently, Paul employs the two-age apocalyptic schema.[144]

Brown continued that Paul's other "references to the cross or crucifixion in 1 Corinthians imply apocalyptic significance in that they concern the true or false perception that arises from the cross as revelatory event."[145] In 1:13, Paul condemns the divisive allegiance of some whom he had baptized with a statement that includes the crucifixion of Jesus as part of his indictment. With this rhetorical move, Paul places Jesus' cross against all systems and alliances. In 1:17, Paul highlights the cross as the central component of his preaching, claiming that it is the operative power in the salvation experience, instead of baptism either by an apostle or by anyone else.

With regard to 1:23, Brown argued that Paul echoes 1:18's word of the cross as an apocalyptic divider when he states that "we preach Christ crucified, a stumbling block to Jews and folly to Gentiles." In 1:23, Paul identifies as the whole world those who misunderstand the cross (i.e., Jews and Greeks)—the whole world seeks signs or wisdom instead of seeking satisfaction in the preaching of the cross. Finally, in 2:2, Paul gives an autobiographical statement about the relationship between the cross and knowledge: "I decided not to know anything among you except Jesus Christ and him crucified." The perceptual or epistemological effects of the cross in the letter reveals both the apocalyptic nature of Paul's vision of the cross and the susceptibility of Paul's gospel in Corinth to perceptual error. Paul "seems to locate the Corinthian error in an insufficient comprehension and experience of the cross. Thus, he adamantly emphasizes his role to preach the gospel . . . lest the cross . . . be emptied (1:17) and, over against, their gnosis, decides to know nothing among [them] except Jesus Christ and him crucified."[146] Paul's word of the cross serves to dismantle the Corinthians' perception of their reality dominated by social status, power, and wealth.[147] Paul argues against their worldview by proffering the message about the crucified Christ (weakness in the Corinthian context) as power, social status, and wealth,

---

144. The entire paragraph comes from Brown, *The Cross & Human Transformation*, 24.
145. Ibid.
146. The entire paragraph comes from ibid., 24–25.
147. Ibid., 1–169.

and by presenting wisdom (power in the Corinthian context) as weakness.[148] However, Brown never addresses whether Paul presents Jesus' death as a representation or a substitution. But she argues that the background behind his word of the cross in 1 Corinthians is apocalyptic thought.

In his famous Galatians commentary in 1997, Louis Martyn discussed the death of Jesus in Gal 3:13. He argued that redemption in 3:13 is a synonym for justify in 2:16.[149] Central to Christ's death in 3:13 is not the standard formulation of substitutionary atonement that results in the forgiveness of sins, but rather victory, "God's victory in Christ and the resultant emancipation of human beings."[150] Apocalyptic warfare is in the foreground in Paul's words. Thus, there are four actors in Paul's redemption theology in 3:13: first, the powerful, enslaving curse of the law, second, human beings enslaved under the power of that curse, third, Christ, who comes to embody the enslaving curse, and fourth, God, who in this Christ powerfully defeats the law's curse, thus liberating human beings from their state of enslavement."[151] Martyn argued that Christ became the law's curse on behalf of us, but he accomplished this not by taking upon himself a punishment due to us. Instead, he embodied the curse in such a way in his crucifixion so as to be victorious over its enslaving power.[152]

Martyn continued that in light of the cosmic battlefield language in 3:6—4:7, Paul stresses that humans need deliverance from the malignant powers that hold them in bondage and not so much forgiveness of sins.[153] The anti-God powers are the law's power to curse (3:10), the law as it pronounces a curse on the crucified Christ (3:13), sin's function as the prison warden over the whole of creation (3:22), and the elements of the cosmos that enslave both Jew and Gentile (4:3). In Gal 3:10—4:5, Paul refers to "being under something" no fewer than eight times, thus referring *seriatim* to anti-God powers that enslave humans.[154] Martyn suggested that Christ's death in 3:13 happened in collision with the law. Paul builds upon a Jewish-Christian atonement tradition and emphasizes with his remarks in 3:13 that humans need deliverance, not forgiveness.[155] Christ by his death has accomplished our redemption from slavery since Paul emphasizes that the

---

148. Ibid.
149. Martyn, *Galatians*, 317.
150. Ibid.
151. Ibid.
152. Ibid., 318 n. 110.
153. Ibid., 272–3,
154. Ibid., 272 n. 175.
155. Ibid., 273.

law has placed us under a curse.¹⁵⁶ With the advent of Christ, his death, and the impartation of his Spirit, God has invaded the present evil age and destroyed the forces of evil in Christ and thereby delivered us from the evil cosmos.¹⁵⁷

In his 2001 monograph on *Cruciformity: Paul's Narrative Spirituality of the Cross*, Michael J. Gorman argued that soteriology in Paul is apocalyptic and participatory. In Gorman's view, Paul—and other Christians—imitate Christ's suffering and self-giving love by participating in his death and living out his sufferings in their daily Christian experiences. "Paul saw himself, then, as a participant in and continuation of the life-giving death of Jesus his Lord that was narrated in the gospel he preached and the hymns his communities sang."¹⁵⁸ Paul chiefly expounds his theology of the cross by showing correspondence between Christ's death and the life of the believing community.¹⁵⁹

Gorman discussed thirteen master patterns under which he argued Paul's understanding of the cross fits.¹⁶⁰ Two of those patterns are interchange/representation and apocalyptic. For example, Gorman stated "substitution per se may or may not be involved in these texts, though some sense of representation and 'interchange' is certainly at work."¹⁶¹ That is, Jesus' death accomplished an interchange between him and believers. Although he was rich, Christ became poor so that the poor would become rich (2 Cor 8:9). Although he was righteous, he became sin so that we would receive the righteousness of God in him (2 Cor 5:21).¹⁶² Regarding the apocalyptic nature of Jesus' cross in Paul, Gorman argued that "Christ's death ended the reign of certain alien and hostile powers, thereby effecting liberation from them and from this age (Gal 1:4) and inaugurating the new age or new creation."¹⁶³ The powers include especially sin and death (Rom 6:9–10) and the old man (Rom 6:6, 1 Cor 6:19; 2 Cor 5:15).¹⁶⁴ The victory through Christ's death transfers believers into the realm of Christ's lordship (2 Cor 5:14–15; Rom 14:9; 1 Thess 5:9–10), which was the purpose for which he

---

156. Ibid.

157. Ibid., 95–105.

158. Michael J. Gorman, *Cruciformity*, 31. For his recent work on cruciformity, see his *Inhabiting the Cruciform God*.

159. Gorman, *Cruciformity*, 75–76.

160. Ibid., 84–86.

161. Ibid., 84.

162. Ibid., 84.

163. Ibid., 86.

164. Ibid.

died.¹⁶⁵ Gorman suggested that Christ's death paradoxically creates life. However, Gorman asserted, the purpose and effect of his death should not be restricted to the forgiveness of sins as if it was only a sacrifice, but his death includes transformation. That is, his death includes "a fundamental renewing and reorienting of life."¹⁶⁶

In his major 2009 work on Paul's soteriology, Douglas A. Campbell discussed martyr theology's influence on Paul's atonement theory in Rom 3:25.¹⁶⁷ He argued that Paul describes Jesus' death in martyrological categories. The categories of faith, blood, execution, and the vindication of a heroic person in Rom 3:21–26 point to a martyrological reading of Rom 3:25.¹⁶⁸ Campbell rejected a direct relationship between Rom 3:25 and 4 Maccabees, for the similarities between the two texts lack the precision needed to support such a claim.¹⁶⁹ He asserted that since 2 Maccabees 6 and 7 indisputably predate Paul and since these chapters contain the atoning efficacy of the martyrs' deaths, to appeal to Greco-Roman influences on Paul is unnecessary to explain Paul's atonement theory. But he contended that a martyrological reading of Genesis 22 is the background in front of which to read Rom 3:25.

Campbell argued that soteriology in Paul is both apocalyptic and participatory. Agreeing with Martyn, Campbell affirmed that salvation in Paul is fundamentally liberative and that it happens in the face of evil powers, from whom God frees humanity. According to Campbell, "God, therefore, is not fundamentally just and the atonement designed to assuage God's righteous anger at transgression; God is fundamentally benevolent and the atonement intended to deliver humanity from bondage to evil powers and to reconstitute it in the age to come."¹⁷⁰ Campbell asserted that although Paul presents Jesus' death in Rom 3:25 as a singular atonement for sin, this is not to be understood as a sacrifice. God appointed Jesus' death to replace the temple cultus.¹⁷¹ However, Paul's use of the term ἱλαστήριον signifies a singular event in relation to atonement and reconciliation.¹⁷² That is, Paul suggests that Jesus' atonement was of an extraordinary nature, like the Yom

---

165. Ibid.

166. Ibid., 86. However, Gorman acknowledged that Paul believed that Jesus' death was an atonement for sins. For example, see Gorman, *Cruciformity*, 163.

167. Campbell, *Deliverance*, 647–56.

168. Ibid., 648.

169. Ibid.

170. Ibid., 192.

171. Ibid., 654.

172. Ibid.

Kippur ritual and the deaths of Isaac and the Maccabean martyrs.[173] This atonement does not refer to a payment in terms of propitiating an angry deity, "although a connotation of sacrifice seems fair (as long as that is correctly nuanced)."[174] According to Campbell, Paul's argument in Rom 3:21–26 is that Jesus' death forensically liberates sinners and that God shows himself to be just in that he delivers Jesus from death by means of resurrecting him from the dead in response to Jesus' faithfulness.[175]

CHAPTER SUMMARIES

Having surveyed the state of scholarship, it may be helpful to outline the journey ahead. Chapter 2 offers an analysis of cultic action and cultic function in the Hebrew cult and in Isaiah 53. The chapter argues that both representation and substitution are present in the Hebrew cult and in Isaiah 53. Chapter 3 investigates all of the relevant Second Temple texts that contain a Jewish martyrology. This chapter argues that a Jewish martyrological tradition existed in Second Temple Judaism prior to Romans. It argues further that just as Isaiah 53 describes the death of YHWH's servant with Levitical cultic language, the Greek version of Daniel 3:1–90 and 2 and 4 Maccabees likewise describe the prospective deaths of Daniel's three friends (LXX Dan 3:1–90) and the deaths of the martyrs (2 and 4 Maccabees) with Levitical cultic language and language from Isaiah 53. Chapter 3 also argues that the relevant Jewish martyrological texts suggest that the Jewish martyrs died as representatives of and as substitutes for Israel's Torah-disobedience and that they functioned as Israel's Yom Kippur.

Chapters 4–6 focus on every text in Romans relevant to the thesis that the Jewish martyrological narratives are Paul's background behind his presentation of Jesus' death as a representation of Jews and Gentiles, as a substitution for Jews and Gentiles, and as Yom Kippur for Jews and Gentiles. Chapters 4–6 argue the preceding by offering historical, lexical, grammatical, and theological evidence to support this premise and by offering a comparative analysis of the relevant Levitical cultic texts, Isaiah 53, and the Jewish martyrological narratives. Chapter 4 argues that the Jewish martyrological narratives are a background behind substitution in Rom 3:21–4:25. Chapter 5 argues that the Jewish martyrological narratives are a background behind substitution in Rom 5:6–11, 8:3, and 8:31–34. Chapter 6 argues that representation is present in Romans 5:12—6:23 and that Paul's

173. Ibid.
174. Ibid.
175. Ibid., 656–56.

presentation of Jesus' death as a representation links Paul's presentation of Jesus' death with the Jewish martyrological narratives. Chapter 7 offers general conclusions from chapters 2–6.

A WORD ABOUT THEOLOGICAL METHOD IN PAUL

Paul's letters are occasional and do not present an exhaustive theology of anything, not even an exhaustive theology of the cross. Instead, all of Paul's comments about the death of Jesus are contextual, and they occur in discourse with other communities. They often occur when he engages in fierce rhetorical polemics against his audience (e.g., 1 Corinthians) or against his opponents (e.g., Galatians). Thus, Paul's presentation of Jesus' death is in critical dialogue with particular audiences at specific times in his ministry.[176] Yet, although Paul's remarks about the death of Jesus are not exhaustive and are culturally conditioned, these non-exhaustive and culturally conditioned statements about Jesus' death actually reflect what he believed about the death of Jesus. Consequently, when we read the Pauline letters in context, we can discern Paul's theology of the death of Jesus by engaging in rigorous exegesis and by analyzing his statements about Jesus' death in the diverse historical contexts of his letters. To this kind of an analysis from Paul's letter to the Romans, I now turn.

---

176. Carroll and Green, *The Death of Jesus in Early Christianity*, 114.

2

Representation and Substitution in the Hebrew Cult and in Isaiah 53[1]

INTRODUCTION

In this chapter, I discuss representation and substitution in the Hebrew cult and in Isaiah 53 by offering a selected analysis of the עלה offering, the חטאת offering, the אשם offering, the Yom Kippur ritual, and Isaiah 53. I analyze the preceding offerings via a discussion of cultic action and cultic function in the Hebrew cult.[2] My thesis in this chapter is threefold. First, in the Hebrew cult, the animal sacrifices (in the עלה, the חטאת, and the אשם) and the Yom Kippur ritual all serve to purify/cover/atone sins and to assuage God's wrath (so long as the sacrificial rituals were offered in accordance with YHWH's instructions).[3] Second, the עלה offering, the חטאת offering, the

---

1. I only discuss the sacrifices in the cult that purify/cover/atone sin.

2. By cultic action, I mean the appropriate performance of the Levitical cultic rituals as prescribed by YHWH in Leviticus and reiterated elsewhere in the Hebrew Bible. By cultic function, I mean the positive results achieved for the community as a result of the appropriate cultic action (e.g., forgiveness, reconciliation, expiation, propitiation, atonement). I presented a small portion of the information in this chapter at the 2013 national meeting of the Society of Biblical Literature in Baltimore, MD in the sacrifice, cult, and atonement study group.

3. Biblical scholars and anthropologists have debated the meaning of sacrifice and whether ritual instead of sacrifice is the best word to describe Israelite religion. I think both sacrifice and ritual are legitimate categories by which to interpret cultic action and cultic function in the Hebrew cult. In this chapter, I use the term sacrifice to describe a

אשם offering, and the sacrificial and scapegoat rituals on Yom Kippur corporately functioned *both* as representatives of *and* as substitutes for the people to expunge the effects of their sin upon the land and to liberate the community from YHWH's wrath. Third, Isaiah 53 presents the death of the Servant as a representative of and as a substitute for those for whom he suffered and died, and in doing so it makes use of Levitical cultic language.

My arguments to support the above threefold thesis are as follows. First, YHWH prescribed the עלה offering, the חטאת offering, and the אשם offering for purification and to purify/cover/atone the sins of YHWH's covenant community due to sin's impurity, and these offerings functioned to assuage his wrath. Second, the Yom Kippur ritual temporarily provided annual purification and purification/covering/atonement from every contamination of sin and deliverance from YHWH's wrath if both the priests performed both the sacrificial ritual and the scapegoat ritual in the appropriate manner. Third, the animals in the Hebrew cult and the Servant of Isaiah 53 functioned as representatives of and as substitutes for non-Torah-observant sinners in both the Hebrew and Greek traditions of Isaiah 53, and both textual traditions applied Levitical cultic language to the Servant.[4]

REPRESENTATION AND SUBSTITUTION IN THE HEBREW CULT[5]

Cultic Action and Cultic Function of the עלה Offering

Cultural anthropologists and biblical scholars have debated the role and function of sacrifice in antiquity for decades.[6] In this chapter, I discuss the

---

specific kind of cultic action and cultic function within the Hebrew cult, and I use the term ritual to refer to the performance whereby cultic action and cultic function occurs in the Hebrew cult. Without the ritual, there would be no cultic action or cultic function. Furthermore, I recognize that sacrifice is a complex category with many different layers. The contexts, within which the category of sacrifice occurs, determine how one should understand sacrifice. The category of sacrifice in Ugaritic, Phoenician, Greek, Roman, Jewish, and Christian communities differed both within the same religious community and when compared to different religious communities. For recent criticism of the category of sacrifice and preference for ritual, see Martin Modéus, *Sacrifice and Symbol: Biblical Šĕlāmîm in a Ritual Perspective*.

4. Unless otherwise indicated, all translations of ancient texts are mine.

5. I am aware of the source-critical discussions regarding the composition of the Pentateuch. This chapter will neither engage nor assume higher critical conclusions about the Pentateuch. I will instead focus on the final form of the text as it has been transmitted to and received by interpreters in the Masoretic textual tradition. Consequently, this chapter will be exegetical instead of higher critical in its approach.

6. For a recent survey and critique of this debate, see James W. Watts, *Ritual and*

role and meaning of cultic action and cultic function of sacrifice in the Hebrew cult.[7] In my view, YHWH prescribed the עלה offering to purify/cover/atone sins and to assuage his wrath. Leviticus 1–7 lists five major offerings.[8] Of these, the עלה offering, the הטאת offering, and the אשם offering purify the community due to sin's contaminating effects within the community. These offerings likewise cover/atone sin.

The עלה offering appears elsewhere in cultic contexts in the Pentateuch besides Leviticus (e.g., Exod 29:18).[9] Exodus 29 speaks of the עלה offering in the context of priestly consecration (29:1). Exodus 29:18 identifies the עלה offering as an offering of fire to YHWH with a sweet-smelling aroma (רֵיחַ נִיחֹחַ אִשֶּׁה). An early Jewish tradition, represented in the LXX, interpreted the עלה offering to be a fragrance of sweet-smelling fruit to YHWH in LXX Exod 29:41 (εἰς ὀσμὴν εὐωδίας κάρπωμα κυρίῳ).[10] In Exodus 30, the sin-offering (not the burnt-offering) is specifically identified as purifying/covering/atoning sin (30:9–10). However, the עלה offering was given a specific cultic function to be executed with specific cultic actions in order to deal with the sins of the people, just as the חטאת offering. The sacrificial system was tied to the holiness code, especially to YHWH's holiness (see Lev 1–16). The people's impurity affected the social body of the community. Thus, appropriate cultic action needed to be followed by the priesthood so that the sacrificial ritual would function appropriately and so that the contagion would not spread throughout the community.[11]

YHWH commanded Moses to instruct the people that the עלה offering should be a male without blemish and that this offering would be a gift

---

Rhetoric in Leviticus, 1–37. For a more thorough survey and critique of sacrificial theories as they relate to the Hebrew cult, see Finlan, *The Background and Content of Paul's Cultic Atonement Metaphors*, 11–72.

7. Against Watts (*Ritual and Rhetoric*, 35–36), who asserted that readers of the Hebrew texts cannot discover the meaning of the ritual "but only read the texts that describe, legislate, and polemicize about them to try to understand how their authors used ritual for rhetorical purposes."

8. Burnt-offering (1:1–17; 6:8–13), grain-offering (2:1–16; 6:14–23), peace-offering (3:1–16; 7:11–36), sin-offering (4:1—5:13; 6:24–30), and guilt-offering (5:14—6:7; 7:1–10).

9. Every Old Testament (OT) reference comes from the Masoretic Text (MT) unless otherwise indicated.

10. The MT associates אִשֶּׁה with the burnt-offering in both Exod 29:18 and in 29:41. However, LXX Exod 29:18 translates אִשֶּׁה as θυσίασμα ("victim"), whereas LXX Exod 29:41 translates the MT's אִשֶּׁה as κάρπωμα ("fruit" or "offering of fruit"). The latter translation suggests that the Jews responsible for this particular LXX tradition understood the burnt-offering in Exodus to function as a non-cultic kind of food-offering to YHWH.

11. For this observation, see Janzen, *The Social Meaning of Sacrifice*, 102–10.

to him (1:3, 10). YHWH required the one presenting the offering to lay his hand on its head to symbolize the offender's identification with the animal (1:4).[12] The text explicitly states that the offering should be a sweet-smelling aroma to YHWH (1:9, 13, 17). If the presenter offered the sacrifice in the appropriate way, YHWH accepted both him and the offering in his presence (1:3–4). The implication is that the wrong posture would result in YHWH's judgment (i.e., the rejection of both presenter and offering).

Since the noun sin is absent in the passages that speak of the עלה offering in Leviticus, the text does not explicitly state that the offering dealt with sin. Nevertheless, the presence of important cultic concepts and vocabulary in the text supports that this offering too dealt with the sin of the individual just as the חטאת offering. For example, the individual identified with the offering by placing his hands on the head of the animal (1:4),[13] and he offered this animal to purify/cover/atone him (1:4). Hand placement alone did not signify atonement for sin in the Hebrew cult since YHWH also instructed the people to place their hands on the peace-offering (3:2).[14] However, the concept of hand placement in 1:4 plus the infinitive לְכַפֵּר implies that the burnt-offering functioned in the cult to deal with the sin of the presenter if the presenter followed YHWH's cultic prescriptions.[15]

Debate exists regarding the meaning of כפר.[16] In general, the root in Leviticus communicates the ideas of purification/covering/atoning when it occurs in the context of purifying the people, the tent of meeting, and the entire community because of impurity (either because of or independent of sin [e.g., Lev 12]). In addition, in Leviticus 16 the root is used to describe the cultic action of the sacrificial and scapegoat rituals that YHWH prescribed to purify the tent of meeting and to provide forgiveness of all the sins of all people within the community.[17] J. H. Kurtz asserted that the object of the purification/covering/atonement is never God but something ungodly (e.g., sin or impurity). He went too far when he stated in footnote 1 on page 67 that it is incorrect to speak of providing atonement for the wrath of God. As

---

12. For the social meanings of sacrifice in the Hebrew Bible, see Janzen, *The Social Meaning of Sacrifice*.

13. Contra Hartley, *Leviticus*, 20.

14. Rightly Hartley, *Leviticus*, 20.

15. Contra Hartley, *Leviticus*, 20. Nevertheless, the phrase לְכַפֵּר עָלָיו occurs in connection with the guilt-offering in Lev 14:21.

16. For example, see Kiuchi, *The Purification Offering in the Priestly Literature*, 87–109.

17. Exod 30:10; Lev 4:20, 26, 31, 35; 5:6, 10, 13, 18, 26; 9:7; 12:7–8; 14:18–20, 31, 53; 15:15, 30; 16:6, 11, 16–18, 24, 32–33; 19:22; Num 6:11; 15:25, 28; 17:11; Deut 32:43; Ps 79:9.

I argue throughout this chapter, the act of purifying/covering/atoning sin with the appropriate cultic action likewise accomplishes the cultic function of delivering Israel from YHWH's wrath. Kurtz agreed with this point since he duly noted that both God's wrath was assuaged by the appropriate cultic function and that Gen 32:21 uses a verbal cognate of כפר in a non-cultic context to express Jacob's desire to cover/atone (i.e., propitiate) Esau's wrath against Jacob because of the latter's wicked schemes against his brother (אֲכַפְּרָה פָנָיו).[18]

Lack of an explicit direct object of the infinitive לְכַפֵּר in Lev 1:4 requires the interpreter to discern from the textual evidence the object of the purifying/covering/atonement.[19] The object appears to be the presenter's sin, because the presenter offered the animal to cover עָלָיו (i.e., for the presenter) and because the burnt-offering pleased YHWH (1:4). LXX Lev 1:4 appears to follow this interpretation when it translates עָלָיו לְכַפֵּר as ἐξιλάσασθαι περὶ αὐτοῦ.[20] MT Lev 5:10 associates the act of purifying/covering/atoning the sin of the offender with the burnt-offering (וְאֶת־הַשֵּׁנִי יַעֲשֶׂה עֹלָה כַּמִּשְׁפָּט וְכִפֶּר עָלָיו). In 5:10, the member of the community presented a lamb to the priest as a burnt-offering, and the priest sacrificed the animal for him because of his sin (אֲשֶׁר־חָטָא מֵחַטָּאתוֹ) to purify/cover/atone his sin (וְכִפֶּר עָלָיו) so that YHWH would forgive his sin (וְנִסְלַח לוֹ).

The cultic function of the burnt-offering required the killing of the animal and the sprinkling of its blood upon and around elements at the tent of meeting. Before the cultic action of the burnt-offering was acceptable to YHWH and functioned appropriately, the animal's blood had to be spilt. The death of the animal illustrates that it functioned as both a representative of and as a substitute for the people. The narrative of the burnt-offering in certain places in the Hebrew cult supports this. A few examples must suffice in light of the large amount of textual material.

YHWH informed Moses to tell the sons of Israel that the burnt-offering should be presented as a gift in his presence in the appropriate way (Lev 1:1, 3, 10, 14; 3:7–8).[21] The preceding cultic action brought YHWH's favor

---

18. Similarly J. H. Kurtz, *Offerings, Sacrifices, and Worship in the Old Testament*, 67. Genesis 32:21 refers to Esau's countenance turning as a result of Jacob's gift to him. In Gen 4:5, Cain's countenance fell (i.e., he became angry) with the result that he murdered his brother, Abel. In the case of Jacob and Esau, the former hoped that his gift to Esau would turn his countenance from anger to friendship.

19. For כפר + ל in texts that reference purification, atonement, and forgiveness, see also Lev 1:4; 6:23; 8:15, 34; 10:17; 14:21, 29; 16:10, 17, 27, 34; 17:11; 23:28; Num 8:12; 15:28; 28:22, 30; 29:5; 31:50; 2 Chr 29:24; Neh 10:34; Ezek 45:15, 17.

20. Cf. LXX Lev 14:21. LXX Num 15:28 uses the phrase to talk about the priest's act of offering a sacrifice to purify/cover/atone the one's soul who has sinned inadvertently.

21. See also Lev 3:12, 14; Num 6:14.

upon the presenter (יַקְרִיב אֹתוֹ לִרְצֹנוֹ לִפְנֵי יְהוָה) (Lev 1:3). After the priest presented the prescribed animal before YHWH, the next cultic action was the shedding of blood. The priests placed their hand upon the animal to symbolize identification, representation, and substitution (Lev 1:4). This is evident by the following. First, the slain animal came from the livestock of the presenter (Lev 1:2–3). Second, the priest received the animal from the offender and brought it in the presence of YHWH for the offender at the door of the tent of meeting (Lev 1:2–3). Third, the priest placed his hands upon the animal before he sacrificed it on behalf of the offender, and the slain animal purified/covered/atoned sin after he placed his hand on the live animal (Lev 1:4). Fourth, the priest slaughtered the animal and sprinkled its blood in the appropriate places for the purification of the people (Lev 1:5). Fifth, the slain animal accomplished purification/covering/atonement for the people's sin (Num 8:12). Sixth, the burnt-offering was a sweet-smelling aroma to YHWH (i.e., he was pleased by it) (Lev 1:9, 13, 17; 8:21; Num 15:3; 19:2; 29:2, 8, 13; 29:36). These cultic actions resulted in both a favorable cultic function on behalf of the offender and in a positive posture for the offender in the presence of YHWH (Lev 1:3).

Leviticus 14:21 supports the claim that both the חטאת offering and the burnt-offering accomplished purification/covering/atonement for the people. Moses describes the acceptable animals when/if the people could not afford the more expensive animals (Lev 14:21–22). In 14:22, Moses says two turtledoves or two pigeons, whichever the people could afford, would be acceptable offerings to YHWH. YHWH prescribed that one of the two animals must be a sin-offering and the other a burnt-offering (14:22) (וְהָאֶחָד עֹלָה). In 14:23, YHWH commands the one presenting the offering to bring both the sin-offering and the burnt-offering to the priest for "his cleansing/purifying" (לְטַהֲרָתוֹ). Leviticus 14:24–29 asserts that the priest should consecrate with blood the one who is being cleansed by the sin-offering and the burnt-offering. In 14:30–31, YHWH states that the priest should offer the sin-offering (אֶת־הָאֶחָד חַטָּאת) and the burnt-offering (אֶת־הָאֶחָד עֹלָה) to purify/cover/atone (וְכִפֶּר הַכֹּהֵן) on behalf of the one who purifies himself (הַמִּטַּהֵר) (Lev 14:31). The one who purified himself was the one who presented the appropriate animals to the priest as a burnt-offering and a sin-offering (14:34).

In 15:1–15, YHWH prescribes the purgative procedures that a man with a discharge should follow. In 15:15 YHWH repeats the cleansing/atoning function of both the sin-offering and the burnt-offering from 14:31. Once more, when giving instructions for the woman who experienced a bodily discharge in 15:30, YHWH reiterates the same cultic function of both the sin-offering and the burnt-offering prescribed for a man with a

Representation and Substitution in the Hebrew Cult and in Isaiah 53

bodily discharge in 15:15. Namely, he commands the woman to offer both a sin-offering (חַטָּאת וְעָשָׂה הַכֹּהֵן אֶת־הָאֶחָד) and a burnt-offering (וְאֶת־הָאֶחָד עֹלָה) to purify/cover/atone on behalf of her (וְכִפֶּר עָלֶיהָ הַכֹּהֵן) in the presence of YHWH (יְהוָה לִפְנֵי) because of her unclean discharge (מִזּוֹב טֻמְאָתָהּ).[22] Leviticus 16:24 associates the burnt-offering with purification/covering/atonement of the priest's personal sin and the sins of the people within the community.[23]

If the presenter's sin remained uncovered, then YHWH's judgment would have surely fallen upon the offender (Lev 10:1; 16:1–34). A blasphemer who cursed the name of God bore his own sin by means of being stoned to death (חֶטְאוֹ כִּי־יְקַלֵּל אֱלֹהָיו וְנָשָׂא) (Lev 24:15–16).[24] The act of a sinner bearing his own sin is illustrated earlier in Leviticus when the sons of Aaron inappropriately offered strange fire before YHWH and his judgment consumed them (Lev 10:1). YHWH begins his instructions regarding the Yom Kippur cultic ritual by warning Moses to inform Aaron to obey precisely his instructions regarding cultic action so that he would not experience the same judgment as his sons (Lev 16:1–34, especially 16:1). YHWH warns in 17:8–12 that if any Israelite or sojourner with him performs inappropriate cultic action with respect to the burnt-offering, then he would be cut off (וְנִכְרַת) by YHWH from the people of the covenant.

Other cultic texts in the Hebrew Bible support the importance of the necessary appropriate cultic action to achieve the appropriate cultic function to spare Israel from YHWH's judgment. In Judges 13, the author associates YHWH's acceptance of the burnt-offering on behalf of Israel with the nation's deliverance from his judgment. Israel was doing much evil in the sight of YHWH in the days of the Judges (e.g., 13:1). Thus, YHWH judged his people in that he gave them into the hands of the Philistines (13:1). Nevertheless, YHWH brought salvation to his people by means of Manaoh, his barren wife, and their son (Samson) (13:2–14). When the angel of YHWH appeared to Manaoh, he attempted to detain the angel (13:15). Instead, the angel urged Manaoh to prepare a burnt-offering for YHWH (13:16), for he did not know that the angel was the angel of YHWH (13:16). After Manaoh and his wife offered the burnt-offering, the angel ascended to heaven in the flame (13:20). Then, Manaoh fell on his face because he knew that the angel was the angel of YHWH and that he had seen God (13:20–22). As a result, Manaoh thought that he would die

---

22. So also MT Num 8:12.

23. וְרָחַץ אֶת־בְּשָׂרוֹ בַּמַּיִם בְּמָקוֹם קָדוֹשׁ וְלָבַשׁ אֶת־בְּגָדָיו וְיָצָא וְעָשָׂה אֶת־עֹלָתוֹ וְאֶת־עֹלַת הָעָם וְכִפֶּר בַּעֲדוֹ וּבְעַד הָעָם

24. For a similar point, see MT Num 5:6.

(מוֹת נָמוּת כִּי אֱלֹהִים רָאִינוּ) (13:22). His wife, however, responded by saying since YHWH received their burnt-offering as an acceptable gift and since he had revealed great things to them, he would not repay them with the judgment of death because God received the offering.

In 2 Kings 5, Naaman, the Syrian, wanted to be cleansed of his leprosy. He obeyed the exhortation of his slave girl to go to Elisha, a prophet of YHWH, in Israel to be cleansed (2 Kgs 5:1–9). Upon his arrival in Israel, Elisha sent word to Naaman that he should wash himself in the Jordan so that his leprosy would be healed (2 Kgs 5:10). At first, Naaman responded to Elisha's exhortation with anger until his servants reminded him that Elisha had spoken a great word to which Naaman would do well to heed (2 Kgs 5:11–12). Naaman obeyed Elisha, washed himself in the Jordan, and he was cleaned from his leprosy (2 Kgs 5:14). After his cleansing, Naaman returned to Elisha, acknowledged that the God of Israel was the only true God, and offered Elisha a gift (2 Kgs 5:15), which Elisha rejected (2 Kgs 5:16). Thus, Naaman proclaimed that from that point forward, he would only offer a burnt-offering (i.e., a sacrifice) to YHWH (2 Kgs 5:17), and he prayed that YHWH would forgive him "by this" (2 Kgs 5:18).

In 2 Kgs 5:17, the phrase עֹלָה וָזֶבַח ("burnt-offering and sacrifice") is a nominal hendiadys. That is, the sacrifice (וָזֶבַח) to which Naaman refers is the burnt-offering (עֹלָה). The LXX's rendering supports the preceding interpretation by using the phrase ὁλοκαύτωμα καὶ θυσίασμα ("burnt-offering and victim"). Naaman's prayer in 2 Kgs 5:18 suggests that Naaman asked YHWH to use the cultic action of the burnt-offering sacrifice to function as a means by which he would be forgiven and escape YHWH's judgment. The grammar of 2 Kgs 5:17–18 supports this interpretation.

The prepositional phrases לְעַבְדְּךָ and לַדָּבָר הַזֶּה modify the verbal clause יִסְלַח יְהוָה. Since the grammatical antecedent וָזֶבַח, which is the second noun within a nominal hendiadys construction עֹלָה וָזֶבַח, identifies the עֹלָה offering as a sacrifice, the phrase לַדָּבָר הַזֶּה should be taken to refer to the entire conceptual package (עֹלָה וָזֶבַח) of 2 Kgs 5:17. This interpretation suggests that Naaman will only offer sacrifices to YHWH. Yet, the phrase also looks forward to Naaman's participation in worship with his master in the house of Rimmon since the phrase לַדָּבָר הַזֶּה precedes this act of idolatry, since the phrase בַּדָּבָר הַזֶּה follows his act of idolatry, and since the verbal clause יְהוָה לְעַבְדְּךָ בַּדָּבָר הַזֶּה יִסְלַח concludes 2 Kgs 5:18. The latter statement is similar to the verbal clause in 2 Kgs 5:17 that introduces 2 Kgs 5:17–18. My reading of the verse suggests that Naaman petitioned YHWH to receive his sacrificial burnt-offering as a means by which he would pardon him and restrain YHWH's wrath when he bowed down at the house of Rimmon with his master to worship.

In 2 Kings 16 and in Jeremiah 14, the burnt-offering sacrifice was ineffective for the people because of the nation's sin. The priest participated in the cultic action of the burnt-offering with the result that YHWH consumed them with his wrath via the judgment of pagan nations (in the case of 2 Kgs 16) and with famine and pestilence (in the case of Jer 14). Ezekiel 43 suggests that the appropriate cultic action of both the sin-offering and the burnt-offering served as a means by which YHWH accepted his people (וְרָצָאתִי אֶתְכֶם, esp. Ezek 43:27). Repentance and appropriate cultic action purified/covered/atoned sin, provided forgiveness for the people, and suspended YHWH's wrath from the offender and the community.[25] However, inappropriate cultic action warranted YHWH's wrath upon the offender and upon the community, because the priest offered the burnt-offering sacrifice to be a representative of and a substitute for the people.

Cultic Action and Cultic Function of the חטאת Offering

YHWH prescribed the חטאת offering to purify his covenant community from sin's contaminating effects and to assuage his wrath against the community by providing purification/covering/atonement of/for the people's sins through the representative and substitutionary חטאת offering. Jacob Milgrom labored to refute the translation sin-offering for חטאת. He argued in many places that the translation of חטאת as sin-offering is "inaccurate on all grounds: contextually, morphologically, and etymologically."[26] First, Milgrom argued from contextual grounds that the range of the term חטאת speaks against the notion of sin since the offering is connected to recovery from childbirth (Lev 12:8), to the successful completion of a Nazarite vow (Num 6:11), and to the dedication of a newly constructed altar (Lev 8:15; cf. Exod 29:36).[27] Based on these scriptural references, Milgrom suggested that the חטאת was "prescribed for persons and objects who could not have possibly sinned."[28] He instead defended the translation "purification-offering." Second, Milgrom argued on grammatical grounds that the root חטאת appears as a piel derivative and that its corresponding verb never occurs in the qal stem, which would translate as "to sin, to do wrong," but in the piel

---

25. Cf. also Philo, *Mut.* 1:233.

26. Jacob Milgrom, *Studies in Cultic Theology and Terminology*, 67; Milgrom, *Leviticus 1–16*, 253–318. Against Milgrom, see Zohar, "Repentance and Purification," 609–18.

27. Milgrom, *Studies in Cultic Theology and Terminology*, 67.

28. Milgrom, *Leviticus 1–16*, 253.

stem, which always translates "to cleanse, to expurgate, to decontaminate" (e.g., Lev 8:15; Ezek 43:22, 26; Ps 51:9).²⁹

However, the texts cited by Milgrom do not prove that the חטאת exclusively refers to purification without regard for the effects of sin. Instead, his observations only demonstrate that there are examples where the חטאת should be translated as purification-offering and refers to the purification of the sancta.³⁰ In my view, the חטאת functioned in certain contexts in the Levitical cult to purify both temple ornaments and YHWH's covenant community *because of* the contaminating effects of sin, even in some texts in which the חטאת offering highlights purification. The offender or the priest presents the חטאת to purify the community (i.e., the offender) and to protect both the sancta and the community from impurity due to sin's contamination. The offering resulted in purification/cleansing/atonement and deliverance from YHWH's wrath.

Milgrom cited Lev 12:8 as proof that the חטאת offering refers exclusively to the purification of the sancta. Purification is certainly present in the text, because the entire context of the חטאת pertains to the purification of an unclean pregnant woman, who gives birth, due to her pregnancy. The woman remained impure after childbirth and was forbidden from entering into the sanctuary of the Lord until after her impurity (Lev 12:1–6). Once the days of impurity expired, she would take the appropriate animals for both the עלה offering and the חטאת offering in order to purify/cover/atone her impurity so that she would be cleansed (וְכִפֶּר עָלֶיהָ וְטָהֵרָה) (Lev 12:7). The sancta, however, was not defiled by the unclean woman during her purification, because she was not permitted to enter into the sanctuary until after her impurity (Lev 12:4). After her days of purification, the priest took the unclean woman's offering and purified/covered/atoned "for her" (וְכִפֶּר עָלֶיהָ) and not for the sanctuary.

Baruch A. Levine proposed that one of the two חטאת offerings was purgative and the other was expiatory because the priests offered one as a safeguard for the sanctuary and to protect the priesthood from contamination, but the people provided the eaten חטאת offering to expiate specific offenses.³¹ Milgrom responded by arguing that neither the eaten חטאת offering nor the burnt חטאת offering has a purificatory purpose for the following three reasons. First, it is burned outside the camp on Yom Kippur though it is brought by the people (16:5, 27). The burning element fits the rule con-

---

29. Ibid., 253–54, esp. 253.

30. I got this thought from Kiuchi (*The Purification Offering*, 40), who got it from A. M. Rodriguez (*Substitution in the Hebrew Cultus*, 104–5).

31. Baruch A. Levine, *In the Presence of the Lord*, 103–4; citation from Milgrom, *Leviticus 1–16*, 263. For Milgrom's objections, see *Leviticus 1–16*, 263.

cerning the blood of the חטאת brought within the sanctuary (6:23; 10:18), a rule alluded to on Yom Kippur when the blood of the sacrificial goat was brought into the sanctuary for purgation (16:27). Second, the burnt חטאת offering did not safeguard anything because it had no apotropaic function. Furthermore, it did not purify the priesthood because the blood, the purgative element, was never sprinkled upon an individual offender, not even upon the priest. Third, there were no offenses for which the eaten חטאת offering was offered to expiate. Milgrom's criticisms of Levine were accurate in that they demonstrated the speciousness of distinguishing between the two חטאת offerings in the context of the Levitical cult. However, both Levine and Milgrom failed to recognize how the חטאת offering functioned within the larger narrative of the Levitical cult.

The cathartic function of the חטאת offering neither determines the offering's function in every context nor precludes the offering from dealing with the effects of the offender's sin. As early as Exodus, YHWH prescribed the חטאת offering to be offered to purify/cover/atone sin (Exod 29:36; 30:10). The חטאת offering specifically functioned in the Levitical cult to purify/cover/atone any offender's unintentional sin (Lev 4:2). YHWH commanded that if the anointed priest sinned in accordance with the people, then he should present the חטאת offering for his specific transgression (Lev 4:3). The priest's חטאת offering purified/covered/atoned his sin that contaminated the entire community, and this offering purified the contaminating effects of sin upon the inanimate objects of the sacrificial cult.

In Lev 4:1–3, the חטאת offering seems to function in a cathartic sense as a sin-offering,[32] because YHWH prescribes it to deal with inadvertent sin against any one of his commandments (מִכֹּל מִצְוֹת יְהוָה). Regardless of whether one sins inadvertently against YHWH's Torah, the consequence of Torah-disobedience was judgment (Lev 10:1–3; 16:1–2; 18:5; Deut 5:1—27:26). Therefore, the priest slaughtered the bull, brought the blood of the bull to the door of the tent of meeting, dipped his finger in the blood, sprinkled it seven times in the presence of YHWH in front of the veil of the holy place, and sprinkled the blood on the designated objects at the tent of meeting to deal with the contaminating effects of sin (Lev 4:4–7). Then, the priest offered the bull's fat as a חטאת offering (Lev 4:8–10), after which he burned the fat outside of the camp (Lev 4:12) so that the sacrificial bull offered as a חטאת offering for sin would not contaminate the purified/covered/atoned community with its presence.[33]

---

32. Against Milgrom, *Leviticus 1–16*, 232, 253–92.

33. George Buchanan Gray argued in the 1970s that the translation of הַחַטָּאת as "the sin-offering" is incorrect since the term means sin and not offering. For his argument, see *Sacrifice in the Old Testament*, 55–66. My exegesis calls into question Gray's

The use of the phrase "outside of the camp" (אֶל־מִחוּץ לַמַּחֲנֶה) in Leviticus and elsewhere in the Hebrew Bible supports the claim that the fat of the sacrificed חטאת was taken outside of the camp so that the community for whom the priest offered the חטאת would avoid contamination. The priest burned the animal offered as a חטאת offering outside the camp (אֶל־מִחוּץ לַמַּחֲנֶה) (Lev 4:12, 21; 6:4; 16:27; cf. Num 19:3). Moses commanded Aaron's nephews to take the dead bodies of Aaron's sons outside of the camp (אֶל־מִחוּץ לַמַּחֲנֶה) after YHWH killed them for inappropriate cultic action (Lev 10:1–5, esp. 10:4–5). YHWH prescribed that a leprous member within the community should go outside of the camp away from the community so that he would not contaminate the clean members within the community, and the priest went outside of the camp (אֶל־מִחוּץ לַמַּחֲנֶה) to evaluate the leprous person (Lev 14:3–4; cf. Num 5:1–4). Members of the Israelite community stoned an Israelite woman's blasphemous son outside of the camp (אֶל־מִחוּץ לַמַּחֲנֶה),[34] and members of the covenant community went outside of the camp (אֶל־מִחוּץ לַמַּחֲנֶה) to meet the unclean captives away from the non-covenant community (Lev 24:10–14, 23, esp. 24:14, 23; cf. Num 15:32–36). Thus, the contamination within the community was taken outside of the camp via the fat of the חטאת.

YHWH also commanded any non-priestly offender within the community to follow the appropriate cultic protocol to purify/cover/atone sin when he broke any of his stipulations and when the offender's sin became known within the community (Lev 4:13–14). YHWH commanded the community to bring his bull to the door of the tent of meeting (Lev 4:14). The elders from the community placed their hands upon the head of the bull in YHWH's presence and slaughtered the bull in his presence (Lev 4:15). Then, the anointed priest received the blood from the elders, brought it to the door of the tent of meeting, dipped his finger in the blood, and sprinkled it seven times before YHWH in the presence of the veil (Lev 4:16–17). The priest repeated the same cultic actions performed for his unintentional sin for the community's sin so that he would purify/cover/atone them so that the people would experience YHWH's forgiveness (Lev 4:18–22).

That the priest's cultic action achieved purification, covering/atonement of sin, and pardon for the people in Lev 4:20–22 is evident in 4:20 from the two verbal clauses וְכִפֶּר עֲלֵהֶם הַכֹּהֵן and וְנִסְלַח לָהֶם. These clauses should be understood a synonymous statements. This interpretation means that the last clause further explains the first with a different statement. Accordingly, וְכִפֶּר עֲלֵהֶם הַכֹּהֵן ("and the priest will atone for them") is defined by וְנִסְלַח לָהֶם

---

claim.

34. For additional support, see MT Num 5:3.

("and it will be forgiven them"). The priest's act of providing purification and a covering/atonement for sin was a provision for YHWH's forgiveness. In fact, the כפר offering provided a covering for one's sins in the presence of YHWH, which is forgiveness (Lev 4:20–22). Thus, Lev 4:13–22 connects the חטאת offering both with the offender's act of committing sin and with the priest's provision for purification because of sin's contaminating effects upon the community. The priest's cultic action purified the community due to sin's contaminating effects by providing purification/covering/atonement so that the community would receive YHWH's forgiveness and escape his judgment. The latter interpretation seems correct, even though כפר in the piel refers to purifying/covering/atoning the altar instead of sin, because the altar needed purification/covering/atoning due to sin's contaminating effects amongst the people, whose sin stained even the most holy objects.[35] The priest provides the חטאת offering to purify/cover/atone the altar (Lev 4:26) and to purify/cover/atone the sins of the people because of their sin (Lev 4:20, 31). The חטאת offering also enables the community to escape YHWH's judgment, which the sentence in 4:20 supports.[36] When sinners break any one of YHWH's divine commandments, "the whole existence of the sinner is at stake."[37] Thus, the sinner is forgiven "because of the expiation of his sin" and because "the expiatory ritual also concerns the salvation of the whole existence of the sinner."[38] This expiation of the sinner's sin, symbolized through the representative and substitutionary sacrificial ritual, likewise achieved propitiation from YHWH's wrath, symbolized by the offender's experience of forgiveness from his sins.

The priest performed the same cultic action for a non-priestly leader who sinned as he did for himself and for those who sinned within the community. The leader brought the appropriate animal to the priest, identified with it to show that the animal and the priest represent the people by placing his hand upon its head, and slaughtered it in the place where the burnt-offering was slaughtered as a sin-offering to YHWH to show that the animals were offered as substitutes for the people. Next, he sprinkled the blood of the animal in the prescribed places in order to purify/cover/atone the sin of the offender and in order to achieve YHWH's forgiveness for him (4:22–27). With the exception of the use of a female lamb without blemish

---

35. So Kiuchi, *The Purification Offering*, 36–37. For further textual support, see Exod 30:10; Lev 4:20, 26, 31, 35; 5:6, 10, 13, 18, 26; 9:7; 12:7–8; 14:18–20, 31, 53; 15:15, 30; 16:6, 11, 16–18, 24, 32–33; 19:22; Num 6:11; 15:25, 28; 17:11; Deut 32:43; Job 38:29; Ps 79:9; Isa 28:18.

36. Rightly Kiuchi, *The Purification Offering*, 36.

37. Ibid., 37

38. Ibid.

instead of a male goat, the priest repeated the same cultic action for any soul that sinned against YHWH (4:28–35).

Leviticus 5:1–13 repeats similar cultic actions for those who sinned by taking YHWH's name in vain or by touching a dead carcass. Leviticus 4–5 suggests that the purpose of the cultic actions of both the offender and the priest was to purify/cover/atone sin and to achieve YHWH's forgiveness for them (4:26, 31; 5:10). Inappropriate cultic action or no cultic action for the offender would have resulted in YHWH's anger against the offender due to the presence of his sin. References to YHWH's pleasure (נִיחֹחַ לַיהוָה לְרֵיחַ) (4:31), YHWH's presence (4:4,6–7, 15, 17–18, 24; 5:26) (לִפְנֵי יְהוָה), forgiveness (4:26; 5:10,31) (נִסְלַח), and references to the offender's guilt (אֶת־אֲשָׁמוֹ) (5:6–7) support that inappropriate cultic action or the absence of cultic action on behalf of the offender would have resulted in no purification of or covering/atonement for sin. Consequently, YHWH would have displayed anger against the offender because of his sin.[39] Finally, Numbers also states that the חטאת offering purified/covered/atoned sin (Num 28:22).[40]

Milgrom's grammatical argument against understanding the חטאת as a sin-offering also fails to convince. He asserted that when the root חטאת occurs in the piel stem, it translates "to cleanse, to expurgate, to decontaminate."[41] Therefore, the verb refers to purification. I offer two brief responses to Milgrom's grammatical analysis.

First, he correctly observed that חטאת refers to purification in the piel stem, just as כפר (Exod 30:10; Lev 5:16).[42] Leviticus 8:15 is one of multiple texts that has a piel form of חטאת (e.g., Lev 9:15; Ezek 43:22). Leviticus 8:15 refers to the purification of the altar since יְחַטֵּא takes אֶת־הַמִּזְבֵּחַ as its direct object. The text elaborates the cathartic nature of 8:15 later when it states that blood should be poured out on the foundation of the altar in order to sanctify the altar by covering over it (וְאֶת־הַדָּם יָצַק אֶל־יְסוֹד הַמִּזְבֵּחַ וַיְקַדְּשֵׁהוּ לְכַפֵּר עָלָיו). The cathartic nature of the חטאת offering appears earlier in 8:1–14 when YHWH gives Moses several instructions regarding ritual purification. However, just as YHWH prescribed the אשם offering to deal with the problem of sin within the community (5:1–7), he likewise prescribed the חטאת offering to deal with sin within the community (5:8). Sin within the community required prescription of the חטאת offering, which YHWH prescribed to function within the cult after sin had already been

---

39. For additional texts that emphasize both the cultic action and the cultic function of the sin-offering in the Hebrew Bible, see Num 8:12; 28:22; 29:5; Ezek 43:25–26; 45:25–26.

40. See also Num 29:11.

41. Milgrom, *Studies in Cultic Terminology and Theology*, 67.

42. For additional texts, see Lev 7:7; 16:30, 33; 17:11; Num 5:8; Ps 78:38.

committed within the community (5:1–8). The entire section of 4:1—5:13 accentuates that the חטאת offering indeed dealt with the effects of sin within the community.[43]

Second, the root חטאת occurs in the qal stem to refer to committing the act of sin (4:2, 27).[44] In 4:27, the verb occurs in the qal stem along with both the אשם offering and the חטאת offering. In 4:27, both the אשם offering and the חטאת offering describe the appropriate cultic action that would rid the community of sin when one of its members sinned. Thus, the translation "to purify" in the piel form does not preclude the חטאת offering from referring to a sin-offering. Even if one rejects sin-offering as a translation for the חטאת offering, the latter still functioned as a solution to the pollution of sin within the community because there are contexts where YHWH prescribes the חטאת offering to deal with the effects of sin (i.e., impurity) in the community, just as he deals with sin through the אשם offering.

Milgrom was insistent that the priest did not present the חטאת to deal with the sin of the offender because individuals offered the חטאת offering under two circumstances: severe physical impurity (Lev 12–15) or the commission of inadvertent sins (Lev 4).[45] He argued that physical impurity was removed by ablution (15:8).[46] Spiritual impurity, on the other hand, did not require a purification rite.[47] The presence of inner guilt proved that the offender had already undergone inner purification.[48] Once more, Milgrom argued that the חטאת offering never purified its presenter because the latter sprinkled its blood on the holy objects (8:15),[49] and the blood was confined to the sanctuary having never been applied to a person.[50] However, although the context in the ritual setting is different in Lev 10:17, Moses states there that the חטאת offering takes away the sin of the assembly (לָשֵׂאת אֶת־עֲוֹן הָעֵדָה) to purify/cover/atone on behalf of them (עֲלֵיהֶם לְכַפֵּר) before them in the presence of YHWH. Leviticus 10:17 overtly states that purification/covering/atonement was for the offender, but Num 18:1 speaks of taking away the sin of the sanctuary (תִּשְׂאוּ אֶת־עֲוֹן הַמִּקְדָּשׁ).

---

43. So Finlan, *The Background and Content of Paul's Cultic Atonement Metaphors*, 34. Contra Milgrom, *Leviticus 1–16*, 254–58.
44. See also Lev 5:1, 17; Num 15:27; 1 Sam 19:5; Job 5:24; Ezek 14:13.
45. Milgrom, *Leviticus 1–16*, 254.
46. Ibid.
47. Ibid.
48. Ibid.
49. Ibid., 254–55.
50. Ibid., 255.

The red cow sacrifice in Numbers 19 further supports the above observations of the חטאת offering. Milgrom argued at first glance that the red cow ritual was not a sacrifice at all since the priest did not sprinkle the cow's blood on the altar. The entire cow and its blood were incinerated outside of the camp after the latter was sprinkled seven times in the direction of the tent of meeting (Num 19:4).[51] Milgrom correctly noted that there are similarities between the red heifer ritual and the חטאת offering that support the proposal that the former is indeed a sacrifice. One similarity is that the priest sprinkled some of the blood in front of the tent of meeting to purify the people.[52]

Additionally, I would add that YHWH commands Moses to instruct the people to take a red heifer (פָּרָה אֲדֻמָּה) without blemish or defect and to give it to the priest (Num 19:1–2). The priest, Eleazar, had to take the heifer outside the camp to slaughter it (Num 19:3). He had to sprinkle the blood in front of the tent of meeting outside of the camp and away from the tent of meeting about seven paces (Num 19:4), after which he burned the remaining part of the cow (Num 19:5–6). Once the priest completed this ritual, he washed both his garments and his flesh with water (Num 19:7). The priest performed this ritual washing after he slaughtered the red heifer because both the red heifer sacrifice and the priest's performance of this ritual symbolically communicated that sin and its effects within the community were being taking away from the community by means of the cultic action of the red heifer sacrifice. Numbers 19:7 supports this interpretation when the text states that the priest would remain unclean until evening after he returned to the camp. In a representative and in a substitutionary manner, the clean priest became unclean for the people when he offered the red heifer sacrifice for the people. Numbers 19:8–9 further affirms this when it states that a pure man would go outside of the camp to gather the ashes of the red heifer outside of the camp in a pure place. Numbers 19:8b describes the red heifer ritual as a חטאת offering that corresponds to one's impurity (לְמֵי נִדָּה). Immediately after his discussion of the red heifer ritual, YHWH discusses the problem of impurity within the community because of death and the process by which the community became pure (Num 19:10–32).

Numbers 19 nowhere states that purification is necessary because of sin or that death is the result of the community's sin. However, the numerous accounts of death in the preceding chapters before Numbers 19 (Num 14:1–37; 15:1–36; 16:1–50) and in the following chapters after Numbers 19 (Num 20:1–29; 21:1–35; 25:1–9; 31:1–42) suggest that the red heifer sacrifice

---

51. Milgrom, *Studies in Cultic Theology and Terminology*, 87.
52. Ibid., 88–89, esp. 89.

and the other ritual washings in Numbers 19 were prescribed because of the presence of death and that death contaminated the community due to the circulation of sin within the community.[53] George Buchanon Gray argued that the red heifer ritual was not a Jewish sacrifice since the cow was not sacrificed on YHWH's altar and since it was not presented to YHWH as an offering. Therefore, it was not a sin-offering or an expiation offering, but an expiatory object.[54] The context of Numbers 19 militates against Gray's arguments.

For example, the people sinned by rebelling against YHWH, and he judged them by killing them (Num 14:1–37). An Israelite sinned against YHWH by breaking the Sabbath, and God judged the offender by having him stoned to death (Num 15:32–36). Korah sinned by leading a rebellion against Moses and Aaron, and YHWH judged him and the rebels by killing them (Num 16:1–35). Moses sinned by striking the rock and YHWH judged him by not allowing him to enter into the Promised Land before his death (cf. Num 20:10–13 with Deut 32). The people sinned by speaking against YHWH and against Moses, and God judged them by killing the offenders in the wilderness (Num 21:4–6). The people sinned by worshipping false gods and by participating in inappropriate relationships with women who did not worship YHWH, and he judged them by killing the offenders (Num 25:1–18). Thus, purification by means of the red heifer sacrifice is necessary in Numbers 19 *because of* sin's contaminating effects upon the entire community, and sin within the community resulted in death within the community. Consequently, the חטאת offering functions in Num 19:9 as an offering of purification *because of* sin.[55] The חטאת offering and the priest both represented and substituted for the people, because the people and the priest identified with the חטאת offering, the priest identified with the offering and the people and became unclean as a result, and the people were purified/covered/atoned by means of the priest's appropriate cultic performance of the red heifer ritual.[56]

---

53. I got the above insight from Gordon J. Wenham.

54. See Gray, *Sacrifice in the Old Testament*, 59–60.

55. Milgrom (*Studies in Cultic Terminology and Theology*, 90) argued that the statement "it is a חטאת" in Num 19:9 refers to the ashes of the red heifer instead of the red heifer since הוּא ("it") is masculine and הַפָּרָה ("heifer") is feminine. The pronoun "it" could be functioning as a synecdoche: a part that refers to the whole. That is, "it" could grammatically refer to the "ashes" (אֵפֶר), which are part of the red heifer sacrifice, but "it" could likewise conceptually refer to the entire red heifer ritual, even though the grammar only points to the ashes.

56. In addition to Lev 4:1—5:13, the חטאת offering occurs in the following texts: Exod 29:10–14, 36–37 (consecration of priests and the altar), Lev 8:14–17 (consecration of priests and the altar), Lev 9:2–3, 7–15 (the eight day service), Lev 10:16–20 (the

Cultic Action and Cultic Function of the אשם Offering

YHWH prescribed the אשם offering to purify/cover/atone sin and to assuage his wrath through representative and substitutionary sacrifices. This offering dealt with the offender's inadvertent sin (יְהוָה וְחָטְאָה בִשְׁגָגָה מִקָּדְשֵׁי יְהוָה כִּי־תִמְעֹל מַעַל) (Lev 5:15). YHWH commanded the offender to offer a compensatory offering (וְהֵבִיא אֶת־אֲשָׁמוֹ) in his presence to purify/cover/atone the offender's guilt (לַיהוָה וְהֵבִיא אֶת־אֲשָׁמוֹ). The offender's incurred guilt was the result of YHWH's declaration against him on account of his transgressions (Lev 5:17–19).[57] This declaration counted the offenders offense against him until he participated in the appropriate cultic action in accordance with YHWH's prescriptions (Lev 5:18–19). Moses accentuates the compensatory nature of both the offender's cultic action and cultic function by using the root אשם three times in Lev 5:19 (אָשָׁם הוּא אָשֹׁם אָשַׁם) and by expressing that the guilt-offering purifies/covers/atones the sin of the guilty (Lev 14:21; 19:21).

Before YHWH accepted this offering, the offender offered a subsequent animal to the priest to restitute his sin against the holy things of YHWH, so that the priest would purify/cover/atone his sin and so that the offender would be forgiven (Lev 5:15–16). Even if the offender was unaware of his transgression, YHWH would have still pronounced him guilty because of his transgression of any one of YHWH's commandments (עָשְׂתָה אַחַת מִכָּל־מִצְוֹת). Consequently, he would have carried his own sin by receiving YHWH's judgment. In this respect, the guilt-offering and the restitution offering placated the judgment of YHWH. The sin-offering and the burnt-offering were the same (כַּחַטָּאת כָּאָשָׁם) in that the priest purified/covered/atoned sin with both offerings (יְכַפֶּר־בּוֹ) (Lev 7:7).[58] The text supports this interpretation for at least three reasons. First, the guilt-offering and the restitution offering purified/covered/atoned the sins of the offender (Lev 5:15–17). Second, the offender bore his own iniquity until he performed the appropriate cultic action (נָשָׂא עֲוֹנוֹ) (Lev 5:1). Third, the offender's appropriate cultic action along with the appropriate cultic function resulted in his receiving YHWH's forgiveness (אָשָׁם הוּא אָשֹׁם אָשַׁם לַיהוָה) (Lev 5:18).

חטאת flesh incident), Lev 12:6, 8; 14:19, 22, 31; 15:15, 30; Num 19:9, 17 (purification from natural uncleanness), Levicus 16 (Yom Kippur), Num 6:11, 14 (purification of the Nazirite), Num 8:7–8, 12 (purification of the Levites), and Lev 23:19; Num 7; 15:22–29 (festive and unique occasions). The preceding information comes from Kiuchi, *The Purification Offering*, 39.

57. Against the idea of incurred guilt, but in favor of feeling guilt, see Milgrom, *Cult and Conscience*, 9–12. Contra Milgrom, see Kiuchi, *The Purification Offering*, 31–34.

58. According to Num 5:7–8, the offender should perform the cultic action of confessing sins to achieve the desired cultic function of restitution with YHWH.

In the Hebrew cult, the one who carried/bore his own sin suffered YHWH's judgment, because the one who carried/bore his own sin did not receive YHWH's forgiveness (Lev 5:1, 17; 17:16).[59]

Numbers 5:7 states that the appropriate cultic action of the אשם offering resulted in the offender's restitution. Isaiah 53:10 applies the אשם offering to the death of YHWH's servant in context where the servant dies (and resurrects) for the sins of others in order to justify them (cf. Isa 53:4–12). Appropriate cultic action resulted in the appropriate cultic function of the אשם offering, which the priest offered as a substitute for the guilt of the people and as a representative of the people.

CULTIC ACTION AND CULTIC FUNCTION AND THE YOM KIPPUR RITUAL[60]

The Yom Kippur ritual temporarily provided annual purification from sin and deliverance from YHWH's wrath for Israel if the offender appropriately performed both the sacrificial ritual and the scapegoat ritual in the prescribed manner. In Leviticus 16, YHWH commanded the priests to atone for all of their personal transgressions, the transgressions of the people, and the impurities of the holy place because of the impurities of the people on Yom Kippur (Lev 16:3–28). YHWH gave Moses specific prescriptions to inform the priests as to how they must conduct appropriate cultic action in order to achieve the appropriate cultic function (Lev 16:3–34). After YHWH stated to Moses how Aaron should perform the Yom Kippur ritual, he confirmed that the day of the ritual should be celebrated every year for the cleansing of sin (Lev 16:29–30). This cleansing through the offering of blood, accompanied by contrition, repentance, and the performance of the scapegoat ritual, achieved and symbolized God's forgiveness for the entire nation (Lev 16:29–30; cf. 1QS 3:4),[61] and the animals functioned as the

---

59. For texts in the Hebrew Bible that associate the action of bearing sin/guilt with YHWH's judgment or forgiveness, see Isa 33:24; 53:4, 12; Mic 7:18.

60. Although critical scholars debate the literary character of Leviticus 16, my concern here is not to engage these scholarly debates since literary critical issues are extraneous to my thesis. Instead, I interpret the information in the final form of the Masoretic text that speaks to cultic action and cultic function on Yom Kippur rather than interact with scholarly conjectures about the various literary strata from which a hypothetical redactor extrapolated to create Leviticus 16.

61. Later Jewish traditions suggested that during Yom Kippur, Jews devoted themselves to communal confession, penitential prayer, and praise to God for lengthy periods of time. *Jubilees* 34:18–19 states that Israel should atone for their sins once a year and that Yom Kippur was decreed "so that they might mourn on it on account of their sin and on account of all of their transgression and on account of all their errors in

nation's representatives and substitutes. In this manner, atonement in the Hebrew cult was a salvation-event (*heilsgeschehen*).⁶²

Cultic Action and Cultic Function on Yom Kippur

The cultic action on Yom Kippur functioned to purify and cover/atone every effect of sin. The action was representative of the people, substitutionary for the people, and it appeased YHWH's wrath. The priest offered the prescribed animals as an offering for sin (16:3, 5–6) to purify and cover/atone on behalf of him and on behalf of his house (16:6, 11) and the prescribed animals for a burnt-offering to cover/atone on behalf of himself and on behalf of the people (16:3, 5, 24). This Day of Atonement was more efficacious than the other cultic rituals performed throughout the year, because the priest performed both the sacrificial ritual to purify and to purify/cover/atone *all* of his sins, *all* the sins of the people, and *all* of the holy ornaments due to the contamination of the sins of the people throughout the community and because he performed the scapegoat ritual whereby *all* of the sins of the people and *all* of their contaminating effects upon the land were carried away from the people into the wilderness to Azazel (16:8, 10, 26). The sacrificial ritual and the scapegoat ritual on Yom Kippur reveal that the priests' daily cultic action of sacrificing the burnt-offering, the offering for sin, and the guilt-offering were unable to eradicate the community's ongoing experience with sin, which in part explains the need for this annual Day of Atonement.

In Lev 16:1–2, YHWH states that inappropriate cultic action in his presence resulted in the death of the offender. The literary prescription in 16:1 refers to the deaths of Aaron's sons when they offered strange fire before YHWH (לִפְנֵי־יְהוָה וַיָּמֻת), and it forges a link with 10:1–3 since the latter text discusses the reason YHWH killed Aaron's sons. Leviticus 10:2 says that YHWH consumed Aaron's sons with his wrath due to their inappropriate offering of אֵשׁ זָרָה before him. Thus, Moses' instructions to Aaron regarding appropriate cultic action on Yom Kippur begin with a reminder of YHWH's wrath if his cultic prescriptions were inappropriately performed.

---

order to purify themselves on this day once a year." Philo expressed that many Jews took up the entire day celebrating Yom Kippur (*Spec.* 2.196). Sirach 50:17–19 states that people fell on their faces to worship the Lord and that the people of the Lord prayed "until the adornment of the Lord was completed and until they completed his service." Such lengthy practices, along with Yom Kippur's cultic sacrifices, were seen by some Jews to effect atonement for sin during the Second Temple period (e.g., 1Q342).

62. For a detailed argument for atonement in the Hebrew cult as a salvation-event, see Bernd Janowski, *Sühne als Heilsgeschehen*.

Representation and Substitution in the Hebrew Cult and in Isaiah 53 55

This reminder would have gotten Aaron's attention since YHWH's wrath consumed his two sons due to their inappropriate cultic action.

Leviticus 16:2 states that YHWH would judge Aaron by killing him, just as he killed his two sons, if he performed inappropriate cultic action in the holy place during the Yom Kippur ritual. If inappropriate cultic action occurred, the sins of the people would not have been purified/covered/atoned and YHWH's wrath would have consumed both the priest and the community (16:1). Leviticus 16:2 states that YHWH's wrath would have absorbed the offender (=Aaron) when YHWH appeared over the mercy seat behind the veil. Leviticus 16:5–9 asserts that Aaron would offer the burnt-offering and the sin-offering to purify/cover/atone sin. Leviticus 16:5–6 continues that Aaron would take two goats from the congregation of Israel to function as an offering for sin and one ram from the congregation of Israel to function as a burnt-offering. The prepositional phrase וּמֵאֵת עֲדַת בְּנֵי יִשְׂרָאֵל in 16:5 suggests that both the sin-offering and the burnt-offering functioned representatively and in a substitutionary manner and that these offerings provided propitiation and expiation for the offender since 16:6 comments that Aaron would offer these animals from the congregation's own livestock *on behalf of* him, *on behalf of* his house (=family),[63] and *on behalf of* the congregation to purify/cover/atone their sin and to receive YHWH's pardon for the people. Leviticus 16:33 states that Aaron would also offer sacrifices to purify/cover/atone *on behalf of* the altar and *on behalf of* the priests.

The scapegoat was not killed, but was sent away into the wilderness. Since Yom Kippur combined the scapegoat ritual and the sacrificial ritual and since the scapegoat symbolically carried away the sins of the people into a deserted place, Yom Kippur was a representative, substitutionary, cultic ritual, although the scapegoat ritual was not a sacrificial ritual.[64] Furthermore, the function and action of the scapegoat ritual symbolized the

---

63. Against Milgrom, *Leviticus 1–16*, 1019, who suggested that "for his house" refers to all of the priests, based on 16:33. The various uses of the construction וְאֶת־בֵּיתוֹ throughout the Hebrew Bible suggests that it has a broader reference than only to the priestly house. For examples, see Gen 12:17; 14:14; 17:23, 27; 18:19; 19:3; 24:2; 29:13; 35:2; 36:6; 39:4, 16; 43:16; 44:1, 4; 45:8; 50:7; Exod 7:23; 12:4; Lev 16:6, 11, 17; 22:11; 27:14–15; Num 22:18; 24:13; Deut 6:22; 24:10; Jos 7:18; 20:6; Jdg 9:16, 19; 11:34; 18:26; 19:29; 1 Sam 1:21; 2:11; 3:12–13; 7:17; 15:34; 24:23; 25:17; 2 Sam 6:11, 20–21; 7:25; 9:9; 11:9–10, 13, 27; 12:15, 17, 20; 14:24; 15:16; 17:23; 19:12, 31, 42; 20:3; 21:4; 1 Kgs 3:1; 4:7; 7:1; 9:15; 16:3, 7; 20:43; 21:4, 29; 2 Kgs 21:18; 1 Chr 16:43; 17:23; 2 Chr. 8:1; 19:1; 33:20; Neh 3:10, 23, 28–29; 7:3; Esth 1:8; 5:10; 6:12; Job 1:10; 8:15; 20:28; 27:18; 38:20; 39:6; Ps 49:17; Prov 6:31; 7:20; 11:25; 15:27; Song 8:7; Jer 22:13; 23:34; Mic 7:6; Zech 5:4.

64. For the latter point, so also Finlan, *The Background and Content of Paul's Cultic Atonement Metaphors*, 77.

efficacy of the sacrificial ritual when Aaron sent it away into the wilderness to Azazel.[65] The preceding interpretation suggests that the scapegoat ritual completed the work of the sacrificial ritual, brought the entire Yom Kippur ritual to a climactic end, and rendered the sacrificial ritual efficacious. The two rituals together reveal that YHWH provided national purification by means of the appropriate cultic action on Yom Kippur.

Kurtz and other scholars proposed two major criticisms against the position that the scapegoat ritual completed the sacrificial ritual.[66] First, they argued that the confession of sins should introduce the sprinkling of blood, since the blood re-established the community's relationship with God instead of vice-versa. Second, they argued that if the sprinkling of blood removed sins away from the people and the sancta, then the scapegoat ritual was superfluous. Conversely, if the scapegoat ritual was necessary to expunge sin, then it should have been required for the ordinary sin-offering (e.g., as in Leviticus 4) and not only for the sin-offering on Yom Kippur.[67] Kurtz articulated these criticisms because he thought that the sancta's purification through the sprinkling of blood completed atonement.

Nevertheless, the scapegoat ritual symbolized the efficacy of the sacrificial ritual. I offer three responses to Kurtz's criticisms. First, his initial criticism begs the question. It assumes that blood in the cult was efficacious only if confession preceded the sacrificial ritual. However, Lev 5:5 (the only other text in Leviticus where וְהִתְוַדָּה occurs) nowhere states that the priest must confess before he offers the burnt-offering or the sin-offering or else YHWH would otherwise reject the ritual.[68] Instead, 5:1–13 stipulates that the sacrificial ritual includes confession without commenting on when confession should take place in the narrative. In fact, the priest does not confess sin, but the offender confesses (5:5), and there the priest performs the appropriate cultic action when the offender brings him the appropriate animals to sacrifice (5:6–13). In the narrative of 5:1–13, YHWH forgives the offender after he confesses his sin and after the priest performs the sacrificial ritual (Lev 5:10).[69]

---

65. Leviticus 16 does not explicitly state the identity of Azazel. For the different views of his identity, see Milgrom, *Leviticus 1–16*, 1020–21.

66. See Kurtz, *Sacrificial Worship of the Old Testament*, 412.

67. Information listed in both criticisms comes from Kiuchi, *The Purification Offering*, 146.

68. However, the root occurs in Lev 5:5; 16:2; 26:40.

69. For a similar point about Lev 5:13 in response to Milgrom, see Gane, "Privative Preposition מִן in Purification Offering Pericopes and the Changing Face of "Dorian Gray,'" 209–22; esp. 216.

Second, in response to Kurtz's second criticism, both the sacrificial ritual and the scapegoat ritual were necessary for the appropriate cultic action on Yom Kippur to accomplish the necessary cultic function (i.e., national purification) precisely because the normal cultic action was not instituted by YHWH to provide national purification from all sins (16:21). The normal offerings in the cult provided forgiveness from specific kinds of sins (e.g., inadvertent), but Aaron confessed over the scapegoat all of Israel's sins (עָלָיו אֶת־כָּל־עֲוֹנֹת בְּנֵי וְהִתְוַדָּה) on Yom Kippur (16:21). The text emphasizes that the scapegoat took away all of the sins of the people by asserting three times that Aaron confessed over it "all of their iniquities" (אֶת־כָּל־עֲוֹנֹת) and "all of their transgressions" (אֶת־כָּל־פִּשְׁעֵיהֶם) "in regard to all of their sins" (לְכָל־חַטֹּאתָם).

Third, Lev 16:10 asserts that the living goat (i.e., the scapegoat) was presented before YHWH to purify/cover/atone "by sending it" to Azazel in the wilderness (לְכַפֵּר עָלָיו לְשַׁלַּח אֹתוֹ). Both the sacrificial and the scapegoat rituals worked together to accomplish the purification/covering/atoning of sin and the necessary propitiation of God's wrath that Israel needed even after the cultic action and the cultic function of the daily sacrificial rituals prior to Yom Kippur, because the act of purifying/covering/atoning sin and YHWH's pardon from his wrath due to the community's sin were experienced by Israel only *after* and *when* the scapegoat carried away the sins of the people and entered into the wilderness (16:10, 17, 20, 22, 26–27, 34). With Kurtz, I agree that the sprinkling of the blood purified the sancta. However, against Kurtz, the scapegoat ritual symbolically communicated to the people that national purification via sacrificial atonement was efficacious since the nation's sins were symbolically taken away by means of confession and the sacrificial ritual.[70] In other words, both the sacrificial ritual and the scapegoat ritual functioned as one special חטאת offering on Yom Kippur.[71]

Stephen Finlan argued that identifying the scapegoat as the חטאת and the scapegoat ritual as a special form of the burning of the חטאת confuses both the terminology and the function of the two rituals, because Hebrew sacrificial rituals dealt with impurity of sin at the temple whereas the scapegoat ritual had nothing to do with the temple but with expulsion beyond

---

70. For criticisms of Kurtz, see Kiuchi, *The Purification Offering*, 147–48.

71. Rightly Kiuchi, *The Purification Offering*, 148–49. But Kiuchi rejected the position that the scapegoat ritual "symbolizes the atonement that has taken place in the sancta." Rather, he asserted that the rituals were symbolically continuous and that the scapegoat ritual was viewed as a special form of the חטאת offering. For criticisms of Kiuchi, see Finlan, *The Background and Content of Paul's Cultic Atonement Metaphors*, 81–82.

the borders of the community.⁷² Likewise, Bernd Janowski argued prior to Finlan's work that the scapegoat ritual was not sacrificial and therefore functioned as a magical principle of identification instead of as a vicarious atonement.⁷³ Finlan's work has offered a necessary corrective to scholars who failed to see the differences between the sacrificial ritual and the scapegoat ritual, but he did not assert that the sacrificial ritual and the scapegoat ritual work together in the narrative of Leviticus 16 to deal with all of the effects of sin upon the community in Leviticus 16 in a non-temple context. Yet, he affirmed that "the dominant cult practice (sacrifice) did partially absorb, or rather surround, the scapegoat ritual."⁷⁴ He continued: "In Leviticus, an assimilation of placement has transpired: the scapegoat rite is inserted into the Temple service and surrounded by sacrifices."⁷⁵ Janowski, on the other hand, appears to have read these rituals in an atomistic way instead of as a collective whole.

For example, Lev 16:5 states that YHWH required Aaron to take two goats from a female (שְׁנֵי־שְׂעִירֵי עִזִּים) for a sin-offering and one ram (אַיִל אֶחָד) for a burnt-offering. He also took one bull (אֶת־פַּר) as a sin-offering to purify/cover/atone for him and for his house (16:6). He then brought both goats (אֶת־שְׁנֵי הַשְּׂעִירִם) to the door of the tent of meeting (16:7). Aaron consecrated one goat for YHWH and the other for Azazel (16:8). He offered one goat to YHWH as a sacrificial sin-offering (16:9), and he presented the second goat to YHWH alive in order to purify/cover/atone עָלָיו by sending it into the wilderness to Azazel (16:10).⁷⁶ The phrase עָלָיו likely refers to Aaron,⁷⁷ mentioned in 16:6, since 16:6 refers to Aaron's act of atoning for himself and his house, albeit with a different animal (אֶת־פַּר), and since in 16:9 עָלָיו modifies Aaron's action of bringing forth the goat (אֶת־הַשָּׂעִיר), which he offered to YHWH, as a sin-offering.⁷⁸ The most important observations for my argument are (a) that the text identifies both the animal presented to YHWH as a sacrifice and the animal devoted to Azazel as a scapegoat as חטאת offerings in 16:5 (לְחַטָּאת יִקַּח שְׁנֵי־שְׂעִירֵי עִזִּים), and (b)

---

72. Finlan, *The Background and Content of Paul's Cultic Atonement Metaphors*, 81–82.

73. So Janowski, *Sühne als Heilsgeschehen*, 210–19. Finlan (*The Background and Content of Paul's Cultic Atonement Metaphors*, 84) pointed me to Janowski's statement.

74. Finlan, *The Background and Content of Paul's Cultic Atonement Metaphors*, 84.

75. Ibid.

76. So Kiuchi, *The Purification Offering*, 151. For a discussion of the different readings of the infinitive, see 149–53.

77. Ibid., 149–50.

78. Cf. also the syntax of Lev 1:4 with 16:10.

that one of these two goats was consecrated to YHWH as a sacrifice and the other as a scapegoat for Azazel in the wilderness (16:8).

Leviticus 16:10 connects purifying/covering/atoning sin with both the sacrificial and the scapegoat rituals because it connects both rituals with כפר. Leviticus 16:11–19 speaks again of the appropriate cultic action that Aaron should follow so that he would achieve the appropriate cultic function and so that he would avoid YHWH's wrath. Leviticus 16:15–26 connects the sin-offering (i.e., the sacrificial ritual) with purifying/covering/atoning (a) the sin of the holy place, (b) all of the impurities of the holy place, and (c) the objects of the tabernacle resulting from sin's impurities. Furthermore, it connects all of the sins of the people with the sin-offering and with the scapegoat ritual. In 16:20–21, YHWH states that after Aaron purified/covered/atoned the holy place, he would bring the living goat to YHWH,[79] place both of his hands on it, confess over it "all of the sins of the sons of Israel and all of their misdeeds for all of their sins, and he would put them on the head of the goat" (16:21a), after which the goat was sent into the wilderness to carry away the sins to Azazel (16:21b).[80]

The sacrificial ritual functioned both as a representation of the people and as a substitution for the people to purify the holy place, to purify the sins of the people, and to placate YHWH's wrath, because the priest sacrificed the animals for the sins of Israel instead of sacrificing the people for their own sins (16:1–7). However, the scapegoat ritual by itself functioned as a representation *of* the people instead of as a substitution *on behalf of* the people. There are several reasons to support this claim.[81] First, the scapegoat purified/covered/atoned the sins of the people by carrying them into the wilderness (16:10) (לַעֲזָאזֵל הַמִּדְבָּרָה לְכַפֵּר עָלָיו לְשַׁלַּח אֹתוֹ יָעֳמַד־חַי לִפְנֵי יְהוָה), not by dying for their sins. Second, Aaron put both of his hands on the head of the goat to signify that he and the people identified with the scapegoat, that sins were transferred, and to signify that the scapegoat would carry

---

79. The word YHWH is not in the text. But context suggests that he presented the living goat in the presence of YHWH.

80. For an argument in favor of transference in Lev 16:21 based on the verb וְהִתְוַדָּה, see Zohar, "Repentance and Purification," 616.

81. Against Kiuchi, *The Purification Offering*, 152–53, who argued for a substitutionary function of the scapegoat ritual by defending the position that Aaron bears the sins of the people and transfers them to the scapegoat, who then takes them away into the wilderness. Likewise, Milgrom (*Leviticus 1–16*, 1082–84) argued that the scapegoat ritual functioned as a substitute or ransom in that it was the substance to which the evil was transferred and thereupon eliminated (Lev 16:10, 21–22). In my view, substitution only applies when someone dies for the transgressions of another. Thus, the sacrificial ritual and the scapegoat ritual together communicate representation and substitution. Against Gaster, "Sacrifices and Offerings, OT," 153.

away from the community sin and its effects, for which the priests performed the sacrificial ritual, and the goat would take away all of their sins (16:10, 21).[82] Third, Aaron confessed over the scapegoat all of Israel's sins (16:21) (יִשְׂרָאֵל עָלָיו אֶת־כָּל־עֲוֺנֹת בְּנֵי וְהִתְוַדָּה). The text emphasizes that the scapegoat took away all of the sins of the people by asserting three times that Aaron confessed over it "all of their iniquities" (אֶת־כָּל־עֲוֺנֹת) and "all of their transgressions" (אֶת־כָּל־פִּשְׁעֵיהֶם) "in regard to all of their sins" (לְכָל־חַטֹּאתָם). Fourth, the scapegoat bore Israel's sins on it and carried them away to an unfertile land after the priest sent the goat into the wilderness outside of the camp (16:22). Fifth, the cultic purpose of both the sacrificial ritual and the scapegoat ritual on Yom Kippur was to purify/cover/atone all of the sins of the people and all of sin's effects within the community, so that the entire community and its associations would be clean in the presence of YHWH, which is another way of stating the people received YHWH's forgiveness resulting in the community's purification (cf. 4:1—5:13 with 16:30 and 19:22). Sixth, the cultic action of both the sacrificial ritual and the scapegoat ritual achieved the purification (and thereby propitiation) for all of the sins of the people after the priest performed both rituals each year, because the priest purified/covered/atoned "the holy sanctuary" (וְכִפֶּר אֶת־מִקְדַּשׁ הַקֹּדֶשׁ), "the tent of meeting" (וְאֶת־אֹהֶל מוֹעֵד), "the altar" (וְאֶת־הַמִּזְבֵּחַ), and "the priests and the people of the assembly" (16:33) (יְכַפֵּר וְעַל הַכֹּהֲנִים וְעַל־כָּל־עַם הַקָּהָל). Leviticus 16:34 emphasizes the comprehensive efficacy of the priest's cultic action for Israel on Yom Kippur by reiterating that the appropriate cultic action should be followed on Yom Kippur "to atone for the sons of Israel because of all of their sins" (יִשְׂרָאֵל מִכָּל־חַטֹּאתָם לְכַפֵּר עַל־בְּנֵי). The scapegoat symbolically carried all of these sinful infirmities away into the wilderness, but the narrative nowhere states that it died (16:10). Thus, the sacrificial ritual and the scapegoat ritual together communicate the ideas of both representation and substitution, for the priests sacrificed the animals for the sins of the people to provide forgiveness and purification, and the priest sent the scapegoat alive into the wilderness away from the people and the community to symbolize that the appropriate cultic action had been performed to accomplish the desired cultic function: purification/covering/atonement and forgiveness for people and objects within the community.

Leviticus 17 sheds further light on the representative and substitutionary nature of cultic action and cultic function of the sacrificial ritual on Yom Kippur. Leviticus 16:34 ends the prescriptions for Yom Kippur. However,

---

82. Similarly Milgrom, *Leviticus 1–16*, 1041–43; D. P. Wright, "The Gesture of Hand Placement in the Hebrew Bible and in Hittite Literature," 433–46. Besides Lev 24:14, 16:21 is the only place in Leviticus where the presenter lays both hands on the head of the animal instead of one (Lev 1:4; 3:2, 8, 13; 4:4, 24, 29, 33, 16:21).

YHWH's instructions in Leviticus 17 connect with Leviticus 16 because YHWH continues to instruct Israel regarding cultic action in Leviticus 17, and his comments relate to his prescriptions for Yom Kippur in Leviticus 16. In addition, the infinitive לְכַפֵּר in 17:11 and in 16:10, 17, 27, and 34 forges a lexical and grammatical link between Leviticus 16–17. Thus, these chapters should be read together.

In Leviticus 17, YHWH instructs Moses regarding the handling of blood. If anyone from the house of Israel killed an ox or a lamb or a goat inside of the camp and yet did not bring the blood to the door of the tent of meeting as a gift to YHWH, then he would reckon to that man's account the verdict of guilty and would cut him off from his people (Lev 17:1–4). In 17:5, YHWH tells Moses what the people should do with their sacrifices. In 17:6, he gives instructions regarding the blood. YHWH commanded Israel to bring the sacrifices to the door of the tent of meeting (17:5), to sprinkle the blood on YHWH's altar, and to burn the fat for a pleasing aroma to him (17:6). YHWH warned again that if the people did not perform the appropriate cultic action precisely the way that he instructed them, then he would cut them off from his people (17:7–9).

In 17:10 –11, YHWH discusses the appropriate way to perform cultic action with the blood of the animals. He forbade Israel from eating the blood, an act which would have resulted in YHWH putting his face against the offender's soul.[83] Leviticus 17:10b states that YHWH would cut off the disobedient from his people (וְהִכְרַתִּי אֹתָהּ מִקֶּרֶב עַמָּהּ). Leviticus 17:11 states two reasons why YHWH would inflict such a harsh judgment upon the one who disobeyed: "because the life of the flesh is in the blood, and I will put it forth on the altar to atone for your transgressions because the blood will atone for the soul." The clause נֶפֶשׁ הַבָּשָׂר בַּדָּם הוּא suggests that the animal died on behalf of and as a representative of Israel. That is, when the animal lost its blood for the people, it likewise lost its life for the people as their representative and substitute.[84] The references to purifying/covering/atoning sin with the infinitive לְכַפֵּר and the verb יְכַפֵּר in 17:11 support the premise that the loss of blood symbolizes the substitutionary and representative death of the animal for Israel, because YHWH gave the blood of the animal on the altar "to atone for" their souls (עַל־נַפְשֹׁתֵיכֶם לְכַפֵּר) and "because the

---

83. וְנָתַתִּי פָנַי בַּנֶּפֶשׁ הָאֹכֶלֶת אֶת־הַדָּם

84. Milgrom argued that בַּדָּם and בַּנֶּפֶשׁ communicate the idea that life's essence is in one's blood. He proposed the translation "For the life of flesh is the blood . . . for it is the blood, as life, that expiates." Milgrom, *Studies in Cultic Theology and Terminology*, 96–101.

blood will atone for the soul" whom the animal represents (כִּי־הַדָּם הוּא בַּנֶּפֶשׁ יְכַפֵּר).[85]

Milgrom cleverly argued that the prohibition not to eat the blood in 17:11 refers to the blood of the peace-offering in 17:1, since this is the only offering regarding which blood prohibition occurs.[86] Regardless of the command not to eat the blood of the peace-offering, Milgrom's suggestion seems to miss the contextual point of the blood prohibition in 17:11. After YHWH commands the people to pour out the blood of beast or animal on the land in 17:13, he echoes 17:11 in 17:14: "because the life of every flesh is his blood; it is in its life" (17:14) (בְנַפְשׁוֹ הוּא כִּי־נֶפֶשׁ כָּל־בָּשָׂר דָּמוֹ). Leviticus 17:14 repeats the inference from 17:12, and 17:14 explains why Israel should not eat blood: the blood is the soul's life, and those who eat the blood would be cut off from the people of God because YHWH designated the blood (i.e., the life of the animal) to provide purification/covering/atonement for the sins of the people by means of the animals representative and substitutionary deaths for the people. Otherwise, the people's impurity would cause them to carry their own sins and to function as their on representatives and substitutes (Lev 17:16; cf. Gen 9:4).

CULTIC ACTION AND CULTIC FUNCTION IN ISAIAH 53

In this section, I offer a concise analysis of Isaiah 53 to advance the argument that Isaiah describes the death of YHWH's servant with Levitical cultic language. My thesis in this section is that Isaiah 53 presents the death of the Servant as a substitute for and a representative of those for whom he suffered and died, and that he does this using Levitical cultic language. I defend this thesis with three primary arguments. First, Isaiah 53 applies substitutionary language to the Servant's death for others. Second, Isaiah 53 applies representative language to the Servant's death for others. Third, Isaiah 53 applies Levitical cultic language to the Servant's death for others.

Isaiah 53 in the Context of Isaiah 40–66[87]

Isaiah 40–66 is one unit that emphasizes the promise of YHWH's future salvation of both his people, Israel, and of the nations. Isaiah 40–66 begins

---

85. So LXX Lev 17:11: τὸ γὰρ αἷμα αὐτοῦ ἀντὶ τῆς ψυχῆς ἐξιλάσεται.

86. Milgrom, *Studies in Cultic Theology and Terminology*, 99.

87. Because of the narrow scope of this chapter, I am only concerned with interpreting the received text of Isaiah. I am not concerned with questions of authorship.

with YHWH exhorting the people to take comfort in the promise of his future salvation of his people in the midst of their judgment (40:1–11). YHWH's judgment of his people is apparent in these chapters. Israel received a strict judgment because of their sin of Torah-disobedience (40:2). Isaiah 1 confirms that YHWH's judgment would take the nation into exile. YHWH proclaims to Isaiah that his people, Israel, rebelled against him (1:2), that they were a sinful nation (1:4), laden with iniquity (1:4), offspring of evildoers (1:4), and corrupt children (1:4). YHWH continues his denouncement of Israel by asserting that the nation had "forsaken the Lord" and that the nation despised YHWH (1:4).

YHWH further continues his indictment of Israel throughout Isaiah. He promises that he would judge Israel because of the nation's sin (1:5–10). He identifies their rulers (i.e., their kings) with the wickedness and the destruction of Sodom and Gomorrah because of their wickedness (1:10). He rejects Israel's cultic worship (1:11–15) because she became a spiritual whore in that she broke the stipulations of his covenant with her (1:21; 54:5–6). As a result of the nation's sin against YHWH, her husband, he promised a judgment in some indeterminate future against her that would be greater than the judgment of exile (2:6–22), and he promised a more immediate judgment against her by means of exile (3:1–26; 5:1–30).[88]

However, Israel's imminent judgment is not the last word in Isaiah. The book promises future salvation. In Isa 2:1–5, YHWH declares that he will establish Jerusalem. He promised to bring the people out of exile after the city's destruction so that Torah would again spring forth from Zion (2:3) as YHWH dwells with his people (4:2–6). In the midst of this judgment, YHWH promises hope for his people (7:14; 9:1–7; 11:1–16; 32:1–8).[89]

In Isaiah 40–66, Isaiah provides a series of statements that point to both Israel's salvation from exile and to a greater eschatological salvation beyond exilic deliverance. For example, in Isa 40:1–5, YHWH exhorts his people to take comfort in the fact that he will deliver them from exile (40:1–2), but most importantly that he will pardon the nation's sin (Isa 40:2). In 40:3, the prophet declares that he is preparing the way for the coming of YHWH, who will bring judgment against his enemies (40:4, 10) and salvation to his people (40:9, 11). YHWH promises to help them with his righteous right hand by destroying those who afflict his people (41:10–11; 43:3–4, 14), by redeeming his people from exile (41:14; 43:1, 14; 44:21, 25;

---

88. For additional judgment texts in Isaiah, see 6:9–13; 8:1–10; 9:8—10:19; 13:1–22; 14:24—21:16; 23:1—25:12; 28:1–13; 29:1–24; 31:1–9; 32:9–20; 34:1–17; 36:1–22; 45:1–13; 47:1–15; 63:1–6; 65:1–16.

89. For additional salvation texts in Isaiah, see 8:11–22; 10:20–4; 11:1–16; 12:1–6; 14:1–2; 26:1—27:13; 30:18–33; 33:1–24; 35:1–10; 40:1—66:24.

49:8–10), and by saving Israel and the nations from his future wrath (49:6; 56:1–8; 61:1—66:24). Isaiah 53 is an integral part of YHWH's promise of future salvation.

Representation and Substitution in MT Isaiah 53

Isaiah 52:13—53:12 is one unit.[90] The unit contains one of the four Servant songs mentioned in Isaiah 40–66. As I have demonstrated elsewhere, much debate exists regarding the Servant's identity.[91] Throughout the Servant songs, Isaiah vacillates in his description of the Servant. He describes the Servant on numerous occasions as Israel or Jacob (41:8-9; 44:1-2, 21; 45:4; 49:6). However, 52:13—53:12 presents the Servant as a distinct figure from Israel by asserting that he will make many righteous and carry the sins of many by his death and resurrection and by asserting that he will bring salvation to the nations (cf. also 42:1-9). The hinge between the notion of the Servant *as* Israel to that of the Servant *to* Israel seems to be Isaiah 49:1ff. In the first part of that oracle, the Servant *is* Israel (v. 3), but then we read that the Servant has a mission *to* Israel (v. 5). Thereafter, the Servant is one who takes on the mission of the nation and ministers to the nation and to the nations. Isaiah 53 describes the Servant as one who would die for the sins of others.[92] The unit applies both representative and substitutionary language to the death of the Servant for others. The substitutionary element of the song is evident by the association of the Servant's suffering for the sins of others with the salvation that he achieved for those for whom he died,[93] and the representative nature of the Servant's suffering is apparent by his innocent suffering by association with the transgressors.

Isaiah 53:3 identifies the Servant as one who suffers for others with multiple parallel stanzas. Isaiah states that the Servant was despised and rejected by men (נִבְזֶה וַחֲדַל אִישִׁים), a man of sorrows (אִישׁ מַכְאֹבוֹת), one who knows affliction (וִידוּעַ חֹלִי), and one from whom men hide their faces (וּכְמַסְתֵּר פָּנִים מִמֶּנּוּ). These three stanzas emphasize the Servant's ignominious suffering. His contemporaries despised and dishonored him. The Servant

---

90. I use the abbreviated Isaiah 53 throughout this section to include 52:13—53:12.

91. For debate regarding the identity of the Servant, see Williams, *Maccabean Martyr Traditions*, 72-77.

92. For stimulating essays on the early Christian receptions of Isaiah 53, see Bellinger and Farmer (eds.), *Jesus and the Suffering Servant*.

93. Contra Hägglund, *Isaiah 53 in the Light of Homecoming after Exile*. Hägglund (ibid., 5) argued that "the image of the suffering Servant describes the people in exile who, in Isa 40:1—52:12, had been expected to return, and the 'we' are the people in the land who encounter those who return."

was sorrowful (i.e., he suffered). He personally experienced affliction, and this affliction was a public spectacle for everyone to see. The verb חֲשַׁבְנֻהוּ ("we considered him") supports the claim that the Servant's suffering was public ridicule. In 53:3, the participles נָגוּעַ ("smitten"), וּמְעֻנֶּה ("afflicted"), and the participial phrase אֱלֹהִים מֻכֵּה ("smitten of God") suggest that the Servant's suffering for others was a public display of suffering inflicted by YHWH.

Two stanzas in 53:4–5 more strongly accentuate the substitutionary nature of the Servant's death than 53:3. YHWH afflicted his Servant with suffering for the sins of others rather than for his own sins. Isaiah asserts that the Servant carried "our sicknesses" (חֳלָיֵנוּ), and he bore "our pains" (מַכְאֹבֵינוּ סְבָלָם).

Fredrik Hägglund has recently argued against substitutionary atonement in 53:4 in part because Isaiah states that the Servant carried (נָשָׂא) sickness and disease. Citing texts from Isa 1:5–6, Jer 6:7; 10:19, and Lam 1:12 and 1:18 that use the language of sickness and disease to describe Israel's situation as a result of Assyrian or Babylonian invasion, Hägglund contended that the language of pain and sickness frequently describes both the condition of the land after Jerusalem fell and as a result of other disasters.[94] The references in Jer 10:19–21 are especially important to Hägglund because he regarded Isaiah 53–54 as a reinterpretation of Jer 10:19–21.[95] In the latter text, Zion vicariously and corporately suffers by association with the guilty because of the sins of the shepherds, not as a substitutionary atoning sacrifice.[96] With a similar critique, Whybray argued years before Hägglund that the "he" and "we" contrast in Isa 53:4 should not lead interpreters to a view of vicarious suffering because "the speakers are the fellow-exiles of the Servant-prophet and therefore themselves by no means free from the afflictions of divine punishment."[97]

However, 53:4 states that YHWH personally afflicted his Servant, which is almost certainly an allusion to Deuteronomy (e.g., Deut 21:22–23; 27:9–26; 28:15–68), an affliction that the Servant suffered along with and on behalf of Israel. John Oswalt rightly emphasized substitution in 53:4, but he sacrificed the representative function of the Servant's suffering on the altar of substitution.[98] In my view, the Servant suffered along with Israel as the nation's representative and on behalf of Israel as the nation's substitute.

94. Ibid., 53–54.
95. Ibid., 54.
96. Ibid.
97. Whybray, *Thanksgiving for a Liberated Prophet*, 58.
98. Oswalt, *The Book of Isaiah Chapters 40–66*, 386.

The reasons for thinking this are that he participated in the same fate as non-Torah-observant Israel, although he was Torah-observant (i.e., righteous), and that his suffering resulted in the justification of the transgressors as he bore their sins (53:4–12).

Isaiah 53:5 raises a specific exegetical challenge for those who dismiss substitution in Isaiah 53, as Hägglund and Whybray, since Isaiah states that the Servant was pierced "because of our transgressions" (וְהוּא מְחֹלָל מִפְּשָׁעֵנוּ) and crushed "because of our guilt" (מְדֻכָּא מֵעֲוֺנֹתֵינוּ).[99] Whybray responded by asserting that the preposition מן is never causal in the sense of exchange in the Hebrew Bible, but the preposition should be understood as the ב of price.[100] Against Whybray, Isaiah speaks of the Servant's affliction as occurring while the author wrote these words. The two prepositional phrases מִפְּשָׁעֵנוּ and מֵעֲוֺנֹתֵינוּ appear to suggest that the Servant's suffering/death was a substitution for others, because he suffered for the transgressions and sins of others instead of his own, an idea that 52:14 expresses when it asserts that the Servant will "sprinkle many nations" (יַזֶּה גּוֹיִם רַבִּים).[101] LXX Isa 53:5 interprets the preposition in a causal sense (διὰ τὰς ἀνομίας ἡμῶν) (cf. MT and LXX Isa 6:4; Ezek 28:18). Most indicting of a non-substitutionary reading of Isa 53:5 (instead of a representative and substitutionary reading) is 53:12, which overtly states that the Servant "carries the sins of many" (הוּא חֵטְא־רַבִּים נָשָׂא). In light of 53:5, one should deduce that the Servant bore the sins of many by experiencing the same afflictions that they experienced and by dying for the transgressors of Torah by suffering with them and for their transgressions in YHWH's judgment and by producing positive results for those for whom he suffered,[102] just as had Daniel and his three friends (LXX Dan 3:1–90) and the Maccabean martyrs (2 Macc 7:32–38; 4 Macc 6:28–29; 17:21–22).

Hägglund's main response to this interpretation is that the phrase in 53:12 to communicate bearing sin occurs eight additional times in the OT (Lev 19:17; 20:20; 22:9; 24:15; Num 9:13; 18:22, 32; Ezek 23:49) and never with reference to suffering on behalf of another, but with reference to

---

99. Against Whybray, *Thanksgiving for a Liberated Prophet*, 61–62.

100. Ibid., 61–62.

101. The verb יָזָה occurs in cultic contexts in Lev 6:20 and 16:14 to refer to the sprinkling of blood. The term occurs in the latter text to refer specifically to the act of sprinkling blood for the cleansing/atoning of sin.

102. While arguing a different point, Whybray (*Thanksgiving for a Liberated Prophet*, 65) indirectly affirmed my point, although he would disagree with the specific argument that I am making about substitution. Likewise, Oswalt (*Book of Isaiah Chapters 40–66*, 388) made a similar point to me regarding substitution, although he rejected any presence of representation in 53:5.

suffering the consequences of one's own sins.[103] Against his argument, Lev 10:17 and 16:22 present the sacrificial ritual (Lev 10:17) and the sacrificial and scapegoat rituals (Lev 16) in both substitutionary and representative language, while speaking of bearing sin, just as Isa 53:12. Thus, the idea of bearing sin in 53:12 can be read as substitution and not simply participatory/shared suffering.

Hägglund unconvincingly argued that Lev 10:17 is not substitutionary because the guilt was not transferred to the victim (i.e., to the animal).[104] But, as I argued above, sin and guilt were transferred to the innocent victim (i.e., to the animal) because the innocent victim died for the sins of the guilty offender. Furthermore, he argued that Lev 16:22 is not substitutionary because the scapegoat was sent away alive to carry the sins of the people into the wilderness.[105] However, as I argued in detail above, both the sacrificial ritual and the scapegoat ritual functioned together in the Hebrew cult to teach substitution and representation, since purification of and covering/atonement for sin occurred after the cultic actions of the slaughtering of the sacrificial ritual and the sending away of the scapegoat rituals. Similarly, R. N. Whybray argued that the scapegoat ritual in Lev 16:22 should not be understood as vicarious suffering because the scapegoat was sent to a "solitary land" and because the text does not state anywhere that the scapegoat suffered and died.[106] Nevertheless, in my view, the scapegoat was sent to a solitary place to take away the sins of the people for which the sacrificial ritual was performed, and both the sacrificial ritual and the scapegoat ritual function together to emphasize substitution and representation. Each element of the Yom Kippur ritual should be interpreted as part of a collective whole. In light of these criticisms, the arguments against substitution in Isaiah 53 do not convince.

Isaiah continues discussing the Servant's death with substitutionary language in 53:5. He states that the Servant received YHWH's chastisement to provide peace/welfare for others (שְׁלוֹמֵנוּ עָלָיו מוּסַר). Isaiah 53:6 communicates the substitutionary and representative nature of the Servant's death by associating his death with the sins of others. Isaiah suggests that the Servant experienced divine judgment (i.e., judgment from YHWH) by asserting that he suffered not for his own sins. For example, 53:6 identifies the guilt and sin of Israel with the words "all of us," "have gone astray as sheep," and everyone has turned to his own way. Then, Isaiah states that

---

103. Hägglund, *Isaiah 53*, 84.
104. Ibid., 86.
105. Ibid., 87–88.
106. Whybray, *Thanksgiving for a Liberated Prophet*, 49.

YHWH has "caused the guilt of us all to fall on him" (הִפְגִּיעַ בּוֹ אֵת עֲוֹן כֻּלָּנוּ). The latter statement is the most devastating verse to Hägglund and others who argue against the substitutionary death of the Servant, for Isaiah gives YHWH credit for laying upon the Servant (an innocent victim) the guilt of the guilty transgressors.

One should not *ipso facto* interpret הִפְגִּיעַ בּוֹ אֵת עֲוֹן כֻּלָּנוּ to refer to substitution, because Isaiah could simply be saying that the Servant suffered the same fate as the transgressors.[107] However, Isaiah has already stated in 53:5 that the Servant suffered *because of* the sins of the transgressors. In addition, אֵת עֲוֹן occurs in Lev 10:17 and in Num 18:1 in sacrificial cultic contexts to refer to substitutionary purification/covering/atonement for Israel. Furthermore, the first part of 53:6 says that "all of us" (כֻּלָּנוּ) have wandered as sheep wander. But the last part of 53:6 states that YHWH caused the guilt of "all of us" (כֻּלָּנוּ) to fall upon his Servant. YHWH's act of causing the guilt of the guilty to fall upon the innocent Servant (אֵת עֲוֹן כֻּלָּנוּ הִפְגִּיעַ בּוֹ) instead of on the guilty was both a representative and a substitutionary act, because the Servant received the payment/penalty for the guilty in spite of his innocence, because the righteous Servant identified with the unrighteousness of the transgressors in that he took their suffering upon himself, because the guilty ones for whom the Servant bore guilt experience exoneration, and because the Servant died for the sins of others and not his own. Isaiah envisages these points in the subsequent verses in the text.[108]

He continues to describe the Servant's death as a representative of and as a substitute for others. Isa 53:7 states "he was crushed and afflicted" (נִגַּשׂ וְהוּא נַעֲנֶה) and led away as a dumb ewe to be slaughtered in the presence of her shearers. Although the Servant was innocent (לֹא־חָמָס עָשָׂה), 53:8 describes him as "cut off" from the land of the living because of the "transgressions of my people" (עַמִּי נִגְזַר מֵאֶרֶץ חַיִּים מִפֶּשַׁע). YHWH, nevertheless, desired to crush him (the innocent one) for the guilty by causing the penalty of the transgressors to fall upon the innocent as an אשם. Isaiah 53:11 states that the Servant's death makes many transgressors righteous (צַדִּיק עַבְדִּי לָרַבִּים יַצְדִּיק) because he died for theirs sins (וַעֲוֹנֹתָם הוּא יִסְבֹּל), which means that he poured out his soul by means of dying for them (נַפְשׁוֹ הֶעֱרָה לַמָּוֶת) (53:12). Isaiah reiterates the substitutionary and representative nature of the Servant's death in 53:12 by reaffirming that the Servant's death "carried the sins of many" (וְהוּא חֵטְא־רַבִּים נָשָׂא). The Servant's act of

---

107. Ibid., 60–61.

108. In favor of substitution and representation in Isaiah 53, so also Janowski, "Er tug unsere Sünden: Jesaja 53 und die Dramatik der Stellvertretung," 36. For a summary of Janowski, see Daniel P. Bailey, "Concepts of Stellvertretung in the Interpretation of Isaiah 53," 223–50, esp. 245–50.

carrying the sins of many should not be understood as merely suffering along with the guilty, for the Servant's act of carrying sins results in exoneration for the guilty (53:11).

Reference to the אשם offering in 53:10 along with Isaiah's earlier remarks about the Servant's suffering and death as a lamb for the transgressions of others in 53:4–12 make the context of Isaiah 53 overtly cultic.[109] The אשם offering in Leviticus functions to rid the community of the guilt that arises because of sin within the community (Lev 5:10; 7:5; 14:21; 19:21). Since Isaiah identifies the Servant's death as an אשם offering in 53:10 and as a death for the sins of others (a sin-offering) in 53:11–12, he seems to suggest that the Servant's death functions the same way as the animals functioned in the Levitical cult: namely, to substitute for the sins of the offenders, to represent the guilty offenders, and to assuage YHWH's wrath. Consequently, the Servant's death personifies the Levitical cult. Whybray dogmatically contended that the Suffering in 53:11 is not vicarious substitution but shared suffering since the Servant (one amongst many) participated in the suffering of the people.[110] However, 53:11 supports the claim that *both* a substitutionary *and* a representative reading is just as likely as Whybray's reading when the verse declares that the righteous Servant (=the innocent victim) suffered with and died for the guilty transgressors (=the offenders) and that his death grants the guilty transgressors the status of righteous,[111] all of which happens as a result of the Servant's guilt-bearing death.

Whybray argued the point that YHWH's revulsion of the idea of acquitting the guilty in other texts excludes יַצְדִּיק as referring to YHWH's justification of the guilty by means of his Servant in 53:11.[112] But regardless of the textual traditions outside of Isaiah 53, יַצְדִּיק in 53:11a should be read in light of 53:11b: "and their punishment he will bear." YHWH makes the guilty righteous by making his Servant suffer with and for the people, for

---

109. Whybray (*Thanksgiving for a Liberated Prophet*, 60, 66) rejected substitution in 53:10 on grammatical, theological, and textual grounds. Regarding the latter, he asserted that the textual tradition is corrupt and that אשם was not part of an earlier textual tradition. However, he asserted that the suggested textual emendations in his day were unacceptable.

110. Ibid., 30.

111. This is not the place to enter into a detailed discussion of justification. But the basic point to grasp is that the innocent Servant's death for the transgressors placed the Servant within the realm of the unrighteous (the guilty) and placed the guilty within the realm of the righteous Servant (the innocent). The innocent and righteous Servant becomes unrighteous and guilty because he dies for the transgressors, but the guilty and unrighteous transgressors become righteous because of the Servant's death for them. For examples of יַצְדִּיק, see Exod 23:7; Deut 25:1; 2 Sam 15:4; 1 Kgs 8:32; 2 Chr 6:23.

112. Whybray, *Thanksgiving for a Liberated Prophet*, 67.

he is reversing the previous order of things in light of the fact that Israel's failure to observe Torah has taken them into exile and eventually put an end to the traditional Hebrew cult. Prior to exile, the centerpiece of Israelite religion was Torah and the Hebrew cult and eventually the Hebrew cult as practiced at the temple. However, Israel's disobedience to Torah resulted in exile, which resulted in an end to temple worship. As a result, YHWH announces to Israel the good news of his salvation for Israel and for the nations through his Servant, who is both Israel (44:1; 53:1–12) and distinct from her (42:1; 53:1–12), and this salvation comes through YHWH's Servant (49:1—53:12).[113]

One reversal of expectations in Isaiah was that YHWH promised to recreate the world afresh (65:17–25). Another reversal from the old ordering of things was that YHWH began to accept the death of a Torah-observant Jew for the benefit of non-Torah-observant people as a means by which he will exonerate the transgressors (e.g., LXX Dan 3:1–90; 2 Macc 7:32–38; 4 Macc 6:28–29; 17:21–22), which YHWH only accepted in both early and Second Temple Judaism during times of exile when the temple cult was dysfunctional (LXX Dan 3:1–90; 2 Macc 7:32–38; 4 Macc 6:28–29; 17:21–22). The transgressors' guilt, sin, and judgment because of the guilt of sin in Isaiah 53 are transferred to the innocent Servant, which Isaiah communicates by stating that the Servant suffered for the transgressors. Therefore, Isaiah presents the Servant as dying a similar kind of substitutionary and representative death as the sacrificial animals in the Levitical cult (e.g., cf. Leviticus 1–16 with Isa 53:4–12). The verbs יָזֶה (Lev 6:20; 16:14; Isa 52:15), נָשָׂא (Lev 10:17; Isa 53:4, 12), the nouns עָוֹן (Lev 10:17; Isa 53:6), אָשָׁם (Lev 5:19; 7:5; 14:21; 19:21; Isa 53:10), חַטָּאת (Lev 4:3, 23, 28; 4:35; 19:22; Isa 53:12), the root שׁלם (Lev 3:1–4; 4:10; 7:37; Isa 53:4), and the concept of an innocent victim suffering a sacrificial death as a representative of and as a substitute for the sins of others (Isa 53:4–6, 8, 11–12) link Isa 53 with the Levitical cult. The representative and substitutionary nature of the Servant's death co-exists in Isaiah 53 as the Servant suffers with and for Israel.

Representation and Substitution in LXX Isaiah 53

Although there are some similarities between LXX Isaiah 53 and MT Isaiah 53, the two traditions are dissimilar at certain points.[114] Perhaps the discrep-

---

113. Oswalt (*Book of Isaiah Chapters 40–66*, 385) makes a similar point about substitution in Isaiah 53 to the neglect of representation.

114. For a comparative analysis of MT Isa 53, 1QIsa, and LXX Isa 53, see Sapp, "The LXX, 1QIsa, and MT Versions of Isaiah 53 and the Christian Doctrine of Atonement,"

Representation and Substitution in the Hebrew Cult and in Isaiah 53

ancies between the two traditions can be explained by affirming that the former used the latter as a source for its translation, that the former added concepts in the process of translation to make the MT tradition speak to the specific unique needs of the Greek-speaking Jews in the diaspora, or by affirming that the LXX tradition used another tradition of Isaiah 53 as its source besides the one found in the MT (e.g., 1QIsa). Regardless of the reasons, there are dissimilarities between the textual traditions. Since the Jewish martyrological narratives used the Greek version of LXX Isaiah 53 and since I argue in chapter 4 of this monograph that Paul applies a Jewish martyrological reading of LXX Isa 53:12 to Jesus in Rom 4:25, I must spend time here discussing representation and substitution in LXX Isaiah 53.[115]

The Servant Identifies with and Dies for Non-Torah-Observant Sinners

The first reference to substitution in LXX Isaiah 53 occurs in 53:4. Isaiah states that the Servant carries ours sins (οὗτος τὰς ἁμαρτίας ἡμῶν φέρει). Substitution is present here even without the "dying for" formula, for the Servant (the righteous one) carries/bears the sins of others by suffering their penalty for them (οὗτος τὰς ἁμαρτίας ἡμῶν φέρει καὶ περὶ ἡμῶν ὀδυνᾶται καὶ ἡμεῖς ἐλογισάμεθα αὐτὸν εἶναι ἐν πόνῳ καὶ ἐν πληγῇ καὶ ἐν κακώσει). LXX Isa 53:5 continues to describe the substitutionary nature of the Servant's death by using the "dying for" formula, which LXX Isa 53:4 uses with the prepositional phrase περὶ ἡμῶν. LXX Isa 53:5 asserts that the Servant was "traumatized for our lawless deeds" (αὐτὸς δὲ ἐτραυματίσθη διὰ τὰς ἀνομίας ἡμῶν) and that he was "made weak for our sins" (μεμαλάκισται διὰ τὰς ἁμαρτίας ἡμῶν). LXX Isa 53:5c–d adds to the substitutionary tone of the Servant's death for others: "the discipline of our peace [came] upon him" (παιδεία εἰρήνης ἡμῶν ἐπ' αὐτόν), and "we were healed by his wound" (τῷ μώλωπι αὐτοῦ ἡμεῖς ἰάθημεν). The latter two statements in LXX Isa 53:5c–d highlight the substitutionary nature of the death of the Servant for others by confirming that his death for the sins of others achieved soteriological benefits (i.e., peace and healing) for those for whom he died. The transgressors went their own way because they were all deceived as sheep (πάντες ὡς πρόβατα ἐπλανήθημεν ἄνθρωπος τῇ ὁδῷ αὐτοῦ ἐπλανήθη), but the Lord gave

---

170–92.

115. My concern in this section is neither the translation technique of the translators of LXX Isaiah 53 nor why the latter disagrees with the former textual tradition. Instead, I simply focus on what LXX Isaiah 53 actually says about substitution.

the innocent Servant to die for the sins of those who were deceived (καὶ κύριος παρέδωκεν αὐτὸν ταῖς ἁμαρτίαις ἡμῶν) (LXX Isa 53:6).

LXX Isa 53:7 confirms that the Lord gave the Servant over to die a substitutionary death for the sins of the transgressors as their representatives by asserting that the Servant did not open his mouth as he was led to be slaughtered like an innocent lamb because he was wounded (καὶ αὐτὸς διὰ τὸ κεκακῶσθαι οὐκ ἀνοίγει τὸ στόμα ὡς πρόβατον ἐπὶ σφαγὴν ἤχθη καὶ ὡς ἀμνὸς ἐναντίον τοῦ κείροντος αὐτὸν ἄφωνος οὕτως οὐκ ἀνοίγει τὸ στόμα αὐτοῦ). He was led for the slaughter as a lamb to die (ὡς πρόβατον ἐπὶ σφαγὴν ἤχθη), and he remained silent as a lamb before his shearer who prepares it for death (ὡς ἀμνὸς ἐναντίον τοῦ κείροντος αὐτὸν ἄφωνος οὕτως οὐκ ἀνοίγει τὸ στόμα αὐτοῦ). LXX Isa 53:8 states that the Servant was judged (ἐν τῇ ταπεινώσει ἡ κρίσις αὐτοῦ ἤρθη) because he was put to death by the lawlessness of the people (ὅτι αἴρεται ἀπὸ τῆς γῆς ἡ ζωὴ αὐτοῦ ἀπὸ τῶν ἀνομιῶν τοῦ λαοῦ μου ἤχθη εἰς θάνατον). Since the Servant was innocent, the Lord provided for him even in death (καὶ δώσω τοὺς πονηροὺς ἀντὶ τῆς ταφῆς αὐτοῦ καὶ τοὺς πλουσίους ἀντὶ τοῦ θανάτου αὐτοῦ ὅτι ἀνομίαν οὐκ ἐποίησεν οὐδὲ εὑρέθη δόλος ἐν τῷ στόματι αὐτοῦ) (LXX Isa 53:9).

LXX Isa 53:10 inserts an additional cultic term (καθαρίσαι) for the MT's וּדַכְּאוֹ. The former means "to cleanse," and the latter means "to crush." The former refers to the cleansing of the priest (LXX Lev 13:7), the cleansing of leprosy (LXX Lev 13:59), the cleansing function of the sin-offering and the burnt-offering (LXX Lev 14:23; 16:30), the cleansing of the house of the Lord (LXX 2 Chr 29:15), the purification of Judah from idolatry (LXX 2 Chr 34:3, 8), the purification of the second temple (1 Macc 4:36), the cleansing of a furnace (Sir 38:30), the Messiah's purification of Jerusalem from Gentile oppression (Pss. Sol. 17:22; 18:5), and to the purification of Israel during the invasion of the Gentiles (LXX Dan 11:35). In the light of its cultic usage in LXX Lev 16:30 and in LXX Isaiah 53's appropriation of Levitical cultic language to the Servant (e.g., carrying/suffering for sins, purification), LXX Isa 53:10 seems to suggest that the Servant would be cleansed from his suffering (καὶ κύριος βούλεται καθαρίσαι αὐτὸν τῆς πληγῆς) and that the Greek-speaking Jewish audience of LXX Isaiah 53 would participate in long life if they give the appropriate offering at the temple for their sins (ἐὰν δῶτε περὶ ἁμαρτίας ἡ ψυχὴ ὑμῶν ὄψεται σπέρμα μακρόβιον). What the translators intended by the clause ἐὰν δῶτε περὶ ἁμαρτίας is not clear. Based on both the plural number of the verb δῶτε and the fact that περὶ ἁμαρτίας refers to the sin-offering on numerous occasions in the LXX, one can conclude that the translators are calling upon the Greek-speaking Jewish audience to participate in the Jewish temple cult even though they are in the Diaspora.

The substitutionary metaphor continues in LXX Isa 53:11d with the statement "their sins he will bear" (τὰς ἁμαρτίας αὐτῶν αὐτὸς ἀνοίσει) and in LXX Isa 53:12 with the words "his soul was given over in death for many" (ἀνθ' ὧν παρεδόθη εἰς θάνατον ἡ ψυχὴ αὐτου), "with the lawless ones he was reckoned" (καὶ ἐν τοῖς ἀνόμοις ἐλογίσθη), "he carried the sins of many" (αὐτὸς ἁμαρτίας πολλῶν ἀνήνεγκεν), and "he was handed over for their sins" (διὰ τὰς ἁμαρτίας αὐτῶν παρεδόθη). The Servant dies to "declare righteous the righteous one" (δικαιῶσαι δίκαιον). As the substitute, the Servant suffers the penalty for the transgressors' transgressions. As the representative, the Servant identifies with transgressors by suffering as one of them.

CONCLUSION

In this chapter, I have discussed cultic action and cultic function in the Hebrew cult by offering a selective analysis of the burnt-offering, the guilt-offering, the sin-offering, the Yom Kippur ritual, and both the Hebrew and Greek versions of Isaiah 53. I defended a twofold thesis. First, I argued that in the Hebrew cult, Israel offered animals as burnt-offerings, sin-offerings, guilt-offerings, and celebrated the Yom Kippur ritual in order to purify/cover/atone sins and to assuage God's wrath (on the condition that the sacrificial rituals were offered in accordance with YHWH's instructions). Second, I argued that the burnt-offerings, sin-offerings, guilt-offerings, and the sacrificial and scapegoat rituals on Yom Kippur corporately functioned both as representatives of and as substitutes for the sins of the people to expunge the effects of their sin upon the land. I presented three major arguments to support this thesis. First, I argued that YHWH prescribed the burnt-offering, the sin-offering, and the guilt-offering to purify/cover/atone sins and to assuage his wrath. Second, I argued that the Yom Kippur ritual temporarily provided annual purification from every contamination of sin and deliverance from YHWH's wrath if both the sacrificial ritual and the scapegoat ritual were offered in the appropriate manner. Third, I argued that the Servant of Isaiah 53 functioned as a substitute for non-Torah-observant sinners in both the Hebrew and Greek traditions of Isaiah 53 and that both textual traditions applied Levitical cultic language to the Servant.

3

Representation and Substitution in Second Temple Jewish Martyrologies

INTRODUCTION

This chapter investigates all of the relevant Second Temple texts that contain a Jewish martyrology. My thesis is that a Jewish martyr theology existed in Second Temple Judaism in texts that indisputably pre-date Romans, and that just as Isaiah 53 describes the death of YHWH's servant with Levitical cultic language, so too LXX Dan 3:1–90 and 2 and 4 Maccabees use Levitical cultic and Isaianic language to describe the deaths of Torah-observant Jews, who died for the soteriological benefit of non-Torah-observant sinners, as representatives of and as substitutes for sinners.[1] In addition, this chapter argues that the Jewish martyrological narratives present the martyrs as functioning as Israel's Yom Kippur. I argue this thesis by means of an exegetical and comparative analysis of the relevant Second Temple texts.

---

1. I am aware that some scholars have argued that the Jewish martyrological narratives are discourses instead of references to history. My thesis is not concerned with whether the Jewish martyrological stories actually happened (maybe they did, maybe they did not), but my focus is how the narratives are actually functioning within LXX Daniel 3 and 2 and 4 Maccabees. For examples of works that argue for the discourse nature of the Jewish martyrological narratives, see Boyarin, *Dying for God*; Rajak, *The Jewish Dialogue with Greece and Rome*, 99–133.

REPRESENTATION AND SUBSTITUTION IN LXX DANIEL 3:24-90[2]

One Jewish martyrology is a story about a Torah-observant Jew who dies as a martyr at the hands of an antagonist Gentile tyrant instead of yielding to the threat of the authorities, when the Tyrant presents the Torah-observant Jew with the choice of renouncing his faith or suffering death as a result of his faith.[3] The Jewish martyr dies to accomplish soteriological benefits for the non-Torah-observant sinner. The Second Temple texts discussed in this chapter share this focus. The first text of investigation is LXX Daniel 3.

LXX Daniel 3 contains approximately sixty-four more verses than MT Daniel 3.[4] The Greek version contains stories and prayers that are absent from the tradition preserved in the Masoretic text.[5] The additional verses in the Greek version of Daniel 3 consist of LXX Dan 3:24–97. The additions resemble the traditional stories about Daniel in MT Daniel 1–6. The author of the LXX versions set the additional stories in context of the Jewish Diaspora; Daniel interacts with foreign monarchs, and Daniel's enemies throw him into the lion's den similar to what MT Daniel 6 records.[6]

LXX Dan 3:24–90 inserts the prayer of Azariah and the Song of the Three Jews.[7] LXX Dan 3:24–40 highlights Daniel's three friends, who are identified in the LXX version as Ananias (Shadrach), Azarias (Meshach), and Misael (Abednego), while they prayed as they suffered in Nebuchad-

---

2. With slight modifications and fresher insights, the material in this chapter comes from my essay "Martyr Theology in Hellenistic Judaism," in *Christian Origins and Hellenistic Judaism*, 493–521, esp. 497–500. I have borrowed the overlapping material from Brill with permission.

3. For a definition of Jewish martyrology, see Rajak, *The Jewish Dialogue with Greece and Rome*, 99–103; Van Henten, *The Maccabean Martyrs as Saviours of the Jewish People*. In this chapter, agreeing with van Henten (*Maccabean Martyrs*, 7–13, esp. 8), I define Jewish martyrdom in LXX Daniel 3 and in 2 and 4 Maccabees as "a person who in an extremely hostile situation prefers violent death to compliance with a demand of the (usually) pagan authorities. This definition implies that the death of such a person is a structural element in the writing about this martyr. The execution should at least be mentioned." See also Jarvis J. Williams, *Maccabean Martyr Traditions in Paul's Theology of Atonement*, 3–4 n. 10.

4. Unless otherwise indicated, I use Rahlf's most recent critical edition of the LXX.

5. Scholars have given these stories and prayers the apocryphal names of The Story of Susanna, the Prayer of Azariah and the Song of the Three Jews, and Bel and the Dragon.

6. This information comes from Henze, "Additions to Daniel," 122.

7. Henze, "The Prayer of Azariah and the Song of the Three Jews," in *Outside the Bible: Ancient Jewish Writings Related to Scripture*, 129.

nezzar's fiery furnace. They refused to worship a golden statue erected by Nebuchadnezzar in Babylon and instead remained faithful to their God. LXX Dan 3:23 states that Nebuchadnezzar seized the three young men with fetters and had them thrown into the fiery furnace.[8] The Babylonian king then expresses shock when he sees four men (Daniel's three friends and an angel) freely walking unharmed in the fiery furnace (LXX Dan 3:24–25).[9] The Greek insertions connect the swift transition from the king's anger and his shock with what happens in the fiery furnace to underscore the miraculous nature of the story.[10]

While Daniel's three friends were in the fiery furnace, they prayed to God. Their prayer acknowledges that Israel suffered the Lord's judgment in exile "because of their sins" (LXX Dan 3:28–37). Azariah blessed the Lord's name and confessed that the Lord was righteous "in all the things" that he had done to them and that the Lord's ways and works were right (LXX Dan 3:27). In LXX Dan 3:28, Azariah continues confessing to the Lord that all of his judgments that he brought upon the holy city were right "because in truth and in judgment you have brought all of these things [upon us] because of our sins" (ὅτι ἐν ἀληθείᾳ καὶ κρίσει ἐπήγαγες πάντα ταῦτα διὰ τὰς ἁμαρτίας ἡμῶν) (brackets mine).

To emphasize that the Lord's judgment of exile came upon his people because of their sins, his prayer continues in LXX Dan 3:29 with the words "we have sinned and we have acted lawlessly so that we turned from you and we missed the mark in all things and we did not hear your commandments" (ὅτι ἡμάρτομεν καὶ ἠνομήσαμεν ἀποστῆναι ἀπὸ σοῦ καὶ ἐξημάρτομεν ἐν πᾶσιν καὶ τῶν ἐντολῶν σου οὐκ ἠκούσαμεν). In LXX Dan 3:30–31, Azariah further prays that "we neither treasured up nor did as you commanded to us so that it would be well with us, and all things that you have brought upon us and all things that you have done to us you have done by means of true judgment" (οὐδὲ συνετηρήσαμεν οὐδὲ ἐποιήσαμεν καθὼς ἐνετείλω ἡμῖν ἵνα εὖ ἡμῖν γένηται πάντα ὅσα ἡμῖν ἐπήγαγες καὶ πάντα ὅσα ἐποίησας ἡμῖν ἐν ἀληθινῇ κρίσει ἐποίησας). In LXX Dan 3:32, Azariah confesses "you have given us over into the hands of lawless enemies, who are the greatest of our enemies and to an unrighteous and most evil king in all of the earth" (καὶ παρέδωκας ἡμᾶς εἰς χεῖρας ἐχθρῶν ἀνόμων ἐχθίστων ἀποστατῶν καὶ βασιλεῖ ἀδίκῳ καὶ πονηροτάτῳ παρὰ πᾶσαν τὴν γῆν).

---

8. καὶ οἱ τρεῖς οὗτοι Σεδραχ Μισαχ καὶ Αβδεναγω ἔπεσον εἰς μέσον τῆς καμίνου τοῦ πυρὸς τῆς καιομένης πεπεδημένοι.

9. Henze, "The Prayer of Azariah and the Song of the Three Jews," 129.

10. Ibid.

In LXX Dan 3:34–35, Azariah begins to pray that God would not break his covenant with his people or withdraw his mercy from them on account of his promise to Abraham, Isaac, and Jacob (μὴ δὴ παραδῷς ἡμᾶς εἰς τέλος διὰ τὸ ὄνομά σου καὶ μὴ διασκεδάσῃς τὴν διαθήκην σου καὶ μὴ ἀποστήσῃς τὸ ἔλεός σου ἀφ᾽ ἡμῶν δι᾽ Αβρααμ τὸν ἠγαπημένον ὑπὸ σοῦ καὶ διὰ Ισαακ τὸν δοῦλόν σου καὶ Ισραηλ τὸν ἅγιόν σου) (cf. also LXX Dan 3:36). In LXX Dan 3:37, Azariah offers a reason for the exile of his people in LXX Dan 3:36: "because, O master, we were reduced in the presence of all the Gentiles, and we are humble today in all the earth because of our sins" (ὅτι δέσποτα ἐσμικρύνθημεν παρὰ πάντα τὰ ἔθνη καί ἐσμεν ταπεινοὶ ἐν πάσῃ τῇ γῇ σήμερον διὰ τὰς ἁμαρτίας ἡμῶν). Azariah's reference to the humility of "today" refers to the Lord's judgment in exile because of sin, the former of which LXX Dan 1:1—2:49 makes abundantly clear and the latter of which Azariah's prayer crystallizes (LXX Dan 3:28; 3:36–37).

In LXX Daniel 3, Azariah and his friends represent the people because he associates them with the sinful nation in exile when he declares that they suffer "because of our sins," even though the text states nowhere that either he or his friends violated Torah. He confesses throughout this prayer that "we" have sinned (ἡμάρτομεν) "because of our sins" (διὰ τὰς ἁμαρτίας ἡμῶν) (LXX Dan 3:27–28, 37), that "we" have broken the law (ἠνομήσαμεν ἀποστῆναι ἀπὸ σοῦ) (LXX Dan 3:28), that "we" have missed the mark (ἐξημάρτομεν) (LXX Dan 3:28), that "we" have not listened to the Lord's commands (τῶν ἐντολῶν σου οὐκ ἠκούσαμεν) (LXX Dan 3:28), that the Lord has handed "us" over into the hands of wicked people (παρέδωκας ἡμᾶς εἰς χεῖρας ἐχθρῶν ἀνόμων ἐχθίστων ἀποστατῶν καὶ βασιλεῖ ἀδίκῳ καὶ πονηροτάτῳ παρὰ πᾶσαν τὴν γῆν) (LXX Dan 3:32), and he prays that the Lord would not destroy him and his people by breaking his covenant with them (καὶ νῦν οὐκ ἔστιν ἡμῖν ἀνοῖξαι τὸ στόμα αἰσχύνη καὶ ὄνειδος ἐγενήθη τοῖς δούλοις σου καὶ τοῖς σεβομένοις σε μὴ δὴ παραδῷς ἡμᾶς εἰς τέλος διὰ τὸ ὄνομά σου καὶ μὴ διασκεδάσῃς τὴν διαθήκην σου) (LXX Dan 3:33–36). Yet, Daniel and his three friends were "young ones without blemish" (νεανίσκους οἷς οὐκ ἔστιν ἐν αὐτοῖς μῶμος) since they were compliant with Torah both prior to and in exile (LXX Dan 1:4). Therefore, they were not individually to blame for exile since they were "without blemish" (LXX Dan 1:4).

LXX Dan 1:8–19 confirms the faithfulness of Daniel and his three friends to Torah in exile when it states that Daniel refused to eat the king's unclean food and to drink his unclean wine. Instead, they complied with Torah and refused to defile themselves. Consequently, God gave favor to Daniel (LXX Dan 1:8–9). LXX Dan 1:12–19 suggests that Daniel's three friends complied with Daniel's Torah-observance, because Daniel includes them in his plot to deceive the king regarding their refusal to eat the unclean food and to drink the unclean wine (cf. MT Lev 11:1–47; *Jub.* 22:16–18).[11] Azariah associates himself and his friends with the sinful nation due to the Deuteronomic principle expressed by Moses in Lev 18:5 and repeated in Deuteronomy: obedience to Torah brings corporate life to Israel in the land (Deut 5:32–33; 8:1; 11:8–9, 18–25, 28; 28:1–14; 30:15–16), but disobedience to Torah results in the Lord's corporate judgment of the people by means of expulsion from the land (Deut 4:25–28; 11:28; 28:15–68; 30:17–20). Both the MT and LXX traditions suggest that Daniel and his three friends were faithful to Torah, but their association with the covenant community meant that they suffered exile along with the people, so that they (Torah-observers) could identify themselves with the sins of the nation.[12] Thus, Azariah's prayer for the nation in exile represents the corporate cry of the Lord's covenant people in exile.

As Azariah continues his prayer, he urges God to deliver Israel from their national suffering in exile (LXX Dan 3:38–40). He laments that the Davidic monarchy has been abolished and that the temple cult had been eradicated (καὶ οὐκ ἔστιν ἐν τῷ καιρῷ τούτῳ ἄρχων καὶ προφήτης καὶ ἡγούμενος οὐδὲ ὁλοκαύτωσις οὐδὲ θυσία οὐδὲ προσφορὰ οὐδὲ θυμίαμα οὐ τόπος τοῦ καρπῶσαι ἐναντίον σου καὶ εὑρεῖν ἔλεος) (LXX Dan 3:38; cf. 2 Kgs 17:22–23; 23:26–25:11; 2 Chr 36:19–20). The eradication of the temple cult resulted in the abolishment of a sacrificial means by which to attain God's mercy for the nation, since YHWH provided cultic sacrifices in order to provide atonement for sin. Note how Azariah's prayer connects God's mercy with Levitical cultic language (e.g., ὁλοκαύτωσις ["burnt-offering"], θυσία ["sacrifice"], προσφορὰ ["offering"], θυμίαμα ["incense"], and καρπῶσαι ["to bear fruit"]).[13] Furthermore, without access to the temple cult, Israel could neither celebrate daily cultic sacrifices of atonement or the traditional Yom Kippur ritual (Lev 1–6, 16). As a result, the absence of the temple cult in exile in LXX Daniel 3 meant that there was not a means by which or a place at which the Lord's people could perform cultic action to receive his mercy. The prayer of the three friends confirm this when they acknowledge that they did not have a place to offer a sacrificial burnt-offering in order to find

---

11. See also 1 Macc 1:11–15, 41–45; 3:58–59; 4:54–60; 2 Macc 5:15–20; 4Q395; CD 4:20; 5:6–9; Pesher Habakkuk 8:8–13; 12:6–10; 4Q390; 4Q385a frag. 3a, C: 6–7; Ep. Arist. 152–53; *Pss. Sol.* 2:2; Jos. *Ant.* 15.5.417; Acts 21:27.

12. Contra Tobit. The setting of Tobit is likewise exile, but Tobit overtly states that he (a Torah-observant Jew) was not to blame either for Israel's or for his exile. To defend this, Tobit highlights his Torah-observance and the Torah-disobedience of others, and he blames the latter for exile.

13. Every word in the above parenthesis occurs in cultic contexts in the LXX (ὁλοκαύτωσις [LXX Lev 6:2]; θυσία [LXX Lev 1:9, 13, 17; 2:1–2, 5–7, 15; 3:1; 5:13; 6:16; Sir 34:18; 35:5; 46:16; 50:13], θυμίαμα [LXX Lev 16:13], and καρπῶσαι [LXX Lev 2:11]).

God's mercy (προσφορὰ οὐδὲ θυμίαμα οὐ τόπος τοῦ καρπῶσαι ἐναντίον σου καὶ εὑρεῖν ἔλεος) (LXX Dan 3:28). This statement alludes to the Levitical cult (cf. LXX Lev 6:2). Thus, the prayer suggests that there is no means by which to receive the Lord's forgiveness through cultic action since the temple cult's absence is parallel with the friends' statement that there is no place to offer a sacrifice to find God's mercy. In this context, Azariah asks God to use his death and the deaths of his friends to perform the necessary cultic action to provide national cleansing for the covenant community in the place of the temple cult, which LXX Dan 3:39 communicates with the optative προσδεχθείημεν in the statement ἐν ψυχῇ συντετριμμένῃ καὶ πνεύματι τεταπεινωμένῳ προσδεχθείημεν ὡς ἐν ὁλοκαυτώμασι κριῶν καὶ ταύρων καὶ ὡς ἐν μυριάσιν ἀρνῶν πιόνων (LXX Dan 3:39).

Furthermore, Azariah asks that God would use their deaths to cleanse the nation while in exile (as long as the temple cult was ineffective) with the prayer, "let our sacrifice be in your presence today also to propitiate behind you because there is no shame in those who trust in you so that we would also consecrate behind you" (οὕτω γενέσθω ἡμῶν ἡ θυσία ἐνώπιόν σου σήμερον καὶ ἐξιλάσαι ὄπισθέν σου ὅτι οὐκ ἔστιν αἰσχύνη τοῖς πεποιθόσιν ἐπὶ σοί καὶ τελειῶσαι ὄπισθέν σου) (LXX Th. Dan 3:40).[14] Azariah wanted God to receive (προσδεχθείημεν) their deaths "just as" (ὡς) he received the function of the burnt-offerings in the Levitical cult (ὡς ἐν ὁλοκαυτώμασι κριῶν καὶ ταύρων καὶ ὡς ἐν μυριάσιν ἀρνῶν πιόνων). The Levitical cultic language (ὁλοκαύτωσις, θυσία, προσφορά, θυμίαμα, καρπῶσαι, ὁλοκαυτώμασι, and ἐξιλάσαι) applied to Daniel's three friends and their identification with the Torah-disobedient nation suggest that they function in the narrative of LXX Th. Daniel 3 as proper representatives and substitutionary cultic sacrifices to bring to Israel the mercy (ἔλεος) and cleansing (ἐξιλάσαι) traditionally provided by the temple cult and Yom Kippur (LXX Th. Dan 3:38–40).

MACCABEAN MARTYRDOM IN HISTORICAL CONTEXT[15]

Scholars of Second Temple Judaism are well aware that 1, 2, and 4 Maccabees record that Antiochus Epiphanes IV (henceforth Antiochus) in the second century BCE persecuted and killed many Jews during the Second

14. For a discussion of the text-variant in the different Greek versions, see my "Martyr Theology in Hellenistic Judaism," 499 n. 12.

15. I am very grateful to Robert Doran for reading and offering critical feedback to much of the material in this section. I am also grateful to him for his gracious comments about my paper on 2 Maccabees in a personal conversation at the 2011 national meeting at the Society of Biblical Literature in San Francisco, CA after we both gave presentations in the Function of the Apocrypha and Pseudepigrapha on Early Christianity.

Temple period because they refused to yield to his Hellenistic reforms and assimilate within Hellenism to the degree he demanded (cf. 1 Maccabees 1).[16] Although certain Jews forsook the religion of their fathers by adopting both the cultural and religious practices of the Gentiles even before Antiochus' crusade for Hellenism (1 Macc 1:11–15), his reforms were nevertheless radical since he required that all people (Jews and Gentiles) everywhere should conform to the Greek way of life (1 Macc 1:20–24, 29–50).[17] He wrote letters and dispatched them throughout his entire kingdom (1 Macc 1:41), which consisted of both Jewish and Gentile territories (1 Macc 1:16–19, 41–42). In these letters, he commanded all nations to adopt Greek customs (1 Macc 1:41).

Antiochus' letters declared that Jews and Gentiles should become one people and that they should surrender their laws and customs (1 Macc 1:41–42). He required the Jews to adopt "other laws in the land" (νομίμων ἀλλοτρίων τῆς γῆς) besides the Torah (1 Macc 1:44). He prohibited the Jews from offering sacrifices and from keeping the Sabbath in compliance with Torah (1 Macc 1:44). He commanded the Jews to defile both the temple's holy place and its priests by building altars for other gods besides YHWH (1 Macc 1:45–47). He gave orders that the Jews could no longer circumcise their children, and he demanded them to forget Torah's prescriptions for their lives (1 Macc 1:48–49). He offered an unlawful sacrifice on the altar in the temple; he burned the books of the Torah; he executed Jews who possessed copies of the Torah, and he hung the infants of those Jews who did not obey his reforms (1 Macc 1:54–61).

To ensure full devotion to his demands, Antiochus concluded his letters by asserting that he would kill anyone who refused to act in accordance with his word (1 Macc 1:50). On the one hand, many Jews yielded to Antiochus' edicts and forsook their religion and their God (1 Macc 1:52). On the other hand, other Jews disobeyed Antiochus and remained faithful to their ancestral traditions (1 Macc 1:62—2:28). Torah-observant Jews were resilient in their commitment to their religion, even in the face of persecution

---

16. I recognize that the reasons behind Antiochus' persecutions are complex. But a basic point that the authors make in 1, 2, and 4 Maccabees is that the persecution was in part the result of the refusal of many Jews to assimilate within Greek culture to the degree that Antiochus desired.

17. 1 Macc 1:11 asserts that renegade Jews approached Antiochus first in pursuit of an alliance with him (ἐν ταῖς ἡμέραις ἐκείναις ἐξῆλθον ἐξ Ισραηλ υἱοὶ παράνομοι καὶ ἀνέπεισαν πολλοὺς λέγοντες πορευθῶμεν καὶ διαθώμεθα διαθήκην μετὰ τῶν ἐθνῶν τῶν κύκλῳ ἡμῶν ὅτι ἀφ᾽ ἧς ἐχωρίσθημεν ἀπ᾽ αὐτῶν εὗρεν ἡμᾶς κακὰ πολλά).

and death. Neither Antiochus' tortures nor his threats of death persuaded them to abandon their religion (4 Macc 5:1—6:30).[18]

When devout Jews in Jerusalem refused to obey his reforms and the reforms of his compatriots, the Gentiles seized the holy city, desecrated the temple, pilfered the holy vessels, and left Jerusalem desolate (1 Macc 1:1–63; cf. 2 Macc 6:1–5). Their plundering devastated Jews throughout the city (1 Macc 1:25–28; cf. 2 Macc 5:11–16). To add insult to injury, two years later, Antiochus deceived many Jews by persuading them that he would extend peace to Israel. He sent a messenger to Judea to execute this deception. Many Jews, unfortunately, believed that Antiochus' gesture of peace was sincere. His deception enabled him to overtake Jerusalem a second time (1 Macc 1:29–32).

After his second attack of the city, Antiochus eventually sacked the temple and desecrated it. He also destroyed the books of the Torah and demanded that Judeans offer sacrifices to him and engage in pagan worship (1 Macc 1:33–50). He promised to kill any Jew who obeyed God's law and who refused to yield full allegiance to his new policies (1 Macc 1:33–50; cf. 4 Macc 4:20, 23),[19] and he forbade the Jews from practicing their festivals and from doing anything that uniquely identified them as Jews (2 Macc 6:6).

Antiochus' abolishment of the law and his desecration of the temple meant that Jews could no longer offer acceptable sacrifices of atonement to God as prescribed in the Torah. Such a prohibition meant that they could not celebrate Yom Kippur. The preceding point is especially true if the latter festival occurred during either the time of Antiochus' desecration or his reforms (1 Macc 1:41–64; 2 Macc 1:5; 5:4, 35; cf. Philo, *Spec.* 1.11.67–69). If Otto Mørkholm is correct that Antiochus suspended temple sacrifices on 15 Chislev (=ca. December 167 BCE)[20] and if this suspension lasted for two full years, then it would have overlapped with the 10th day of Tishri (=September-October) when Yom Kippur would have likely been celebrated.[21] In support of this assertion, in a recent essay, while speaking of Yom Kippur during pre-Antiochus Second Temple Judaism, Albert I. Baumgarten comments that the Jews viewed it as unacceptable to celebrate Yom Kippur on a different date from the one determined by the central temple authorities.[22] The date of celebration enforced by the temple authorities would have likely

---

18. Jewish resiliency in the face of persecution and death also appears in History of Susanna and Bel and the Dragon.
19. Cf. 1 Macc 1:36—2:13; 4 Macc 1:11; 17:22.
20. So Mørkholm, "Antiochus IV," 286.
21. Sanders, *Judaism, Practice and Belief: 63BCE-66CE*, 140.
22. See Baumgarten, "Setting the Outer Limits," 90–2, esp. 91.

been the day prescribed by YHWH in the Torah since pious Jews zealously devoted to the Torah during Antiochus' reign would have honored Moses's prescriptions in the Torah regarding this most important Jewish festival until their very death (e.g., 1 Maccabees 1–2), for, as Philo states, Yom Kippur was the "highest of the festivals" (*Spec.* 2:193–94).[23]

The words of Mattathias during the Maccabean revolt supports the assertion that Jews during the revolt would have likely observed Yom Kippur on the exact day prescribed by YHWH in Torah, which would have been the 10th day of Tishri (cf. Lev 16:29). After Antiochus threatened the Jews and desecrated the temple (cf. 1 Macc 1:10–64), Mattathias responds by saying: "And I and my sons and my brothers will walk in the covenant of our fathers. Far be it from us to forsake the law and the ordinances. We will not obey the king's words so that we would abandon our worship with respect to the right or the left" (1 Macc 2:20–22). By refusing to abandon "our worship/service," Mattathias means sacrificial worship as prescribed by YHWH in Torah and this sacrificial worship would have included the precise time to celebrate Yom Kippur. Both points seem right because Mattathias utters these words immediately after the king's threat against the Jews who participate in cultic worship in compliance with Torah (1 Macc 1:41–47, 51) and immediately after he (Mattathias) vociferates that he and his family would continue to worship YHWH in compliance with Torah, even if all of the king's nations should turn away from the "worship/service" of its fathers (1 Macc 2:19–22).

In support of the above, with the exception of two occurrences (LXX Exod 13:5; 3 Macc 4:14), the term λατρείαν ("worship/service") in 1 Macc 2:22 occurs in the LXX in reference to cultic worship. For example, in LXX Exodus 12 when giving Moses instructions regarding the feast of Passover, YHWH asserts that Israel will keep this "worship/service" and that when their children ask them about this "worship/service," Israel shall explain to them that it is a Passover (LXX Exod 12:25–26). In LXX Jos 22:27, λατρείαν refers to approaching YHWH with "burnt-offerings," "sacrifices," and "sacrifices of salvation." In LXX 1 Chr 28:13, the Chronicler(s) uses λατρείας in connection with the divisions of the priests and Levites and with the cultic "service" in YHWH's temple.[24]

Appropriate cultic worship at the temple was extremely important for all Torah-observant Jews during the Second Temple period, because the

---

23. Ben Ezra (*Yom Kippur*, 16) pointed me to the above citation from Philo. For Philo, however, Yom Kippur is "the fast" and not the day of propitiation. For this latter thought, see Tiwald, "Christ as *HILASTERION* (Rom 3:25)," 198.

24. In 1 Macc 1:43, 2 Macc 2:19, and 2 Macc 2:22, λατρείας refers to cultic "worship/service."

temple was central to their religious life, which included their social and political status as God's people.²⁵ The temple was especially essential for Israel's cultic worship during the Second Temple period.²⁶ The temple symbolized that YHWH dwelt with his people (cf. 11QT 25:12—31:10).²⁷ Thus, the desecration of the temple in Second Temple Judaism suggested both that YHWH no longer dwelt with his people due to the nation's sin (cf. LXX Dan 3:28–90) and that he put an end to the temple sacrifices and religious festivals that involved the temple due to the nation's sin (cf. 2 Macc 7:33). The sacrificial system, especially Yom Kippur, was central to Jewish identity and particularity.²⁸ Consequently, Antiochus' desecration of the temple ended Jewish particularity and identity as they knew it (i.e., their religious life as they practiced it in compliance with the Torah in distinction from the nations). Yom Kippur focused on fasting, prayer, and confession and on both individual and corporate atonement for sins (LXX Lev 16:2–34).²⁹

Since, therefore, Antiochus desecrated the temple and ended the cult, Torah-zealous Jews would have considered the temple to be unfit for temple worship.³⁰ They would have considered it to be defiled because of its contamination by the Gentiles and apostate Jews (1 Macc 4:36–58; 2 Macc 6:4–6; cf. Acts 21:27),³¹ whose contamination would have overlapped with the daily sacrifices and the yearly celebration of Yom Kippur. Torah-observant Jews believed that all sin defiles the temple, especially the sin of mingling with Gentiles.³² For example, observe the following excerpt from *Jub.* 22:16–18 and from the *Epistle of Aristeas* 139, 142.

> Separate yourself from the Gentiles, and do not eat with them,
> and do not perform deeds like theirs, because their deeds are
> defiled, and all of their ways are contaminated and despicable

---

25. Cohen, *From The Maccabees to the Mishnah*, 101–2; Klawans, *Purity, Sacrifice, and the Temple*, 103–74. See also Ezra-Nehemiah; Hag 1–2; 1–4 Maccabees.

26. Jos. *Ag. Ap.* 2.24.193; Philo, *Spec.* 1.11.67–69.

27. The above citations come from Klawans, *Purity, Sacrifice, and the Temple*, 145–74, esp. 147–48, 153–55.

28. Sir 50:14–21; 4Q508; 11QTemple 25:10—27:10. See also Sanders, *Judaism*, 143.

29. *Jub.* 5:17–18; 34:18–19; 11Q5 27:2–11; *Pss. Sol.* 3:8; Philo, *Spec.* 193–203; *Mos.* 2.23–24; *Legat.* 306; *L.A.B.* 13:6. See also Falk, "Festivals and Holy Days," 642.

30. For sins that some Second Temple Jews thought would defile the temple and for the relevant primary texts, see Klawans, *Purity, Sacrifice, and the Temple*, 147–74.

31. The above citation of 1 Macc 4:41–59 comes from Schiffman, *Texts and Traditions*, 160–61.

32. The above statement does not imply that Second Temple Jews believed that the sin of mingling with the Gentiles was the only sin that defiled the temple. For example, see texts cited in Klawans, *Purity, Sacrifice, and the Temple*, 147–74.

and abominable. They slaughter their sacrifices to the dead, and to the demons they bow down. And they eat in tombs. And all their deeds are worthless and vain. And they have no heart to perceive, and they have no eyes to see what their deeds are, and where they wander astray, saying to the tree "you are my god," and to a stone "you are my lord, and you are my savior," and they have no heart (*Jub.* 22:16–18).[33]

In his wisdom, the legislator, in a comprehensive survey of each particular part, and being endowed by God for the knowledge of universal truths, surrounded us with unbroken palisades and iron walls to prevent our mixing with any of the other peoples in any matter, being thus kept pure in body and soul, preserved from false beliefs, and worshipping the only God omnipotent over all creation. . . . So, to prevent our being perverted by contact with others by mixing with bad influences, he hedges us in on all sides with strict observances connected with meat and drink and touch and hearing and sight after the manner of the Law (Ep. *Arist.* 139, 142).

As YHWH prescribed in Leviticus 1–6 and 16, appropriate cultic action leads to appropriate cultic function. In addition, as YHWH prescribed in Leviticus 16, during Yom Kippur, the priests would atone for all of their personal transgressions, the transgressions of the people, and the impurities of the holy place because of the impurities of the people (Lev 16:3–28).[34] In Leviticus 16, YHWH commands Aaron to offer specific animals as atonement for sin, so that the nation and the holy place would be purified and cleansed (Lev 16:3–34).[35] After YHWH instructs Moses how Aaron should perform the Yom Kippur ritual, he states that the day of the ritual should be celebrated every year for the cleansing of sin (Lev 16:29–30). This cleansing through the offering of blood accompanied by contrition and repentance achieved and symbolized God's forgiveness for the entire nation (Lev 16:29–30; cf. 1QS 3:4).[36]

---

33. See also 1 Macc 1:11–15, 41–45; 3:58–59; 4:54–60; 2 Macc 5:15–20; 4Q395; CD 4:20; 5:6–9; Pesher Habakkuk 8:8–13; 12:6–10; 4Q390; 4Q385a frag. 3a, C: 6–7; Ep. *Arist.* 152–53; *Pss. Sol.* 2:2; Jos *Ant.* 15.5.417; Acts 21:27.

34. Exod 30:10; Lev 23:27–32; 25:9–10; Num 29:7–11. For a discussion of the rituals of Yom Kippur during both Second Temple and post Second Temple Judaism, see Ben Ezra, *Yom Kippur*, 28–67.

35. See Hartley, *Leviticus*, 241.

36. These sacrifices were not *ipso facto* efficacious to provide forgiveness, but repentance was the fundamental prerequisite for the efficacy of the sacrifices (cf. Psalm 51; Amos 5:21–22; Hos 6:6; Isa 1:10–17; Mic 6:6–8; Jer 7:21–23). For this point, see

Later Jewish traditions suggest that during Yom Kippur, Jews devoted themselves to communal confession, penitential prayer, and praise to God for lengthy periods of time.[37] *Jubilees* 34:18-19 states that Israel should atone for their sins once a year and that Yom Kippur was decreed "so that they might mourn on it on account of their sin and on account of all of their transgression and on account of all their errors in order to purify themselves on this day once a year." Philo expresses that many Jews took up the entire day celebrating Yom Kippur (*Spec.* 2.196). Sirach 50:17-19 states that people fell on their faces to worship the Lord and that the people of the Lord prayed "until the adornment of the Lord was completed and until they completed his service." Such lengthy practices, along with Yom Kippur's cultic sacrifices, were seen by some Jews to effect atonement for sin during the Second Temple period.[38] Philo attests to the efficacy of Yom Kippur during this period when he expresses that much prayer was offered on the Day of Atonement to propitiate the Father of the universe to pardon former sins and to ensure new blessings (*Mos.* 2.24).[39]

As to the importance of temple purity in the Second Temple period, further support emerges from 1 and 2 Maccabees and Josephus. *Hannukah*, the Festival of Dedication, memorializes the restoration of the Second Temple and the dedication of the altar by Judas Maccabaeus in 164 BCE during the reign of Antiochus.[40] The feast was celebrated with much feasting, sacrifices, rejoicing, praise, and music due to both the restoration and deliverance of the temple from the hands of the Gentiles (1 Macc 4:36-59; 2 Macc 1:10—2:18; Jos *Ant.* 12.316-26). Regarding the importance of the temple and its purity, Philo describes the purgative rituals of the priest before he entered into the Holy of Holies (*Somn.* 1.216-17; *Legat.* 306),[41] and he states that "*as God is one*, his temple should also be *one*. In the next place, he does not permit those who desire to perform sacrifices in their own houses to do so, but orders all men to rise up, even from the furthest

---

Milgrom, *Cult and Conscience*.

37. For a recent collection of essays devoted to Yom Kippur in early Judaism and in early Christianity, see Hieke and Nicklas (eds.), *The Day of Atonement*.

38. Possibly also 4Q507, 4Q509 frgs. 5-6 ii., 7; 4Q508 frgs. 2, 22 + 23. For additional texts, see Falk, "Festivals and Holy Days," 642.

39. For the importance of long prayers of confession at Yom Kippur in Second Temple Judaism, see also Philo, *Spec.* 1:186; 2:196-99, 203; 7:431. Additionally, as Ben Ezra (*Yom Kippur*, 114) points out, Philo emphasizes the symbolic meanings of Yom Kippur due to his allegorical exegesis, but he likewise maintains the literal meanings and institutions of Yom Kippur.

40. Falk, "Festivals and Holy Days," 644-45, esp. 644.

41. Ibid., 641.

boundaries of the earth, and to come to this temple . . . ." (*Spec.* 1.11.67–69). Philo states elsewhere that Jews would be willing to sacrifice their entire family to preserve the purity of the temple (*Legat.* 308). Josephus says that "there ought to be but one temple for *one God* . . . ." (*Ag. Ap.* 2.24.193).

The above comments from 1 and 2 Maccabees, Philo, and Josephus suggest that Torah-observant Jews would have withdrawn from the temple when Antiochus desecrated it, for they would offer sacrifices only in a sanctified and in a purified temple that symbolized the presence of the one and only God of Israel (cf. Tob 1:4; 1 Macc 4:36–58; cf. Acts 21:27–30).[42] Since Antiochus forbade the Jews from offering sacrifices and from celebrating their festivals in compliance with Torah when he gained control of the temple (1 Macc 1:41–59; 2 Macc 6:4–6), 2 and 4 Maccabees suggest that it was both unfit and unavailable for the Jews to practice cultic worship in compliance with the Torah (1 Macc 1:41–59). Thus, if there was no temple cult due to its impurity, YHWH's prescribed forms of cultic action would not happen. Without cultic action, then there could be no Yom Kippur ritual.[43] Without the Yom Kippur ritual, there would be no cultic function that offered national purification for the nation's sin. This becomes conspicuous in a Second Temple text like LXX Dan 3:24–90, where Daniel's three friends offer *themselves* as atoning sacrifices for the sins of the nation while in exile without access to the temple. This is likewise true in Tobit, where Tobit expresses, while in exile, that almsgiving accomplishes atonement for sin for those in exile without access to the temple (Tob 4:10–11; 12:9). The preceding traditions offer alternatives to the traditional Yom Kippur cult at the temple because there was no sanctified temple in the land of exile at which Jews could celebrate Yom Kippur.[44]

JEWISH MARTYRDOM AND RECONCILIATION

2 and 4 Maccabees present the Jewish martyrs as Israel's representatives, substitutes, and as the nation's Yom Kippur. After killing Eleazar in 2 Maccabees 6, Antiochus tried to compel a mother and her seven sons to eat unlawful foods (2 Macc 7:1). They were faced with death if they disobeyed. Yet, they rebelled against Antiochus. As a result, each suffered torture and

---

42. See Baumgarten, "Setting the Outer Limits," 92–93.

43. For a list of Rabbinic texts that likewise find other means of offering atonement due to the temple's destruction in post-70 CE Judaism, see David Janzen, *The Social Meanings of Sacrifice in the Hebrew Bible*, 1.

44. Ben Ezra (*Yom Kippur*, 115–18) argues that Leviticus 16 and the Yom Kippur ritual were instructive for the vicarious deaths of the martyrs in 4 Maccabees.

death (2 Macc 7:2–41). While encouraged by his mother to trust God as he faced Antiochus' wrath (2 Macc 7:28–29), the seventh son stated that "we suffer because of our own sins" (ἡμεῖς γὰρ διὰ τὰς ἑαυτῶν ἁμαρτίας πάσχομεν) (2 Macc 7:32; cf. 2 Macc 5:17). His words echo the cry of Daniel's three friends in LXX Dan 3:28–29 and 3:37 (2 Macc 7:32; cf. 2 Macc 5:17).[45] The seventh son's confession is almost exactly the same as his older brother's (the sixth son), who was martyred earlier in the narrative, in 2 Macc 7:18 (ἡμεῖς γὰρ δι' ἑαυτοὺς ταῦτα πάσχομεν ἁμαρτόντες εἰς τὸν ἑαυτῶν θεόν ἄξια θαυμασμοῦ γέγονεν). Just as the confession of Daniel's three friends, the confession of both the sixth and the seventh sons acknowledges that sin is the foundational reason that the martyrs suffer in the narrative of 2 Maccabees at the hands of Antiochus and that the martyrs' deaths are the foundational reason why God "will be reconciled again to his servants" (εἰ δὲ χάριν ἐπιπλήξεως καὶ παιδείας ὁ ζῶν κύριος ἡμῶν βραχέως ἐπώργισται καὶ πάλιν καταλλαγήσεται τοῖς ἑαυτοῦ δούλοις) (2 Macc 7:33; cf. 2 Macc 1:5; 7:37–38; 8:29).

References to the Lord's servants, who were Torah-observant Jews, as dying for the soteriological benefit of non-Torah-observant sinners in 2 Macc 7:33 conceptually connects with Isaiah 53. Isaiah 53 asserts that YHWH's Servant will serve as the means by which the nation's sin is forgiven and the means by which YHWH will declare many righteous to be in the right (LXX 53:4–6, 8, 10–12). Although the verb καταλλαγήσεται in 2 Macc 7:33 is absent in LXX Isaiah 53, the infinitive δικαιῶσαι and the adjective δίκαιον in LXX Isa 53:11 communicate the concept of reconciliation between God and sinners because the soteriological reality communicated with the words δικαιῶσαι and δίκαιον is the result of the Servant's death for the sins of others. In other words, the act of YHWH declaring to be in the right those for whom the Servant dies in order to take away their sins results in reconciliation between YHWH and the transgressors for whom the Servant dies. In addition to the Isaianic language, 2 Maccabees appropriates Levitical cultic language.

The seventh son's statements that "we suffer because of our sins" and that "he will again be reconciled to his servants" refer to Israel as a nation, which includes the martyrs.[46] This seems right because of the first person

---

45. Similarly Kraus, *Der Tod Jesu als Heiligtumsweihe*, 35. However, Kraus argues against a cultic background behind 2 Macc 7:32–38.

46. So van Henten, *Maccabean Martyrs*, 137–38. Against Schwartz, *2 Maccabees*, 314, who without substantiation asserts that 2 Macc 7:32 only refers to the Jews' sins in contrast to 7:33. But, as van Henten (*Maccabean Martyrs*, 137 n. 51) astutely points out, "the verb ἁμαρτόντες occurs only in 2 Macc 7:18 and 10:4, where it also refers to the sinning of the people as a body."

plural ἡμεῖς, the phrase διὰ τὰς ἑαυτῶν ἁμαρτίας, and the first person plural verb πάσχομεν. The need for God to be reconciled again to his servants reveals that enmity exists between God and his people in the narrative due to the apostasy of many Jews away from their God to follow Antiochus' Hellenistic policies (1 Macc 1; 2 Macc 5:18; 6:12–16). However, the martyrs were individually innocent of religious apostasy (cf. 1 Macc 1–2; 2 Macc 7; 4 Macc 6), which is evident by their Torah-observance in the face of death. Their suffering was a corollary of their refusal to embrace Greek culture as many of their kinsmen had begun to embrace it (cf. 2 Macc 5:1—8:5; 4 Macc 6).[47] The reconciliation needed by their martyrdom is the cessation of God's wrath against the people because of the sin of some within the community and a return of friendship between YHWH and the nation. In this respect, the seventh son interprets the situation of the nation and his brothers in light of Deuteronomy 32, and he interprets the vindication of YHWH's servants in Deut 32:36 to be accomplished by means of his faithful death and the faithful deaths of his brothers, who are both *representatives of* and *substitutes for* the nation.

In LXX Deut 32:36a, in his final words to Israel, Moses states that the Lord will vindicate his people, and "he will feel compassion for his servants" (καὶ ἐπὶ τοῖς δούλοις αὐτοῦ παρακληθήσεται), whereas 2 Macc 7:33 stresses that the Lord "will be reconciled again by means of his servants" (καὶ πάλιν καταλλαγήσεται τοῖς ἑαυτοῦ δούλοις). The former accentuates *what* God will do for his people (namely, show them mercy) (cf. 2 Macc 7:6), but the seventh son's prayer stresses *the means* by which God will show mercy (namely, through his servants, the faithful martyrs). The veracity of the statement that the martyrs would be the means by which God would be reconciled to his nation is strengthened by the noun καταλλαγή and the verb καταλλαγήσεται in 2 Maccabees, both of which always concern reconciliation between the Lord and his people in 2 Maccabees (cf. 2 Macc 1:5; 7:33; 8:29).[48]

Before the seventh son utters these words in 2 Macc 7:32–38, the author places a panegyric speech in the mouth of both Eleazar in 2 Maccabees 6 and in the mouths of the mother and her seven sons in 2 Maccabees 7. Prior to these speeches, the author lucidly asserts that the sin for which the martyrs suffered torturous death was the nation's rebellion against the Torah (2 Macc 5:20—7:32; cf. 1 Macc 1:11–15). The respective texts in 2 and 4 Maccabees do not state anywhere that the martyrs themselves actually

---

47. O'Hagan, "The Martyr in the Fourth Book of the Maccabees," 94–120, esp. 108. Against Baumeister, *Die Anfange der Theologie des Martyriums*, 41–42.

48. For more detailed discussions of reconciliation in 2 Maccabees and for alternative interpretations of the nature of reconciliation in 2 Maccabees, see Breytenbach, *Versöhnung*; Porter, *Καταλλασσω in Ancient Greek Literature*.

violated Torah along with the rest of the nation. Nevertheless, the "we" in "we suffer because of our sins" (2 Macc 7:32) includes the martyrs along with rebellious Israel for the following reasons. First, the martyrs were members of YHWH's covenant community for which they suffered (cf. 2 Macc 7:16, 30, 30-32, 38). Second, Antiochus is called the adversary of the Hebrews and not simply the adversary of the martyrs (2 Macc 7:31). Third, the martyrological narratives begin with the author's statements about the positive role of suffering in the lives of the Lord's covenant people (2 Macc 6:12-17).[49] Thus, 2 and 4 Maccabees' presentations of the martyrs' suffering echo Israel's antecedent Deuteronomic history, thereby fulfilling the Deuteronomic curses set forth in Deuteronomy 27-28 and 32 against Israel via the nations due to the disobedience of some within the nation (cf. Deut 28:1-14 with 28:15-68).[50] The seventh son's words demonstrate that the principle set forth in Leviticus and reiterated in Deuteronomy (namely, when a few in the covenant community sinned against God and suffered the consequences of their sin, the entire covenant community, including the martyrs, suffered the consequences of this sin) was still alive and well in 2 Maccabees.[51] The martyrs' suffering was a result of their refusal to embrace Greek culture as many of their kinsmen had begun to embrace it (cf. 2 Macc 5:1—8:5; 4 Macc 6),[52] and their kinsmen's acceptance of Antiochus' Hellenistic regime resulted in God's judgment of the entire nation through Antiochus (cf. 1 Macc 1), as promised in Deut 28:1-68. Therefore, the martyrological narratives present the seventh son and the other martyrs as representatives of the nation and as substitutes for the nation to pay for Israel's sin, which also became a payment for their sins by virtue of their membership within the covenant community (cf. 2 Macc 7:32).[53] 2 Maccabees 5:1—7:38 supports this interpretation.

As a result of the nation's rebellion against God's law, the temple and the land were dishonored (2 Macc 5:27—6:6). When Antiochus and Menelaus (a Jewish high priest) entered the temple in Jerusalem, they profaned it (2 Macc 5:15-16). To eradicate God's judgment against the nation, the

---

49. So van Henten, *Maccabean Martyrs*, 139.

50. To see the Deuteronomic thesis argued in more detail, see Jarvis J. Williams, *Christ Redeemed 'Us' from the Curse of the Law* . . . (forthcoming).

51. Cf. Num 25:11; Isa 1:1-26; LXX Dan 3:24-90; Wis 3:1-6; 1QS 1.6-11.

52. O'Hagan, "The Martyr," 94-120, esp. 108. Against Baumeister, *Die Anfange*, 41-42.

53. So de Jonge, *Christology in Context*, 181-82; Kellermann, "Zum traditionsgeschichtlichen Problem des stellvertretenden Sühnetodes in 2 Makk 7:37," 63-83, esp. 69; van Henten, *Maccabean Martyrs*, 137. Against Williams, *Jesus' Death*, 79 n. 29; Seeley, *The Noble Death*, 87.

seven sons voluntarily offer themselves to die for Israel to achieve God's forgiveness (2 Macc 7:32–38).[54] 2 Maccabees 7:32–38 suggests that the seventh son was confident that God would be reconciled again to the nation through the martyrs' deaths because he asserts that God "will be reconciled again to his servants" in 2 Macc 7:33 and because 2 Macc 7:37–38 affirms that the seventh son wants God to end his wrath against the nation by means of the deaths of him and his brothers on behalf of the nation (ἐγὼ δὲ καθάπερ οἱ ἀδελφοί καὶ σῶμα καὶ ψυχὴν προδίδωμι περὶ τῶν πατρίων νόμων ἐπικαλούμενος τὸν θεὸν ἵλεως ταχὺ τῷ ἔθνει γενέσθαι καὶ σὲ μετὰ ἐτασμῶν καὶ μαστίγων ἐξομολογήσασθαι διότι μόνος αὐτὸς θεός ἐστιν ἐν ἐμοὶ δὲ καὶ τοῖς ἀδελφοῖς μου στῆσαι τὴν τοῦ παντοκράτορος ὀργὴν τὴν ἐπὶ τὸ σύμπαν ἡμῶν γένος δικαίως ἐπηγμένην).[55]

The most important parts of the above prayer in 2 Macc 7:37–38 for my thesis are the seventh son's statements "be merciful quickly to the nation" in 7:37 and "to end the wrath of the Almighty in me and in my brothers" in 7:38. The grammatical construction in 2 Macc 7:37 is similar to the one in 4 Macc 6:28. Eleazar asks God in the latter text to provide mercy for the nation through his death (ἵλεως γενοῦ τῷ ἔθνει σου). In 2 Macc 7:37, the seventh son prays that God would "quickly be merciful to the nation" (ἵλεως ταχὺ τῷ ἔθνει γενέσθαι) through his death. In both 4 Macc 6:28 and 2 Macc 7:37, the martyrs urge God to grant mercy to the nation through their deaths for it. They offered themselves to God to pay for the nation's sin, which also became a payment for their sin by virtue of their membership within the community (cf. 2 Macc 7:32). Thus, the function of the martyrs' deaths for Israel parallels the function of Yom Kippur for Israel. That is, the martyrs represent and stand in the place of rebellious Israel, and they are the means by which and the place at which atonement is made for the nation to achieve YHWH's reconciliation, just as the animals stand in the place of Israel (=the sacrificial ritual), represent the people (=the scapegoat ritual), and is the means by which Israel's sins are purified/covered/atoned during Yom Kippur (Leviticus 16),[56] just as the Servant stands in the place

---

54. Similarly Lohse, *Märtyrer und Gottesknecht*, 67–69; Gnilka, "Martyriumsparänese und Sühnetod in synoptischen und jüdischen Traditionen," 223–46; Downing, "Jesus and Martyrdom," 279–93, esp. 288–89; van Henten, *Maccabean Martyrs*, 140–44. Against a sacrificial reading of 2 Macc 7:32–38, see Sam Williams, *Jesus' Death*, 82–88; Goldstein, *2 Maccabees*, 316; Seeley, *The Noble Death*, 87–91, 145; Versnel, "Making Sense," 258–59.

55. Schwartz, *2 Maccabees*, 317.

56. Contra Sam Williams, *Jesus' Death*, 79 n. 29; Seeley, *The Noble Death*, 87. Rightly de Jonge, *Christology in Context*, 181–82; Kellermann, "Zum traditionsgeschichtlichen Problem des stellvertretenden Sühnetodes in 2 Makk 7:37," 63–83, esp. 69; van Henten, *Maccabean Martyrs*, 137.

Representation and Substitution in Second Temple Jewish Martyrologies 91

of Israel as the means by which the nations' sins are purified/covered/atoned in Isaiah 53. As the ensuing narrative of 2 Macc 8:1–5 suggests, the martyrs' deaths are the means by which YHWH's wrath ceases against Israel and the means by which reconciliation is achieved in the narrative of 2 Maccabees.

Scholars debate the meaning of 7:38.[57] The debate pertains to how one should interpret the seventh son's statement that God's wrath would end ἐν ἐμοὶ δὲ καὶ τοῖς ἀδελφοῖς μου (2 Macc 7:38). As I have discussed elsewhere, Sam K. Williams argued in the latter part of the 1970s that the seven sons do not avert God's wrath away from the nation by means of their deaths. According to Williams, the phrases ἐν ἐμοὶ δὲ καὶ τοῖς ἀδελφοῖς μου do not suggest the *means by which* the wrath of God is averted away from Israel, but the *point at which* the wrath of God is averted.[58] He simply affirms that the wrath of God would end "with" him and "with" his brothers. That is, the seventh son urges God to let the martyrs be the last ones upon whom or the final point at which God pours out wrath. Williams maintains his view partly because he rejects that 2 Maccabees teaches vicarious atonement.[59] According to him, 2 Maccabees only presents the martyrs' suffering and death as exemplary for their fellow Jews to imitate when they face their own suffering and death.[60]

Williams' analysis is partially correct in two ways. First, the author of 2 Maccabees states that the suffering and deaths of the martyrs were exemplary (2 Macc 6:28, 31; cf. 2 Macc 6:24–31). Eleazar's death was an example of nobility for the entire nation to follow (2 Macc 6:28, 31). Even 4 Maccabees, where martyrdom is glamorized, speaks of the martyrs' deaths as exemplary for others (4 Macc 6:18–21; 9:23; 10:3, 16; 11:15; 12:16; 13:8–18; 17:23). Second, Williams is correct to note that the preposition ἐν in the phrase ἐν ἐμοὶ δὲ καὶ τοῖς ἀδελφοῖς μου στῆσαι τὴν τοῦ παντοκράτορος ὀργὴν has more meanings than "by means of."

In response to Williams' first observation, the exemplary nature of the martyrs' deaths in 2 and 4 Maccabees does not preclude their deaths from functioning as representatives of the nation and as substitutes for the nation. Their deaths could in fact be exemplary, representative, and substitutionary. In response to Williams' second observation, the preposition ἐν likely conveys instrumentality in 2 Macc 7:38 ("by means of") for multiple reasons. First, the preceding meaning occurs in numerous places in 2 Maccabees

---

57. Sam Williams, *Jesus' Death*, 83–88; Surkau, *Martyrien in jüdischer und frühchristilicher Zeit*, 59.

58. Sam Williams, *Jesus' Death*, 83–88.

59. Ibid.

60. Ibid.

(2 Macc 1:28; 5:20; 7:29; 15:11; cf. 4 Macc 9:22; 16:15). Second, the prepositional phrases occur in a context where the seventh son urges God to be reconciled to the nation again (2 Macc 7:33).[61] Third, the term should be translated as "by means of" in 2 Macc 7:29, which is a text in close proximity of 2 Macc 7:38. If the translation "by means of" is correct in 2 Macc 7:38, then the seventh son's prayer should be interpreted to mean that he wanted God to end his wrath "by means of" his death and "by means of" the deaths of his brothers. This interpretation suggests that the seventh son wants his death and the deaths of his brothers to satisfy God's wrath against the nation in a substitutionary manner since the martyrs die as representatives of the nation.

2 Maccabees 5:1—8:5 supports that God fulfilled the seventh son's expectation through the martyrs' deaths, for the latter text states that God was reconciled to the nation after the martyrs die (2 Macc 8:1–5).[62] In light of this, the martyrs' deaths are a foundational reason God ended his wrath against the nation.[63] For example, 2 Macc 1:5 begins with a prayer that God "would be reconciled" to his people and not forsake them during an "evil time" in the first letter in the book prior to the epitome in 2:19—15:37. The "evil time" spoken of in 2 Macc 1:5 probably refers to Hellenization on account of the distress that consequently came upon Torah-zealous Jews when apostate Jews revolted against the holy city and embraced Antiochus' Hellenistic policies (2 Macc 1:7–8; 2:17–18).

Before the epitome, the author reminds his fellow Jews in Egypt (to whom he is writing) that God has saved his people from the Greek tyrant, restored temple-worship, and he expresses hope that God would soon show his mercy to all Jews scattered throughout the world by gathering them at his holy temple in Judea (2 Macc 2:17–18). The epitome begins with a recounting of how God showed his mercy to the Jews through Judas and his brothers during the Maccabean crisis (2 Macc 2:19-22), and the author suggests that he intends to set forth this story by summarizing Jason of Cyrene's five-volume work (2 Macc 2:23). The epitome ends with the author asserting that the Hebrews possessed the city of Judea after Judas and his army

---

61. For other examples where the preposition conveys means or instrumentality, see Robertson, *A Grammar of the Greek New Testament in the Light of Historical Research*, 589–91; Smyth, *Greek Grammar*, 376–77.

62. Schwartz (*2 Maccabees*, 317) observes that 2 Macc 8:4–5 applies 7:38.

63. Van Henten, "Tradition-Historical Background," 117–21, esp. 117. Against Sam Williams, *Jesus' Death*, 85–89; Seeley, *The Noble Death*, 88. Kellermann, *Auferstanden in den Himmel*, 54–55; Cummins, *Paul and the Crucified Christ*, 88. William H. Brown ("From Holy War to Holy Martyrdom," 287–88) states that "Judas and his men are asking God to accept the present national suffering as sufficient, not only to atone for the nation's sins, but as sufficient to invoke his wrath upon the Syrian armies."

cut off Nicanor's (a Gentile king's) head and cut out his tongue (2 Macc 15:32-37). Thus, reconciliation with God in 1:5, God's mercy and salvation in 2:18, and God's mercy and salvation in 15:37 frame the martyrological sections of the epitome in 6:18—7:42. Such an arrangement could suggest that the author wants to communicate that the means by which God's reconciliation, mercy, and salvation came to the covenant community through Judas and his brothers was the faithful martyrs, which the ensuing narrative of 5:1—8:5 supports.[64]

While Antiochus was finishing his second invasion of Egypt in the narrative of 2 Maccabees, he heard that Judea was in revolt (2 Macc 5:1-11). He immediately left Egypt to seize Jerusalem (2 Macc 5:11b-14). Antiochus entered the holy temple and profaned it, for he was oblivious to the fact that God was using him to defile the temple on account of his anger with Israel (2 Macc 5:17-18). Just as the temple suffered pollution and judgment because of the nation's sin, it also experienced God's blessings when he pardoned the nation (2 Macc 5:20a; cf. Lev 16:16, 30). 2 Maccabees 5:20b states that God's wrath ended, and the glory of Israel was restored to the nation "by means of the reconciliation of the Great Lord" (2 Macc 8:5; cf. Lev 9:1—10:2).

After the author describes the reversal of the abominations that Antiochus committed against Israel (2 Macc 5:21—6:11), he discusses why the Jews suffered by means of Antiochus. He offers this explanation immediately before he writes about the martyrdoms of Eleazar, the mother, and her seven sons (2 Macc 6:18—8:2). In 2 Macc 6:12-17, the author urges his readers not to be discouraged by the calamities that God brought against the nation by asserting that God provided the calamities against the nation for her benefit. The author also states that God would soon judge the Gentile nations when they reach the full measure of their sins, but he would not deal with Israel in this way. Instead, God judged Israel through Antiochus, and the martyrdom of some was representative of his divine judgment against the entire nation. The author explains that God neither withdrew his mercy from his people nor forsook them (2 Macc 6:13-16). The author, then, highlights the deaths of the martyrs in 2 Macc 6:18—8:2 to demonstrate how God's mercy was achieved for the nation (2 Macc 5:20; 8:5-7). 2 Maccabees 6:18—8:5 suggests that God reveals his mercy to Israel by his reconciliatory acts toward the nation, because after the seventh son promises God's future judgment of Antiochus (2 Macc 7:33), he states that he (just as his brothers) offers his life to God with the prayer that God would be merciful to the

---

64. In 1 Maccabees, the wrath is ascribed to Antiochus (1:64), and Judas' valor ends wrath against the nation and not his death (3:8). I owe this thought to Schwartz, *2 Maccabees*, 317.

nation through their deaths (2 Macc 7:37). His optimistic prayer in 2 Macc 7:37 follows the seventh son's confident assertion in 2 Macc 7:33 that the "Lord will be reconciled to his own servants." Subsequent to the author's presentations of the martyrdoms of Eleazar, the mother, and her seven sons (2 Macc 6:18—7:42), the author immediately discusses the response of the Torah-zealous Jews to the martyrs' deaths.

In 2 Maccabees 8, Judas Maccabaeus reappears in the narrative. He and other Torah-zealous Jews ask God to be merciful to the martyrs, the temple, and the city (2 Macc 8:2–3). They also pray that the Lord would hear the blood of the martyrs, that he would remember the destruction of the innocent babies, that he would remember the blasphemies against his name, and that he would hate all of the evil committed against Israel (2 Macc 8:4). The reconciliation for which the author prays in 2 Macc 1:5, the mercy of which the author speaks in 2 Macc 2:18, 5:20, 6:12–16, and 15:37, the mercy for which the martyrs die in 2 Macc 7:32–38, and the mercy for which Judas prays in 2 Macc 8:1–4 becomes a reality when God is reconciled again to the nation by reversing his wrath away from the Jews against Antiochus and his army (2 Macc 5:1—8:5).[65]

Against the view that the deaths of the martyrs atoned for Israel's sin, some scholars have argued that the effective prayer of Judas was the means by which the Lord granted mercy and reconciliation to the nation.[66] Indeed, the reconciliation that the seventh son asserts his death and the deaths of his brothers would achieve for the nation becomes a reality for Israel in the narrative after Judas' prayer, and God's glory was again restored to both the temple and the nation through their deaths after Judas' prayer. However, to make Judas' prayer the primary basis upon which God becomes reconciled to Israel in the narrative is too narrow a reading of 5:1—8:5, because God's reconciliation does not take place in this section until *after* the martyrs die (cf. 2 Macc 5:20—8:5; 4 Macc 17:21—22).

Judas' prayer was effective. But the exegetical question remains: *why* is his prayer effective? The narrative suggests that the prayer is efficacious in the narrative because the martyrs died for the nation. Thus, the efficacy of Judas' prayer does not disprove that the martyrs' deaths functioned as Israel's Yom Kippur. In fact, Philo notes that prayers were offered at Yom Kippur, along with fasting, to propitiate God (ἱλασκόμενοι τὸν πατέρα τοῦ παντὸς) as the participants asked him to forgive their old sins and to bring new blessings (*Moses* 2:24).

---

65. Contra Seeley, *The Noble Death*, 87–8.
66. Most recently, see Schwartz, *2 Maccabees*, 329.

Therefore, the text of 2 Macc 7:32–38 teaches that the martyrs function in the martyrological narratives as representatives of and as substitutes for sinful Israel and that they function as the nation's Yom Kippur. This claim can be supported by the following six reasons. First, the temple cult was dysfunctional. Second, the seventh son and his brothers suffered and, eventually, died because of the nation's sin (2 Macc 7:32; cf. Lev 16:3, 5, 6, 9, 21, 25, 34). Third, the martyrs offered their lives to God in death to achieve reconciliation for the nation (2 Macc 7:37; cf. Lev 16:30). Fourth, the seventh son asserted that God would again be reconciled to the nation through his death (2 Macc 7:37b; cf. Lev 16:30). Fifth, the seventh son prayed that God would deliver the nation from his wrath through his death and through the deaths of his brothers (2 Macc 7:38; cf. Lev 16:30).[67] Sixth, God was reconciled to the nation once again by means of the martyrs' deaths (2 Macc 5:1–8:5; cf. Lev 16:30).

JEWISH MARTYRDOM, GOD'S MERCY, SATISFACTION, AND PURIFICATION

The evidence that the martyrs functioned as representatives of, as substitutes for, and in the place of Israel's Yom Kippur in the martyrological narratives is even stronger in 4 Maccabees than in 2 Maccabees because of the explicit cultic language applied to the martyrs' deaths. In 4 Maccabees, the author describes the martyrdom of Eleazar in 4 Maccabees 6 and offers his concluding interpretation regarding the function of their deaths for the nation in 4 Macc 17:21–22. The author describes Eleazar as a scribe of high rank (2 Macc 6:18), from a priestly family, and an expert in the law (4 Macc 5:4, 35). Antiochus urges him to disobey the Torah and eat swine (2 Macc 6:18; 4 Macc 5:6). Instead, Eleazar voluntarily chooses death. As a result, Antiochus severely tortures him (4 Macc 6:1–8). As he bleeds profusely from the scourges that tore his flesh and from being pierced in his side with a spear (4 Macc 6:6), Eleazar prays that God would use his death to achieve three benefits for Israel: (1) mercy (4 Macc 6:28), (2) satisfaction (4 Macc 6:28), and (3) purification (4 Macc 6:29).

---

67. Similarly van Henten, *Maccabean Martyrs*, 143–44. Against Sam Williams, *Jesus' Death*, 83–88.

Eleazar's Death and God's Mercy

In the face of death, Eleazar urges God in 4 Macc 6:28 to be merciful to Israel through his death (ἵλεως γενοῦ τῷ ἔθνει σου) (2 Macc 4:1—6:31; 4 Macc 5:4—6:40). Numerous texts throughout 4 Maccabees support that Eleazar's request for mercy is a request for deliverance from God's wrath (2 Macc 4:16-17; 6:12-17; 4 Macc 17:21-22), a wrath that he pours out on Israel in the narrative through Antiochus in order to chasten his people (1 Macc 1:1-64; 2 Macc 6:12-17; 7:32). In 4 Macc 4:19-20, Jason, the high priest, changed the nation's way of life from Torah-observance to compliance with the Greek way of life so that he both constructed a gymnasium in Judea and abolished the care of the temple (καὶ ἐξεδιήτησεν τὸ ἔθνος καὶ ἐξεπολίτευσεν ἐπὶ πᾶσαν παρανομίαν ὥστε μὴ μόνον ἐπ' αὐτῇ τῇ ἄκρᾳ τῆς πατρίδος ἡμῶν γυμνάσιον κατασκευάσαι ἀλλὰ καὶ καταλῦσαι τὴν τοῦ ἱεροῦ κηδεμονίαν). As a result, the Lord's divine anger caused Antiochus to make war on Israel (ἐφ' οἷς ἀγανακτήσασα ἡ θεία δίκη αὐτὸν αὐτοῖς τὸν Ἀντίοχον ἐπολέμωσεν) (4 Macc 4:21). Hence, Antiochus issued a decree that anyone practicing Judaism would die (δόγμα ἔθετο ὅπως εἴ τινες αὐτῶν φάνοιεν τῷ πατρίῳ πολιτευόμενοι νόμῳ θάνοιεν) (4 Macc 4:23).

4 Maccabees 6:28 supports the claim that Eleazar's prayer urges God to use his death to provide salvation for Israel from God's wrath expressed through Antiochus. He asks God to be satisfied with the martyrs' judgment for the nation (ἀρκεσθεὶς τῇ ἡμετέρᾳ ὑπὲρ αὐτῶν δίκῃ).[68] With this request, Eleazar expresses that he offers his life to God as both a representative of and a substitute for Israel to achieve God's mercy, and he hopes that his provision would satisfy God's wrath against the nation. This interpretation seems correct for at least three reasons: First, Eleazar offers this petition to God while he faces his judgment for the people and as a representative of the people by means of Antiochus' persecution (4 Macc 6:28; 17:22; cf. 1 Macc 6:60; Ps 68:32; Jer 18:4; Dan 4:2). Second, judgment (δίκη) consistently refers to divine judgment throughout 4 Maccabees (4 Macc 4:13, 21; 8:14, 22; 9:9, 15, 32; 11:3; 12:12; 18:22).[69] Third, the author applies the cultic language of blood to Eleazar in 4 Macc 6:29 to refer to the cleansing power of Eleazar's death for the nation.[70]

---

68. For other possible substitutionary uses of ὑπὲρ in atonement texts, see LXX Exod 21:20; Lev 26:25; Deut 32:41, 43; Mic 7:9; Wis 1:8; 14:31; 18:11; cf. 1 Macc 5:32; 2 Macc 1:26; 3:32; Rom 5:6-11; 8:32; 1 Cor 1:13; 11:24; 15:3; 2 Cor 5:14-15, 21; Gal 1:4; 2:20-21; 3:13; 1 Thess 5:10.

69. cf. 2 Macc 8:11, 13.

70. Since Eleazar's first request that God would be merciful to the nation (ἵλεως γενοῦ τῷ ἔθνει σου) is the main clause in the sentence ἵλεως γενοῦ τῷ ἔθνει σου ἀρκεσθεὶς

Eleazar's Death and Israel's Purification

4 Maccabees 6:29 states that Eleazar asks God to make his blood to be Israel's purification (καθάρσιον αὐτῶν ποίησον τὸ ἐμὸν αἷμα).[71] Since Eleazar has already prayed that God would bring mercy to Israel and end his wrath against Israel through his death, Eleazar's request in 4 Macc 6:29 suggests that he urges God to make his death a substitute for the nation's violation of Torah to accomplish national purification and salvation. Eleazar's request likewise urges God to let his death function as Israel's Yom Kippur. The substitutionary nature of Eleazar's request is apparent when he asks God to make his αἷμα to be Israel's purification (2 Macc 5:17–18; 6:15; 7:32; 12:42; 4 Macc 5:19; 17:21; cf. Lev 16:16, 30),[72] and the function of his death as "the" Yom Kippur for the nation is conspicuously set forth with the words purification and blood and in 17:21–22, when the author states that the martyrs died propitiatory deaths to purify the homeland and to save the nation—language and concepts straight from Leviticus 16. The blood of the animals in Leviticus 16 served to purify the nation from all of its sins and to provide salvation from the looming judgment of YHWH if Yom Kippur was not performed in compliance with Torah (cf. Lev 9:1—16:34). Eleazar asks God to use his blood to be Israel's Yom Kippur by granting the nation mercy and satisfaction as a result of his blood (4 Macc 6:28–29), and 4 Macc 17:21–22 in fact states that the martyrs propitiated God, saved the nation, and accomplished national purification for the homeland.

τῇ ἡμετέρᾳ ὑπὲρ αὐτῶν δίκῃ, the adverbial participial clause (ἀρκεσθεὶς τῇ ἡμετέρᾳ ὑπὲρ αὐτῶν δίκῃ) is a continuation of the first request in 4 Macc 6:28a and likewise takes the tone of a prayer of entreaty, as the first part of the prayer. Other uses of the adjective ἵλεως elsewhere in 4 Maccabees support that in 4 Macc 6:28, Eleazar asks God to accept his death as the means through which he would save the nation from his judgment. For example, (1) prior to Antiochus' torture of the seven sons in 4 Macc 8:14, he urges them to provide mercy for themselves by eating unclean meat. Obedience to Antiochus would have ensured their salvation from his judgment. (2) In 4 Macc 9:24, as Antiochus inflicts torture upon one of the seven sons, he exhorts his brothers to follow his example of godliness and he stated that through his godliness God's mercy would save the nation. (3) After the seventh son refuses to obey Antiochus in 4 Macc 12:4–16, he hurls himself into Antiochus' fire that Antiochus used to threaten him and to the other brothers. As he entered the fire, the seventh son prays that God would be merciful (ἵλεως) to save the nation through his death (4 Macc 12:17). For other connections in the LXX between God's mercy and deliverance from judgment, see Exod 32:12, 33; Num 14; Deut 21:1–8; 2 Chr 6:25–27, 39; 7:14; Amos 7:2; Jer 5:1, 7; 27:20; 38:34; 43:3.

71. See also 4 Macc 1:11; LXX Dan 3:38–40.
72. Against Seeley, *The Noble Death*, 97–98.

As I have argued elsewhere,[73] besides 4 Macc 6:29, καθάρσιον occurs nowhere else in the LXX. However, καθάρισμος is a cognate of καθάρσιον. The latter occurs in the LXX and in the New Testament to refer both to the purification of Israel and to Christians. In both testaments, one receives purification through cultic blood (Exod 29:36; 30:10; cf. 2 Pet 1:9), through ritual cleansing (Lev 14:32; 15:13; cf. Mark 1:44; Luke 2:22; 5:14; John 2:6; 3:25), through God's forgiveness (Num 14:18), through the cleansing of holy utensils (1 Chr 23:28), through the purification of the temple (2 Macc 1:18; 2:16, 19; 10:5), or through one's piety (4 Macc 7:6; cf. 1QS 1–3, 10). Eleazar's expertise in the law, his priestly status, and his priestly familial heritage in the narratives of 2 and 4 Maccabeees (2 Macc 6:18; 4 Macc 5:4, 35) suggest that his comments about his death in 4 Macc 6:28–29 are overtly cultic.[74] Moreover, since the narrative of 4 Macccabees states that Antiochus abolished the sacrificial system, killed anyone who yielded allegiance to the Torah (1 Macc 1:41–64; 2 Macc 5:4, 35), controlled the temple, and prohibited compliance with the Torah (2 Macc 1:5; 7:32–38; 4 Macc 6:28–29; 17:20–21), Eleazar's request likely, then, urges God in 4 Macc 6:28–29 to use his death and the deaths of the other martyrs to substitute for the absence of temple sacrifices, which would have included the Yom Kippur ritual since Antiochus forbade all sacrifices, so that the nation would corporately experience God's cleansing of forgiveness through the martyrs as the Yom Kippur sacrifices.

Eleazar's Death as a Ransom for Israel

In the final part of his prayer in 4 Macc 6:29b, Eleazar asks God to receive his death as a ransom for the nation (καὶ ἀντίψυχον αὐτῶν λαβὲ τὴν ἐμὴν ψυχήν). The term ἀντίψυχον ("ransom") in 4 Macc 6:29b likewise occurs in 4 Macc 17:21. There the term suggests that the martyrs' deaths purified and saved the nation, because the author connects ἀντίψυχον with both the nation's purification from sin and with its salvation and because the author identifies the nation's death as a propitiatory offering (καὶ διὰ τοῦ αἵματος τῶν εὐσεβῶν ἐκείνων καὶ τοῦ ἱλαστηρίου τοῦ θανάτου αὐτῶν ἡ θεία πρόνοια τὸν Ισραηλ προκακωθέντα διέσωσεν). Furthermore, 4 Macc 6:29b reveals an explicit lexical connection with Yom Kippur with the compound ἀντίψυχον, which occurs as two different words (ἀντὶ τῆς ψυχῆς) in LXX Lev 17:11 in

---

73. Williams, *Maccabean Martyr Traditions*.
74. See also 2 Macc 6:18; 4 Macc 5:4, 35.

a context where the author discusses Yom Kippur (Lev 16) and the atoning function of blood on behalf of one's life (Lev 17:11).[75]

The restriction not to eat blood in LXX Lev 17:11 due to its redemptive effect for the soul (ἀντὶ τῆς ψυχῆς) includes the blood that atones for sin at Yom Kippur, for in Leviticus 16–17 YHWH's prohibition not to eat blood emerges to highlight the importance of the function of the animal's blood offered as atonement. This point is supported by YHWH's statement in Leviticus 16–17 that the blood makes atonement (Lev 16:5–20; 17:12). Similarly, the blood of the martyrs in 4 Macc 6:28–29 and 17:21–22 accomplishes atonement and thereby functions as the nation's Yom Kippur, for the martyrs' blood achieves the same effect as the animals' blood during the Yom Kippur ritual: namely, national purification and salvation (cf. Lev 16:5–34; 4 Macc 17:21–22). The narrator states this in a straightforward way in 4 Macc 17:21–22 with his assertion that the martyrs purified the homeland by means of their deaths (τὴν πατρίδα καθαρισθῆναι ὥσπερ ἀντίψυχον γεγονότας τῆς τοῦ ἔθνους ἁμαρτίας καὶ διὰ τοῦ αἵματος τῶν εὐσεβῶν ἐκείνων καὶ τοῦ ἱλαστηρίου τοῦ θανάτου αὐτῶν ἡ θεία πρόνοια τὸν Ἰσραηλ προκακωθέντα διέσωσεν).

A function of ἀντίψυχον in 4 Macc 6:29 and 17:21, then, is to communicate that the blood of the martyrs was the required price paid to achieve both Israel's purification and salvation (cf. 4 Macc 17:21–22), just as the sacrificial ritual on Yom Kippur required the blood of the animal to cover/atone the sins of the people (Leviticus 16).[76] In fact, 4 Macc 17:21 asserts that the homeland was purified "just as" (ὥσπερ) the martyrs became a ransom for the sin of the nation.[77] As I have discussed in detail elsewhere, Williams, followed by Seeley, argued that the adverb ὥσπερ in 4 Macc 17:21 suggests that the author of 4 Maccabees metaphorically means that God received the martyrs' deaths "just as" (ὥσπερ) he received sacrifices, since he deemed their deaths as an act of expiation. The adverb, they argue, should not be interpreted to mean that their deaths *literally* expiated sin in the narrative. However, 4 Macc 17:22 speaks against this reading since the author states that "through the blood of these godly ones" (i.e., the martyrs) and "through their propitiatory death," God saved the nation from his wrath (καὶ διὰ τοῦ αἵματος τῶν εὐσεβῶν ἐκείνων καὶ τοῦ ἱλαστηρίου τοῦ θανάτου αὐτῶν ἡ θεία πρόνοια τὸν Ἰσραηλ προκακωθέντα διέσωσεν). Consequently, the author of

75. So Campbell, *Deliverance*, 650–51.

76. For a different emphasis, see Rajak, *The Jewish Dialogue with Rome and Greece*, 109–11. She argues that the primary function of the ἀντίψυχον in 4 Maccabees "was to establish a connection between persecution, in the Diaspora, and victory, in Palestine, and to bridge the awkward geographical disjunction between two locations."

77. Williams, *Jesus' Death*, 177–78; Seeley, *The Noble Death*, 97.

4 Maccabees appears to be echoing Leviticus 16–17, especially the feast of atonement and the Yom Kippur ritual, when he discusses the martyrs' deaths since he repeatedly uses similar cultic language from Leviticus 16–17 to describe the function of the martyrs' deaths for the nation in a cultic setting without a functional temple.[78]

4 Maccabees 17:21–22: The Author's Interpretation of the Martyrs' Deaths

The author of 4 Maccabees interprets the martyrs' deaths to be both sacrificial in nature and a saving event for the nation in 4 Macc 17:21–22 (καὶ τὸν τύραννον τιμωρηθῆναι καὶ τὴν πατρίδα καθαρισθῆναι ὥσπερ ἀντίψυχον γεγονότας τῆς τοῦ ἔθνους ἁμαρτίας καὶ διὰ τοῦ αἵματος τῶν εὐσεβῶν ἐκείνων καὶ τοῦ ἱλαστηρίου τοῦ θανάτου αὐτῶν ἡ θεία πρόνοια τὸν Ισραηλ προκακωθέντα διέσωσεν). He describes their deaths by using the phrase τοῦ ἱλαστηρίου τοῦ θανάτου.[79] The term ἱλαστήριον occurs in 4 Macc 17:22 with other cultic vocabulary (e.g., "sin [ἁμαρτίας]," "blood [διὰ τοῦ αἵματος]," and "to purify [καθαρισθῆναι]"), a cultic concept [ἀντίψυχον γεγονότας τῆς τοῦ ἔθνους ἁμαρτίας]), and a soteriological term (διέσωσεν). Additionally, the cultic concept of consecration occurs in 4 Macc 17:19–20 (καὶ γάρ φησιν ὁ Μωυσῆς καὶ πάντες οἱ ἡγιασμένοι ὑπὸ τὰς χεῖράς σου καὶ οὗτοι οὖν ἁγιασθέντες διὰ θεὸν τετίμηνται οὐ μόνον ταύτῃ τῇ τιμῇ ἀλλὰ καὶ τῷ δι' αὐτοὺς τὸ ἔθνος ἡμῶν τοὺς πολεμίους μὴ ἐπικρατῆσαι). The idea of the consecration of the martyrs in 4 Macc 17:19–20 joins with the other cultic concepts mentioned above to make the context of the martyrs' deaths overtly cultic and similar to Yom Kippur.

4 Maccabees 17:22 and Rom 3:25 are the only places in available literature where an author applies ἱλαστήριον to the death of Torah-observant Jews in a cultic context for the soteriological benefit of non-Torah-observant sinners. The term ἱλαστήριον refers to the mercy seat in contexts in the LXX where priests atoned for sin through the sacrifice of blood (Lev 16:14–15). God commands Israel to put the ἱλαστήριον above the ark of the covenant in the holy of holies, the place where only the high priest could enter (Exod 25:17–20; 37:6). God commands the priest to make atonement

---

78. Against Kraus, *Der Tod Jesu*, 38–39. Rightly Campbell, *Deliverance*, 650–51. For further evidence, see 4 Macc 6:28–29; 7:8; 17:10; 17:21–22; 18:4; cf. Exod 33:12—34:9; *As. Mos.* 9.6–7; 10:2–10; 2 Macc 5:20—7:38.

79. In 4 Macc 17:22, a major textual variant exists pertaining to the function of ἱλαστήριον. For a discussion, see H. J. Klauck, *4 Makkabäerbuch*, 753; van Henten, "The Tradition-Historical Background," 101–28, esp. 123, and DeSilva, *4 Maccabees*, 250.

Representation and Substitution in Second Temple Jewish Martyrologies   101

on the ἱλαστήριον to provide cleansing for sin (Exod 25:18–22; 31:7; 35:12; 37:6–8; Lev 16:14–15), and God appears above the ἱλαστήριον to show his acceptance of atonement (Exod 25:22; Lev 16:2; Num 7:89). The term also occurs in LXX Ezek 43:14–20 in reference to a place at which atonement takes place by the pouring out of blood.[80]

In his now famous unpublished doctoral thesis, Daniel P. Bailey argues that ἱλαστήριον in 4 Macc 17:22 and in Rom 3:25 have distinct meanings.[81] The author of 4 Macc 17:22 uses the term consistent with its occurrence in the Hellenistic world (i.e., propitiatory), but Paul uses the term consistent with its occurrence in the biblical world (i.e., mercy seat).[82] According to Bailey, to argue that ἱλαστήριον refers to sacrificial atonement in 4 Macc 17:22 is a mistake. After reviewing the evidence in the relevant Hellenistic literature that supports reading the term as a propitiatory, Bailey argues that various inscriptions in the Hellenistic world affirm that ἱλαστήρια were offered either to propitiate the wrath of offended deities or to gain their favor.[83] He also argues that -τήριον words do not regularly refer to actions,

---

80. The occurrence of ἱλαστήριον in the context of 4 Macc 17:21–22 is certainly cultic for the above reasons, but also since the term itself is part of a semantic family of ἱλας-words that often occur in cultic contexts in the LXX that speak of atoning for sin, since these words often translate from the Hebrew root, which often means "to atone," and since some form ἱλαστήριον occurs in Leviticus' prescriptions regarding Yom Kippur (cf. LXX Lev 16:2, 13–15). I am not asserting that the ἱλας-words group always translates from the Hebrew that means "to atone" (cf. LXX Exod 32:14; 2 Kgs 21:3; 1 Chr 6:34; 2 Chr 29:24; Ps 105:30; Ezek 43:14–20; Zech 7:2; 8:22). I am neither affirming that the ἱλας-words group always conveys the idea of atoning sacrifice (cf. LXX Exod 32:14; Prov 16:14). For example, ἐξιλάσασθαι is often cultic and often refers to the cleansing that takes places when sins are atoned (LXX Exod 30:10; Lev 1:4; 4:20, 26, 31, 35; 5:6, 10, 13, 16, 18, 26; 6:23; 7:7; 16:29; Num 5:8; 6:11; 8:12, 19, 21; 15:25, 28; 17:11, 12; 28:22, 30; 29:5, 11; 31:50; 1 Kgs 3:14; 2 Kgs 2:13; 1 Chr 6:34; 2 Chr 29:24; 30:18; 2 Esd 20:34; Ps 105:30; Ezek 43:20, 22; 45:17; Sir 3:3, 30; 5:6; 20:28; 28:5; 34:19; 45:16, 23). However, the one occurrence of ἱλάσθη in the LXX is not cultic, and it is altogether void of sacrificial ideas (LXX Exod 32:14). In LXX Exod 32:14, ἐξιλάσασθαι translates from a root that means "to repent" and highlights YHWH's mercy to Israel in spite of the nation's idolatry. Rather, my point is simply that the ἱλας-words often occurs in cultic texts and often speaks of sacrificial atonement when this word group occurs with explicit cultic vocabulary, as it does in 4 Macc 17:21–22. Thus, 4 Macc 17:21–22 speaks of the martyrs' deaths with specific sacrificial/cultic language that closely resembles the Old Testament cult and that echoes Yom Kippur, especially since 4 Macc 17:21–22 states that the martyrs brought divine favor to Israel via blood and purification when they died for the nation.

81. Many thanks to Dan Bailey for e-mailing me a copy of his dissertation.

82. Bailey, "Mercy Seat" 5–12, esp. 11–2.

83. For the above analysis and summary of Bailey's view, see DeSilva, *4 Maccabees*, 250–51, who cites Bailey ("Mercy Seat," 31–75).

but to places.⁸⁴ Bailey concludes that the meaning of ἱλαστήριον in 4 Macc 17:22 as it relates to the martyrs' deaths "should be sought against a non-sacrificial background."⁸⁵ According to Bailey, 4 Maccabees nowhere states that the martyrs died as atoning sacrifices for Israel's sin.

Bailey's doctoral thesis is a careful and thorough contribution to scholarship. To my knowledge, it provides the most extensive lexical analysis of ἱλαστήριον based on ancient texts and ancient inscriptions in English speaking scholarship. Bailey's concern, though, is exclusively a lexical one. His work seeks to offer a better translation of ἱλαστήριον in Rom 3:25 by analyzing every ancient text and inscription that has lexical affinity to it. I agree with his argument that the occurrence of the same term in different texts (i.e., 4 Macc 17:22 and Rom 3:25) does not necessitate that the term should be translated the same way in both texts. Nevertheless, Bailey's thesis and arguments (if I correctly understand them) seem to pit his lexical analysis against the context within which ἱλαστήριον occurs. Therefore, his analysis prevents the term from conveying its contextual theme. In my view, regardless of how one translates ἱλαστήριον in 4 Macc 17:22, since the term occurs in the same context as several atonement words and concepts found in Leviticus 16–17 (e.g., judgment, purification of the nation, ransom, vicarious death, sin, and blood), ἱλαστήριον in 4 Macc 17:22 at least alludes to the Yom Kippur ritual; it at least suggests that the martyrs' deaths are functioning as Israel's Yom Kippur, and it at least suggests that the martyrs die in the narratives as representatives of and as substitutes for Israel.⁸⁶

4 Maccabees 6:28–29 speaks of the martyrs' deaths in the context of blood, purification, and ransom. Likewise, 4 Macc 17:21–22 speaks of the martyrs' deaths in the context of purification for the nation, ransom, blood, and salvation.⁸⁷ The author's reference to the consecration of the martyrs for God in 4 Macc 17:20 (ἁγιασθέντες διὰ θεὸν) and the participle προκακωθέντα in reference to the mistreatment of the nation in 4 Macc 17:22 recall the imagery of setting apart the animals for atonement and terminology of the afflictions at Yom Kippur (cf. LXX Lev 16:29–32).⁸⁸ Therefore, the contextual evidence in 4 Macc 6:28–29 and 17:21–22 challenges the conclusion that ἱλαστήριον in 4 Maccabees should be understood as a pagan reference

---

84. Finlan, *Atonement Metaphors*, 200–203, who cites Bailey.

85. The above quote comes from DeSilva (*4 Maccabees*, 251), who summarizes Bailey's view.

86. Similarly Ben Ezra, *Yom Kippur*, 115. DeSilva (*4 Maccabees*, 250–51) argues that the author uses the cultic language from the Yom Kippur ritual to describe the effect of the martyrs' deaths.

87. DeSilva, *4 Maccabees*, 202.

88. Ben Ezra, *Yom Kippur*, 116.

Representation and Substitution in Second Temple Jewish Martyrologies 103

to a non-cultic/non-sacrificial background. I suggest that 4 Macc 6:28–29 and 17:21–22 together affirm that the martyrs offered themselves to God as representatives of the nation, as substitutes for the nation, and that the martyrs functioned as Israel's Yom Kippur in the narrative of 4 Maccabees.[89]

CONCLUSION

In this chapter, I have argued that a Jewish martyr theology existed in Second Temple Judaism in texts that indisputably pre-date Romans. Furthermore, I have defended the claim that just as Isaiah 53 describes the death of YHWH's Servant with Levitical cultic language, LXX Dan 3:1–90 and 2 and

---

89. DeSilva, *4 Maccabees*, 202–3; similarly de Jonge, "Jesus' Death for Others and the Death of the Maccabean Martyrs," 142–51, esp. 150–51. Although Wisdom of Solomon technically does not contain a Jewish martyrology that accords to the definition of martyr theology used in this chapter or a theology of representation and substitution, this work deserves to be mentioned since it contains the idea of righteous Torah-observers who die at the hands of the wicked (i.e., Torah-breakers), whose deaths God received as burnt-offerings. Wisdom of Solomon is a Jewish text that was written to Jews in the Diaspora to promote Torah-observance and Judaism. In light of the strong language of persecution throughout the book, the author could have written it during a time when Second Temple Judaism experienced much imperial persecution. In 1:1, Wisdom urges its readers to love righteousness, by which the author means Torah-observance (cf. 2:11; 14:16). In 2:12–16, the author personifies Torah-disobedience by presenting the ungodly as predators who wait for an opportunity to ambush the righteous (i.e., Torah-obedient-ones), because the latter rebuke the former when they sin. In 2:17–20, evil commands the ungodly ones to persecute the righteous. In 2:19, evil specifically commands the ungodly to inflict mistreatment and torture upon the righteous. In 2:20, evil commands the ungodly to condemn the righteous to a shameful death. In 2:20b and in 3:1–6, Wisdom states that God will vindicate the righteous as they die for Torah because the souls of the righteous are in God's hand, and he will not allow the ungodly to torment the righteous (3:1). The righteous suffer and die at the hands of the persecutors (2:17–20), but the righteous are in peace after they die (3:2–3). Wisdom 3:6 suggests that the hope of the righteous will be full of immortality because God would find them to be worthy of himself since he tested them "just as" gold in a furnace and since he would receive them through the test "just as" he received "a burnt-offering of sacrifice" (ὡς χρυσὸν ἐν χωνευτηρίῳ ἐδοκίμασεν αὐτοὺς καὶ ὡς ὁλοκάρπωμα θυσίας προσεδέξατο αὐτούς) (3:6; cf. LXX 16:24). The *Assumption of Moses* is a Jewish text written in response to severe persecution during the Second Temple period. Some scholars admit that the book was written in anticipation of Antiochus Epiphanes' attack upon Israel. *Assumption of Moses* 9:6—10:10 speaks to the death of Torah-observant Jews for the benefit of Torah-breakers to save them. Similar to 2 and 4 Maccabees, *Assumption of Moses* portrays Antiochus' siege of Jerusalem to be the result of the nation's disobedience to Torah (*As. Mos.* 9:1–5). A character in the narrative, Taxo (a Levite), informs his fellow Jews that their fasting and dying would avenge the Lord's anger (*As. Mos.* 9:6–7). When they die, their deaths inaugurate God's kingdom and destroy the devil (*As.* Mos. 10:1). God uses their deaths to avenge their enemies (*As.* Mos. 10:2–10).

4 Maccabees likewise use Levitical cultic language to describe the deaths of Torah-observant Jews. These martyrs die for the soteriological benefit of non-Torah-observant sinners—as representatives of and as substitutes for them—and their deaths function as Israel's Yom Kippur. The following eight conclusions can be inferred from the analysis in this chapter.

First, Antiochus desecrated the temple and forbade the Jews from offering sacrifices in compliance with Torah (1 Macc 1:41–59). As a result, many Jews in the narratives of 2 and 4 Maccabees viewed the temple as unclean and unfit for temple worship until its purification in compliance with Torah (cf. *Jub.* 22:16–18; *Ep. Arist.* 152–53; *Pss. Sol.* 2:2; Acts 21:27). Second, in 2 and 4 Maccabees, Antiochus forbade the Jewish people from offering any cultic sacrifices in compliance with Torah, which included Yom Kippur (1 Macc 1:41–59). Third, the martyrs suffered and died because of the nation's sin (2 Macc 7:18, 32; 12:39–42; 4 Macc 4:21; 17:21–22), just as the high priest offered the animal's blood for sin on Yom Kippur (Lev 1:1—7:6; 8:18–21; 16:3–24). Fourth, the martyrs' blood was the required price for the nation's national purification, forgiveness, and salvation (2 Macc 7:32–38; 4 Macc 6:28–29; 7:8; 17:21–22), just as the animals' blood was the required price for Israel's forgiveness on Yom Kippur (Lev 16:30). Fifth, the martyrs' deaths provided purification and cleansing for the nation (4 Macc 6:28–29; 17:22), just as the animals' blood provided purification and cleansing for Israel on Yom Kippur (Lev 16:16, 30). Sixth, the martyrs' deaths ended God's wrath against the nation (1 Macc 1:1–64; 2 Macc 7:32–38; 8:5; 4 Macc 17:21–22), just as the animals' blood when appropriately offered at Yom Kippur placated God's wrath against the nation (Lev 9:1—16:30). Seventh, the martyrs died as representatives of and vicariously for the nation (2 Macc 7:18, 32; 4 Macc 4:21; 17:21–22), just as the animals were representatives of and were substitutes for the sins of the nation on Yom Kippur (Lev 16:1–30). Eighth, God judged sin and granted forgiveness through the martyrs' deaths in the narratives (2 Macc 6:12—7:38; 4 Macc 17:21–22), just as YHWH judged sin and granted forgiveness through the animals' deaths on Yom Kippur (Lev 16:1–30).

4

Jewish Martyrology and Substitution in Romans 3:21—4:25

INTRODUCTION

In this chapter, I argue that the Jewish martyrological narratives are a background behind substitution in Rom 3:21—4:25. I support this by an exegetical and theological analysis of selected texts in Rom 3:21—4:25 and by a comparative analysis of these texts with the Jewish martyrological narratives.

ROMANS 3:21—4:25 IN CONTEXT

In Rom 1:18—3:20, Paul offers a strong indictment against both Jews and Gentiles.[1] After introducing his gospel to the Romans as a gospel of the revelation of God's saving righteousness and as a gospel of Jesus Christ, the Son of David, in 1:1-17, Paul explains God's judging righteousness in 1:18—3:20. He highlights the dominating power of sin through sinful actions and the judgment that comes to Jews and Gentiles alike because of sin in the argument of 1:18—3:20. He asserts that he is eager to preach the gospel to the Roman Christians (1:15), whom he had not met prior to his

---

1. For recent monographs on judgment according to works in 1:18—3:20 or in the NT, see Kim, *God Will Judge Each One according To Works*; McFadden, *Judgment according to Works in Romans*.

letter (1:10–11; 15:24), because he is not ashamed of the gospel and because the gospel is God's saving power for Jews and Greeks who believe (1:16). Paul explicates the saving power of the gospel in 1:17 by stating that God's saving righteousness is revealed in it by faith. In 1:18—3:20, he places the saving power of the gospel alongside of the universal power of sin that results in God's present and eschatological wrath for those under Torah and outside of Christ.

Paul states that God's wrath is presently revealed upon all unrighteousness (1:18).[2] In 1:19–32, he argues that God's wrath is revealed by his judgment of the offender by handing him over to the desires of his heart *after* he suppresses the truth (1:18–20), *after* he fails to honor God (1:21), and *after* he exchanges the truth of God for a lie (1:21–23). Instead of worshipping the creator, the ungodly commit idolatry (1:21–23). Paul, thus, states in 1:24, 26, and 28 that God's wrath is revealed in the current age against those who suppress the truth in that he gives them over to a depraved mind to practice a rebellious lifestyle against God.[3]

---

2. God's wrath in Paul is primarily eschatological (2:5–16; 3:5; 4:15; 5:9; Eph 2:3; 5:6; Col 3:6; 1 Thess 1:10; 2:16; 5:9). In 1:18, wrath refers to his personal, retributive wrath that he unleashes in the present evil age upon those who suppress the truth. Against Dodd, *The Epistle of Paul to the Romans*, 21–24; Dodd, *The Bible and the Greeks*, 82–95; Travis, *Christ and the Judgment of God*, 60–70, 74–84. For an argument against Dodd and Travis, see Jarvis Williams, *Maccabean Martyr Traditions in Paul's Theology of Atonement*; Jarvis Williams, *One New Man*, chapter 3; Jarvis Williams, "Martyr Theology in Hellenistic Judaism and Paul's Conception of Jesus' Death in Romans 3:21–26,"; Jarvis Williams, "Violent Atonement in Romans: The Foundation of Paul's Soteriology," 579–99, esp. 588.

3. For example, Rom 1:24 states that "God gave" the ungodly over "in the lusts of their hearts to impurity so that their bodies would be dishonored." Paul immediately thereafter states that "they exchanged God's truth for a lie and worshipped and served the creation rather than the creator" (Rom 1:25). In Rom 1:26, Paul states again that "God gave" the ungodly over to "dishonorable passions," and he immediately says that both men and women began to practice unnatural sexual relations with one another, namely, homoerotic acts (Rom 1:27). Finally, Paul states for a third time in the text that "God gave" the ungodly over to an unapproved mind to practice unlawful deeds (Rom 1:28), and immediately thereafter he states that they practiced "unrighteousness," "evil," "covetousness," "envy," "murder," "deceit," "selfishness," and "meanness" and that they were "gossipers," "slanderers," "haters of God," "insulters," "arrogant," "prideful," "schemers of evil," "disobedient to parents," "foolish," "unfaithful," "without affection," and "unmerciful" (Rom 1:29–31). Thus, God reveals his wrath in the current age upon those who suppress the truth by giving them over to immorality. Romans 1:32 also supports the idea that sin manifests its power through sinful actions when Paul states that those who know God's righteous requirement demand death for those who practice unrighteousness, and yet they still both practice unrighteousness and approve of those who practice unrighteousness.

In 2:1—3:8, Paul argues that God judges Jews and Gentiles in accordance with the same standard and that neither group will be exonerated by God in the judgment by means of law. Paul infers from 2:1—3:8 in 3:9-20 that Jews and Gentiles (i.e., the entire world) stand condemned before God.[4] He first asks in 3:9a if Jews have an advantage over Gentiles in the judgment since the latter group is not Jewish. He offers an emphatic "by no means" in 3:9b![5]

The main argument of 2:1—3:20 pertains to God's universal judgment of both Jews and Gentiles because of sin.[6] Romans 2:1-10 begins the argument by focusing on Jewish condemnation of Gentile vices mentioned in 1:24-31,[7] because these are precisely the types of sins for which Jews often indicted Gentiles (Wis 11:1—16:1; *Jub.* 22:16-23; *Sib. Or.* 3.595-606). Paul also argues this way because 2:1 transitions from speaking of the judgment of the group who practices immorality in 1:24-32 to speaking of the judgment of a different group that practices similar vices as the first group mentioned in 1:18-32 (e.g., 2:1-3). Yet, Paul starkly criticizes the Jew in 1:18-32 alongside of the Gentile because God impartially saves (1:16) and judges Jews and Gentiles (2:6-16) and because both groups will be without excuse when they stand before God's righteous judgment (1:20; 2:1).[8] Romans 2:9-10 confirms this interpretation. These verses confidently assert

---

4. So Dunn, *Romans*, 1:144-45; Moo, *Romans*, 196-210; Schreiner, *Romans*, 161. Against, however, Stowers, *A Rereading of Romans*, 176-93.

5. Paul states earlier in 3:1-2 that Jews have an advantage over Gentiles. Romans 3:9 does not contradict 3:1-2. Romans 3:1-2 occurs in a context in which Paul lists the privileges that Jews have over Gentiles (cf. 2:17-18). Paul contends, however, that such ethnic and national privileges are not sufficient for a right standing before God (cf. 2:19-29). Yet, Jewish ethnic privileges grant them an advantage over the Gentiles in that "the oracles of God were believed" by the Jews and some Jews were in fact saved (3:2). On the other hand, notwithstanding that Jews have certain privileges, they are equally condemned before God because of their sin (cf. 3:9-18). In *this* sense, Jews will have no advantage over Gentiles in the judgment (3:9).

6. Against Bassler, "Divine Impartiality in Paul's Letter to the Romans," 43-58, who thinks the theme is divine impartiality and against Snodgrass, "Justification by Grace—to the Doers," 72-93, who thinks that the theme is the vindication of God. Yinger rightly argues that Romans 1-4 functions to destroy distinction, privilege, or advantage in God's law court based on racial or religious differences and that the chapters are Paul's defense of God's impartial judgment and salvation of a universal sinful world, but he emphasizes that Paul's indictment "is not against a world claiming 'we have sinned' . . . , but against Jews or Jewish-Christians claiming that they will not be treated the same as the 'sinners' in the judgment of God . . ." (*Paul, Judaism, and Judgment according to Deeds*, 152-53).

7. So VanLandingham, *Judgment and Justification in Early Judaism and the Apostle Paul*, 217.

8. Nygren, *Romans*, 118.

that both Jews and Gentiles will receive God's judgment if they disobey God (2:10) but eternal life if they obey (2:10; cf. 2:1–10), "because there is no partiality with God" (2:11).[9]

Romans 2:3–16 develops 2:1–2. One of the main arguments in 2:3–16 is that Jews (alongside of Gentiles) will be judged in accordance with the same standard of righteousness, because God is impartial.[10] Paul begins 2:3 by asking those who judge (i.e., Jews) and commit the same sins whether they will escape God's judgment. Romans 2:3 should be read as sarcasm because Paul previously stated in 2:2 that "God's judgment is according to the truth," whereas now he asks his Jewish interlocutor whether he will escape God's judgment. He follows the question from 2:3 with a subsequent question in 2:4 pertaining to whether the one who judges despises God's goodness and patience because he is ignorant that God's goodness leads him

---

9. For compelling arguments supporting the indictment of both Jews and Gentiles, see Das, *Paul, the Law, and the Covenant*, 170–77. As I already noted above, certain Jewish literature indicts the Gentiles for similar sins as Paul's interlocutor in 1:24–31 (Wis 11:1—16:1; *Jub.* 22:16–23; cf. *Ep. Aris.* 142, 152–53; *Bar.* 4:4; *T. Naph.* 3:3; 4:1–2). Paul offers a similar indictment of Gentiles elsewhere in his letters. Paul states that Gentile Christians were before their conversion "fornicators" (1 Cor 6:9; Col 3:5; cf. Rom 1:24, 26, 29), "idolaters" (1 Cor 6:9; cf. Rom 1:21–25, 30), "adulterers" (1 Cor 6:9; cf. Rom 1:29), "homosexual perverts" (1 Cor 6:9; cf. Rom 1:26–27), "male sexual perverts" (1 Cor 6:9; cf. Rom 1:26–27), "thieves" (1 Cor 6:10; cf. Rom 1:29), "coveters" (1 Cor 6:10; cf. Rom 1:29), "drunkards" (1 Cor 6:10; cf. Rom 1:29), "revilers" (1 Cor 6:10; cf. Rom 1:29–31), lewd children of darkness (Eph 4:17–5:8), "swindlers" (1 Cor 6:10; cf. Rom 1:29–30), and were devoted to tenacious impurities and passions (Col 3:5; cf. Rom 1:26–31). In the OT, Israel likewise practiced idolatry and all sorts of evil (cf. Exod 32; Num 25; 1 Kings–2 Chronicles). In fact, YHWH warns the nation not to associate with Gentiles because they would lead them away from serving their God (Deut 6). In 1, 2, and 4 Maccabees, Israel suffers because the nation turned from serving YHWH faithfully in compliance with his law and followed the way of the Gentile ruler Antiochus Epiphanes IV (cf. 1 Macc 1, 2 Macc 7:32–38; 4 Mac 6:28–29; 17:21–22). Jews indicted fellow Jews for teaching commandments that are opposed to God's just ordinances (*T. Levi* 14:4), such as stealing the Lord's offerings and eating them with whores (*T. Levi* 14:5–6), profanation of married women (*T. Levi* 14:6), promiscuous relationships with whores and adulteresses (*T. Levi* 14:6), marriages to Gentile women (*T. Levi* 14:6), inflation of pride because of the priesthood (*T. Levi* 14:7), and a derision of sacred things (*T. Levi* 14:8). In the New Testament, Jesus (Matt 23) and Paul (1 Cor 10:1–22) condemn the Jews for numerous activities that are contrary to the Torah. Thus, the Jew who knows God's righteous requirement and yet still both approves of those who disobey and likewise disobeys is guilty (Rom 1:32), and the one who judges is guilty himself since he does the same things as the Gentile (Rom 2:1).

10. Jewett (*Romans*, 196–218) argues that 2:1–16 can be explained by "Paul's rhetorical goal of creating an argument that provides the premises for an ethic of mutual tolerance between the competitive house and tenement churches in Rome, which could enable them to participate with integrity in the Spanish mission."

to repentance and because Second Temple Jews knew very well that those who disobey Torah would not escape his wrath.[11]

Romans 2:5—3:20 develops the argument that Torah condemns both Jews and Gentiles. In 2:5, Paul answers his earlier questions pertaining to whether the Jew would escape God's judgment by stating "you" are storing up wrath for "yourself" in the day of wrath.[12] Paul indicts the Jew first in 2:9-10. Jewish condemnation is the focus of 2:1—3:8, because Jews were notorious for judging Gentiles on account of their unrighteousness (e.g., *Jub.* 22:16-23).

Paul elaborates the impartiality of God's judgment in accordance with Torah in 2:12-29 although he introduced this theme in 2:11. The latter verse functions as a theme verse for the ensuing argument of 2:12-29.[13] According to *some* early Jewish texts, the only thing that would provide blessing for Israel in the land (Deuteronomy 6) and eschatological exoneration in God's law court (Rom 2:13) was obedience to Torah (*T. Jud.* 13:1-5; 26:1; *T. Iss.* 5:1-2; *T. Dan* 5:1; *T. Ash.* 2:1-10; 6:1-5; *T. Jos.* 11:1). This does not mean that all Jews believed that their obedience was apart from God's supernatural empowerment.[14] Nevertheless, Paul's argument at this point emphasizes that YHWH's expectation both in the OT and maintained in some versions of early Judaism was that Jews must obey Torah to live long in the land. Their obedience would merit the reward that Torah set forth for those who obeyed.[15]

---

11. Cf. Deut 30:16; Isa 13:6-16; 34:8; Dan 7:9-11; Joel 2:1-2; Zeph 1:14—2:3; 3:8; Mal 4:1; *Jub.* 5:10-16; *Pss. Sol.* 15:8; *1 En.* 90:20-27.

12. For the idea of storing up heavenly rewards in Jewish thought, see Tob 4:9-10; *Pss. Sol.* 9:3-5; *4 Ezra* 6:5; 7:77; 8:33, 36; *2 Bar.* 14:12.

13. Bassler, *Divine Impartiality*, 137, 152. But she goes too far when she argues that divine impartiality is the central theme of the letter.

14. A point that Das persuasively argues regarding early Judaism ("Paul and Works of Obedience in Second Temple Judaism" 795-812, esp. 797-801). See also recently Sprinkle, *Paul and Judaism Revisited*.

15. I find Paul L. Owen's recent argument from Deuteronomy against perfect obedience (that Moses means that all of God's words are precious and therefore should not be ignored and that one's intent to keep the law is the issue) to be unpersuasive ("The 'Works of the Law' in Romans and Galatians" 560-61), for Deuteronomy and Paul appear to suggest more than simply one's intent to obey the law by their emphasis that all of Torah must be obeyed. Moses emphasizes that disobedience to one of YHWH's commands would result in judgment in the land (Deut. 28:15-68); certain segments of early Judaism placed confidence in their ability to obey God's laws in order to receive the reward of life (Sir 11:26; 17:23; Tob 1:3, 5-18; 4:5-11; Bar 4:1-2; *Pss. Sol.* 14:2-3, 10; 15:4, 16; *Jub.* 30:21-22; 4Q215a ii 2-7; *4 Ezra* 6:7—9:25), and Paul states that God would give the appropriate reward to Jews and Gentiles in accordance with their works (Rom 2:6-10, 13). The work of obedience results in eternal life (Rom 2:7, 10), but the work of disobedience will result in condemnation (Rom 2:8-9). Paul A. Rainbow

Rom 2:12–16 argues that Gentiles who sin without the law will perish without the law, just as God through the law condemns Jews who sin with the law, because doing (not hearing or possessing) the law justifies (2:13–15). The work of the law, then, written on the hearts of the Gentile means that he, even without a written Torah, follows some of the precepts in the written Torah, because Gentiles obey certain moral norms of Torah.[16] This is supported by the subsequent language in the text that describes the coming judgment of Jews and Gentiles, who disobey Torah (cf. 2:16).

Beginning with a conditional statement in 2:17,[17] Paul suggests that the Jew relies upon Torah and boasts in God (Rom 2:17; cf. *Pss. Sol.* 17:1; *2 Bar.* 48:22–24),[18] that he knows the will of God and approves of the excellent things since he is taught by Torah (Rom 2:18; cf. Deut 6; Bar 4:4; Wis 15:2–3),[19] that he persuades himself to be a teacher and a light of the spiritually blind (Rom 2:19; cf. Isa 42:6–7; 49:6; *1 En.* 105:1; *T. Levi* 14:3–8; Wis 18:4; Sir 24:27; *Sib. Or.* 3.194–95; Jos. *Ag. Ap.* 2.291–95; Philo, *Abr.* 98; *Mos.* 1.149), a light for those in darkness (Rom 2:19; cf. 1QS 1:9; 2:16; 3:13, 24–25; 1QM 1:1, 7, 11, 13–15),[20] an instructor of the foolish (Rom 2:20; cf. 1QH 2:9; 1QS 3:13), and a teacher of infants (1QpHab 7:4–5), because they have the truth in Torah (Rom 2:20; cf. Sir 17:11; 45:5; Bar 3:36; *2 Bar.* 44:2–15).[21] The spiritually blind, the foolish, and the infants most certainly refer to Gentiles.[22] This Jewish caricature of Gentiles was a typical description of them in Second Temple Judaism (*Jub.* 22:16–23; Isa 49:6), and this description fits with Paul's earlier indictment of Gentiles in 1:18–31. In 2:21–24, Paul indicts the Jew for failing to obey Torah. He accuses him of

---

argues that Paul holds to a double justification (an initial positive verdict in the present age, followed by sanctification in the present age, which results in a second positive verdict on the last day). See Rainbow, *The Way of Salvation*, 107–98. Although I *strongly* disagree with his overall thesis (that works in the Old Testament, early Judaism, and in Paul determine election and final justification), VanLandingham rightly understands 2:6–11 to refer to a positive verdict in the judgment based on one's deeds. For this point, see *Judgment*, 218–24.

16. He does not use the phrase "moral norms of Torah," but see also Bell, *No One Seeks for God*, 153–9.

17. The unit is an anacoluthon. Jewett, *Romans*, 221 n. 16.

18. On Jewish boasting in 2:17, see Bell, *No One Seeks for God*, 185–88.

19. A point vividly expressed in 2 Macc 1:3–4.

20. DSS references in Jewett, *Romans*, 225.

21. So Wright, "Romans," 446–47. For an example of Jewish confidence, see Bar 4:1–4.

22. *Pace* Jewett, *Romans*, 225, who thinks that Paul's remarks refer to Jews and Gentiles since the Old Testament prophets often refer to disobedient Israelites as blind (Zeph 1:17; Isa 43:8; 56:10; 59:9–10).

violating Torah while boasting in Torah (Rom 2:21–23a), of dishonoring God through transgression of Torah (Rom 2:23b; cf. *T. Levi* 14:1–8), and consequently of provoking the Gentiles to blaspheme the God of Torah on account of Jewish disobedience to Torah (Rom 2:24; cf. Isa 52:5; Ezek 36:20; *T. Levi* 14:1–8). His point here is not that every Jew or most Jews violate Torah and not even that the Jews were legalistically trying to earn their salvation by keeping the law,[23] but that neither Jewish identity nor effort will privilege Jews over Gentiles in God's law court.[24]

In 2:25–29, Paul directly takes up the question of the benefit of circumcision in the judgment, one of the stipulations in Torah (Exod 12:48; Lev 12:3; Josh 5:2) and one of the marks of covenant membership (Gen 17:1–14; *Jub.* 15:1–34; Jdt 14:10; 1 Macc 1:48, 60–61; 2:46; 2 Macc 6:10; Jos. *Ant.* 13.257–58). LXX Deut 30:16 records that Moses urges Israel that if the nation hears "the commandments of the Lord," goes in "all his ways," and keeps "his righteous requirements," then the people would live and inherit the land. Since circumcision was one requirement of Torah, by obedience to Torah Paul means that if a Jew wants his circumcision to benefit him in God's eschatological law court, then he must obey other stipulations in Torah in addition to circumcision (cf. Gal 5:2–4).[25]

In 2:25, Paul states that if the Jew does not obey Torah, then his circumcision is viewed as lack of circumcision (sign of non-covenant membership). Paul does not mean in 2:25 that the Jew literally becomes uncircumcised if he fails to obey Torah, but he means that his physical circumcision is not enough to grant him covenant membership within the eschatological people of God, for a Jew who violated other portions of Torah (i.e., adultery, murder, etc. [cf. Rom 2:21–23]) was still circumcised and still had the physical sign of covenant membership. Paul neither means in 2:26 that the Gentile who obeys Torah becomes physically circumcised when he states that his lack of circumcision is reckoned as circumcision if he obeys Torah, because Paul states that the Gentile who obeys Torah is still an uncircumcised Gentile since he asserts that "his un-circumcision will be reckoned as circumcision."

In 2:26, Paul states that the uncircumcised Gentile condemns the circumcised Jew "as a transgressor of the law through the writing and circumcision because the [uncircumcised Gentile] fulfills the law" (brackets mine). Paul cannot literally mean that an uncircumcised Gentile condemns

---

23. Rightly Das, *Paul*, 184.

24. Against Dunn, *Romans*, 1:114.

25. Against Barrett (*Romans*, 58) who states that for Paul, to do the law means to have faith. Rightly Schreiner, *Romans*, 138.

a circumcised Jew as a transgressor of Torah because the uncircumcised Gentile cannot literally or even hypothetically obey Torah, for an uncircumcised Gentile is guilty of breaking Torah by virtue of being uncircumcised (cf. Eph 2:11–12). Rather, the Gentile condemns the Jew as a violator of Torah because Jews have not obeyed Torah, but the Gentile in 2:27 fulfills Torah. It is exegetically significant that Paul does not say here that the Gentile condemns the Jew because the former obeys Torah, but rather because he "fulfills" it.[26] The Gentiles in 2:27 fulfill Torah because they have received the new covenant promise of the Spirit (Jer 31:31–34 [LXX Jer 38:31–34]; Ezek 36–37; Joel 2), which is fulfilled in Jesus Christ and of which one partakes if he obeys the gospel in the power of the Spirit (Rom 8:1–4).[27] Romans 2:28–29 supports this when Paul stresses that Jewishness (i.e., covenant membership) is not marked merely by external commands and physical circumcision as demanded by Torah (Rom 2:28–29), but by the internal (spiritual) work of the Spirit (Rom 2:29; cf. Jer 31:31–34; Ezek 36–37; Joel 2), and this internal, spiritual circumcision results in God's approval in the judgment.[28]

26. For a different reading, see Jewett, *Romans*, 234; Schreiner, *Romans*, 140.

27. Against Moo, *Romans*, 169–71.

28. In Rom 8:1–4, Paul states that Torah does not condemn those in Christ Jesus (as opposed to those in Adam), "for the law of the Spirit of life in Christ Jesus has freed you from the law of sin and death since God did what the law was incapable of doing in that he sent his Son in the likeness of sinful flesh and he condemned sin in [Jesus'] flesh, so that the righteous requirement of the law would be fulfilled in us who walk not according to the flesh, but according to the Spirit." This paragraph is significant in Paul's argument for many reasons, but one is that it reveals a connection with the argument of Rom 2:25–29 and with the new covenant promises of the Spirit in the OT. Paul mentions the law (Rom 8:2–3; cf. 2:25–29; 8:4; cf. 1:32; 2:26), fulfillment language (Rom 8:4; cf. 2:27), and the Spirit in both texts (Rom 2:29; 7:6; 8:4). Another connection with 2:25–29 and with the new covenant promises of the Spirit in the Old Testament occurs in the argument of Romans 9–11. After expressing that Israel has a zeal for God, but not in accordance with knowledge since the nation is ignorant with respect to God's righteousness by faith in Jesus (9:30—10:3), Paul states that the "goal/end" in 2:27 "of the law is Christ resulting in righteousness for everyone who believes" (Rom 10:3). In 10:5–13, Paul continues the argument that he began in 9:30 by pitting Israel's unsuccessful pursuit of righteousness in Torah because of the nation's disobedience against the Gentiles' successful pursuit of righteousness by faith in Jesus Christ (Rom 9:30—10:13). Paul cites a portion of LXX Joel 2:32 (a text that prophesies about the new covenant promise of the Spirit for all the nations who call upon the name of the Lord) in Rom 10:13 when he states that everyone who calls on the Lord will be saved. He states in Rom 10:8–9 that this Lord is Jesus Christ. In Rom 10:14—11:36, Paul continues the discussion of Jewish unbelief, Gentile salvation, and the future salvation of Israel. Thus, it seems most likely that Rom 2:25–29 refers to a spiritual obedience to Torah that finds its fulfillment in Jesus Christ and those who have united themselves to him by faith and who thereby receive the gift of the Spirit. By arguing in this way, Paul highlights the

Romans 3:1–8 considers whether the Jew has an advantage over Gentiles (Rom 3:1). On the one hand, Paul states that Jews have a real advantage over Gentiles in that they were given the oracles of God (3:2). The phrase "oracles of God" in 3:2 refers to God's words as revealed to Israel in Torah.[29] But Paul's answer raises the question as to whether God's faithfulness to Israel is nullified on account of the faithlessness of some Jews (3:3; cf. chapters 9–11). The argument of 2:1—3:4 asks and answers the question whether God is just to condemn Jews in his law court and to vindicate Gentiles, and specifically whether he has forsaken his promises to provide salvation for Israel. The question in 3:3 anticipates Paul's detailed argument in Romans 9–11 where he provides a *tour de force* in defense of God's faithfulness to Israel in spite of the fact that many Jews reject Jesus as the Jewish Messiah, to whom God's oracles pointed (10:4). His answer in 3:4 (as in Romans 9–11) regarding God's unfaithfulness is "No!" He asserts that God is true and mankind is a liar so that God's words vindicate him (God) and he (God) will conquer when he (God) is accused of unrighteousness in the judgment (cf. LXX Ps 115:2; 50:6; CD 20; 1QH 7, 9, 14).[30] Thus, Jewish disobedience to Torah and God's judgment of the Jew because of disobedience does not nullify his faithfulness to his people (Rom 3:3; cf. 9:11—11:36), for he is right to judge Gentiles and even Jews for their unrighteousness or else he would not be able to judge the world for its unrighteousness. Both Jews and Gentiles are guilty of disobedience (Rom 3:4–8; cf. *Pss. Sol.* 8:1–34; 9:1–11).

Romans 3:9–20 concludes the unit of 2:1—3:20 by emphasizing Torah's universal condemnation of Jews and Gentiles. In 3:10–18, Paul recalls the condemnation of Gentiles in 1:18–32 and extends condemnation to the Jews by arguing that they and Gentiles are guilty before God.[31] In light of his stark indictment of Jews in 2:1—3:8, Paul asks in 3:9 if the Jews have an advantage over Gentiles in God's judgment.[32] He responds with a sharp

---

condemnation of Jews (Torah insiders) outside of Christ now that Torah has entered salvation-history by accentuating that Gentiles (Torah outsiders) have in fact fulfilled Torah by receiving the Spirit by faith in Jesus.

29. Against Dunn (*Romans*, 1:130–31), who takes the phrase to include both Torah and the prophets and against Jewett (*Romans*, 244, 247), who interprets the phrase to refer to God's promise concerning Messiah. For a reference to God's words, see LXX Num 24:4, 16; Pss 11:7; 17:31; 104:19; 106:11; 118:11; Isa 28:13.

30. DSS references in Sanders, *Paul and Palestinian Judaism*, 305–12.

31. Jewett, *Romans*, 260–61.

32. For the different ways to translate 3:9a, see Barrett, *Romans*, 66–68 and Jewett, *Romans*, 256–58. See also Bell (*No One Seeks for God*, 211–3) who creatively argues that Paul's question in 3:9 pertains to whether he will circumvent God's judgment in response to the charge in 3:8 that Paul was antinomian. For the relationship between 3:1 and 3:9 and the latter's meaning, see rightly Schreiner, *Romans*, 163–64.

"No" and then offers a reason: "because we have already charged in advance both Jews and Greeks, all, to be under sin" (Rom 3:9).[33] Paul charged both groups to be under the power of sin in the previous argument of 1:18—3:8.[34]

To bolster the charge of Torah's universal condemnation of Jews and Gentiles, he cites in 3:10–18a a catena of OT texts that refer to the wicked in their contexts (cf. CD 5:13–17; 4 *Ezra* 7:22–24).[35] Paul applies these texts to both Gentiles and (especially to) Jews to highlight the universal condemnation of both groups. Although, after the catena, Paul refers to Torah in 3:19, this catena of texts is from other parts of the Jewish Scriptures. Paul broadens the indictment of Jews and Gentiles by appealing to sections of the Jewish Scriptures that speak of the condemnation of the wicked.[36] His usage of Torah in 3:19 makes the point that the entire body of the Jewish Scriptures pronounces universal judgment upon all who disobey God.

Paul concludes the argument of 1:18—3:20 with 3:19-20. Based on his argument that Gentiles (and Jews) are guilty of suppressing the truth about God and of disobeying his righteous requirement (1:18–32), that God judges Jews and Gentiles in accordance with the same standard (2:1–29), that God universally condemns Jews and Gentiles by the same standard (3:1–18), that his solution to the spiritual plight of both Jews and Gentiles is justification by faith in the crucified and resurrected Jesus (3:21—4:25), and based on his fuller exposition of how Torah is rightly fulfilled in the people of God (Jews and Gentiles) who possess the Spirit by faith in Jesus (8:4; 9:1—11:36), Paul confirms in 3:19-20 that Torah speaks to those in the realm of Torah. Although Torah was especially given to the Jews, all Jews and Gentiles who have not received the new covenant promise of the Spirit are in the realm of Torah,[37] which means that the entire world (Jews and Gentiles) will be without excuse and accountable to God in the judgment

---

33. Against Dunn's translation (*Romans*, 1:146–47). Bell (*No One Seeks for God*, 213–14) insightfully argues that Paul's point in 3:9b is that every single person without exception is under the power of sin.

34. Similarly Dunn, *Romans*, 1:148; Wright, "Romans," 457; Moo, *Romans*, 203; Schreiner, *Romans*, 164. Against Räisänen, *Paul & the Law*, 98–99; Watson, *Paul, Judaism, and the Gentiles*, 223. Watson argues that Paul *only* refers back to his comments in Rom 3:4 and not to his earlier comments in Romans 1–2.

35. For the specific texts cited, see Schreiner, *Romans*, 165.

36. See Rom 3:10–12 with Pss 14:1–3; 53:1–3; Eccl 7:20, Rom 3:13 with Pss 5:9; 140:3; Rom 3:14 with Ps 10:7; Rom 3:15–17 with Isa 59:7–8; Prov 1:16, and Rom 3:18 with Ps 36:1.

37. Regarding the above analysis of 3:19, against Käsemann, *Romans*, 87–88; Barrett, *Romans*, 70; Dunn, *Romans*, 1:152; Wright, "Romans," 459; Moo, *Romans*, 205–6; Schreiner, *Romans*, 168.

(3:19).³⁸ Thus, Paul can say that "no flesh will be justified in his presence by works of law, for knowledge of sin comes through the law" (Rom 3:20; cf. LXX Ps 142:2; *2 Apoc. Bar.* 51:3).³⁹

Paul diminishes any remains of Jewish optimism in 3:19-20 regarding the soteriological function of the law. He concludes that although a real promise of final justification awaits the one who obeys Torah (2:6, 13), absolutely *no one* will be vindicated in God's law court by Torah because Torah reveals that one has broken specific commands of God (cf. 3:20; 4:15; 5:13-14; 7:7-23).⁴⁰ Torah does not provide salvation, but his gospel about Jesus Christ saves all who believe (1:16-17). Thus, 1:18—3:20 suggests that Jews and Gentiles are guilty before God and will be judged by the same standard in God's law court apart from faith in Christ.

---

38. Dunn (*Romans*, 1:152) sees a reference to God's judgment of the entire creation with his use of "entire world," not just his judgment of Jews and Gentiles. But the phrases "every mouth" (3:19) and "all flesh" (3:19) together with "the entire world" (3:19) seem to emphasize in this text God's judgment against Jews and Gentiles, for these groups have been the subject of 1:18—3:18.

39. Jewett (*Romans*, 265-66) argues that "not any flesh" refers to circumcised flesh and is a specific attack against the Judaizers, because Paul alters the original word from LXX Ps 142:2b from "everyone who lives" to "any flesh," which fits Paul's earlier discussion of circumcision in 2:28. Paul's denial that one could stand on his own terms before God in the judgment was not novel with him, but this idea was also denied by some within early Judaism (1QH 9:14-16). However, as we have already seen above, there was *a* strong Jewish perspective that Jews would be exonerated in God's law court because they were distinctively Jewish and because they yielded obedience to Torah. This perspective is evident by their trust in Torah, by their emphasis on circumcision and proselytizing, by their disdain for Gentiles, and by their optimistic view of their ability to keep Torah to the fullest (Gen 17:1-14; Exod 24; Isa 42:6-7; 49:6; *Ep. Aris.* 139, 142; *Jub.* 14:10; 15:1-34; 22:15-23; Tobit; Wis 18:4; Sir 24:27; Bar 4:4; *Sib. Or.* 3.195; Jos., *Ag. Ap.* 2.293; Philo, *Abr.* 98; *Mos.* 1.149; 1QH 2:9; 1QS 3:13). For a similar point, see Das, "Paul and Works of Obedience," 798-801.

40. Dunn (*Romans*, 1:155-56) takes the phrase "a knowledge of sin through the law" to refer to the "typical Jewish attitude which saw the law as the means and measure of life within the covenant (as in Sir. 45:5; *Pss. Sol.* 14:2) and as a bulwark and hedge against the sinfulness of the Gentiles (as in *Let. Aris.* 139, 142)." In contrast, Paul argues, says Dunn, that Torah was not given to elicit a sense of distinctiveness and security for the Jew, but to make the Jew to whom Torah was addressed aware that he was still in need of God's grace even as a member of God's covenant, just as the Gentile sinner is in need of God's grace.

SUBSTITUTION, YOM KIPPUR, AND MARTYR THEOLOGY IN ROMANS 3:21-26

Paul presents Jesus' death as a substitution, and he suggests that his death functioned as Yom Kippur for Jews and Gentiles in Rom 3:21-30. He presents Jesus' death this way by appropriating ideas from Jewish martyrological traditions. The most significant verses in 3:21-30 that contain Jewish martyrological ideas are 3:24-25. However, I discuss these two verses in the context of Paul's very condensed argument in 3:21-26.

God's Righteousness, Justification, Redemption, Blood, and ἱλαστήριον

In Rom 3:24-26, Paul conflates several metaphors as he discusses Jesus' death for Jews and Gentiles. He combines ἀπολυτρώσεως (a broad slavery metaphor) in 3:24 with the cultic metaphors of ἱλαστήριον and αἵματι in 3:25 while commenting on God's saving righteousness in 3:21-22 and 3:24-26. He contends that God justifies sinners by faith because he offered Jesus to die for their sins (3:21-25). In 3:23-24, Paul states that all sinners must be freely justified "by God's grace through the redemption which is in Christ Jesus." The statement "all have sinned" universally refers to Jews and Gentiles, because Paul's argument in 1:18—3:20 focuses on the condemnation of both groups due to their inability to meet Torah's demands and because he explicitly states in 3:30 that God is the God of Jews and Gentiles, whom he justifies by faith. Justification, says Paul, is God's gracious gift and comes to all sinners freely (3:23-24). This justification is possible by faith because Jesus provides redemption for those who are justified by his blood (3:24-25). God's act of justification by the offering of Jesus proves God to be just and the one who justifies the one who has faith in Jesus (3:26). God's free act of justification through Christ excludes all forms of boasting (3:27), because he justifies Jews and Gentiles by faith apart from Torah-observance (3:28-30).

The centerpiece of Paul's entire argument in 3:21-30 is the substitutionary death of Jesus in 3:24-25. He argues that Jesus' death for others is the reason why God justifies Jewish and Gentile sinners by faith in Jesus Christ.[41] Paul embeds Jesus' death between numerous statements about justification (3:20, 24) and God's righteousness (3:21-22, 25-26), which both refer to God's salvation. The first substitutionary statement in 3:21-26 is

---

41. For the πίστις Ἰησοῦ Χριστου debate, see Bird and Sprinkle, *The Faith of Jesus Christ*.

ἀπολυτρώσεως in 3:24.[42] Its occurrence here suggests that Jesus' redemption is the means through which God justifies all who have sinned and that faith is an efficacious necessity for justification, since Paul connects God's free gift of justification in 3:24 with διὰ τῆς ἀπολυτρώσεως τῆς ἐν Χριστῷ Ἰησοῦ and with διὰ [τῆς] πίστεως ἐν τῷ αὐτοῦ αἵματι in 3:25. Neither the justification of the sinner nor the redemption in Christ is possible without his shed blood for sinners, because the phrase διὰ τῆς ἀπολυτρώσεως τῆς ἐν Χριστῷ Ἰησοῦ modifies δικαιούμενοι δωρεὰν τῇ αὐτοῦ χάριτι and because Paul attaches ἀπολυτρώσεως to Jesus' blood with a relative clause (ὃν προέθετο ὁ θεὸς ἱλαστήριον διὰ [τῆς] πίστεως ἐν τῷ αὐτοῦ αἵματι εἰς ἔνδειξιν τῆς δικαιοσύνης αὐτοῦ διὰ τὴν πάρεσιν τῶν προγεγονότων ἁμαρτημάτων), which modifies Χριστῷ Ἰησοῦ in 3:24.

In the early part of the twentieth century, Adolf Deissmann argued that Paul's background for redemption-language was the Greco-Roman religious cult. He suggested that slaves in the Greco-Roman world could be liberated by paying or depositing money in the sanctuary of Apollos' shrine. This transaction made slaves the property of Apollos.[43] Leon Morris offered one of the most detailed responses to Deissmann. He argued that Paul's background was explicitly the Jewish Scriptures.[44] In my view, both Deissmann and Morris were incorrect.

Of course, Paul's use of ἀπολυτρώσεως in 3:24 provides a lexical connection with Exodus and a conceptual connection with Israel's redemption from slavery. The lexical connection with Exodus is apparent from the occurrence of a cognate verb in LXX Exod 21:8. There the translators use the verb ἀπολυτρώσει to render the Hebrew וְהֶפְדָּהּ in a context that discusses the redemption of a daughter from the man to whom the father betrothed her as a slave if she was unacceptable to the man. The conceptual connection with Israel's deliverance from slavery is apparent when Israel describes the nation's salvation from slavery as YHWH's purchasing of a people (LXX Exod 15:13, 16). LXX Exod 15:13 uses a verb from the λυτρ-word group (ἐλυτρώσω) to describe YHWH's deliverance of Israel as an act of redemption from slavery, while LXX Exod 15:16 uses the verb ἐκτήσω ("you acquired") to refer to the same act instead of using terms from the λυτρ-word group as LXX Exod 21:8 and as Rom 3:24. The preceding evidence, and the occurrence of ἐκτήσω with αἵματι in Sir 33:31 in a context that refers

---

42. See also Luke 21:28; Rom 8:23; 1 Cor 1:30; Eph 1:7, 14; 4:30; Col 1:14; Heb 9:15, and 11:35. Paul also, however, suggests elsewhere that Jesus' death was a ransom (1 Cor 6:20; 7:23; Gal 3:13; cf. 4:5; 5:16; Col 4:5; Titus 2:14).

43. Deissmann, *Light from the Ancient East*, 319–30.

44. Morris, *The Apostolic Preaching of the Cross*, 11–64, esp. 9–26; Morris, "Redemption," 784–86.

to the redemption of a slave with the price of blood, confirms that ἐκτήσω was synonymous with ἀπολυτρώσει at least in some texts written during the Second Temple period and that both verbs referred to redemption in the Second Temple period along with other words from the λυτρ-word group.[45]

However, the concept of redemption was fluid in the OT world. Redemption was applied in the OT to various situations: redemption from bondage (Lev 25:47–55; Exod 21:1; Deut 15:12–18), redemption of property (Lev 25:23–34; Ruth 4:1–6; Jer 32:6–15), redemption of something previously devoted to God (Lev 27:15–33; Judg 11:29–40), and Levirate marriage was a redemption by which a family was delivered from the threat of extinction (Gen 38:1–30; Deut 25:6; Ruth 3:10—4:12).[46] This evidence suggests that Paul's ἀπολυτρώσεως is a general allusion to redemption in the Greco-Roman and Jewish worlds and a specific allusion to the redemption of Israel from slavery and the redemption of slaves. This interpretation is confirmed by numerous references in the OT where slaves were purchased/redeemed/bought by a kinsman or redeemer for a monetary price (cf. LXX Lev 25:47–52), although Paul's exact word (ἀπολυτρώσεως) only occurs in the LXX in Dan 4:34 to refer to Nebuchadnezzar's praise of YHWH upon the exhortation of an angel. Paul employs the metaphor of redemption to accentuate the claim that Jesus redeemed Jewish and Gentile sinners from the universal, malefic effects of sin (cf. Rom 6:1—8:11). The term ἀπολυτρώσεως in 3:25 is also a substitutionary term, because Jesus achieved ἀπολυτρώσεως for Jews and Gentiles by means of his blood/death for others to achieve a soteriological benefit for them (cf. Rom 3:24–25 with 3:29–30).[47]

In spite of his echo of Greco-Roman and Jewish concepts of slavery, Paul's background behind redemption is neither Greco-Roman nor only the OT,[48] but also martyrological. Paul appropriates both Levitical cultic lan-

---

45. E.g., see LXX Exod 6:6; 15:13; Deut 7:8; 9:26; 15:15; 24:18; Isa 43:1; 44:22; 63:9; Mic 6:4. David J. Williams, *Paul's Metaphors*, 138 n. 112 pointed me to these texts.

46. Preceding information comes from D. J. Williams, *Paul's Metaphors*, 138 n. 111.

47. A similar observation is in Lee, *Paul's Gospel in Romans*, 221–22.

48. Josephus uses the exact term in the exact case and number in *Antiquities* to refer to the freeing of slaves (*Ant.* 12.27). However, the price of the redemption was money instead of a human life: πλειόνων δ' ἢ τετρακοσίων ταλάντων τῆς ἀπολυτρώσεως γενήσεσθαι φαμένων ταῦτά τε συνεχώρει καὶ τὸ ἀντίγραφον τοῦ προστάγματος εἰς δήλωσιν τῆς τοῦ βασιλέως μεγαλοφροσύνης ἔγνωσαν διαφυλάξαι ἣν δὲ τοιοῦτον ὅσοι τῶν συστρατευσαμένων ἡμῶν τῷ πατρὶ τήν τε Συρίαν καὶ Φοινίκην ἐπέδραμον καὶ τὴν Ἰουδαίαν καταστρεψάμενοι σώματα λαβόντες αἰχμάλωτα διεκόμισαν εἴς τε τὰς πόλεις ἡμῶν καὶ τὴν χώραν καὶ ταῦτα ἀπημπόλησαν τούς τε πρὸ αὐτῶν ὄντας ἐν τῇ ἐμῇ βασιλείᾳ καὶ εἴ τινες νῦν εἰσήχθησαν τούτους ἀπολυέτωσαν οἱ παρ' αὐτοῖς ἔχοντες ὑπὲρ ἑκάστου σώματος λαμβάνοντες δραχμὰς ἑκατὸν εἴκοσι οἱ μὲν στρατιῶται μετὰ καὶ τῶν ὀψωνίων οἱ δὲ λοιποὶ ἀπὸ τῆς βασιλικῆς τραπέζης κομιζόμενοι τὰ λύτρα.

guage and language from Isaiah 53 to the death of a Torah-observant Jew for the soteriological benefit of non-Torah-observant sinners condemned by Torah, just as the Jewish martyrological narratives apply both Levitical cultic language and language from Isaiah 53 to the deaths of Torah-observant Jews for the soteriological benefit of non-Torah-observant sinners condemned by Torah.[49] In a recent book on Rom 1:16—8:39, Jae Hyun Lee assumed that there was a straight line from Leviticus 16 to Rom 3:24–25. He dismissed in a footnote a Jewish martyrological influence upon Paul in 3:24–25 since "it is more plausible to think that Paul interprets the role of Jesus in the process of God's salvation through the lens of the OT than that of contemporary writing."[50] Indeed, Yom Kippur imagery in 3:24–25 is apparent by both the lexical and conceptual parallels, but the presence of this imagery does not disprove the proposition that Paul interpreted Jesus' death through the lens of a Jewish martyrological reception and appropriation of Leviticus 16.

For example, in the final part of Eleazar's prayer in 4 Macc 6:29b, he asks God to receive his death as a ransom for the nation (καὶ ἀντίψυχον αὐτῶν λαβὲ τὴν ἐμὴν ψυχήν). The term ἀντίψυχον ("ransom") in 4 Macc 6:29b likewise occurs in 4 Macc 17:21. In my view, ἀπολύτρωσις in Rom 3:24 and the phrase ἐν τῷ αὐτοῦ αἵματι in Rom 3:25 function together as a circumlocution for ἀντίψυχον in 4 Macc 6:29b and 17:21, because the author associates ἀντίψυχον with the martyrs' blood (διὰ τοῦ αἵματος) in 4 Macc 6:28–29 and in 17:21, with the nation's sin (τῆς τοῦ ἔθνους ἁμαρτίας) in 17:21, with τοῦ ἱλαστηρίου in 17:22, with national salvation (διέσωσεν) in 17:21, and with national purification (καθαρισθῆναι) in 17:22 in order to accentuate the idea that the martyrs' deaths were sacrificial for Israel and the means by which God purified and saved the nation in the Jewish martyrological narratives. Paul associates Jesus' death for Jewish and Gentile sinners with the above categories in Rom 3:24–25 by combining ἀπολύτρωσις and ἱλαστήριον with ἐν τῷ αὐτοῦ αἵματι. Bishop Ignatius, a Christian martyr, referred to his martyrdom as a substitutionary ransom (ἀντίψυχον) in that he prayed that his death would take the place of his audiences' death (*Eph.* 21.1; *Smyr.* 10.2; *Pol.* 2.3; 6.1). However, the overt cultic language found in the Jewish martyrological narratives and in Paul is absent in Ignatius. In the Levitical cult, in the Jewish martyrological reception of the Levitical cultic traditions, and in Rom 3:24–25, blood is a central element of cultic action in that life was lost to achieve the desired cultic function: namely, salvation.[51]

---

49. For a connection between Jewish martyrology and redemption in Rom 3:25, see I. Howard Marshall, "The Development of the Concept of Redemption," 163; Hill, *Greek Words and Hebrew Meanings*, 41–48.

50. Jae Hyun Lee, *Paul's Gospel in Romans*, 222, esp. n. 21.

51. Keener, *Romans*, 60.

The martyrological narratives suggest that the martyrs' deaths represented the nation because they did not violate Torah. Their deaths were substitutes for the nation to achieve national salvation because the authors of 2 and 4 Maccabees explicitly state that the martyrs suffered the curses of Torah along with the nation to achieve national salvation for the people (4 Macc 17:21–22). Therefore, the function of ἀντίψυχον in 4 Macc 6:29 and 17:21 suggests that the blood of the martyrs was the required price paid to achieve Israel's redemption (i.e., purification and salvation) just as the sacrificial ritual on Yom Kippur required the blood of the animal to purify/cover/atone the sins of the people and the effects of sin within the community (Leviticus 16) and just as the Servant's death liberates many nations from their sins (Isa 53:4–12). In fact, 4 Macc 17:21 asserts that the homeland was purified "just as" (ὥσπερ) the martyrs became a ransom for the sin of the nation.

Likewise, Paul's association of Jesus' death (a Torah-observant-Jew) with ἀπολυτρώσεως in 3:24, with αἵματι and ἱλαστήριον in 3:25, and with his assertion that Jesus' death accomplished justification before God and salvation from sins make 3:24 a Jewish martyrological statement. Paul presents Jesus' death as a substitution for Jews and Gentiles, and he suggests that he functions as Yom Kippur for Jews and Gentiles because his blood accomplishes their redemption (3:25). In the NT, only Paul connects ἀπολυτρώσεως with blood (Rom 3:24 and Eph 1:7), just as the author of 4 Macc 6:28–29 and 17:21–22 connects ἀντίψυχον with blood. Paul states that Jesus (a Torah-observant-Jew) paid the price of ἀπολυτρώσεως for sinners with his death (3:23–25), which Paul supports with a reference to Jesus' blood in 3:25. Contrary to the redemption of slaves in both the Greco-Roman and in Jewish worlds, Paul states in 3:24 that Jesus was the agent of ἀπολυτρώσεως instead of its object (διὰ τῆς ἀπολυτρώσεως τῆς ἐν Χριστῷ Ἰησοῦ). And Paul suggests that Jesus (a Torah-observant Jew) paid the price of redemption with his blood, whereas YHWH killed Pharaoh and his army to accomplish the nation's redemption (Exod 14–15) and whereas slaves paid money to the gods to achieve their emancipation without the shedding of blood in the Greco-Roman world.[52]

Paul asserts that justification comes to sinners through the redemption accomplished by means of Jesus' blood (3:24–25) and that God appointed Jesus to function as a ἱλαστήριον to take away sin (3:25).[53] Since Paul uses ἀπολυτρώσεως in 3:24 in the context of blood (3:25) and since the redemp-

---

52. Deissmann, *Light*, 119–30.

53. I take προέθετο as "he appointed/planned" instead of as "he put forth," because the term means this in the only other occurrence in Romans (1:13).

tion that Jesus has accomplished for Jews and Gentiles by his blood was the means through which God provided justification for them (cf. 3:21-22, 24), ἀπολυτρώσεως likely suggests in 3:24 that Jesus' death accomplished redemption because he was a substitutionary payment (i.e., a ransom), which God appointed to purchase justification for all who have sinned and to deal with previously committed sins (3:23-25). As a result of Jesus' substitutionary death, God liberated in Christ those who were otherwise guilty before God (cf. 1:18—3:26).[54]

Some scholars have rejected the notion that Jesus' death was a ransom.[55] Nevertheless, the very argument and structure in 3:24-25 militates against their objection. For example, ἀπολυτρώσεως in 3:24 was the accomplishment achieved by Jesus' blood in 3:25. Reading 3:24-25 together suggests that the blood was the necessary price paid for both justification and redemption in 3:24.[56] Paul does not state to whom the ransom was paid in 3:24. Yet, he explicitly states in 3:24-25 that God put forth Jesus as the price of redemption for Jewish and Gentile sinners.

Paul conflates ἀπολυτρώσεως into a condensed cultic statement in 3:24-25 about the salvation accomplished for Jewish and Gentile non-Torah-observant sinners with two words that make an explicit connection with Yom Kippur (αἵματι and ἱλαστήριον) in 3:25 and consequently a connection with the Jewish martyrological narratives (cf. LXX Lev 16:14-15; 4 Macc 6:28-29 and 17:21-22).[57] The relative clause in 3:25 reinforces the Jewish martyrological influence upon Paul's substitutionary presentation of Jesus' death in 3:25, and Paul continues his thought from 3:24 with a relative clause (ὃν προέθετο ὁ θεὸς ἱλαστήριον διὰ [τῆς] πίστεως ἐν τῷ αὐτοῦ αἵματι εἰς ἔνδειξιν τῆς δικαιοσύνης αὐτοῦ διὰ τὴν πάρεσιν τῶν προγεγονότων ἁμαρτημάτων). The relative clause includes a word (ἱλαστήριον) that explicitly links 3:24-25 with the Yom Kippur tradition as appropriated in the Jew-

---

54. Mark A. Seifrid ("Romans," 619) does not discount the idea of ransom in Rom 3:24, but he places the accent on liberation. I think Paul's point in 3:24-25 is that liberation takes place (3:24) because Jesus' blood paid the price (3:25).

55. For example, see Hill, *Greek Words and Hebrew Meanings*, 49-81. Hill primarily rejects the idea of ransom in Rom 3:24 on lexical grounds.

56. Cf. Warfield, "The New Testament Terminology of Redemption," 327-98; Morris, *Apostolic Preaching*, 11-64, esp. 9-26; Moo, *Romans*, 229; Finlan, *The Background and Content of Paul's Cultic Atonement Metaphors*, 164-69. Against the idea of ransom, see Swallow, "Redemption in St. Paul," 21-27; Hill, *Greek Words*, 49-81.

57. God commands the priest to make atonement on the ἱλαστήριον to provide cleansing for sin (Exod 25:18-22; 31:7; 35:12; 37:6-8; Lev 16:14-15), and God appears above the ἱλαστήριον to show his acceptance of atonement (Exod 25:22; Lev 16:2; Num 7:89). The term also occurs in LXX Ezek 43:14-20 in reference to a place at which atonement takes place by the pouring out of blood.

ish martyrological narratives. Because both the author of 4 Macc 17:22 and Paul apply ἱλαστήριον to the death of a Torah-observant Jew for the soteriological benefit of sinners with language that resembles Yom Kippur, both texts conflate the Yom Kippur tradition with the Levitical cultic tradition to emphasize that the martyrs (4 Macc 17:22) and Jesus (Rom 3:25) were substitutes for the sins of others and functioned as Yom Kippur.

As I have argued elsewhere, 4 Macc 17:22 and Rom 3:25 are the only places in available Greek literature where an author applies ἱλαστήριον to the death of a Torah-observant Jewish human in a cultic context for the soteriological benefit of non-Torah-observant sinners. In the LXX, the term ἱλαστήριον refers to the mercy seat. The priests purified/covered/atoned sin through the sacrifice of blood and sprinkled the blood over the mercy seat (Lev 16:14–15). God commands Israel to put the ἱλαστήριον above the ark of the covenant in the holy of holies, the place where only the high priest could enter (Exod 25:17–20; 37:6). God commands the priest to make atonement on the ἱλαστήριον to provide cleansing from sin (Exod 25:18–22; 31:7; 35:12; 37:6–8; Lev 16:14–15), and God appears above the ἱλαστήριον to show his acceptance of atonement (Exod 25:22; Lev 16:2; Num 7:89).

In LXX Ezek 43:14–20, ἱλαστήριον refers to a place at which atonement takes place by the pouring out of blood.[58] In Jos. Ant. 16.182, ἱλαστήριον describes μνῆμα and refers to a propitiatory monument erected to placate

---

58. The occurrence of ἱλαστήριον in the context of 4 Macc 17:21–22 is certainly cultic for the above reasons, but also since the term itself is part of a semantic family of ἱλας-words that often occur in cultic contexts in the LXX that speak of atoning for sin, since these words often translate from the Hebrew root, which often means "to atone," and since some form of ἱλαστήριον occurs in Leviticus' prescriptions regarding Yom Kippur (cf. LXX Lev 16:2, 13–15). I am not asserting that the ἱλας-words group always translates from the Hebrew that means "to atone" (cf. LXX Exod 32:14; 2 Kgs 21:3; 1 Chr 6:34; 2 Chr 29:24; Ps 105:30; Ezek 43:14–20; Zech 7:2; 8:22). I am neither affirming that the ἱλας-words group always conveys the idea of atoning sacrifice (cf. LXX Exod 32:14; Prov 16:14). For example, ἐξιλάσασθαι is often cultic and often refers to the cleansing that takes places when sins are atoned (LXX Exod 30:10; Lev 1:4; 4:20, 26, 31, 35; 5:6, 10, 13, 16, 18, 26; 6:23; 7:7; 16:29; Num 5:8; 6:11; 8:12, 19, 21; 15:25, 28; 17:11, 12; 28:22, 30; 29:5, 11; 31:50; 1 Kgs 3:14; 2 Kgs 2:13; 1 Chr 6:34; 2 Chr 29:24; 2 Chr 30:18; 2 Esd 20:34; Ps 105:30; Ezek 43:20, 22; 45:17; Sir 3:3, 30; 5:6; 20:28; 28:5; 34:19; 45:16, 23). However, the one occurrence of ἱλάσθη in the LXX is not cultic, and it is altogether void of sacrificial ideas (LXX Exod 32:14). In LXX Exod 32:14, ἐξιλάσασθαι translates from a root that means "to repent" and highlights YHWH's mercy to Israel in spite of the nation's idolatry. But ἱλας-words often occur in cultic texts and often speak of sacrificial atonement when this word group occurs with explicit cultic vocabulary, as it does in 4 Macc 17:21–22. Thus, 4 Macc 17:21–22 speaks of the martyrs' deaths with specific sacrificial/cultic language that closely resembles the Old Testament cult and that echoes Yom Kippur, especially since 4 Macc 17:21–22 states that the martyrs brought divine favor to Israel via blood and purification when they died for the nation.

the offended deity.⁵⁹ In Philo, ἱλαστήριον functions as a noun and refers to the mercy seat both with (*Cher.* 1:25; *Her.* 1:166; *Fug.* 1:101) and without the article (*Fug.* 1:100; *Mos.* 2:95, 97).

In my view, regardless of how one translates ἱλαστήριον in 4 Macc 17:22 and in Rom 3:25, since the term occurs in the same context as several cultic vocabulary and concepts found in Leviticus 16–17 (e.g., judgment, national purification, ransom, vicarious death, sin, salvation, and blood), ἱλαστήριον in 4 Macc 17:22 at least alludes to the Yom Kippur ritual and it at least suggests that the martyrs' deaths function as Israel's Yom Kippur in the context of 4 Maccabees.⁶⁰ The appropriate way to translate ἱλαστήριον in Rom 3:25 in English is no trivial matter.⁶¹ An accurate translation of the term in part depends upon Paul's background behind 3:25. If a Jewish martyrological background is correct, as I am arguing, then one should render ἱλαστήριον in English in a way that communicates the substitutionary nature of Jesus' death and the Yom Kippur function of his death in the soteriological narrative of 3:21–26. However, the question of translation is separate from the question of how the martyrs and Jesus are functioning in their soteriological narratives.

4 Maccabees 6:28–29 speaks of the martyrs' deaths in the context of national sin due to Torah disobedience, blood, purification, and ransom. 4 Maccabees 17:21–22 speaks of the martyrs' deaths in the context of national purification, national salvation, ransom, and blood/death.⁶² Likewise, Paul identifies Jesus as a ἱλαστήριον in Rom 3:25 in a context where he asserts that Jesus' blood accomplished universal salvation for non-Torah-observant Jewish and Gentile sinners (cf. 1:18–3:31). Therefore, Bailey's lexical analysis prohibits ἱλαστήριον in 4 Macc 17:22 and in Rom 3:25 from functioning in its unique thematic way in the distinct contexts of 4 Maccabees and Romans.⁶³ Both textual traditions emphasize substitution by means of appropriating Levitical cultic and Isaianic language to the deaths of Torah-observant Jews, who died for the soteriological benefit of non-

59. καὶ τοῦ δέους ἱλαστήριον μνῆμα λευκῆς πέτρας ἐπὶ τῷ στομίῳ κατεσκεύασατο πολυτελὲς τῇ δαπάνῃ.

60. Similarly Ben Ezra, *Yom Kippur*, 115. DeSilva (*4 Maccabees*, 250–51) argues that the author uses the cultic language from the Yom Kippur ritual to describe the effect of the martyrs' deaths.

61. For the different translation options and advocates of each position, see Jarvis J. Williams, "Martyr Theology in Hellenistic Judaism and Paul's Conception of Jesus' Death in Romans 3:21–26," 514–15.

62. DeSilva, *4 Maccabees*, 202.

63. For a similar critique, see also Finlan, *Atonement Metaphors*, 200. In agreement with the Yom Kippur imagery in 4 Macc 17:22 and the effective nature of their deaths, similarly Ben Ezra, *Yom Kippur*, 115; DeSilva, *4 Maccabees*, 250–51.

Torah-observant sinners in order to present them as Yom Kippur in their distinct soteriological narratives.

The Jewish martyrological concept of the substitutionary death of a Torah-observant Jew for the soteriological benefit of non-Torah-observant sinners conflated with Levitical cultic language in 3:25 is further evident by the words that modify ἱλαστήριον in 3:25–26. The Greek sentence reads as follows: ὃν προέθετο ὁ θεὸς ἱλαστήριον διὰ [τῆς] πίστεως ἐν τῷ αὐτοῦ αἵματι εἰς ἔνδειξιν τῆς δικαιοσύνης αὐτοῦ διὰ τὴν πάρεσιν τῶν προγεγονότων ἁμαρτημάτων ἐν τῇ ἀνοχῇ τοῦ θεοῦ, πρὸς τὴν ἔνδειξιν τῆς δικαιοσύνης αὐτοῦ ἐν τῷ νῦν καιρῷ, εἰς τὸ εἶναι αὐτὸν δίκαιον καὶ δικαιοῦντα τὸν ἐκ πίστεως Ἰησοῦ. The sentence is a complex and condensed relative clause, which takes προέθετο as its main verb. The relative clause begins with ὃν in 3:25 and ends with Ἰησοῦ in 3:26. The relative pronoun (ὃν) and ἱλαστήριον work together to form a double accusative construction. The former term is the direct object of the verb, and the latter functions as a predicate adjectival-accusative with an implied to be verb between both terms. The translation would suggest that God appointed Jesus to be a ἱλαστήριον. Reading the grammar this way avoids a strict translation of ἱλαστήριον as mercy-seat (against Bailey), because it identifies ἱλαστήριον as an adjective instead of as a noun.

With the exception of the absence of the article in Rom 3:25, an adjectival construction fits with its occurrence in 4 Macc 17:22 although ἱλαστήριον is an attributive adjective there since it takes an article and modifies a noun (e.g., τοῦ ἱλαστηρίου τοῦ θανάτου). Joseph Fitzmyer strongly objected to an allusion to 4 Macc 17:22 in Rom 3:25 since he asserted that ἱλαστήριον in the former text is clearly an adjective.[64] Instead, he argued that it is best to interpret the term in light of its LXX usage as a reference to God's act of setting Jesus forth as the new means of expiation in light of the textual connections with Yom Kippur imagery.[65]

Markus Tiwald assumed that the Yom Kippur ritual was the only background behind Rom 3:25. He argued that the background behind Paul's use of ἱλαστήριον in Rom 3:25 is not martyrological for at least two reasons: grammar and date. First, if Rahlfs' critical edition to the Septuagint is correct in that an article should precede ἱλαστήριον, then the latter is an adjective describing θανάτου in 4 Macc 17:22 (τοῦ ἱλαστηρίου θανάτου). The preceding construction makes a connection with Romans 3 unlikely since ἱλαστήριον is not attributive in Rom 3:25. Second, if most scholars are correct, then we should date 4 Maccabees to the latter part of the first century (e.g., 90–100 CE). According to Tiwald, therefore, 4 Maccabees

---

64. Fitzmyer, *Romans*, 120–22, 349–50.
65. Ibid., 121, 349–50.

should no longer be seen as a reference text for Paul in Romans 3, contrary to Eduard Lohse in a monograph on martyrdom in 1955 and again in his Romans commentary in 2003.[66] Against Bailey's thesis, Tiwald argued that ἱλαστήριον in Rom 3:25 refers to the Yom Kippur ritual instead of to the mercy seat.[67] As Tiwald stated:

> Yom Kippur was the most important celebration in the second temple. And כַּפֹּרֶת was the holiest place of the temple. Even if it no longer existed in the second temple, its mythic importance continued unbroken. Therefore, by using the expression that God has displayed Christ publicly as ἱλαστήριον, Paul maintains that in Jesus' death the apex of fulfillment of all the expectations of redemption has now been reached. Christ is the fulfillment of all hopes to obtain salvation and atonement. In this *pars pro toto* view two different aspects of interpretation, which sometimes have been seen as a contradiction, may also coexist: Christ now becomes the eschatological atonement for our sin ... and he also becomes the place of the presence of God in this world.[68]

Tiwald's thesis is correct in so far as it goes, but his essay failed to highlight the Jewish martyrological background as a foundation underneath Paul's presentation of Jesus' death as Yom Kippur for Jews and Gentiles.

Regarding the part of speech of ἱλαστήριον, unless I have overlooked something, every articular occurrence of the term in the canonical LXX refers to the mercy-seat.[69] The only anarthrous occurrence of ἱλαστήριον in the canonical LXX is an adjectival occurrence in LXX Exod 25:17 describing ἐπίθεμα (ἱλαστήριον ἐπίθεμα, "propitiatory covering"). As I argued above, Jos. *Ant.* 16:182 uses an anarthrous ἱλαστήριον as an adjective, and Philo uses ἱλαστήριον as a noun to refer to the mercy seat both with (*Cher.* 1.25; *Her.* 1.166; *Fug.* 1.101) and without the article (*Fug.* 1.100; *Mos.* 2.95, 97). Thus, the absence of the article in Rom 3:25 gives no insight into the part of speech of ἱλαστήριον in Rom 3:25. Instead, context suggests that ὃν is the direct object of προέθετο, and ἱλαστήριον is a predicate adjective describing ὃν. This interpretation takes ἱλαστήριον to function in a similar way as it does in 4 Macc 17:22: namely to identify a Torah-observant Jew as the propitiatory for non-Torah-observant sinners with Levitical cultic language and with both Yom Kippur language and imagery. A Jewish martyrological

---

66. Tiwald, "Christ as *HILASTERION*," 189–208, esp. 192.

67. Ibid., 194, 198.

68. Ibid., 205.

69. Exod 25:18–21, 22; 31:7; 35:12; 38:5, 7–8; Lev 16:2, 13–15; Num 7:89; Ezek 43:14, 17, 20; Amos 9:1.

background in Rom 3:25 highlights the substitutionary function of Jesus' death for others in that a Torah-observant Jew's death (similar to but greater than the martyrs) dealt with every contaminating effect of the sin on behalf of Jewish and Gentile sinners, because he functioned as the sacrificial means by which God's wrath was propitiated and because his death "provided a new means of access to God that reached far beyond the sins of Israel,"[70] just as the sacrificial and scapegoat rituals on Yom Kippur.

In an important book on Paul's soteriology in 2009, Douglas A. Campbell discussed martyr theology's influence on Paul's atonement theory in Rom 3:25.[71] He rightly argued that Paul describes Jesus' death in Jewish martyrological categories. The categories of faith, blood, execution, and the vindication of a heroic person in Rom 3:21–26 point to a Jewish martyrological reading of Rom 3:25.[72] Campbell rejected a direct relationship between 3:25 and 4 Maccabees, for the similarities between the two texts lack the precision needed to support such a claim.[73] He asserted that since 2 Maccabees 6 and 7 indisputably predate Paul and since these chapters contain the atoning efficacy of the martyrs' deaths, an appeal to Greco-Roman influences on Paul is unnecessary to explain Paul's atonement theory. He further contended that a Jewish martyrological reading of Genesis 22 is the appropriate background in front of which to read 3:25.

Campbell's work on 3:25 is extremely important for the question of the origins and the function of Jesus' death in 3:25 because he argued that soteriology in Paul is both apocalyptic and participatory. Agreeing with Louis Martyn, Campbell affirmed that salvation in Paul is fundamentally liberative and that it happens in the face of evil powers, from which God frees humanity. According to Campbell, "God, therefore, is not fundamentally just and the atonement designed to assuage God's righteous anger at transgression; God is fundamentally benevolent and the atonement intended to deliver humanity from bondage to evil powers and to reconstitute it in the age to come."[74] Campbell asserted that although Paul presents Jesus' death in 3:25 as a singular atonement for sin, this is not to be understood as a sacrifice. God appointed Jesus' death to replace the temple cultus.[75] However, Paul's use of the term ἱλαστήριον signifies a singular event in relation to atonement

---

70. Although contrary Jewett, above citation comes from Jewett (*Romans*, 286), who relied upon Kraus, *Der Tod Jesus als Heiligtumsweihe*, 166–67.

71. Campbell, *Deliverance*, 647–56.

72. Ibid., 648.

73. Ibid.

74. Campbell, *Deliverance*, 192.

75. Ibid., 654.

and reconciliation.⁷⁶ That is, Paul suggests that Jesus' atonement was of an extraordinary nature, like the Yom Kippur ritual and the deaths of Isaac and the Maccabean martyrs.⁷⁷ This atonement does not refer to a payment in terms of propitiating an angry deity, "although a connotation of sacrifice seems fair (as long as that is correctly nuanced)."⁷⁸ According to Campbell, Paul's argument in 3:21–26 is that Jesus' death forensically liberates sinners and that God shows himself to be just in that he delivers Jesus from death by means of resurrecting him from the dead due to Jesus' faithfulness.⁷⁹ However, in my view, the rest of the argument in 3:25–26 challenges Campbell's suggestions.

For example, several modifiers in 3:25–26 support a Jewish martyrological reading and a substitute reading of 3:25, and they support that Paul presents Jesus as God's bloody ἱλαστήριον to assuage his wrath along the lines of the Jewish martyrological narratives. The seven prepositional phrases (διὰ [τῆς] πίστεως ἐν τῷ αὐτοῦ αἵματι εἰς ἔνδειξιν τῆς δικαιοσύνης αὐτοῦ διὰ τὴν πάρεσιν τῶν προγεγονότων ἁμαρτημάτων ἐν τῇ ἀνοχῇ τοῦ θεοῦ, πρὸς τὴν ἔνδειξιν τῆς δικαιοσύνης αὐτοῦ ἐν τῷ νῦν καιρῷ) in 3:25–26 follow the words ὃν προέθετο ὁ θεὸς ἱλαστήριον. These phrases possibly connect with the main verb προέθετο in 3:25 since prepositional phrases normally modify verbs in NT Greek. Upon this reading, the text states the means by which, the purpose for which, and the time on which God "appointed/planned" (προέθετο) Jesus to be ἱλαστήριον: namely, through faith, by means of his blood, for the demonstration of his righteousness, because he overlooked previously committed sins, by the forbearance of God, for the demonstration of his righteousness, and in the present age.⁸⁰ However, since I take ἱλαστήριον in 3:25 as a predicate adjective with an implicit "to be" verb and since the prepositional phrases are closer to ἱλαστήριον than to προέθετο, I understand the seven phrases in 3:25–26 as modifying ἱλαστήριον.

The above understanding of the grammar suggests that Paul places the accent on the function of Jesus' death in God's soteriological plan for sinners instead of placing the accent solely on God's action. To clarify, Paul is emphasizing what God has done in history to demonstrate his saving righteousness and to deal with the problem of universal sin apart from the law (3:21–24). In fact, God's action to appoint Jesus as the bloody ἱλαστήριον in 3:25 and God's action to justify Jews and Gentiles in 3:30 surround

76. Ibid.
77. Ibid.
78. Ibid.
79. Ibid., 656–76.
80. For "he planned" as the meaning of προέθετο, see Keener, *Romans*, 59.

ἱλαστήριον and its modifiers. Still, my point is that Paul in 3:25–26 especially emphasizes what God has done *in* and *through* Christ at a particular time in history for the particular purpose of providing the final solution to sin and to his wrath due to law's exacerbation of the humanity's plight. As a result, Paul places the accent in 3:25–26 on God's action to manifest his saving righteousness to all (Jews and Gentiles) *in* and *through* Christ's bloody, martyrological, and substitutionary death for them to emphasize that Jesus functions as the Yom Kippur for all non-Torah-observant Jewish and Gentile sinners who have faith in Christ (e.g., 1:18—3:26)!

N. T. Wright acknowledged in his Romans commentary that Paul presents Jesus both as an atoning sacrifice and as Israel's Day of Atonement in place of Yom Kippur in 3:25. In addition, Wright affirmed that Paul interprets Jesus' death along the lines of the Jewish martyrs in 2 and 4 Maccabees.[81] However, Wright forcefully argued that these two backgrounds (Yom Kippur and Jewish martyrological) cannot entirely explain Paul's sequence of thought in 3:25.[82] Instead, interpreters should look to the traditions of Dan 11:35, 12:1–12, and Isaiah 40–55 as the background in front of which to read ἱλαστήριον in Rom 3:25.[83] He argued that just as Isaiah 40–55 offers a robust exposition of God's righteousness by describing in sacrificial terms a suffering figure who would represent and fulfill YHWH's promise that Israel would be a light to the nations, Paul presents Jesus the same way.[84]

Wright correctly recognized that the multifarious imagery in Rom 3:21–26 (e.g., Levitical cultic, Isaianic, and Jewish martyrological) does not mean that Paul's fundamental background behind 3:25 was OT cultic, Yom Kippur, or Isaianic apart from the Jewish martyrological narratives. First, unlike OT cultic sacrifices, Jesus and the martyrs were Torah-observant Jews who died for the soteriological benefit of non-Torah-observant sinners. Second, unlike the mercy seat in Leviticus 16, neither the Jewish martyrs nor Jesus was sprinkled with blood to be purified due to the effects of sin within the community, but their innocent, Jewish blood was sprinkled to provide purification/covering/atonement for non-Torah-observant sinners in order to restore the sinners' broken relationship with God and to assuage his wrath. Third, unlike Isaiah 40–55, Paul specifically applies ἱλαστήριον to the vicarious death of a Torah-observant Jew in a similar vein as 4 Macc 17:22.[85] Thus, the parallels between the Jewish martyrological narratives and

---

81. Wright, "Romans," 171–2. Also Dunn, *Romans 1–8*, 170–73, 180–82.
82. Ibid., 475.
83. Ibid.
84. Ibid.
85. For Jewish martyrological parallels in Rom 3:25, see also van Henten, "Jewish

Rom 3:21–26 are too strong to dismiss them as an important background for Paul.

Robert K. Jewett too simplistically dismissed a Jewish martyrological influence on Paul because martyr texts emphasize that the martyrs died for the sins of Israel, whereas Paul highlights that Jesus died for Jews and Gentiles.[86] Instead, Jewett argued that 4 Maccabees 17 presents a precedent for "replacing the Day of Atonement ritual with a martyr's death, making clear that the hymn [of Rom 3:25–26] proclaims Jesus' blood as a new institution of atonement" (brackets mine).[87] Jewett's critique of a Jewish martyrological background assumed that Paul must appropriate the Levitical cultic metaphor to the Jewish martyrological narratives the exact same way as the metaphor functioned in its original social setting. In my view, Paul borrowed the Jewish martyrological reading of Yom Kippur, but he reconstructed it and applied it to Jesus to accentuate Jesus' superior soteriological achievement of his death for Jews and Gentiles in contrast to the martyrs' deaths in 4 Maccabees. Jewett also overlooked the fact that even if Paul relied independently upon his own reading of Leviticus 16 apart from any antecedent or contemporary interpretative traditions, the same problem remains for his (Jewett's) reading of Rom 3:25: namely, Israel celebrated Yom Kippur by performing the sacrificial ritual and the scapegoat ritual to deal with Israel's sins instead of the sins of Jews and Gentiles via the death of humans. If Paul's presentation of Jesus' death in Rom 3:25 is the result of his independent reading of Leviticus 16, he would still be using a text (i.e., Leviticus 16) in his social setting to explain the death of Jesus for others in a different way from how the text functioned in its original social setting.

In my view, Paul uses the Jewish martyrological narratives to articulate that God appointed Jesus to be the ἱλαστήριον for Jews and Gentiles who receive him through faith, to be a ἱλαστήριον by means of blood, to be a ἱλαστήριον for the purpose of demonstrating God's righteousness, to be a ἱλαστήριον because of the passing over of previously committed sins, to be a ἱλαστήριον in God's forbearance, and to be a ἱλαστήριον in the present age (cf. 3:21). The infinitive clause concludes the complex sentence by providing the purpose for which God appointed Jesus to be a bloody ἱλαστήριον: εἰς τὸ εἶναι αὐτὸν δίκαιον καὶ δικαιοῦντα τὸν ἐκ πίστεως Ἰησοῦ. With the preceding understanding of the syntax in mind, I will now discuss the meaning of each prepositional phrase and how each sheds light on a Jewish martyrological

---

Martyrdom and Jesus' Death, 139–68.

86. Jewett, *Romans*, 286–87. Rightly Kraus, *Der Tod Jesus als Heiligtumsweihe*, 41.
87. Jewett, *Romans*, 286–87.

understanding of substitution as the background behind Paul's remarks in 3:25.

The first prepositional phrase in 3:25 is διὰ [τῆς] πίστεως. Scholars debate whether one should translate it as a reference to the faith of a sinner (i.e., "faith in" Christ) or as a reference to the faithfulness of Jesus. A third option is that God appointed Jesus to be a ἱλαστήριον through his (i.e., God's) faithfulness. The first interpretation suggests that God appointed Jesus to be a ἱλαστήριον to be received by faith. The second interpretation suggests that God appointed Jesus to be a ἱλαστήριον through his faithfulness (i.e., through Jesus' faithfulness). The third interpretation suggests that God faithfully appointed Jesus to be a ἱλαστήριον. The context seems to support that διὰ [τῆς] πίστεως refers to the faith of an individual sinner, but the entire argument from Rom 3:1–30 suggests that God's faithfulness to deal universally with the problem of sin should not be discounted as a theme in Romans 3. The following arguments will defend this interpretation. First, I will defend the interpretation that διὰ [τῆς] πίστεως in 3:25 refers to the faith of individual Jewish and Gentile sinners in Jesus, God's appointed ἱλαστήριον for their sin. Second, I will defend the interpretation that the argument of Romans 3 includes the idea of God's faithfulness to deal universally with the problem of sin by his offering of Jesus as the ἱλαστήριον.

First, διὰ [τῆς] πίστεως refers to the faith of the individual sinner in Jesus, God's appointed ἱλαστήριον for their sin. In 3:20—4:25, Paul contrasts works (=doing) with faith (=believing). In 3:20, after a detailed argument against justification by works of law, Paul asserts that God will not justify anyone "by works of law" (ἐξ ἔργων νόμου). In 3:21–22, Paul states that God's righteousness comes to the sinner "through faith in Jesus Christ" (διὰ πίστεως Ἰησοῦ Χριστοῦ). Although many contest the latter translation, the prepositional phrase (εἰς πάντας τοὺς πιστεύοντας, "to all who believe") in 3:22b clarifies the meaning of διὰ πίστεως Ἰησοῦ Χριστοῦ in 3:22a. Many scholars have lamented that the preceding interpretation makes Paul too tautological.[88] His redundancy is here for emphasis. In 3:26–31, Paul refers to the individual's justification by faith apart from works of law with the prepositional phrases τὸν ἐκ πίστεως Ἰησου (3:26), διὰ νόμου πίστεως (3:27), ἐκ πίστεως (3:29), διὰ τῆς πίστεως (3:30–31), and with the infinitive clause δικαιοῦσθαι πίστει (3:28).

In 4:1–25, Paul continues the contrast of believing versus doing. He emphasizes justification by faith in Christ apart from works of law with the Abrahamic example. He introduces the doing versus believing antithesis in

---

88. For a discussion of "faith in" versus "faithfulness of" Christ, see Bird and Sprinkle, *The Faith of Jesus*.

4:1-2 by asking if Abraham found favor with God based on works (Τί οὖν ἐροῦμεν εὑρηκέναι Ἀβραὰμ τὸν προπάτορα ἡμῶν κατὰ σάρκα γὰρ Ἀβραὰμ ἐξ ἔργων ἐδικαιώθη, ἔχει καύχημα, ἀλλ' οὐ πρὸς θεόν). In 4:3, Paul answers the question with a scriptural citation from Gen 15:6 that affirms Abraham's faith (τί γὰρ ἡ γραφὴ λέγει; Ἐπίστευσεν δὲ Ἀβραὰμ τῷ θεῷ καὶ ἐλογίσθη αὐτῷ εἰς δικαιοσύνην). Just as in 3:20-31, Paul interchangeably uses the verb δικαιοω and the noun δικαιοσύνη in 4:2-25 along with the noun πίστις and a participial form of πιστευω to accentuate justification by faith in Christ apart from justification by Torah. Paul asserts that Abraham believed in God (Ἐπίστευσεν δὲ Ἀβραὰμ τῷ θεῷ) and that God counted Abraham's faith as righteousness (4:3).

In 4:5, Paul asserts that God reckons as righteousness the faith (λογίζεται ἡ πίστις αὐτοῦ εἰς δικαιοσύνην) of the one who believes (πιστεύοντι) in the one who justifies the ungodly (ἐπὶ τὸν δικαιοῦντα τὸν ἀσεβῆ). In 4:9-12, Paul asserts that Abraham's faith was reckoned as righteousness before he was circumcised as a sign of the righteousness that would come to Jews and Gentiles who believe. In 4:13-17, Paul asserts that God's promise to Abraham was realized by him by his individual faith apart from works of Torah. In 4:18-19, he asserts that Abraham believed in God and that he was not weak in the faith. In 4:20, Paul states that Abraham did not doubt God's promise with unbelief (οὐ διεκρίθη τῇ ἀπιστίᾳ) but he was strengthened in faith (ἀλλ' ἐνεδυναμώθη τῇ πίστει). Finally, 4:23-24 concludes that the kind of righteousness reckoned to Abraham by faith will be reckoned to those who believe in God who raised Jesus from the dead. Thus, the phrase διὰ [τῆς] πίστεως refers to the individual faith of a Jew and a Gentile.

Second, I will defend the interpretation that the idea of God's faithfulness to deal universally with the problem of sin is also present in Romans 3, although the phrase διὰ [τῆς] πίστεως in Rom 3:25 exclusively refers to the individual faith of Jewish and Gentile sinners in Jesus, God's appointed ἱλαστήριον. The argument of 1:18—3:20 emphasizes God's universal judgment of Jews and Gentiles due to their inability to do what the law says. Within this argument, Paul mentions God's faithfulness (3:2) and truth (3:4) in response to his question whether the unfaithfulness of Jews means that God is being unfaithful when he judges them. By this question, he means: does God's judgment of his covenant people for disobeying Torah mean that God has broken his promises to Jews, his covenant people, since a symbol of his faithfulness to the Jew was the giving of his oracles, codified in Torah (3:1)?

Paul's answer is emphatically no! God's judgment of the Jew for disobeying Torah does not speak against his faithfulness to Israel. To the contrary, God's judgment of Torah-disobedience proves him to be faithful and everyone else (Jew and Gentile) to be a liar (3:4-17). Paul confirms this observation about the faithfulness of God in 3:4 by citing LXX Ps 115:2 (cf. LXX Ps 50:6). The entire Psalm expresses David's remorse for his sin against Uriah and his wife. David confesses in the Psalm that the Lord has forgiven his lawlessness, which he committed in God's presence, in accordance with his great mercy and that the Lord is vindicated by his words of judgment against him. Paul likewise uses this citation with its verb δικαιωθῇς to refer to God being vindicated by his judgment of Jews (ὅπως ἂν δικαιωθῇς ἐν τοῖς λόγοις σου καὶ νικήσεις ἐν τῷ κρίνεσθαί σε) instead of using it to refer to the sinner's justification by God, which is how Paul most often uses this verb in Romans (2:13; 3:20; 5:1, 9). But Paul interjects LXX Ps 115:2 (cf. LXX Ps 50:6) in the argument to prove the veracity of God's faithfulness even in the judgment of the Jew for Torah-disobedience.

Paul's response to his question of God's faithfulness in 3:1-4 fits with what Torah actually says to those under its jurisdiction: namely, obedience results in life and disobedience results in death (2:12-16; 3:20; 10:4-5). Paul definitively answers in 3:25-26 the question regarding God's faithfulness and truth in 3:1-4 by stating the action that God took both for Jews and Gentiles to deal with the sins that he previously passed over. Thus, in Paul's view, God ultimately displays his faithfulness to his covenant people and to Gentiles by offering Jesus to be the universal ἱλαστήριον as the climactic act of God in his soteriological drama. The preceding suggests that the similarities with 3:20-31 in the argument of 4:1-25 are a continuation of the same argument from 3:21-26: namely, faith in Christ versus works of Torah as the means of justification for Jews and Gentiles. Additionally, these similarities and the interchange between faith and believing versus works of law in 3:20-21 strongly suggest that διὰ [τῆς] πίστεως in 3:25 refers to the individual Jewish and Gentile sinner's response in faith to Jesus as God's ἱλαστήριον. But the faithfulness of God provides a background behind the entire argument of 1:18—11:36, even if not evident in the phrase διὰ [τῆς] πίστεως (cf. Rom 3:3-6).

The addition of the phrase ἐν τῷ αὐτοῦ αἵματι makes διὰ [τῆς] πίστεως different from any other occurrence of διὰ [τῆς] πίστεως in the NT. The latter phrase in 3:25 joins with ἐν τῷ αὐτοῦ αἵματι as a modifier of ἱλαστήριον in order to state that God's saving righteousness comes to Jews and Gentiles in the present age apart from Torah through Jesus, God's appointed ἱλαστήριον. Faith is the only means by which Jesus' blood functions as Yom Kippur for Jews and Gentiles and deals with the universal problem of sin for them. The martyrological component of the verse is evident in that Jesus, a Torah-observant Jew, functioned as the ἱλαστήριον for the benefit of non-Torah-observant sinners (cf. 2 Macc 7:32-38; 4 Macc 6:28-29; 17:21-22).

The substitutionary element of the verse is evident in that Jesus functioned as the ἱλαστήριον for sinners and extends God's saving righteousness to Jews and Gentiles who have faith in him (and thereby in God's provision) as the ἱλαστήριον. The Jewish martyrological narratives are the only explicit texts in Second Temple Judaism where a Torah-observant Jew died for the soteriological benefit of non-Torah-observant sinners.

The third prepositional phrase in 3:25 (εἰς ἔνδειξιν τῆς δικαιοσύνης αὐτοῦ) and the sixth prepositional phrase in 3:26 (πρὸς τὴν ἔνδειξιν τῆς δικαιοσύνης αὐτοῦ) state one of the two purposes in 3:25–26 for which God appointed Jesus as the ἱλαστήριον to be universally received by faith ("for the demonstration of his righteousness "). The seventh prepositional phrase states the time when God appointed Jesus as the ἱλαστήριον ("in the present time)." That the phrases εἰς ἔνδειξιν τῆς δικαιοσύνης αὐτοῦ and πρὸς τὴν ἔνδειξιν τῆς δικαιοσύνης αὐτοῦ communicate purpose is confirmed by the uses of these prepositions in NT Greek and by the infinitive of purpose in 3:26 (εἰς τὸ εἶναι αὐτὸν δίκαιον καὶ δικαιοῦντα τὸν ἐκ πίστεως Ἰησοῦ).[89] The noun ἔνδειξιν is uniquely Pauline in the NT.[90] It means "proof/demonstration/sign." The only other occurrence of the term in the NT is in 2 Cor 8:24.[91] There it refers to the "demonstration/proof/sign" of the Corinthians' love for the churches being made manifest through their financial ministry to the churches. Both occurrences of ἔνδειξιν in Rom 3:25–26 take τῆς δικαιοσύνης αὐτοῦ as their genitival modifiers. Thus, God's appointment of Jesus as the ἱλαστήριον reveals that God's saving righteousness manifested to Jews and Gentiles by faith apart from the law was a "demonstration/proof/sign" of "his righteousness."

The phrase τῆς δικαιοσύνης αὐτοῦ in 3:25 and in 3:26 is an elaboration of God's righteousness mentioned earlier in 1:17, 3:5, 3:21–22, and later in 10:3–6. As I argued earlier, δικαιοσύνη θεοῦ in 3:21–22 refers to God's saving righteousness (cf. 1:16–17). The phrase is another way of talking about the verdict of justification (a specific element of God's saving righteousness). Although the phrase τῆς δικαιοσύνης αὐτοῦ in 3:25–26 continues Paul's discussion of his saving righteousness in 3:21–24, it reveals the negative aspect of God's salvation of Jews and Gentiles: namely, judgment. In other words, God's appointment of Jesus as the ἱλαστήριον manifests both his righteous judgment against Jewish and Gentile sinners and his faithfulness to deal with the sins of Jewish and Gentile sinners previously committed during

89. For a few examples of εἰς as purpose in Romans, see 1:5, 16; 3:7. For an example of πρός as purpose in Romans, see 15:2.

90. The only other occurrence of the word in the NT is in 2 Cor 8:24.

91. Its verbal cognate form appears in LXX Jos 7:15; Exod 9:16; Dan 3:44; Ep Jer 1:25; 2 Macc 9:8; Wis 12:17, and in the NT in 2 Cor 8:24 to mean "to demonstrate."

the age of Torah. In order to accomplish these things, God appointed Jesus as the ἱλαστήριον for Jews and Gentiles. When God appointed Jesus as the ἱλαστήριον for Jews and Gentiles, he judged sin in the present age, vindicated his character, and proved himself to be faithful and just (e.g., 3:3–6). The latter point Paul's interlocutor could have challenged since Paul has forcefully argued in 1:18—3:20 that God reveals his righteousness apart from Torah and since he asserts that God overlooked previously committed sins (3:20–22, 25–26).

The only occurrence of the noun πάρεσιν in the NT is in Rom 3:25. By my count, the term occurs twice in Josephus and three times in Philo (Jos. *Ant.* 9:240; 11:236; Philo *Pep.*1:143, 45; *Pot.* 1:168). Although Josephus associates the term with salvation from physical harm in a context that speaks of God's judgment through military warfare (*Ant.* 9:240),[92] Paul is the only author (to my knowledge) who associates the term with both salvation from God's wrath and with the concepts of sin, blood, and ἱλαστήριον. Because of the close connection to the argument against Torah as a means of justification, because of the genitival modifiers προγεγονότων ἁμαρτημάτων, and because of the reference to God's patience in 3:26, the entire phrase should be translated as "because of [God's] overlooking of previously committed sins." But what were these previously committed sins?

The entire argument from 1:18—3:20 to 5:1—11:36 supports the proposal that these previously committed sins refer to sins committed during the age of Torah. For example, Paul asserts his thesis in 1:16–17, which is the gospel is the power of God for salvation for believing Jews and believing Gentiles (1:16), because God's saving righteousness is revealed by means of the gospel (1:17). He defends this thesis throughout 1:18—15:13, and he specifically discusses the new Jewish and Gentile reality within the people of God in 12:1—15:13 as a result of the gospel of God's saving righteousness, the center of which is Jesus Christ, apart from Torah. In 1:18—3:26, he argues that Torah will not exonerate a Jew or a Gentile in God's law court because exoneration comes by faith in Jesus Christ, God's appointed ἱλαστήριον, whom he appointed/planned to be the means by which he would universally manifest his saving righteousness to Jews and Gentiles by faith in Jesus and to satisfy his wrath in the death of Jesus. In 3:21–22 and in 3:26, he contends that God's act of universally dealing with the sin problem in Jesus Christ has introduced a new age, which he identifies as Νυνὶ δὲ ("but now!") in 3:21 and as ἐν τῷ νῦν καιρῷ ("in the present time") in 3:26. In 3:26, Paul states that God's demonstration of his righteousness in the precise way

---

92. σῴζειν γὰρ αὐτῶν ἐθελήσουσι τὰς ψυχὰς μᾶλλον ἢ τὰ κτήματα δεινὴ γὰρ αὐτοὺς ἐν ἀλλήλοις ἔρις ἕξει καὶ θρῆνος πάρεσίς τε τῶν μελῶν αἵ τε ὄψεις ὑπὸ τοῦ φόβου μέλαιναι τελέως αὐτοῖς γενήσονται.

described in 3:25–26 proves that he is both a righteous God and that he justifies sinners by faith in Jesus. Romans 3:27–31 states that God's act of justifying Jewish and Gentile sinners in the definitive act of appointing Jesus as a ἱλαστήριον also shows that God is the one God of Jewish and Gentile sinners apart from Torah.[93] Thus, the entire argument of 3:21–26 uses the Jewish martyrological narratives to emphasize Jesus' death as a substitute for Jewish and Gentile sinners.

Additional parallels between the Jewish martyrological narratives and 3:21–26 support the idea that the former is a background in front of which to read his substitutionary presentation of Jesus' death in 3:21–26.[94] Paul states that Jesus (a Torah-observant Jew) died for sinners in a soteriological narrative (3:20–24). Likewise, 2 and 4 Maccabees present Torah-observant Jews who died for the sins of non-Torah-observant sinners in a soteriological narrative (2 Macc 7:32–38; 4 Macc 6:28–29; 17:21–22). The noun δικαιοσύνη refers to God's judgment and justice in Rom 3:25b–26, just as the noun δίκη refers to judgment (e.g., 4 Macc 4:13, 21; 6:28–29; 8:14, 22; 9:9, 15, 32; 11:3; 12:12; 18:22) and the noun δικαιοσύνη refers to justice in 4 Maccabees (4 Macc 1:4, 6, 18; 2:6; 5:24).[95] Participial forms of πιστεύω occur in 2 Macc 3:12 (τοὺς πεπιστευκότας), 2 Macc 3:22 (τὰ πεπιστευμένα τοῖς πεπιστευκόσιν), in 4 Macc 4:7 (οἱ πιστεύσαντες), and in 4 Macc 7:19 (πιστεύοντες), and a participial form of πιστεύω occurs in Rom 3:22 (τοὺς πιστεύοντας). 2 Maccabees 2:8 and 4 Macc 1:2 refer to God's glory, and Rom 3:23 refers to God's glory. 2 and 4 Maccabees metaphorically refer to a human's death with a reference to blood (2 Macc 1:8; 8:3; 12:16; 14:18, 45; 4 Macc 6:6; 7:8; 9:20; 10:8; 13:20), and Rom 3:25 metaphorically refers to Jesus' death with a reference to his blood.

ISAIAH 53, JEWISH MARTYROLOGY, AND SUBSTITUTION IN ROMANS 4:24–25

A Jewish martyrological background behind Paul's presentation of Jesus' death as a substitution in Romans is present in Rom 4:24–25. The primary argument that I develop to support this claim is that Paul appropriates a Jewish martyrological reading of Isaiah 53 to the death of Jesus for sinners to achieve for them the soteriological benefit of justification. The argument

---

93. For a recent analysis of Rom 3:27–31, see Bruno, *God is One*.

94. All of the material in this paragraph comes from Jarvis Williams, "Martyr Theology in Hellenistic Judaism and Paul's Conception of Jesus' Death in Romans 3:21–26," 512–20.

95. See also 2 Macc 8:11, 13.

integrates the analysis of Isaiah 53 in chapter 2 of this monograph and the analysis of the Jewish martyrological narratives in chapter 3.

Handed Over for Our Transgressions and Raised for Our Justification

A Jewish martyrological background behind Paul's presentation of Jesus' death and substitution are present in Rom 4:24–25. This background is apparent in the following ways. First, as he concludes a detailed argument about justification by faith in Christ apart from works of law in 3:21—4:25, Paul frames his statement about Jesus' death in 4:25 with two references to the resurrection of Jesus in 4:24 and in 4:25. In 4:24, Paul states that the event of God reckoning Abraham as righteous was written down for all who believe in the one who raised Jesus, our Lord, from the dead (ἀλλὰ καὶ δι' ἡμᾶς, οἷς μέλλει λογίζεσθαι, τοῖς πιστεύουσιν ἐπὶ τὸν ἐγείραντα Ἰησοῦν τὸν κύριον ἡμῶν ἐκ νεκρῶν). In 4:25b, he asserts that Jesus was raised "for our justification" (ἠγέρθη διὰ τὴν δικαίωσιν ἡμῶν). In 4:24, between the two statements about Jesus' resurrection, Paul inserts a reference to Jesus' death for the transgressions of others (ὃς παρεδόθη διὰ τὰ παραπτώματα ἡμῶν), which resembles LXX Isa 53:12.

In an essay on the Septuagint version of Isaiah 53, Cilliers Breytenbach has argued that the Greek version of Isaiah 53 radically departs from the Hebrew version due to the influence of Greek culture on the translators. Indeed, he says that early Christian reception and appropriation of LXX Isa 53:12 to the death of Jesus was not due to an independent Israelite or Jewish tradition, because of the fluidity of the "dying for" formula rampant throughout Greco-Roman secular literature (e.g., Dio Cassius 63 [64]. 13.1–3).[96] In response to Breytenbach's detailed and helpful analysis, I contend that once Jews or Jewish Christians applied Jewish cultic categories to a Greco-Roman "dying for" formula and then appropriated the formula to the death of Torah-observant Jews, the formula becomes explicitly Jewish, in the case of the Jewish martyrs in 2 and 4 Maccabees, and explicitly Jewish-Christian, in the case of Jesus in Romans. In addition, Breytenbach's essay did not acknowledge that the combination of the death of a Torah-observant Jew for the soteriological benefit of non-Torah-observant sinners alongside of the category of resurrection is an explicit *Jewish* martyrological concept, since the martyrs' deaths for non-Torah-observant sinners and the resurrection of the martyr-servants occur in 2 and 4 Maccabees, although

---

96. Breytenbach, *Grace, Reconciliation, Concord*, 83–94.

the resurrection of the Suffering Servant is altogether absent from LXX Isaiah 53, but occurs in MT Isaiah 53.

For example, both 2 and 4 Maccabees either explicitly mention or indirectly allude to the resurrection of those Torah-observant Jews martyred for the salvation of non-Torah-observant sinners.[97] These books record the manifestation of God's wrath against Judea through the fierce persecution of Antiochus Epiphanes IV on account of Torah-disobedience of some within Israel. Ironically, the narrators of both works suggest that Antiochus persecuted the Jews in part because of their refusal to assimilate to his Hellenistic regime and that God judged Israel through Antiochus because of Jewish assimilation.

The second argument in favor of a Jewish martyrological background behind Rom 4:24–25 and in favor of substitution in 4:24–25 is the presence of the Suffering Servant language both in the Jewish martyrological narratives and in 4:24–25. Paul appropriates language from LXX Isaiah 53 to the death of Jesus (a Torah-observant Jew) for the soteriological benefit of Jewish and Gentile transgressors, just as the Jewish martyrological narratives appropriate language from LXX Isaiah 53 to the deaths of Torah-observant Jews for Jewish transgressors. Many scholars suggest that Rom 4:25 is part of a confessional formula created with reference to LXX Isa 52:13—53:12 and that Paul reconstructs the formula for his purposes.[98] The following citations from LXX Isa 53:12 and from Rom 4:25 highlight the similarities:

διὰ τὰς ἁμαρτίας αὐτῶν παρεδόθη (LXX Isa 53:12)[99]

ὃς παρεδόθη διὰ τὰ παραπτώματα ἡμῶν (Rom 4:25)

Both traditions contain διὰ plus a noun for sin. Both traditions have the verb παρεδόθη, and both traditions state that someone died for the offenses of others. However, too often, scholars assume without any substantiation that Paul independently applies LXX Isa 53:12 to Jesus without being influenced by any antecedent Second Temple Jewish receptions of Isaiah's Suffering Servant.[100] To the contrary, Nihls Dahl argued in a very stimulating essay that the *Aqedah* Tradition (i.e., the binding of Isaac) forms

---

97. For a more detailed history, see chapter 2.

98. For a recent example, see Hultgren, *Paul's Letter to the Romans*, 191–92.

99. LXX Isa 53:6 (κύριος παρέδωκεν αὐτὸν ταῖς ἁμαρτίαις ἡμῶν) communicates the same point with a different grammatical sentence.

100. See major Greek text commentaries on Rom 4:25 to see this very point. For Jewish-Christian reception of Isaiah 53, see Janowski and Stuhlmacher (eds.), *The Suffering Servant*.

the backdrop of the dying for formula in the NT.[101] Although Dahl specifically focused on Rom 8:32a, his premise regarding the origins of the NT authors' "dying for" formula is relevant here. He argued that instead of a Jewish martyrological background that functioned as the atoning cult in the place of the Hebrew cult, God's offering of his Son corresponds to Abraham's offering of his son.[102] The offering of both results in a reward for others.[103] Of course, the obvious problem with Dahl's thesis is that the correspondence between Abraham, Isaac, and Jesus breaks down since Jesus actually died and Isaac did not and since God appointed Jesus to die for non-Torah-observant Jewish and Gentile sinners, whereas God commanded Abraham to offer Isaac to prove his faithfulness to him (cf. Gen 15:6; 22:1–24).

In my view, Paul re-contextualized a Second Temple Jewish martyrological reading of LXX Isa 53:12 for his soteriological purpose of presenting Jesus as a substitute for Jewish and Gentile transgressors to achieve the justification of both groups. This interpretation is supported by Paul's insertion of Jesus' resurrection as the basis underneath the justification of transgressors in 4:25b. Paul states that Jesus was "handed over for our transgressions" (ὃς παρεδόθη διὰ τὰ παραπτώματα ἡμῶν) (Rom 4:25a) and that "he was raised for our justification" (καὶ ἠγέρθη διὰ τὴν δικαίωσιν ἡμῶν) (Rom 4:25b).[104] A hint at the resurrection of the Servant is present in MT Isa 53:10 with the words "his soul will see his seed, and he will cause days to be long," but the resurrection of the Suffering Servant is altogether absent from LXX Isa 53:10. The pronoun "your" in the phrase "your life" in LXX Isa 53:10 is a plural word (ἡ ψυχὴ ὑμῶν). Thus, LXX Isa 53:10 should be read to mean that Israel's seed will resurrect themselves (ἡ ψυχὴ ὑμῶν ὄψεται σπέρμα μακρόβιον). I readily admit, however, that Paul's formulation in Rom 4:24–25 could be the result of his own independent reading of MT

---

101. Dahl, "The Atonement—An Adequate Reward for the Aqedah," 146–66, 184–89.

102. Ibid.

103. Ibid.

104. In his essay on the "for us" phrases in Paul's soteriology, Breytenbach seemed to argue that Jesus' death benefits those for whom he died without functioning as a substitute and as a functional sinner. But in Rom 4:25 (and in Rom 5:6–11), Paul associates the death of Christ for sins with the soteriological benefits received by sinners for whom Jesus died. The concept of a death of a righteous human for sinners for the latter's soteriological benefit is by definition a substitutionary death, because the substitute received the penalty of a condemned sinner that he did not deserve on behalf of the transgressors, and the transgressors received the soteriological benefit of the righteous, which they did not deserve, as a result of the righteous substitute's personal sacrifice. See Breytenbach, *Grace, Reconciliation, Concord*, 76–79.

Isaiah 53. Even still, Paul's independent reading resembles a Jewish martyrological reading of Isaiah 53.

2 Maccabees 7:32–33, on the other hand, appropriates Isaiah 53's Suffering Servant language to the Jewish martyrs to emphasize that the martyrs' function in the narrative as the faithful Torah-observant servants who die for the sins of the people to reconcile God to them (ἡμεῖς γὰρ διὰ τὰς ἑαυτῶν ἁμαρτίας πάσχομεν εἰ δὲ χάριν ἐπιπλήξεως καὶ παιδείας ὁ ζῶν κύριος ἡμῶν βραχέως ἐπώργισται καὶ πάλιν καταλλαγήσεται τοῖς ἑαυτοῦ δούλοις), and their deaths guarantee that God will resurrect them from the dead because of their substitutionary deaths for non-Torah-observant Jews (ἐν σὺ μέν ἀλάστωρ ἐκ τοῦ παρόντος ἡμᾶς ζῆν ἀπολύεις ὁ δὲ τοῦ κόσμου βασιλεὺς ἀποθανόντας ἡμᾶς ὑπὲρ τῶν αὐτοῦ νόμων εἰς αἰώνιον ἀναβίωσιν ζωῆς ἡμᾶς ἀναστήσει) (2 Macc 7:9). To my knowledge, this reading of LXX Isa 53:12 is only found in the Jewish martyrological narratives and in Rom 4:25.

Paul applies LXX Isa 53:12 to Jesus, which is further supported by Paul's reference to justification in 4:25.[105] Paul's reading of LXX Isa 53:12 is a Jewish martyrological reading. He appropriates this martyrological reading of LXX Isa 53:12 to the death of Jesus to emphasize that his death was a substitute for non-Torah-observant Jewish and Gentile transgressors. A Jewish martyrological background is evident both by the similar appropriations of Isaiah 53 to Torah-observant Jews who died for the benefit of non-Torah-observant transgressors and by the explicit reference to the resurrection of the one who suffered for the soteriological benefits of others. According to the martyrological narratives, the martyrs' deaths and resurrection brought reconciliation (2 Macc 7:32–38), purification (4 Macc 6:28–29; 17:21–22), and salvation to Israel (4 Macc 17:21–22). According to Paul, Jesus' death and resurrection for Jewish and Gentile transgressors brought justification to Jews and Gentiles who believe in the God who raised Jesus, "our Lord," from the dead (Rom 4:24–25).

CONCLUSION

Jesus' substitutionary death for sinners as a Torah-observant Jew who died for the soteriological benefit of non-Torah-observant Jews and Gentiles, his function as their Yom Kippur, and the efficacy of his death and resurrection link Paul's remarks with the Jewish martyrological narratives. Paul uses similar Levitical cultic language, imagery from Yom Kippur, lexical similarities, and conceptual similarities, along with a Jewish martyrological reading of Isaiah 53 in his presentation of the death of Jesus, a Torah-observant Jew,

---

105. Cf. LXX Isa 53:12 with Rom 4:25.

for the soteriological benefit of non-Torah-observant Jewish and Gentile sinners in Rom 3:21—4:25. These similarities between the Jewish martyrological narratives and Paul support the thesis that the Jewish martyrological narratives are a background in front of which interpreters should understand Paul's presentation of Jesus' death as a substitute in Rom 3:21—4:25.

5

Jewish Martyrology and Substitution in Romans 5:6–11, 8:1–4, and 8:31–34

INTRODUCTION

This chapter discusses Jewish martyrology and substitution in Rom 5:6–11, 8:1–4, and 8:31–34. My thesis is that the Jewish martyrological narratives are a background behind Paul's presentation of Jesus' death as a substitution in Rom 5:6–11, in 8:1–4, and 8:31–34. I support this thesis by an exegetical, conceptual, and comparative analysis of these texts.

JEWISH MARTYROLOGY AND SUBSTITUTION IN ROMANS 5:6–11

In Rom 5:6–11, Paul supports his preceding argument in 5:1–5 that Christians have hope in suffering. He introduces a reason for hope in 5:5: "because God's love has been poured out in our hearts through the Holy Spirit who was given to us." In 5:6–11, Paul provides an additional reason for hope: Jesus died for sinners. In the argument of 5:6–11, Paul states that Jesus' substitutionary death for sinners guarantees future salvation. Paul presents Jesus' death as a substitute for the soteriological benefits of the unrighteous for whom he died with the Jewish martyrological concept of the death of a Torah-observant Jew for the soteriological benefit of non-Torah-observant sinners.

Jesus' Death for the Ungodly and Its Soteriological Benefits

In the argument of 5:6–11, Paul introduces the death of Jesus in 5:6 with the words "Christ still died at the right time for the ungodly while we were still weak" (Ἔτι γὰρ Χριστὸς ὄντων ἡμῶν ἀσθενῶν ἔτι κατὰ καιρὸν ὑπὲρ ἀσεβῶν ἀπέθανεν). Paul identifies the weak and the ungodly from 5:6 as sinners in 5:8 by using the adjective ἁμαρτωλῶν and by repeating the verb ἀπέθανεν from 5:6 in order to specify that Jesus died for sinners. He emphasizes the uniqueness of Jesus' death for the ungodly with a tautological use of the adverb ἔτι, the first of which modifies the participle ὄντων and the second modifies ἀπέθανεν.[1] Jesus' death for the ungodly happened while they were still in a state of ungodliness, but he, nevertheless, still died for the ungodly in God's appointed time.[2]

In a collection of essays published in 1989, Otfried Hofius discussed atonement and reconciliation.[3] In an essay titled *Sühne und Versöhnung: Zum paulinischen Verständis des Kreuzestodes Jesus*, Hofius discussed Rom 5:8–10 and 2 Cor 5:18–20. He took Rom 5:8–10 as his starting point for his discussion of the death of Jesus. He began by acknowledging that Paul describes in Rom 5:8 Jesus' death as an apparent proof of God's love. After he noted that Rom 5:9 speaks of atonement and 5:10 speaks of reconciliation, Hofius asked: in what sense is the apostle Paul speaking of atonement and reconciliation? With this question, Hofius meant: according to Paul, what kind of death did Jesus die?

In Hofius' view, the death of Jesus should be understood in the following four ways in Rom 5:8–10 and in 2 Cor 5:18–21. First, the OT sin-cult was a participatory (*Mitbeteiligung*) atonement-action.[4] The man, who offered atonement, identified himself with the offering by placing his hands on it, and the priest would execute this act as God's representative of the blood-ritual.[5] In the occurrences of atonement by means of Jesus' crucifixion, God alone is the doer of atonement (*Im Sühnegeschenen des Kreuzestodes Jesu ist Got allein der Handelnde*).[6] God himself takes the initiative and gives his own Son in death, and he identifies with sinful humanity with the crucifixion and the resurrection of Christ.[7] Needy mankind receives atone-

---

1. Against Powers, *Salvation through Participation*, 93.

2. For "at the right time" as a reference to God's appointed time, rightly Hultgren, *Paul's Letter to the Romans*, 209.

3. Otfried Hofius, *Paulusstudien*, 25–49.

4. Ibid, 48.

5. Ibid.

6. Ibid.

7. Ibid.

ment and reconciliation in a completely passive way from God through the representative or inclusive-place taking (*stellvertretenden*), atoning death of Jesus. This is why Paul asserts in 2 Cor 5:18 that τὰ δὲ πάντα ἐκ τοῦ θεοῦ.[8] Second, the OT atonement cult has a certain inner logic to it.[9] Israel relies upon the repetition of the sacrificial cult.[10] The atoning offering of Jesus, however, happens once and for all.[11] His death actualizes an eternal, valid, atonement and reconciliation. In the word of the cross, the message of reconciliation is proclaimed (1 Cor 1:18; 2 Cor 5:19).[12] Third, Jesus is the sin-offering for all sins unlike the OT sin-offering.[13] In the crucifixion of Jesus Christ, God has acted to grant atonement and reconciliation for sinful men.[14] Fourth, The OT sin-offering was only for Israel and not for the heathens.[15] Jesus' representative and crucifying death is a universal action of atonement for Jews and heathens.[16]

Hofius' analysis astutely pointed out the continuity and the discontinuity between the death of Jesus and the OT cult. But his analysis dismissed the substitutionary nature of Jesus' death and the Jewish martyrological background behind Jesus' death in Rom 5:8–10. The following arguments respond to Hofius' understanding of the death of Jesus in Rom 5:8–10.

First, as I argued in chapter 2, cultic action in the Hebrew cult was both participatory and substitutionary as the priests and animals represented the people and as the animals were slain on behalf of the sins of the people. In the case of the Yom Kippur ritual, both the sacrificial ritual and the scapegoat ritual functioned together to emphasize both representation and substitution (Leviticus 16) as the priests sacrificed the animals for all of the sins of their house, the people, and the community and for all of sins' effects upon the community, whose sins the scapegoat symbolically carried away into the wilderness (Lev 16:1–34). Second, third, and fourth, Paul's presentation of Jesus' death in Rom 5:8–10 has both continuity and discontinuity with the Hebrew cult. It provided atonement for Israel by means of animal sacrifices, whereas Paul states that Jesus provided atonement for Jews and Gentiles by means of his own blood.

8. Ibid.
9. Ibid., 48.
10. Ibid., 49
11. Ibid.
12. Ibid.
13. Ibid.
14. Ibid.
15. Ibid.
16. Ibid.

Citing Daniel G. Powers' work as the authoritative source on the issue,[17] Robert K. Jewett asserted that "the widely used formula of Christ dying on behalf of others should be understood in terms of representation and not in terms of substitution."[18] Jewett argued that Paul's citation is a well-established formula integrated into his larger argument that Jesus' death on behalf of sinners demonstrates God's love, and his death overcomes their disgraceful status as enemies by providing the basis "for a revolutionary new form of boasting."[19] Since the formula was widely used throughout early Christianity and was similar to the words of institution at the love feasts in the house tenement churches, the expression of Christ dying "on our behalf" communicates "a sense of participationism and solidarity that Paul wishes to be felt to include everyone in the various branches of the community, and even Paul himself."[20] Jewett's analysis of 5:8 completely ignored the fact that Paul states in 5:6–11 that Jesus, a Torah-observant Jew, died for the benefit of non-Torah-observant sinners to accomplish their soteriological benefits. In response to Jewett, Paul's repetition of the "Christ died for" formula (Χριστὸς ἀπέθανεν ὑπὲρ) in Rom 5:8 does not by itself support substitution.[21] However, because Paul states that Christ, a Torah-observant-Jew (i.e., a righteous one [5:6–8]), died for ungodly sinners to accomplish their soteriological benefits and because he states that his death for these sinners actually achieves for them the soteriological benefits of justification (5:9), deliverance/salvation from God's future wrath (5:9), and reconciliation with God (5:1, 10–11), the "Christ died for" formula should be read as a substitutionary formula instead of only as a representative statement in 5:8.[22]

17. Powers, *Salvation through Participation*, 233.
18. Jewett, *Romans*, 362.
19. Ibid., 362.
20. Ibid.
21. For a list of texts that contain a death formula in Paul's letters, see Hultgren, *Romans*, 209.
22. Although Morna Hooker's work has focused primarily on 2 Cor 5:20 and Pauline texts other than Rom 5:8–10, she argued in a similar vein as Hofius. In a 1994 book on interpretations of Jesus' death, she argued against substitution in favor of representation. Commenting on 1 Thess 5:9–10, she contended that Paul presents Jesus' death as a sharing in the experiences of those for whom he died instead of as dying as a substitute for others. She supported this by suggesting that Jesus' death does not eliminate the possibility of one's physical death and by suggesting that one still dies with Jesus. Hooker argued that Christ gives life to those who participate in his death. "He has been raised from the dead, and we share that resurrection life. It is not, then, a question of Christ and the believer exchanging places; it is rather a sharing of experiences. Christ died, and we live with him." In her discussion on the death of Jesus in Galatians, Hooker clearly stated that Jesus' death was a representation instead of a substitution. According to her, Paul believed that he participated in the death of Jesus when he was

Contrary to Henk S. Versnel's very elaborate defense of the Greco-Roman pagan heroic death as the background behind the NT authors' presentation of Jesus' death,[23] with the Χριστὸς ἀπέθανεν ὑπέρ-formula, Paul does not offer a generic statement about a pagan noble/patriotic/heroic death, of which he speaks in 5:7 when he contrasts the kind of death that Jesus died for the ungodly with a Greco-Roman patriotic death.[24] Rather, with the Χριστὸς ἀπέθανεν ὑπέρ-formula in 5:6 and in 5:8, Paul identifies Christ (the righteous one) as the one who suffered the fate of the weak and ungodly sinners on behalf of the weak and ungodly as a substitute for sinners so that the weak and ungodly sinners would be justified, saved, and reconciled to God through the blood of Christ.

After a detailed analysis of soteriology in Paul, Powers dogmatically claimed that "there is no compelling evidence that Jesus' death was understood as being vicarious in the sense that Jesus died in the place of or instead of sinners,"[25] and he just as dogmatically asserted that Paul fails to explain both how the death of Christ is demonstrative of God's love and how the death of Christ benefits believers.[26] Arguing for participation/representation instead of substitution in 5:6–11, Powers insisted that Paul's understanding of the cross and resurrection in this section as a total event suggests that he emphasizes the believer's participation in the death of Christ, even when he uses a "dying for" formula.[27] Participation is additionally evident, said

---

crucified with Christ (Gal 2:20). In her own words, "he died as our representative, on our behalf." In Hooker's view, Jesus died so that those redeemed from the curse in Gal 3:10–14 would participate in his life giving resurrection. "Christ shared our humanity, our estrangement from God, in order that we might share his sonship, his relationship with God." She argued the same point when she discussed other Pauline texts that have traditionally been interpreted to refer to substitution. See Hooker, *Not Ashamed of the Gospel*, 28–9; Hooker, "Interchange in Christ," 13–25; Hooker, "On Becoming the Righteousness of God," 358–75.

23. Versnel, "Making Sense of Jesus' Death," 213–94.

24. Romans 5:7 is likely a reference to Greco-Roman Heroic death instead of to Jewish martyrology. An entire monograph could be written on this topic alone. Work has already been done in this regard. Although I disagree with his analysis on several points, see Seeley, *The Noble Death*. For an essay that develops as a *tour de force* the Greco-Roman background behind Jesus' death, see Versnel, "Making Sense of Jesus' Death," 215–94. For a recent discussion of the similarities and differences between Rom 5:6–8 and classical texts and for analysis of the classical texts, see Gathercole, *Defending Substitution*.

25. Powers, *Salvation through Participation*, 233–34.

26. Ibid., 97.

27. Ibid., 104–5, esp. 105.

Powers, by Paul's use of the preposition ἐν, which he admitted has an instrumental idea in 5:6–11 (e.g., in 5:9–10 in conjunction with διά).[28]

However, along with Paul's assertion in 5:6, his argument in 5:7–11 begs to differ with those who affirm representation/participation instead of substitution in this section. In my view, although participatory and representative ideas could be present in 5:6–11, especially since 5:12–21 emphasizes Jesus as humanity's representative, my thesis simply acknowledges that substitution is present too in 5:6–11. Paul confirms his affirmation of the substitutionary nature of the death of Jesus in 5:7. Here he denies that the kind of death that Jesus died in 5:6 and in 5:8 (a death for sinners) was commonly practiced in the ancient Greco-Roman and Jewish worlds in which he lived and wrote his letter. In 5:7, he affirms the uniqueness of Jesus' death for the ungodly by declaring the rarity of such a death in Greco-Roman antiquity. He agrees in 5:7 that someone rarely died for a righteous person and that maybe someone would even dare to die for a good person, which is another way of repeating the first proposition from 5:7a.

Romans 5:7 presents a translation problem. The gender of the adjectives δικαίου and τοῦ ἀγαθοῦ is grammatically ambiguous. Christina Eschner has recently argued in an impressive two volume set on the Greco-Roman background behind the death of Jesus that 5:7 does not contrast Jesus' death with the death of the good, rather, his death was for the good. She understood τοῦ ἀγαθοῦ as a neuter reference to an ideal/concept/thing instead of as a reference to a person.[29] She offered numerous examples of the neuter use of ἀγαθοῦ from Romans and classical literature to bolster her case. Powers, however, speciously argued against substitution in part because the two nouns, to which ὑπέρ connects in 5:7, could be neuter.[30]

Regardless of the gender of the nouns, based on context, I understand 5:6 to contrast Jesus' death with an honorific noble death for the noble city-state and/or for a good person.[31] In 5:6, Paul refers to Jesus' death as a death

---

28. Ibid., 105–6.

29. For example, see Eschner, *Gestorben und hingegeben for die Sünder*, 278–79. Gathercole pointed me to Eschner's argument.

30. Powers, *Salvation through Participation*, 107. Another specious element to his argument is that he appealed to 5:12–21 to argue against a substitutionary reading of ὑπέρ in 5:6–7 even though 5:12–21 never even uses the preposition (a point Powers acknowledged but nevertheless ignored in his critique of substitution). As I argue in chapter 6, 5:12–21 emphasizes the representative function of Jesus' death. An affirmation of substitution in Rom 5:6–11 does not require one to deny representation in Romans. But Powers' work (as so many scholars before and after him) sacrificed substitution on the altar of representation. For his full argument against substitution in Rom 5:6–11, see 105–9.

31. For example, as you see in classical literature. See Gathercole, *Defending*

for ungodly and unrighteous sinners. In 5:7, he contrasts Jesus' unique death with other kinds of unique deaths in Greco-Roman antiquity.[32] In 5:7, Paul likely references the Greco-Roman heroic death motif, which contained the death-for-another concept in a non-cultic substitutionary context.[33] Greco-Roman literature in antiquity is latent with examples of heroic or patriotic death.[34] However, unlike the kind of death mentioned in 5:7, Paul states in 5:6 and in 5:8–11 that Jesus (a Torah-observant Jew) died for unrighteous people to achieve their justification, salvation, and reconciliation, which greatly distinguishes his death from the pagan Greco-Roman heroic/patriotic/noble death to which Paul alludes in 5:7.[35] Jesus did not die a mere patriotic death for a noble city-state. Rather, he died for the ungodly sinners (5:6, 8). Those who died noble-deaths in Greco-Roman antiquity died for the good or the noble city-state to preserve or protect the noble city-state from some kind of dishonor, either divine dishonor or human dishonor.[36]

In 5:9–11, Paul mentions the soteriological benefits received by those for whom Jesus died.[37] Each soteriological benefit (justification, salvation, and reconciliation) falls underneath Paul's umbrella of soteriology. Each is closely related, but each represents a specific component of his soteriology. Justification refers to God's verbal exoneration of the sinner in his law court (e.g., 1:18—3:20); salvation refers to deliverance from God's wrath on the Day of Judgment (e.g., 2:5–10), and reconciliation refers to the friendship that exists between God and the sinners as a result of justi-

---

Substitution, for classical texts.

32. See recently Gathercole, *Defending Substitution*.

33. Gathercole suggested that Paul may specifically have in mind Alcestis' substitutionary death for her husband. Gathercole, *Defending Substitution*. Other NT scholars have also acknowledged that Alcestis was part of the common culture of the Greco-Romans world. So Cilliers Breytenbach, "The Septuagint Version of Isaiah 53 and the Early Christian Formula: He Was Delivered for Our Transgressions," 339–51, esp. 341. See additional sources in Gathercole, *Defending Substitution*, n. 190 in chap. 3.

34. For examples in classical Greek literature, see Eur. Iph. taur. 3–24; *Phoeni.* 968–75; *Alc.* 1–36; *Iph. aul.* 1553–556; *Hec.* 38–41, 367–78, 484–582; *Heracl.* 501–50; Pl. *Menex.* 237a, 246b; *Symp.* 179b; Hor. *Carm* 3.19.2. For a Roman example, see Livy, *History of Rome* 8.9.9–10, 13–14; 10.28.18.

35. Against Seeley, *The Noble Death*.

36. Jeffrey Gibson's essay ("Paul's Dying Formula," 20–41) forcefully demonstrated this point! Many thanks to Jeffrey for both making me aware of his essay and emailing me a copy of it in 2010 after a dialogue with him at the national meeting of SBL 2010 about my paper on the Jewish martyrological influence on the death of Jesus in Rom 3:21–26.

37. For an argument that Paul's application of the soteriological benefits to those for whom Jesus died supports that he believed that Jesus died exclusively for the elect, see Jarvis J. Williams, *For Whom Did Christ Die?*.

fication. This friendship is achieved by faith because of Jesus' death for the ungodly, and this friendship between the ungodly and God will serve as a means by which the reconciled friend will be delivered from God's wrath in the judgment (5:9–10). A close relationship between justification and reconciliation in 5:9–10 is evident when Paul states that both justification by Jesus' blood guarantees the sinner's future salvation from wrath (πολλῷ οὖν μᾶλλον δικαιωθέντες νῦν ἐν τῷ αἵματι αὐτοῦ σωθησόμεθα δι' αὐτοῦ ἀπὸ τῆς ὀργῆς) and reconciliation with God by the death of Jesus guarantees the sinner's future salvation by means of Jesus' resurrection (εἰ γὰρ ἐχθροὶ ὄντες κατηλλάγημεν τῷ θεῷ διὰ τοῦ θανάτου τοῦ υἱοῦ αὐτοῦ, πολλῷ μᾶλλον καταλλαγέντες σωθησόμεθα ἐν τῇ ζωῇ αὐτοῦ). The parallel clauses πολλῷ οὖν μᾶλλον δικαιωθέντες ... σωθησόμεθα ... in 5:9 and πολλῷ μᾶλλον καταλλαγέντες σωθησόμεθα in 5:10 strongly suggest that justification and reconciliation at least in 5:9–10 are two different metaphors (judicial and relational) to communicate the same soteriological reality of future deliverance from God's wrath, a deliverance accomplished by means of the death and resurrection of Christ (cf. 4:25).[38]

In 5:9, Paul refers to justification, which means to declare to be in the right. Paul states that justification comes to the sinner by means of Jesus' blood (δικαιωθέντες νῦν ἐν τῷ αἵματι αὐτοῦ). Justification is primarily a future verdict in Romans that has invaded this present evil age (e.g., 2:13; 3:20, 24; 5:1, 9). In 5:9, Paul continues his thoughts in 5:1 about the present reality of justification for those who have faith in Christ, and he uses the verb for future salvation (σωθησόμεθα) to state that justification by Jesus' blood results in future deliverance from God's wrath. Salvation, like justification, is primarily a future hope that has invaded this present evil age in Romans (e.g., 5:9–10). Although justification is a soteriological category, Paul's reference to salvation with the verb σωθησόμεθα means deliverance, which the phrase "from wrath" supports in 5:9. The phrase δι' αὐτοῦ in 5:9 asserts that sinners will be delivered from God's wrath through Jesus who shed his blood to this end. The antecedent of αὐτοῦ is likely Christ in 5:8, but the dead Christ, attested to by αἵματι, who lives, is the one through whom God accomplishes soteriological benefits for the ungodly and weak sinners (cf. 5:6, 8, 9–11). The wrath from which Jesus' death and resurrection will deliver/save those for whom he died is God's eschatological wrath

---

38. Corneliu Constantineanu (*The Social Significance of Reconciliation in Paul's Theology*, 120) pointed out the parallelism to me. Stanley E. Porter (καταλλασσω in *Ancient Greek Literature*, 156) pointed him in this direction. However, Constantineanu criticizes Porter for limiting justification and reconciliation to vertical realities. Against Constantineanu, Paul emphasizes the vertical reality in Rom 5:9–10 and says nothing about the horizontal reality of justification and reconciliation until 12:1—15:21.

since 1:18—3:20 has focused on God's condemnation of Jews and Gentiles for their disobedience to the law (e.g., 2:7–10).[39] The combination of the concepts of the justification of the ungodly by the blood of Jesus and deliverance/salvation from God's wrath through the blood of Jesus vis-à-vis his death for the ungodly speaks to the substitutionary nature of his death in 5:8–9. The ungodly and weak sinners who are enemies of God and who are deserving of the penalty of his wrath (2:7–10) will be delivered from it because Jesus died for them (5:6, 8–10).

Paul's remarks in 5:10 support the above interpretation when he states that because of Jesus' death and resurrection, those who were once enemies with God are now reconciled to God and therefore will be saved by Jesus' life (=by his resurrection). Corneliu Constantineanu has recently argued that justification, peace, and reconciliation refer to both vertical and horizontal realities in 5:1–10.[40] But the prepositional phrase πρὸς τὸν θεὸν, which modifies εἰρήνην ἔχομεν in 5:1, and the clause κατηλλάγημεν τῷ θεῷ challenge his interpretation. These statements assert that God is the one to whom justified sinners have been reconciled and that this same group will be delivered/saved from his wrath.

Arland J. Hultgren offered an unconvincing argument against understanding reconciliation in 5:9 in a dual sense: reconciliation occurs between enemies who are hostile to God and between God who is hostile toward his enemies. He instead argued that since the text states while "we" were enemies, "we" were reconciled to God, the hostility was only directed toward God from his enemies instead of from the enemies to God.[41] Hultgren's argument is somewhat shocking since Paul argued that the ungodly and the weak sinners will be saved from God's future wrath.[42] Since 1:18—3:20 has strongly emphasized God's retributive judgment against disobedience, since he emphasizes in 1:18 that the ungodly are currently under his wrath, and since he states in 5:9–10 that the reconciled sinners will be saved from wrath, I think it is likely that reconciliation occurs by means of the blood of Christ between two groups who were both hostile toward one another. The ungodly sinners show their hostility to God by disobeying him, and God

39. A point that Stephen H. Travis overlooked in his monograph about divine retribution. Travis, *Christ and the Judgment of God*. For a response to Travis' thesis, see Jarvis Williams, *For Whom Did Christ Die?*, 48–49.

40. Constantineanu, *The Social Significance of Reconciliation in Paul's Theology*, 123–26.

41. Hultgren, *Romans*, 212. Similar to Hultgren, see also Jewett, *Romans*, 364. Contra Cranfield, *Romans*, 267; Dunn, *Romans*, 258, Fitzmyer, *Romans*, 401; Moo, *Romans*, 312.

42. Hultgren, *Romans*, 212.

shows his hostility toward them by handing them over to his current wrath (1:18) and by reserving them for a future day of wrath (2:7–10; 5:9). With 5:9–10, Paul writes that salvation from wrath happens because of justification by the blood of Christ, because of Jesus' resurrection, and because of reconciliation between God and the justified. Paul in 5:9–10 puts forth Jesus' death for sinners (and his resurrection) as the basis upon which friendship occurs between God and sinners and as the basis upon which they will be justified and thereby saved from God's future wrath by faith.[43]

Jewish Martyrology, Salvation, Reconciliation, and Resurrection

Speaking specifically of 5:7 in his defense of substitution, Simon Gathercole insightfully argued that the closest parallels with Paul's remarks are the vicarious deaths in the classical tradition. Yet, in his discussion of 5:8–11, he nowhere critically engaged the numerous parallels between the Jewish martyrological narratives and 5:8–11, narratives that would have strengthened his argument for substitution in Paul.[44] Throughout Paul's discussion of the substitutionary nature of Jesus' death in 5:8–11, he shows two theological connections with the Jewish martyrological narratives and six lexical connections with them. The two theological connections are the death of a Torah-observant Jew for the sins of others for their soteriological benefit and the resurrection of the one who died for non-Torah-observant sinners. The six lexical connections are ἁμαρτία, καταλλασσω, σῴζω/διασῴζω, ὀργη, καταλλαγη, and αἷμα.

In 2 Macc 7:18, the sixth son affirms that the martyrs suffered because of ἁμαρτία (ἡμεῖς γὰρ δι' ἑαυτοὺς ταῦτα πάσχομεν ἁμαρτόντες εἰς τὸν ἑαυτῶν θεόν). In 2 Macc 7:32, the seventh son echoes his brother's affirmation (ἡμεῖς γὰρ διὰ τὰς ἑαυτῶν ἁμαρτίας πάσχομεν). The same sentiment is expressed in LXX Daniel 3. In LXX Dan 3:28, Azariah confesses to the Lord that all of his judgments that he brought upon the holy city were right "because in truth and in judgment you have brought all of these things [upon us] because of our sins" (ὅτι ἐν ἀληθείᾳ καὶ κρίσει ἐπήγαγες πάντα ταῦτα διὰ τὰς ἁμαρτίας ἡμῶν). He continues in LXX Dan 3:29 with the words "we have sinned and we have acted lawlessly so that we turned from you and we missed the mark

---

43. Arguing against substitution in 5:6–11, Powers (*Salvation through Participation*, 104) asserted that Paul never explicitly states in the text how the death and resurrection of Jesus benefits believers, but only that the Christ-event does. To the contrary, Paul overtly states in 3:21–22, 3:24, and 5:1 that the death of Jesus benefits sinners by their expression of faith in Christ, who delivers sinners from wrath.

44. Gathercole, *Defending Substitution*.

in all things and we did not hear your commandments" (ὅτι ἡμάρτομεν καὶ ἠνομήσαμεν ἀποστῆναι ἀπὸ σοῦ καὶ ἐξημάρτομεν ἐν πᾶσιν καὶ τῶν ἐντολῶν σου οὐκ ἠκούσαμεν).

After the king killed the first son (2 Macc 7:3–6), he summoned the second son (2 Macc 7:7). He too threatened the second with death lest he assimilate as he did his older brother (2 Macc 7:7). The second son replied in the Hebrew language that God will resurrect him and the other martyrs because they die for his laws (ἐν ἐσχάτῃ δὲ πνοῇ γενόμενος εἶπεν σὺ μέν ἀλάστωρ ἐκ τοῦ παρόντος ἡμᾶς ζῆν ἀπολύεις ὁ δὲ τοῦ κόσμου βασιλεὺς ἀποθανόντας ἡμᾶς ὑπὲρ τῶν αὐτοῦ νόμων εἰς αἰώνιον ἀναβίωσιν ζωῆς ἡμᾶς ἀναστήσει) (2 Macc 7:9). In 2 Macc 7:23, the mother repeated the second son's remarks regarding the resurrection of the martyrs who died for God's law. The martyrs' death for the law in 2 Maccabees is also described as a death for sins (2 Macc 7:23, 32, 37; cf. Rom 7:7—8:3). In 2 Macc 7:29, the mother urges her youngest son to be faithful to die for Torah so that she will receive him back again, which in context refers to the resurrection. The seventh son states that he and the other martyrs suffered because of their own sins (2 Macc 7:32); he prays that God would be reconciled to the martyrs through the martyrs' deaths (2 Macc 7:33), and he prays that God would use his death and the deaths of his fellow martyrs to be the means by which God assuaged his wrath against Israel (2 Macc 7:37–38).

The author of 4 Maccabees likewise speaks of the death of Torah-observant Jews for non-Torah-observant people in tandem with the resurrection of those who died for others. In 4 Macc 6:28–29, Eleazar asks God to use his death to function as Israel's purification. In 4 Macc 13:13, the Jewish martyrs state that Abraham, Isaac, and Jacob will welcome them in the afterlife. In 4 Macc 17:21–22 and in 18:3–5, the author states that God purified and saved Israel from his wrath through the martyrs' propitiatory deaths for Israel. Thus, just as Paul states that God resurrected Jesus, a Torah-observant Jew who died for sinners to achieve their soteriological benefits (Rom 5:6, 8, 10), the authors of 2 and 4 Maccabees state that the martyrs, Torah-observant Jews who died for the soteriological benefit of non-Torah-observant Jews, will be resurrected from the dead.

Paul's second, third, fourth, fifth, and sixth lexical connections in Rom 5:6–11 with the Jewish martyrological narratives are his use of the verb καταλλάσσω in 5:10 (cf. 2 Macc 1:5; 7:33; 8:29), which only occurs in 2 Maccabees in the LXX and in Paul in the NT (cf. Rom 5:9–10; 1 Cor 7:11; 2 Cor 5:18–20),[45] the noun καταλλαγή in 5:11 (cf. 2 Macc 5:20), which only

---

45. As I will discuss below, reconciliation language occurs in numerous places in Greco-Roman literature.

occurs in Paul in the NT (Rom 5:1; 11:15; 2 Cor 5:18–19),[46] the verb σῴζω in 5:9–10 (cf. 2 Macc 2:17–18; διασῴζω in 4 Macc 17:22), and the noun ὀργή in 5:9 (cf. 2 Macc 7:38). Regarding Paul's background behind καταλλασσω and καταλλαγη, in a series of publications dating from 1989 to 2010,[47] Cilliers Breytenbach argued that the reconciliation terminology in 2 Maccabees was not Paul's background. Instead, he argued that non-religious Hellenistic literature influenced Paul. In those texts, reconciliation terminology only appears in political or military contexts. According to Breytenbach, the reconciliation terminology in Paul is different from its occurrence in 2 Maccabees, Philo, and Josephus, each of which emphasizes the need for God to be reconciled to his people, but Paul emphasizes the need for sinners to be reconciled to God. He additionally argued that Paul's use of this terminology is not sacrificial.[48]

In a 2010 essay, Breytenbach argued that Paul's reconciliation metaphor should be understood as two different domains: target domain and source domain. The target domain is the audience to which the reconciliation metaphor is directed. The source domain is the place from which the metaphor emerges. Paul's target domain determined how he structured parts of the source domain to appropriate to his target domain. The result was that Paul used a non-religious metaphor from one target domain and religiously applied it to a different target domain. Consequently, Breytenbach concluded that some scholars have misinterpreted Paul's use of the reconciliation metaphor in that they required "the reproduction of the source domain in the target domain. In terms of the rules and functions of mapping across semantic boundaries, it is inappropriate to demand the target to be described as a replica of the source."[49]

By means of an impressive analysis of a few secular Hellenistic and Roman texts, Breytenbach argued that Paul's usage of the reconciliation metaphor in 2 Cor 5:18–20 is similar to the usage in Hellenistic and Roman polis-diplomacy texts. For example, he cited texts in Diodorus Siculus (5.75.1; 16.82.3), Cassius Dio (41.16.4; 48.11.1–2), 2 Maccabees (4:11; 5:17; 8:17), Dionysius of Halicarnassus (*Ant. Rom.* 2.45.6; 3.9.2; 3.50.4; 5.21.1; 5.31.1–2; 5.62.1; 6.67.2; 6.88.2), Josephus (*Ant.* 15.136), private letters from the CE era (*P.Mich.* 8.502.7–8; *P.Giss.* 17.13–14), Plutarch (*Pel.* 26.2), Chersias the poet (*Mor.* 156f), and Aelius Aristides (*Orationes* 3.344) that

---

46. The only other occurrence in the LXX is in Isa 9:4.

47. Breytenbach, "Salvation of the Reconciled," 171–86.

48. Breytenbach, *Versöhnung*, 40–83; Breytenbach, "Versöhnung," "Stellvertretung," 59–73; Breytenbach, "Christus starb für uns," 447–75; Breytenbach, "Salvation of the Reconciled," 271–86; Breytenbach, "Salvation of the Reconciled" 177–79.

49. Breytenbach, "Salvation of the Reconciled," 173.

discuss reconciliation with similar or the same vocabulary as Paul. These texts express that ambassadors pursued reconciliation by politically negotiating peace between two parties by begging or urging the estranged party to be reconciled to the offended party.⁵⁰ Breytenbach, therefore, concluded that "there can be little doubt that Paul depicts his role as apostle to the Corinthians metaphorically in the language of the Hellenistic and Roman polis-diplomacy."⁵¹ He based his conclusion on the use of the verbs πρεσβεύομεν, παρακαλοῦντος, and δεόμεθα, which occur in 2 Cor 5:20 and in secular texts that he discussed. The lexical parallels suggest that Paul borrowed from the domain of Greco-Roman political diplomacy to depict his mediating role to the Corinthians, not from the domain of sacrificial ritual. According to Breytenbach, the latter point explains why sacrificial language is absent in 2 Cor 5:18–20 and Rom 5:10–11. Accordingly, the language of reconciliation "has in fact no cultic background. Furthermore, it rarely transferred to relationships between gods and between gods and humans."⁵²

Ralph Martin's classic work on reconciliation in Paul discussed the similarities between martyr theology and Paul with regard to reconciliation.⁵³ Martin limited his study to Rom 5:9–11 and 2 Cor 5:18–21. He acknowledged that the presence of καταλλάσσω, the concepts of God's wrath, judgment, and vicarious suffering for sin seem to support a connection between 2 Macc 7:32–33 and Paul. However, he argued that the distinctions between the traditions suggest otherwise. For example, Martin first pointed out that in 2 Macc 7:33, the martyrs asked God to be reconciled to him (καὶ

50. Dio Halicarnassus *Ant. Rom.* 2.45.6; 3.9.2; 3.50.4; 5.21.1; 5.31.1–2; 5.62.1; 6.67.2; 6.88.2; 2 Macc 4:11.

51. Breytenbach, "Salvation of the Reconciled," 175.

52. Ibid., 175–76. Breytenbach argued that a few secular texts in Greco-Roman literature describe reconciliation as the actions of a deity or the relationship between the gods. But the emphasis in these texts is on human action instead of divine action. The former's actions alter the relationship between these two parties from enmity to friendship. For his discussion of these texts, see "Salvation of the Reconciled," 176–79. Breytenbach's 2010 essay further contended that Paul's Christ died ὑπὲρ πάντων language in 2 Cor 5:14 does not refer to atonement since his background is the Greek tradition of "dying for," albeit that he gives the Greek tradition an awkward twist when he uses it to describe how humanity benefits from Christ's death for all. Breytenbach offers three unconvincing reasons. First, in 2 Cor 5:14, Paul states that Christ died "for all" instead of "for our sins" as in 1 Cor 15:3. Second, ὑπὲρ in 2 Cor 5:14 communicates the benefit of Christ's death for every sinner. By this, Paul universalizes and personalizes the efficacy of Jesus' death. Third, Paul substitutes εἷς for Χριστός. See his, "Salvation of the Reconciled," 180. For his discussion of non-sacrificial vicarious suffering in Paul's letters, see his 2010 essay ("The 'For Us' Phrases in Pauline Soteriology," 59–81).

53. Martin, *Reconciliation*, 105–6. Against a martyrological background behind Paul's reconciliation terminology, see also Beale, "Reconciliation in 2 Corinthians 5–7," 550–81.

πάλιν καταλλαγήσεται τοῖς ἑαυτοῦ δούλοις). The martyrs did not ask God to reconcile them to him. Second, Martin noted that the martyrs offered themselves to God as vicarious acts of piety and merit. Third, Paul and the other apostles emphasize that God initiates reconciliation and that he is never the object of reconciliation in the New Testament.[54]

In a series of publications in 1981, 1996, and 2002, Seyoon Kim discussed the origins of Paul's gospel.[55] With regard to reconciliation, Kim argued that it is unlikely that Jewish martyrological traditions influenced Paul's understanding of Jesus' death. Although he acknowledged the possibility of a martyrological reading of reconciliation in Paul, he asserted that such a reading cannot explain either the means by which Paul soteriologically applies the reconciliation terminology to the death of Jesus or the reason that Paul describes his ministry as a τὴν διακονίαν τῆς καταλλαγῆς.[56] Kim specifically defended his thesis that the Damascus-Road experience is the background behind Paul's reconciliation terminology instead of Jewish martyrological traditions by asserting that Paul uses the terminology to suggest that God reconciles humans to himself or to other human beings and never to declare that God is reconciled or that God reconciles himself to human beings.[57] For example, in 2 Macc 7:32–33, the seventh martyr utters: εἰ δὲ χάριν ἐπιπλήξεως καὶ παιδείας ὁ ζῶν κύριος ἡμῶν βραχέως ἐπώργισται καὶ πάλιν καταλλαγήσεται τοῖς ἑαυτοῦ δούλοις.[58]

---

54. For further observations about the differences between reconciliation in 2 Maccabees and Paul's letters, see Porter, καταλλάσσω, 39–77; Breytenbach, Versöhnung, 40–83; Breytenbach, "Versöhnung, Stellvertretung," 59–73; Breytenbach, "Christus starb für uns," 447–75; Breytenbach, "Salvation of the Reconciled," 271–86; Beale, "Reconciliation in 2 Corinthians 5–7," 550–81; Thrall, Second Corinthians, 429–39, esp. 429–30.

55. Kim, "2 Cor. 5:11–21 and Reconciliation," 360–84; Kim, The Origins of Paul's Gospel, 215–238. The latter work is a revised version of his 1977 doctoral thesis submitted at the University of Manchester and originally published in 1981 by Mohr Siebeck. My discussion from Kim primarily comes from his 2002 edition.

56. Kim is reacting to I. Howard Marshall's view here (to be discussed later) in his "Reconciliaiton," 129ff.

57. Kim (The Origin of Paul's Gospel, 220) acknowledged that Hofius ("Erwägungen," 14) first suggested this idea but that he did not defend it.

58. Kim, The Origins of Paul's Gospel, 217.

Contrary to Paul's usage of the reconciliation terminology in 2 Cor 5:18–20[59] and Rom 5:10–11,[60] Kim asserts that the Hellenistic Jewish usage and the profane Hellenistic usage affirm that God needs to be reconciled to the people.[61] These distinctions between Paul and the Hellenistic Jewish traditions suggest that "Paul deliberately makes a fundamental correction of the Hellenistic Jewish conception of reconciliation between God and human beings: it is not God who needs to be reconciled to human beings, but it is human beings who need to be reconciled to God; and it is not by repentance, prayers, or good works on the part of the human beings that reconciliation is brought between God and human beings, but it is by his grace that God reconciles human beings to himself."[62] Kim thinks 2 Cor 5:11–21 provides the earliest and the best access to the origin of reconciliation in Paul.[63]

In his 2011 monograph on Romans, Richard N. Longenecker likewise distinguished between the use of reconciliation language among the Jews in 2 Maccabees and Josephus and Paul's use. According to the former, God is reconciled, whereas God reconciles sinners to God in Paul. Since Paul is the only NT author to use the reconciliation language and since the language does not appear in the earliest Christian writers, Paul probably learned this language because of its inclusion in early Christian confessional material. He came to appreciate such language as accurately expressing what he personally experienced in his relationship with God through Christ by the Spirit. Longenecker stated four reasons why Paul likely borrowed his reconciliation language from early Christian confessions, all of which he based on 2 Cor 5:18–20 rather than Rom 5:9–10, even though his arguments are in his Romans commentary. First, Paul states in 2 Cor 5:20 a certain balance structure. Second, Paul introduces the verse with the particle ὅτι, which Paul and other NT writers used to introduce a quotation from traditional

---

59. τὰ δὲ πάντα ἐκ τοῦ θεοῦ τοῦ καταλλάξαντος ἡμᾶς ἑαυτῷ διὰ Χριστοῦ καὶ δόντος ἡμῖν τὴν διακονίαν τῆς καταλλαγῆς, ὡς ὅτι θεὸς ἦν ἐν Χριστῷ κόσμον καταλλάσσων ἑαυτῷ, μὴ λογιζόμενος αὐτοῖς τὰ παραπτώματα αὐτῶν καὶ θέμενος ἐν ἡμῖν τὸν λόγον τῆς καταλλαγῆς. Ὑπὲρ Χριστοῦ οὖν πρεσβεύομεν ὡς τοῦ θεοῦ παρακαλοῦντος δι' ἡμῶν· δεόμεθα ὑπὲρ Χριστοῦ, καταλλάγητε τῷ θεῷ.

60. εἰ γὰρ ἐχθροὶ ὄντες κατηλλάγημεν τῷ θεῷ διὰ τοῦ θανάτου τοῦ υἱοῦ αὐτοῦ, πολλῷ μᾶλλον καταλλαγέντες σωθησόμεθα ἐν τῇ ζωῇ αὐτοῦ· οὐ μόνον δέ, ἀλλὰ καὶ καυχώμενοι ἐν τῷ θεῷ διὰ τοῦ κυρίου ἡμῶν Ἰησοῦ Χριστοῦ δι' οὗ νῦν τὴν καταλλαγὴν ἐλάβομεν.

61. Kim, *Origins of Paul's Gospel*, 217.

62. Ibid.

63. Ibid., 220. On the similarities and differences between Paul's reconciliation motif and 2 Maccabees' reconciliation motif, see Barnett, *Second Corinthians*, 303 n. 10.

material. Third, the verse formally incorporates early Christian proclamation. Forth, 5:19 is central to 5:18 and 5:20.⁶⁴

The works of Breytenbach, Martin, Kim, and Longenecker offered helpful insights to the political, Christian, and confessional backgrounds behind Paul's reconciliation language. However, their works made at least two methodological mistakes. First, they assumed that Paul was limited to one background. This mistake caused them to limit their investigation to the backgrounds that they assumed were the context in front of which to understand Paul's reconciliation terminology. In my view, Paul uses a variety of metaphors from a variety of traditions (Hebrew Bible, Jewish martyrological, Greco-Roman economic, slave, legal, etc.), and he often conflates and/or reconstructs them to fit his polemical and theological purposes.⁶⁵ Second, the above scholars let 2 Cor 5:18–20 largely determine Paul's reconciliation vocabulary in Rom 5:8–11 instead of letting the latter text speak on its own terms and in its own historical and epistolary context. Although Rom 5:8–11 and 2 Cor 5:18–21 use either the same or similar vocabulary, the latter should not determine how Paul uses the same vocabulary in the former text. Third, they basically ignored the overt parallels between Paul's reconciliation terminology in Rom 5:8–11 and the Jewish martyrological narratives.

The Jewish martyrological narratives and Paul are the only traditions that associate ἁμαρτία, καταλλασσω, σῴζω/διασῴζω, ὀργη, καταλλαγη, and αἵμα to the substitutionary death of a Torah-observant Jew for the soteriological benefits of non-Torah-observant sinners. Such associations occur nowhere else (to my knowledge) in any secular or religious Greco-Roman or Jewish source in reference to the death of Torah-observant Jews for the benefit of non-Torah-observant sinners. Paul, instead, specifically associates καταλλασσω and καταλλαγη with the death of Jesus for sinners, and he states that Jesus' death for sinners accomplished reconciliation and salvation from God's wrath for those for whom he died (5:6–11), just as the Jewish martyrological narratives state about the martyrs' deaths for Israel.

In 2 Macc 7:33, the seventh son martyred asserts that God will be reconciled to his servants (καταλλαγήσεται τοῖς ἑαυτοῦ δούλοις). In 2 Macc 7:38, the seventh son states that this reconciliation would take place through the martyrs, whose deaths would end the wrath of the Almighty (ἐν ἐμοὶ δὲ καὶ τοῖς ἀδελφοῖς μου στῆσαι τὴν τοῦ παντοκράτορος ὀργὴν τὴν ἐπὶ τὸ σύμπαν ἡμῶν γένος δικαίως ἐπηγμένην). 2 Maccabees 5:1—8:5 supports the claim that God fulfilled the seventh son's expectation through the martyrs' deaths,

---

64. For Longenecker's discussion, see *Introducing Romans*, 337–43.
65. For example, he calls Christ the Passover lamb in 1 Cor 5:8.

Jewish Martyrology and Substitution in Romans 5:6–11, 8:1–4, and 8:31–34   157

because the section states that God was reconciled to the nation after the martyrs died (e.g., 2 Macc 7:32—8:5).

2 Maccabees 1:5 begins with a prayer that God "would be reconciled" to his people in an evil time (καὶ ἐπακοῦσαι ὑμῶν τῶν δεήσεων καὶ καταλλαγείη ὑμῖν καὶ μὴ ὑμᾶς ἐγκαταλίποι ἐν καιρῷ πονηρῷ) and that he would not forsake them during an "evil time" in the first letter prior to the epitome in 2:19—15:37. Before the epitome, the author reminds his fellow Jews in Egypt that God previously saved his people from the Greek tyrant and restored temple-worship, and he expresses hope that God would soon show his mercy to all Jews scattered throughout the world by gathering them at his holy temple in Judea (ὁ δὲ θεὸς ὁ σώσας τὸν πάντα λαὸν αὐτοῦ καὶ ἀποδοὺς τὴν κληρονομίαν πᾶσιν καὶ τὸ βασίλειον καὶ τὸ ἱεράτευμα καὶ τὸν ἁγιασμόν καθὼς ἐπηγγείλατο διὰ τοῦ νόμου ἐλπίζομεν γὰρ ἐπὶ τῷ θεῷ ὅτι ταχέως ἡμᾶς ἐλεήσει καὶ ἐπισυνάξει ἐκ τῆς ὑπὸ τὸν οὐρανὸν εἰς τὸν ἅγιον τόπον ἐξείλετο γὰρ ἡμᾶς ἐκ μεγάλων κακῶν καὶ τὸν τόπον ἐκαθάρισεν) (2 Macc 2:17-18). The epitome begins with a recounting of how God showed his mercy to the Jews through Judas Maccabeus and his brothers during the Hellenistic crisis (2 Macc 2:19-22).

In 2 Macc 5:20, the author expresses hope that Israel would no longer be consumed by God's wrath through Antiochus but that they would again experience his reconciliation (διόπερ καὶ αὐτὸς ὁ τόπος συμμετασχὼν τῶν τοῦ ἔθνους δυσπετημάτων γενομένων ὕστερον εὐεργετημάτων ἐκοινώνησεν καὶ ὁ καταλειφθεὶς ἐν τῇ τοῦ παντοκράτορος ὀργῇ πάλιν ἐν τῇ τοῦ μεγάλου δεσπότου καταλλαγῇ μετὰ πάσης δόξης ἐπανωρθώθη). The epitome ends with the author asserting that the Hebrews possessed the city of Judea after Judas and his army cut off Nicanor's head and cut out his tongue (2 Macc 15:32-37). Thus, reconciliation with God in 1:5, God's mercy and salvation in 2:18, and God's mercy and salvation in 15:37 frame the martyrological sections of the epitome in 6:18—7:42. In 4 Macc 6:28-29, Eleazar asks God to make his blood a ransom for Israel. In 17:21-22, the author states that the martyrs' propitiatory deaths for Israel saved the nation through their blood (καὶ διὰ τοῦ αἵματος τῶν εὐσεβῶν ἐκείνων καὶ τοῦ ἱλαστηρίου τοῦ θανάτου αὐτῶν ἡ θεία πρόνοια τὸν Ἰσραηλ προκακωθέντα διέσωσεν). Likewise, Paul asserts that Jesus' death (the death of a Torah-observant Jew) for sinners justifies by faith (Rom 5:1, 6, 8), delivers from God's wrath (Rom 5:9, 10), and reconciles to God those sinners for whom he died (Rom 5:10-11).

Furthermore, Breytenbach and others have made too much of the fact that 2 Maccabees refers to the need for God to be reconciled to Israel and Paul the need for sinners to be reconciled to God (cf. 2 Macc 1:5; 7:33; 8:29 with Rom 5:10) as an argument against the former's influence upon the latter.⁶⁶ 2 Maccabees likely uses the passive voice to refer to God being reconciled to his people because the author emphasizes throughout his abridged history that Hellenistic assimilation offended Israel's God and brought his wrath upon them via Antiochus (2 Macc 6:12-17). As a result, God needed to be reconciled to his people so that the wrath of God through Antiochus would cease (2 Macc 6:12—7:38). On the other hand, Paul exposits his gospel throughout Romans (cf. Rom 1:16-17), a crucial element of which is God's salvation of sinners through Christ apart from works of law (Rom 1:18—4:25).

The primary aim of Romans is not to articulate to the Romans that a righteous God needs to be appeased in order to accept sinners in his presence, although this is a central component of the gospel that Paul proclaimed (e.g., 1:16—4:25). Rather, Paul's primary aim in the letter is to acquaint the Romans with his gospel so that they would assist his missionary endeavors to Spain when/if he passed through Rome to Spain (cf. 1:1-17; 15:22-24, 28), and his primary message throughout the letter is that his apostolic gospel centers on the revelation of God's saving righteousness in and through Jesus Christ, the Son of David; Jews and Gentiles participate in this righteousness by faith in Jesus, the wrath-bearing and resurrected Christ who died as a substitute for the sins of Jews and Gentiles to achieve their soteriological benefits (e.g., 1:1-17; 3:21—4:25), apart from Torah-observance (3:20), and they ought to live out faithfully in unity the new identity of what God has done for them in Christ as Jewish and Gentile Christ-followers in society in the context of the church (5:1—15:21). Therefore, regardless of the voice of καταλλασσω, both 2 Maccabees (2 Macc 1:5; 7:33; 8:29) and Rom 5:10-11 speak of the accomplishment of reconciliation between God and non-Torah-observant sinners by means of the death of Torah-observant Jews whose deaths put an end to God's wrath and provides reconciliation between both the offenders and the offended. 2 Maccabees states that the Lord was angry with his people for a little while (6:12-17) and that he would be reconciled to his servants again by ending his wrath by means of them (2 Macc 7:32-38). Paul states that God reconciled sinners to himself through Christ's death while they were enemies with God and that because he reconciled sinners to God through Christ's death, they will be saved by his life from his wrath (Rom 5:9-11).⁶⁷

---

66. Breytenbach, *Versöhnung*, 40–83; Breytenbach, "Versöhnung, Stellvertretung," 59–73; Breytenbach, "Christus starb für uns," 447–75; Breytenbach, "Salvation of the Reconciled," 271–86; Breytenbach, "Salvation of the Reconciled," 177–79.

67. Neither Philo (*Decal.* 1:87; *Ebr.* 1:208; *Leg.* 3:134) nor Josephus (*Ant.* 6:143, 353; 5:137; 7:184; 11:195; 14:278) ever applies καταλλασσω to the death of a Torah-observant Jew for the benefit of non-Torah-observant people to reconcile a hostile relationship

JEWISH MARTYROLOGY AND SUBSTITUTION IN ROMANS 8:1-4[68]

Jesus' Death as a Sin-Offering

In Rom 8:1-4, Paul suggests that Jesus' death was not only a substitute for sinners but also a penal substitute in that he identifies his death as a sin-offering that delivers sinners from God's condemnation pronounced upon them by Torah (cf. 7:1—8:11).[69] This identification links Paul's presentation of Jesus' death mainly with the Levitical cult and secondarily to the Jewish martyrological narratives. Although the phrase sin-offering (περὶ τῆς ἁμαρτίας) never occurs in the Jewish martyrological narratives, the authors of those narratives identify the martyrs as offerings for sin that would deliver the nation from God's wrath. As a result, their deaths function as sin-offerings in the Jewish martyrological narratives. In the face of persecution and in the face of death, the Torah-observant Jewish martyrs state that they suffered for sins (LXX Dan 3:28-37; 2 Macc 7:28-29). They ask God to use their deaths as means by which he would be reconciled to his servants again (LXX Dan 3:28-37; 2 Macc 7:32-38; 4 Macc 6:28-29), and the author of 4 Maccabees states that God purified and saved the nation by means of their propitiatory deaths (4 Macc 17:21-22).

Although one can successfully argue that penal substitution is present in Rom 3:24-26 and 5:6-11, Paul overtly affirms the penal substitutionary nature of Jesus' death for sinners when he states that no condemnation exists for those in Christ Jesus. Paul laments in 7:1-25 that the law enslaves and kills the Jew in Adam outside of Christ (and all people) under its jurisdiction, but he victoriously proclaims in 8:1 that Christ delivers from its condemnation. He, therefore, declares in 8:1 that "condemnation" (κατάκριμα) no longer exists for those who are in Christ Jesus, "because the law of the Spirit of life by means of Christ Jesus freed you from the law of sin and of death." He reiterates the penal nature of Jesus' substitutionary death in 8:3 with the words κατέκρινεν τὴν ἁμαρτίαν ἐν τῇ σαρκὶ ("he condemned sin in the flesh"). Paul explains 8:2 in 8:3 by stating how those in Christ Jesus received such freedom: "For God [did] what the law was incapable [of doing] because it was weak through sinful flesh in that he sent his own

---

between God and non-Torah-observant people. To my knowledge, no ancient source does the latter with the exception of 2 Macc 7:32-38, Rom 5:9-11, and 2 Cor 5:18-20.

68. This section overlaps with Jarvis J. Williams, "Violent Atonement in Romans," 579-99. I have borrowed the overlapping material with permission.

69. N. T. Wright has acknowledged the strong penal substitutionary language in Rom 8:1. For example, N. T. Wright, "Reading Paul, Thinking Scripture," 372-73.

Son to deal with sin in the likeness of sinful flesh, and he condemned sin in [Jesus'] flesh" (Τὸ γὰρ ἀδύνατον τοῦ νόμου ἐν ᾧ ἠσθένει διὰ τῆς σαρκός, ὁ θεὸς τὸν ἑαυτοῦ υἱὸν πέμψας ἐν ὁμοιώματι σαρκὸς ἁμαρτίας καὶ περὶ ἁμαρτίας κατέκρινεν τὴν ἁμαρτίαν ἐν τῇ σαρκί). The syntax of 8:3 is complex.[70] The basic point of the verse seems more direct than the syntax: namely, God sent Jesus to identify with sinners and to die for their sins to liberate them from both God's and Torah's condemnation.

As Paul argues in 7:1–24, sin uses Torah to bring death to those under its jurisdiction and outside of Christ. But God exonerates those in Christ because he frees sinners from Torah through Christ's death for their sin by offering Jesus as a sin-offering (7:25—8:3). In 8:3, Paul uses several terms that identify Jesus' death as a penal substitute and that link his death with the Jewish martyrological narratives. First, in 8:3, Paul states that God sent Jesus in the "likeness of sinful flesh" (ἐν ὁμοιώματι σαρκὸς ἁμαρτίας). The noun (ὁμοιώματι) in 8:3 is uniquely Pauline in the NT.[71] Every occurrence in Romans and elsewhere refers to the "image/likeness/form" of something. In 1:23, ὁμοιώματι refers to the "image/likeness/form" of corruptible creation (ἐν ὁμοιώματι εἰκόνος φθαρτοῦ ἀνθρώπου καὶ πετεινῶν καὶ τετραπόδων καὶ ἑρπετῶν). In 5:14, ὁμοιώματι refers to the "image/likeness/form" of Adam's transgression (ἐπὶ τῷ ὁμοιώματι τῆς παραβάσεως Ἀδὰμ). In 6:5, ὁμοιώματι refers to the "image/likeness/form" of Jesus' death (τῷ ὁμοιώματι τοῦ θανάτου αὐτοῦ). In Phil 2:7, ὁμοιώματι refers to Jesus' incarnation (ἀλλὰ ἑαυτὸν ἐκένωσεν μορφὴν δούλου λαβών, ἐν ὁμοιώματι ἀνθρώπων γενόμενος). The latter use in Phil 2:7 is closest to Paul's use in Rom 8:3, which the following citations reveal:

> ὁ θεὸς τὸν ἑαυτοῦ υἱὸν πέμψας ἐν ὁμοιώματι σαρκὸς ἁμαρτίας (Rom 8:3).

> ἀλλὰ ἑαυτὸν ἐκένωσεν μορφὴν δούλου λαβών, ἐν ὁμοιώματι ἀνθρώπων γενόμενος καὶ σχήματι εὑρεθεὶς ὡς ἄνθρωπος (Phil 2:7).

In Rom 8:3, Paul suggests that God sent Jesus in the "image/likeness/form" of sinful flesh. This statement means that Jesus became a man and consequently functioned in the role of the sinner. Jesus was not ontologically a sinner. However, he functioned as a sinner in that he took on sinful flesh by taking the form of humanity (hence, the phrase ἐν ὁμοιώματι σαρκὸς

---

70. See critical commentaries on the Greek text of Romans for different ways to understand the syntax.

71. The noun ὁμοίωμα in 8:3 is used elsewhere to mean similar in copy (LXX Deut 4:15–18, 23, 25; 5:8; Jos 22:28; 1 Kgs 6:5; Ps 105:20; Sir 34:3; Rom 1:23; 5;13; 6:5).

ἁμαρτίας).⁷² Paul's remarks in 8:3 are strongly incarnational. Although a different context, his words in Phil 2:7 shed light on an incarnational reading of Rom 8:3. Paul highlights the incarnation in Phil 2:7 with the words Jesus emptied himself (ἑαυτὸν ἐκένωσεν), by taking on the form of a slave (μορφὴν δούλου λαβών), by coming into the "image/likeness/form of men" (ἐν ὁμοιώματι ἀνθρώπων γενόμενος), and by being found in appearance as a man (καὶ σχήματι εὑρεθεὶς ὡς ἄνθρωπος). In Phil 2:7, the noun σχήματι ("form/appearance/shape") is a synonym for ὁμοιώματι, which Paul supports by identifying Jesus' ὁμοιώματι and σχήματι with taking on a human form (ἐν ὁμοιώματι ἀνθρώπων/σχήματι εὑρεθεὶς ὡς ἄνθρωπος).⁷³

In Rom 8:3, the participial phrase (πέμψας ἐν ὁμοιώματι σαρκὸς ἁμαρτίας) emphasizes Jesus' incarnation (cf. Phil 2:7),⁷⁴ but the main verb (κατέκρινεν) accentuates his death on the cross.⁷⁵ The entire sentence highlights the incarnation and the cross, because the sentence argues that Jesus fully identified with sinful humanity by taking upon himself God's condemnation/judgment for humanity's sin and by being judged/condemned as a sinner (cf. Gal 4:5–6; Phil 2:5–9).⁷⁶ Jesus identified with sinful humanity by becoming human, by submitting to the sinful realm of existence, and by going to the cross to take upon himself God's death penalty for humanity's sin (cf. Rom 5:12—8:3). Unlike Adam and the rest of humanity, Jesus remained free from the act of committing sin (cf. Rom 5:12–21; 2 Cor 5:21), and his sin-less-ness explains why his death on the cross delivers from the law those who were condemned by it (cf. Rom 7:1—8:10). However, like Adam and like the Jewish martyrs, Jesus paid a severe penalty for the problem of sin: namely, God's judgment in death. But, unlike Adam and the Jewish martyrs, Jesus' death universally reversed Adam's universal curse for both Jews and Gentiles under Torah's jurisdiction (cf. Rom 5:12—8:4), just as the deaths of the Jewish martyrs exclusively reversed God's curse of judgment through Antiochus away from Israel (2 Macc 7:32—8:5; 4 Macc 6:28–29; 17:21–22).

Second, Paul presents Jesus' death as a penal substitute and links his presentation of Jesus' death with the Jewish martyrological narratives by

---

72. I understand this phrase to affirm representation so that both representation and substitution occur in 8:1–4 (cf. with 5:14).

73. For further examples of σχήματι as "form/image/likeness," cf. Philo, *Migr.* 1:48–49; Jos. *Ant.* 8:195 with LXX Isa 3:17 and Jos. *Ant.* 1:129, 324; Philo, *Opif.* 1:120.

74. So Bell, "Sacrifice and Christology in Paul," 7–8.

75. Against Bell, "Sacrifice and Christology in Paul," 8. Bell did not emphasize the importance of the cross-event in Rom 8:3, but he thinks that Paul refers both to the incarnation and to the cross-event. However, rightly Fitzmyer, *Romans,* 486–87; Schreiner, *Romans* 404.

76. Cf. Jewett, *Romans* 483–84.

identifying Jesus as a sin-offering through whom God condemned sin: "And concerning sin [God] also condemned sin in [Jesus'] flesh" (καὶ περὶ ἁμαρτίας κατέκρινεν τὴν ἁμαρτίαν ἐν τῇ σαρκι). In his famous Romans commentary, C. E. B. Cranfield rejected a reference to the sin-offering in Rom 8:3 in spite of the fact that the LXX often uses περὶ ἁμαρτίας to refer to the sin-offering (e.g., LXX Lev 5:9; 14:31; Ps 39:7).[77] Cranfield argued that a sacrificial reading is a forced reading in 8:3 since the context of Paul's argument does not support it. He argued instead that περὶ ἁμαρτίας in 8:3 should be connected to the clause πέμψας ἐν ὁμοιώματι σαρκὸς ἁμαρτίας and that 8:3 refers to Jesus' mission instead of his penal death for sin.

Thomas R. Schreiner rightly agreed with Cranfield's reading of the syntax, but he rejected his understanding of the verse. Instead, he argued that the phrase περὶ ἁμαρτίας identifies Jesus as a sin-offering since the phrase refers to a sin-offering in forty-four of fifty-four occurrences in the LXX (e.g., LXX Lev 5:6–11; 7:37; 9:2–3; 12:6, 8; 14:13, 22, 31; 15:15, 30; 16:3, 5, 9; 23:19) and since Paul uses the phrase to refer to Jesus' death for sin in Rom 8:3.[78] In addition to Schreiner's arguments, the phrase ἐν τῇ σαρκι refers to Jesus' flesh (=his incarnation) as a sin-offering because 8:1–3 states that there is no condemnation for those "in Christ Jesus" since God sent Jesus "in the likeness of sinful flesh." The phrase περὶ ἁμαρτίας most likely refers to the OT sin-offering since the LXX uses this phrase on numerous occasions either to refer to one's individual sin (LXX Exod 32:30; Lev 4:3, 14) or to the sin-offering that covered/purified/atoned sin (LXX Lev 6:18, 23; 7:7) and since Paul associates this phrase with Jesus' flesh. Paul's reference to Jesus' flesh in 8:3 links his incarnation to the OT sin-offering (cf. LXX Lev 5:9).[79] This connection fits nicely with Paul's argument in Romans 7 that the "I" under the law commits sin ignorantly/unintentionally, for the sin-offering dealt with ignorant/unintentional sins in the OT (cf. LXX Lev 5:7–8; 6:25 [MT Lev 6:18]).[80]

Third, Paul presents Jesus' death as a penal substitute and links his death with the Jewish martyrological narratives by connecting the death of a Torah-observant Jewish man with penal language. The Torah-observant

---

77. Cranfield, *Romans* 378–90, esp. 382.

78. Schreiner, *Romans* 401–3; Stuhlmacher *Römer*, 107; N. T. Wright, *The Climax of the Covenant*, 220–25; Bell, "Sacrifice and Christology in Paul," 1–27, esp. 5–8. Against Barrett, *Romans*, 156; McLean, *The Cursed Christ*, 46.

79. Rightly, see Käsemann, *Romans*, 216; Schreiner, *Romans*, 401–3; Moo, *Romans*, 480; Finlan, *Paul's Cultic Atonement Metaphors*, 114; Peter Stuhlmacher, *Römer* 107; Dunn, *Romans*, 422; N. T. Wright, *The New Testament and the People of God*, 220–25; idem, "Romans" 579; Bell, "Sacrifice and Christology in Paul" 1–27, esp. 5–8.

80. So Wright, "Romans," 579.

Jewish martyrs died to end God's wrath against Israel because of the nation's sin, which was Torah-disobedience (2 Macc 1:1—8:5; 4 Macc 1:1—6:29). The narrator of 4 Maccabees states that their propitiatory deaths saved the nation and purified the homeland (4 Macc 17:21-22). Salvation through the deaths of Torah-observant Jews for non-Torah-observant sinners in 2 and 4 Maccabees communicates a penal/judicial idea, because disobedience to Torah results in God's judgment against the offender through Antiochus and his army, but the deaths of the Jewish martyrs ends God's judgment and brings salvation to the nation in the Jewish martyrological narratives (cf. 4 Macc 17:21-22).

Likewise, Paul states that God "judged/condemned" (κατέκρινεν τὴν ἁμαρτίαν ἐν τῇ σαρκί) sin in Jesus' flesh. The majority of appearances of this verb in the LXX suggests a penal judgment.[81] The verb or its cognate noun (κατάκριμα) elsewhere in the NT supports that those to whom κατέκρινεν and its cognate κατάκριμα are applied would either receive the penalty of judgment (Rom 2:1; 8:34; 14:23; cf. Matt 12:41; 20:18; 27:3; Mark 10:33; 14:64; Luke 11:31; Heb 11:7; 2 Pet 2:6) or would be delivered from the penalty of judgment (Rom 8:1; 1 Cor 11:32). The Jewish martyrological narratives state that the martyrs died to put an end to God's wrath (2 Macc 7:32-38; 4 Macc 6:28-29; 17:21-22). Thus, the phrase περὶ ἁμαρτίας in Rom 8:3 in connection with the judicial language in 8:1 (κατάκριμα) and in 8:3 (κατέκρινεν) support that Jesus' death (the death of a Torah-observant Jew for the soteriological benefits of those condemned by Torah) was a penal substitutionary death.

The penal substitutionary element of the death of the martyrs and the death of Jesus and both traditions' strong reliance upon the Levitical cult's sin-offering motif is further evident since Lev 4:1-35 and Lev 5:9 state that the sin-offering should be slaughtered and its blood should be presented before YHWH in order to provide atonement for sin (cf. Lev 4:26, 35). Sin deserved death (Gen 2:17), and the sin-offering delivered the sinner from death (LXX Lev 16:6, 11, 15, 27; 19:22). YHWH required the animal to be slaughtered for the sins of others and its blood to be shed to rectify the unintentional/ignorant wrongs. The Jewish martyrological narratives in 2 Macc 7:32-38, 4 Macc 6:28-29, and 17:21-22 identify the martyrs as functional sin-offerings without using the phrase περὶ ἁμαρτίας in that the authors state that the martyrs died for the nation to save the nation. Paul in Rom 8:3 likewise identifies Jesus with the περὶ ἁμαρτίας at the functional level, so that Jesus' identification with the sinner by his participation in human existence makes his death an offering for sin that accomplished a soteriological

---

81. For example, see LXX Est 2:1; Wis 4:16; *Pss. Sol.* 4:2; Sus 1:41, 48, 53.

benefit for those for whom he died (namely, exoneration in God's law court from his eschatological wrath at the end of history), just as the Jewish martyrological narratives suggest that the Torah-observant martyrs died for sin to achieve a soteriological benefit for those for whom they died (namely, deliverance from God's temporal wrath within history) (2 Macc 7:32–38; 4 Macc 6:28–29; 17:21–22).

N. T. Wright stressed that Paul says that God condemned sin, not that he condemned Jesus.[82] Wright correctly acknowledged what the text actually says: namely, sin was condemned in Jesus' flesh. However, Wright argues that this does not mean "that God desired to punish someone and decided to punish Jesus on everybody else's behalf."[83] Instead, Wright asserted that in Jesus' cross, God judged sin by rendering it powerless as a power so that sin would no longer take up residence in human beings and consequently produce their death.[84]

Wright's work correctly pointed out that Paul states that God condemned sin, not Jesus. He also correctly noted that contrary to some translations, the phrase "in the flesh" in the clause "God condemned sin in the flesh" refers to Jesus' flesh (not to humanity's flesh), because the entire context of Paul's argument explains why condemnation no longer exists for those in Christ Jesus (cf. 7:1—8:4). Nonetheless, even if Paul places the accent in the argument on God's condemnation of sin in the cross of Jesus in 8:3 instead of on God's condemnation of Jesus, one should not separate God's condemnation of sin in Jesus' flesh from God's condemnation of Jesus in 8:3, because Paul states that God "judged" sin "in Jesus' flesh." To speak of judgment in Jesus is a penal expression. Consequently, Wright appears to have overlooked that Paul presents Jesus' death penalty as the only way that God's condemnation of sin in Jesus' flesh could have effectively condemned sin and thereby made its power inoperative in humanity, because Jesus functioned as a sinner and died the death that sinners deserved. Condemnation of Torah no longer exists for those "in Christ Jesus" because God offered Jesus for sin and condemned sin in Jesus' flesh (8:1–3). This argument fits with Paul's earlier argument in 5:12–21 that Adam brought death to all because of his disobedience, but Jesus brings life to all because of his obedience. God's plan to overcome the power of sin in humanity was incomplete and ineffective until God "condemned sin" in Jesus' flesh (cf. 3:25–26; 8:3).

Richard H. Bell likewise argued against the idea that Paul refers to "a satisfaction theory of the atonement" in 8:3 when he states that "God

82. Wright, "Romans," 578.
83. Ibid.
84. Ibid.

condemned sin in Jesus' flesh."[85] Bell posited that Paul's theory of atonement in 8:3 reflects the P source, which (he asserted) suggests that the sin-offering dealt with the essence of sin in a human (rather than the human's doing of sin). Bell's view, however, seems to dichotomize falsely between the concept of sin and the act of doing sin when in fact Paul himself discusses sin in complex ways in Romans. Paul states that God will repay evil deeds in the judgment with wrath (2:6–10), and he affirms that everybody sins (3:23). The preceding evidence seems to emphasize the individual's participation in sin. Paul also states that sin should not reign over believers (6:12), which seems to present sin as a power and thereby focuses on the essence of sin. Bell's view also fails to take seriously the divine penal language of 5:12—8:4. Adam's disobedience brought "judgment" and "death" upon everyone (5:12–21). Torah's presence only increases the power of sin and the severity of God's judgment against sin (5:12–21; 7:1–23), but Jesus' death frees those under Torah from its condemnation because Jesus fulfilled the righteous requirement of the law in those who walk not in accordance with the flesh but in accordance with the Spirit (7:24—8:4).

Furthermore, Paul's words "in the likeness of sinful flesh" in 8:3 additionally support the penal nature of Jesus' death. Paul connects God's condemnation of sin in Jesus' death with Jesus' participation within the realm of sinful humanity.[86] Bell rightly argued that the phrase "in the likeness of sinful flesh" refers to Jesus' "full identity and resemblance" with sinful humanity. Accordingly, Paul is concerned with "the sending of Christ into the area of human existence" and that part of such an existence was indeed sin.[87] Bell did not argue that Jesus' experience with sin was ontological. Instead, he correctly identified functional sinfulness with Jesus.[88] That is, Jesus participated in the realm of sin in that he functioned as a sinner. Jesus' functional sinfulness is supported by the rest of 8:3: "he judged sin in the flesh."

In 8:4, Paul states that God's purpose of condemning sin in Jesus' flesh was to fulfill the righteous requirement of the law in "us who are not walking according to the flesh but according to the Spirit." Since the entrance of the law into history increased the power of sin (1:18—7:25; esp. 3:20; 4:15; 5:12–21; 7:7–25; Gal 3:19), God sent Jesus to overcome the power of sin and death and to fulfill the law's demands in us who live according to

---

85. Bell, "Sacrifice and Christology in Paul," 6–8 n. 40.
86. Ibid., 7–8.
87. Ibid., 6–7.
88. Bell, "Sacrifice and Christology in Paul," 6–7. See, in contrast to Bell, Branick, "The Sinful Flesh of the Son of God [Rom 8:3]," 246–62, esp. 251.

the Spirit (5:12—6:23). Scholars debate whether Christ's active obedience or Christian obedience is in view in 8:4.[89] Regardless of the position that one takes, the point remains that foundational to the fulfillment of the law's righteous requirement in us who walk according to the Spirit is Jesus' penal death for sin, which Paul mentions in 8:3, because God fulfills the righteous requirement of the law "in us" by means of his condemnation of sin in Jesus' flesh and by means of the obedience of those who live out what God has done for them in Christ in the power of the Spirit. Romans 8:3 discusses God's work of defeating the power of sin by condemning sin in Jesus' flesh (humanity's representative man), and 8:4 states that the purpose for which God condemned sin in Jesus' flesh was to fulfill the righteous requirement of the law "in us" who walk according to the Spirit. Jesus' identification with functional sinfulness can be seen by God's judgment of sin in his flesh (8:2–3). Jesus paid a price as a representative man for those in Christ who were otherwise condemned by the law and his death for those in him fulfilled in them and on their behalf the law's righteous requirement (8:1–3). He took upon himself their condemnation by means of his death for them so that they would receive in themselves the law's fulfillment by means of their Christian obedience (8:4).

JEWISH MARTYROLOGY AND SUBSTITUTION IN ROMANS 8:31–34

Jewish Martyrology, Jesus' Death for Others, and His Resurrection

The text of Rom 8:31–34 further supports the substitutionary nature of Jesus' death and a connection with the Jewish martyrological narratives. Paul asserts that God did not spare his own son, but he gave him up in death "for us all." God gives over (παρέδωκεν) in wrath those who suppress the truth to practice their sinful desires (1:24, 26, 28), but God handed over (παρέδωκεν) his Son in death to give us freely "all things." The phrase τὰ πάντα at least refers to the soteriological blessings mentioned in 8:29–30 (foreknowledge, predestination, calling, justification, and glorification), and maybe even to the certainty of the future redemption and salvation of believers who suffer (8:12–25), because 8:28–30 explains why everything works out for the good for those who love God by emphasizing God's act of salvation for those in Christ. Paul's connection of soteriological blessings with legal language in

---

89. For a recent discussion of this debate and for an argument in favor of Christian obedience, see McFadden, "The Fulfillment of the Law's Dikaiōma:," 483–97.

8:33–34 in conjunction with a reference to Jesus' death in 8:32 and 8:34 support the penal substitutionary nature of Jesus' death for others.

Focusing his critique of substitution in 8:32 on the preposition ὑπέρ, Powers argued that there are two factors in the immediate context of 8:32 that militate against a substitutionary understanding of the preposition. First, the immediate context of 8:32 is unique in that the expression ὑπὲρ ἡμῶν is not restricted to the surrender formula. The same phrase occurs in 8:31 and in 8:34.[90] The expression ὑπὲρ ἡμῶν in 8:31 occurs in tandem with καθ' ἡμῶν in response to Paul's question "if God is for us (ὑπὲρ ἡμῶν), then who is against us (καθ' ἡμῶν)?"[91] In 8:34, in response to his question regarding "who shall bring a charge against God's elect?" Paul answers by saying that Jesus, who died and was resurrected from the dead and sits at God's right hand, prays for us (ὑπὲρ ἡμῶν).[92] The entire passage communicates that God is for/on the side of his people. God demonstrated that he is for his people in that he did not spare his Son, but gave him up for them in death, the proof of which in this text is the cross, resurrection, ascension, and Christ's intercession for the believer.[93] Thus, Powers concluded, "the immediate context of the surrender formula in Rom 8:32 does not favor a substitutional reading of the phrase ὑπὲρ ἡμῶν; rather the context promotes the notion that God's surrender of Christ was done 'on our behalf' or 'for our benefit.'"[94] Second, Powers argued that the phrase σὺν αὐτῷ refers to the believer's identification and union in Christ and with Christ. The believer's identification and participation in the fate of Christ, who died, was resurrected, and is exalted, are the source of his assurance.[95]

However, Powers' first criticism of substitution in 8:31–34 begged the question. He assumed that the exegetical weight in favor of substitution is on Paul's use of ὑπέρ. From this assumption, he argued against substitution by demonstrating that ὑπέρ means "in favor of" in 8:31 since it is paired with καθ' ἡμῶν in 8:31 and since it occurs in a statement about prayer in 8:34, whose context answers the question whether God is in favor of his people. Yet, he ignored the fact that Jesus' death for believers in 8:32 and resurrection in 8:34 provide the foundational reason why believers will be exonerated in God's law court.

---

90. Powers, *Salvation through Participation*, 138.
91. Ibid., 138–39.
92. Ibid.
93. Ibid.
94. Ibid., 139.
95. Ibid., 139–41, esp. 140.

An argument in support of substitution in 8:31–34 is not solely dependent upon a substitutionary reading of ὑπέρ. In fact, my argument places no weight on a substitutionary function of ὑπέρ at all in the context of Rom 8:31–34. Rather, my understanding of the contextual argument in Rom 8:31–34 shapes how I understand ὑπέρ in this section.

As I argued above regarding 8:3, Paul can communicate substitutionary ideas with the preposition περί (e.g., in the phrase περὶ τῆς ἁμαρτίας) if the context warrants it. Regarding the substitutionary context of 8:31–34, after stating that God surrendered his Son "for us" in 8:32, Paul uses legal/forensic language in 8:33 with the verbs ἐγκαλέσει ("bring a charge") and δικαιω ("I declare to be in the right") and in 8:34 with the participle κατακρινῶν ("I condemn"),[96] the latter of which appears in its nominal cognate form in 8:1 (κατάκριμα) and in its finite verbal form in 8:3 (κατέκρινεν). Since Paul has already stated that God offered Jesus in death to free those under Torah's jurisdiction from condemnation (7:1—8:3), Paul likely, therefore, speaks of substitution in 8:32.

Furthermore, because of the legal/forensic language of 8:33–34, Paul likely suggests that Jesus' substitutionary death was penal. Jesus' penal substitutionary death for sin is foundational to receiving the soteriological blessings of 8:28–34 for the following reasons: (1) Paul mentions Jesus' death in 8:32 and in 8:34 in the context of legal language (8:33–34). (2) Paul states in 8:29–34 why all things work together for the good for God's people. Romans 8:31 begins with the question of who is "against us," followed in 8:32 with a statement about Jesus' death "for us all," followed in 8:33 by another question about who can bring charges "against God's elect" in the law court, followed by the statement in 8:33 that God "justifies," and these series of comments are followed by the question of who "condemns" God's people in his law court. The section culminates in 8:34 with a reference to Jesus' death for God's elect against whom no charge can be made in God's law court. All things work together for the good for God's elect because he is the author of their salvation, and no one condemns God's elect in his law court because Jesus was condemned for them in death and because his death exonerates (i.e., justifies) them in God's judgment. This affirmation of substitution (and more specifically, penal substitution) does not deny

96. For examples of this with ἐγκαλέω, see LXX Exod 22:8; 2 Macc 5:8; Prov 19:5; Wis 12:12; Sir 46:19; Zech 1:4; Acts 19:38, 40; 23:28–29; 26:2, 7; with δικαιω, see LXX Gen 44:16; Exod 23:7; Deut 25:1; 1 Kgs 8:32; Isa 1:7; 5:23; 43:9; Sir 1:22; 7:3; 9:12; 10:29; 13:22; 23:11; 26:29; 31:5; 42:2; *Pss. Sol.* 8:26; Matt 12:37; Acts 13:38–39; Rom 2:13; 3:4, 20, 24, 26, 28, 30; 4:2, 5; 5:1, 9; 8:30, 33; 1 Cor 4:4; 6:11; Gal 2:16–17; 3:8, 11, 24; 5:4; Tit 3:7; Jas 2:21, 25; and with κατακρινω, see LXX Est 2:1; Wis 4:16; *Pss. Sol.* 4:2; Sus 1:41, 48, 53; Matt 12:41–42; 20:18; 27:3; Mark 10:33; 14:64; Luke 11:31; Rom 2:1; 8:34; 14:23; Heb 11:7; 2 Pet 2:6.

participation or representation. Nor does this affirmation suggest that one view is superior to another in this text. Instead, my argument is simply that penal substitution is present in 8:31–34.

Powers' second criticism wrongly played participatory/representative notions in the phrase σὺν αὐτῷ in 8:32 against substitution in 8:31–34. To the contrary, even if 8:32 emphasizes representation/participation, substitution could still be present in the text (e.g., as in the case of 8:3). After Paul asks who condemns God's elect (8:33–34), he states that God justifies (i.e., declares to be in the right) the elect in 8:33 and that Jesus died and was raised in 8:34. Paul's reference to the death and resurrection of Jesus in context of justification in 8:33–34 recalls 4:25: "[Jesus] was handed over for our transgressions and raised for our justification." His reference to the justification of the elect in tandem with both Jesus' death for non-Torah-observant transgressors and his resurrection connects Paul's remarks in 8:31–34 with the Jewish martyrological narratives, which likewise present the martyrs as both representatives of and substitutes for Israel in the context of a future resurrection.

The Torah-observant Jewish martyrs died for non-Torah-observant sinners to reconcile God to them (LXX Dan 3:27–40; 2 Macc 7:32–38; 4 Macc 6:28–29; 17:21–22). Their deaths secured their participation in the resurrection (2 Macc 7:9). After the king killed the first son (2 Macc 7:3–6), he summoned the second son (2 Macc 7:7). He too threatened the second with death lest he assimilate (2 Macc 7:7). The second son replied in the Hebrew language that God will resurrect him and the other martyrs because they die for his laws (ἐν ἐσχάτῃ δὲ πνοῇ γενόμενος εἶπεν σὺ μέν ἀλάστωρ ἐκ τοῦ παρόντος ἡμᾶς ζῆν ἀπολύεις ὁ δὲ τοῦ κόσμου βασιλεὺς ἀποθανόντας ἡμᾶς ὑπὲρ τῶν αὐτοῦ νόμων εἰς αἰώνιον ἀναβίωσιν ζωῆς ἡμᾶς ἀναστήσει) (2 Macc 7:9). In 2 Macc 7:23, the mother repeated the second son's remarks regarding the resurrection of the martyrs who died for God's law. The martyrs' death for the law in 2 Maccabees is also described as a death for sins (2 Macc 7:23, 32, 37; cf. 7:7—8:3). In 2 Macc 7:29, the mother urges her youngest son to be faithful to die for Torah so that she will receive him back again, which in context refers to the resurrection. The seventh son states that he and the other martyrs suffered because of their own sins (2 Macc 7:32); he prays that God would be reconciled to the martyrs through the martyrs' deaths (2 Macc 7:33), and he prays that God would use his death and the deaths of his fellow martyrs to be the means by which God assuaged his wrath against Israel (2 Macc 7:37–38).

The author of 4 Maccabees likewise speaks of the death of Torah-observant Jews for non-Torah-observant people vis-à-vis the resurrection of those who died for others. In 4 Macc 6:28–29, Eleazar asks God to use his death to function as Israel's purification. In 4 Macc 13:13, the Jewish martyrs state that Abraham, Isaac, and Jacob will welcome them in the afterlife. In 4 Macc 17:21–22 and in 18:3–5, the author states that God purified and saved Israel from his wrath through the martyrs' propitiatory deaths for Israel. Thus, just as Paul states that God resurrected Jesus, a Torah-observant Jew and that he died for the soteriological benefits of non-Torah-observant sinners, the authors of 2 and 4 Maccabees state that the Jewish martyrs, Torah-observant Jews who died for the soteriological benefit of non-Torah-observant Jews, will be resurrected from the dead.

CONCLUSION

In this chapter, I discussed Jewish martyrology and substitution in Rom 5:6–11, 8:1–4, and 8:31–34. I argued that the Jewish martyrological narratives were a background behind Paul's presentation of Jesus' death as a substitute in Rom 5:6–11, in 8:1–4, and 8:31–34. I supported this thesis by an exegetical, conceptual, and comparative analysis of these texts.

6

Jewish Martyrology and Representation in Romans 5:12—6:23[1]

INTRODUCTION

In chapters 4–5, I argued that Paul presents Jesus' death as substitute for sinners and that the Jewish martyrological narratives are a background in front of which interpreters should read his presentation of Jesus' death as a substitute. As with the earlier chapters on substitution, I simply argue here that representation is within Paul's understanding of Jesus' death and that his presentation of Jesus' death as a representation in Romans forges a link with the Jewish martyrological narratives. I argue these points by means of an analysis of Rom 5:12—6:23.

REPRESENTATION IN ROMANS 5:12-21

James D. G. Dunn wrote the following in an essay on representation: "The thesis put forward in what follows is that Paul's understanding of Jesus' life as having representative significance is the key which opens up to us his understanding of the significance of Jesus' death. Or to put the point in more technical shorthand: Paul's Adam Christology is integral to his theology of

---

1. Representation occurs elsewhere in Romans besides 5:12—6:23 (e.g., 8:3). But the former section is perhaps the clearest.

Jesus' death as an atoning sacrifice."[2] Although Dunn may have overestimated the importance of representation for Paul, he was certainly correct to emphasize that representation is important for Paul's understanding of Jesus' death. In my view, the most sustained place representation occurs in Romans is in 5:12–21.[3] His emphasis on the representative function of Jesus' death in this section reveals another connection with the Jewish martyrological narratives. The representative function of Jesus' death in 5:12–21 is evidenced by both Paul's presentation of Jesus as the new Adam and by his contrasting of him with the old Adam. As the new Adam, Jesus reversed the old Adam's universal curse of judgment by his own righteous obedience. To defend this thesis, I offer an exegetical and comparative analysis of the Jewish martyrological traditions and Rom 5:12–21.

Representation and the Adam-Christ Antithesis

As I have argued in more detail elsewhere,[4] Paul's argument in 5:12–21 is grammatically complex. He introduces this section with the prepositional phrase διὰ τοῦτο, follows this phrase with a comparative adverbial clause in 5:12, truncates the comparison in 5:13–17, and again takes up the comparison in 5:18–21 in order to emphasize that Adam brought universal death to all but Christ brought universal life to all.[5] Paul links 5:12–21with 5:1–11 and more importantly with the Jewish martyrological narratives by beginning 5:12 with the phrase διὰ τοῦτο. The latter phrase also points to the argument that follows in 5:12–21.[6] The phrase διὰ τοῦτο makes 5:6–21 one martyrological unit because the phrase links both the martyrological categories of the substitutionary death of Torah-observant Jews for the soteriological benefit of non-Torah-observant sinners with representation. If this is correct, Paul's remarks in 5:12–21 flow from 1:18—5:11, most immediately connect with 5:1–11, and anticipate in 5:12a the comparison in 5:18–21.

---

2. Dunn, "Paul's Understanding of the Death of Jesus as Sacrifice," 35–56; esp. 35.
3. So Dunn, "Paul's Understanding," 36.
4. See Jarvis J. Williams, *For Whom Did Christ Die?*
5. For a different reading of the syntax, see Leithart, "Adam, Moses, and Jesus," 264–65 n. 15.
6. Similarly Nygren, *Commentary on Romans*, 206–12. Against Karl Barth, *The Epistle to the Romans*, 164–65; Käsemann, *Commentary on Romans*, 141–42; Porter, "The Pauline Concept of Original Sin," 20–21; Cranfield, *Romans*, 1:271–72; Witherington, *The Problem with Evangelical Theology*, 12. For a kataphoric use of the phrase, see Matt 13:13; 24:44; Mark 12:24; John 5:16, 18; 8:47; 10:17; 12:18, 39; Rom 1:26; 13:6; Eph 6:13; 1 Thess 2:13; 3:7–8; 2 Thess 2:11; 1 Tim 1:16; 2 Tim 2:10; Phlm 1:15; Heb 2:1; 9:15; 1 John 3:1.

Paul's argument in the entire unit appears to be that just as Adam's disobedience introduced sin and death to all, so also Jesus' obedience conquered the power of sin, introduced to humanity by Adam's disobedience, and produced life for all (5:12–21). The argument presents Adam as humanity's representative who introduced a curse to his progeny and Christ as humanity's representative who reversed Adam's curse away from his progeny.

Both the representative functions of Adam and Jesus are evident throughout the section. Paul refers to the "one man" who sinned in 5:12, and he states that the "one man" is indeed "Adam" in 5:14.[7] He continues by speaking of the "transgression of Adam" (5:14), "the transgression of the one" (5:15, 17), "judgment from the one" (5:16, 18), "the one who sinned" (5:16), the "reign of death through the one" (5:17), and "the disobedience of the one man" (5:19). He refers to Jesus' obedience as "the gift from the one man" (5:15, 17), "acquittal through the one man" (5:18), and "the obedience of the one" (5:19). Paul's use of the adverbs ὥσπερ (5:12, 19), ὡς (5:15–16, 18–19), and οὕτως καὶ (5:15, 18) throughout 5:12–20 elucidate the Adam-Christ antithesis.

Paul states that "sin entered into the world through one man, death through sin, and so death spread to all men with the result that all sin" (Rom 5:12; cf. 2 Esdr 3:7–8 [NRSV]; 4 *Ezra* 3:21). Since the "one man" who introduced sin to the creation is Adam (cf. 5:14), Paul is alluding to Genesis 2–3 in Rom 5:12. Adam's disobedience introduced sin into God's good creation (cf. Gen 1–3), and a universal reign of sin immediately followed his disobedience. After Adam sinned, God first curses his good creation (cf. Gen 3:14–21). This curse and the events that followed suggest that the human condition after the disobedience of Adam radically changed after his transgression. Prior to sin's entrance into the creation, Adam enjoyed God, his presence, and his creation, but after he sinned he fled from God's presence and he cultivated God's creation by the sweat of his brow (cf. Gen 3). Because of his transgression, God cursed (1) the animals (Gen 3:14), (2) the woman (Gen 3:16), (3) the man (Gen 3:17), and (4) the ground (Gen 3:17–19). This universal curse fulfilled God's promise to Adam in Gen 2:17 that if he should eat from the forbidden tree, he would certainly die.

Paul does not use a Greek word for representation/participation anywhere in 5:12–21, but he presents Adam as humanity's representative along the same lines of Genesis 1–3 and certain texts in Second Temple Judaism. He also presents Jesus as the representative new Adam in whom human beings must participate to be freed from the curse of the first Adam. In

---

7. Although I disagree with his criticisms of substitution in Romans 5, Powers (*Salvation through Participation*, 107–8) offered helpful comments about representation/participation in 5:12–21.

Genesis 3, God curses the entire creation because of Adam's transgression. The author of *Jub.* 3:17–32 blames Adam, Eve, and the serpent for sin, but Paul highlights Adam's representative role in bringing a curse upon the entire creation when he says that "sin" entered the world "through one man" and "death" entered the world "through sin" with the result that "all sin" (Rom 5:12). The phrase "through sin" in 5:12 refers back to the sin that entered into the world through the one man in 5:12a.

Paul expresses in 5:12 that the agent through whom sin and death entered the world was Adam and the manner by which sin entered the world and brought a universal curse upon the entire creation was his disobedience.[8] Adam's disobedience brought a curse upon him and a universal curse upon the entire cosmos. In Paul's view, Adam's curse exercises itself in history by means of sin's universal reign as a power over the entire creation, especially over human-beings (the pinnacle of God's creation in Genesis 1–2) and by means of individual transgressions (e.g., cf. 3:23 with 5:12). These propositions emphasize that Paul presents Adam as humanity's representative. Thus, his logic runs as follows: (1) Adam's sin brought sin into the world. (2) Adam's sin resulted in death for Adam and his progeny. (3) Adam's sin and its curse spread to all of humanity. (4) Adam's sin and the spread of sin and death to all men resulted in humanity's bondage to sin's power.

The latter clause in 5:12 has been the subject of intense debate among NT scholars because of the relative clause ἐφ' ᾧ πάντες ἥμαρτον.[9] The most important option for my thesis in this chapter is the Adamic interpretation of the text. This view has different nuances,[10] but each proponent interprets ἐφ' ᾧ to refer to Adam. The Adamic interpretation has its origins in Augustine who could not read Greek well but relied on the Latin translation *in quo* ("in whom"). He understood "in whom" in the clause ἐφ' ᾧ πάντες ἥμαρτον to refer to Adam. Accordingly, this view suggests that Paul asserts that Adam was humanity's federal head in that he represented them. In my view, Augustine grammatically misunderstood the clause ἐφ' ᾧ πάντες ἥμαρτον. Yet, he rightly understood Adam's representative role in bringing the curse of sin against Adam and the entire creation. The entirety of 5:12 proposes that Adam was humanity's representative, not the phrase ἐφ' ᾧ.

---

8. I take οὕτως καὶ in a modal sense (cf. Acts 7:8; 27:44; Rom 11:26; 1 Cor 11:28; 14:25; 15:11; Gal 6:2; 1 Thess 4:17; Heb 6:15; Jas 2:12; Rev 9:17).

9. For a summary of the interpretive options, see Vickers, "Grammar and Theology in the Interpretation of Rom 5:12," 271–88.

10. For the different nuances of the same view, see Danker, "Rom 5.12: Sin under Law," 428; Bultmann, "Adam and Christ according to Romans 5," 143–65, esp. 153; Cambier, "Péchés des hommes et péches d' Adam en Rom v. 12," 246–53.

For example, the ἐφ' ᾧ construction occurs in the NT epistles only in the Pauline letters. Every occurrence in Paul refers to a thematic or conceptual antecedent instead of a grammatical antecedent (Rom 5:12; 2 Cor 5:4; Phil 3:12; 4:10).[11] These occurrences support the claim that the phrase has a conjunctive construction. The phrase points to the entire theological concept in 5:12: namely, sin entered the world through Adam, death through sin, and Adam's sin that lead to death results in the fact that all sin.[12] Consequently, this reading proposes that Paul fundamentally blames Adam for the problem of sin and death because he was humanity's representative. But because of Adam's sin, everyone has become his own Adam in that everyone participates in Adam's sin both inherently and experientially in the here and now (cf. 2 Bar. 54:15, 19). Paul's remarks that "all have sinned and fallen short of the glory of God" in 3:23 support this point.

Paul states in 5:13–14 that the entrance of the law into history exacerbated the problem of sin. He argues that sin was in the world even before the giving of Torah and that it was not counted as transgression, whereas sin's universal reign over the entire creation was still evident even before the giving of Torah since death reigned from Adam until Moses.[13] Paul's argument in 5:15–21 contrasts Jesus' obedience with Adam's disobedience in order to highlight the superiority of the gift of justification provided through Jesus' obedience over the universal condemnation of sin resulting from Adam's disobedience.[14] Paul first pits Adam's transgression against Jesus' gift in 5:15. He asserts that God's gift, provided through Jesus' obedience, will supremely abound for many since "many died because of the transgression of the one man." Since the grace and gift of God that come to humanity as a result of the obedience of the "one man" in 5:15 refer to justification and eternal life (5:17), the death that all died as a result of Adam's sin must include spiritual death in 5:12.

Paul states that the transgression of the one man results in condemnation for all in 5:16. Romans 5:16–21 affirms the universal impact of Adam's transgression on humanity. Here Paul contrasts Jesus' gift with Adam's sin. Judgment comes as a result of the one who sinned, but the gift results in acquittal "from many transgressions" (5:16).[15] Prior to 5:16, Paul has only spo-

11. The phrase occurs in Acts 7:33.

12. For a detailed discussion of ἐφ' ᾧ that resists committing to any antecedent, see D. L. Turner, "Adam, Christ, and US," 129–49. This reference is cited in Daniel B. Wallace, *Greek Grammar Beyond the Basics*, 342–43, esp. 343 n. 75.

13. Against Leithart, "Adam, Moses, and Jesus," 257–73, who argues for a positive role of Torah's entrance into salvation-history.

14. Similarly Cranfield, *Romans*, 1:270.

15. J. R. Daniel Kirk argues that *dikaiōma* means "reparation" accomplished by a

ken of transgression in the singular, which is his way of referring to Adam's sin (Rom 5:12–16a). But now, Paul mentions in 5:16 Adam's sin and God's judgment beside of the phrase "from many transgressions." This combination suggests that the "many transgressions" do not refer to Adam's sins, but to the transgressions of all who sin because of Adam's transgression. Adam's transgressions result in both the condemnation of all and in humanity's personal experience with sin because (in Paul's view) a real Adam sinned as humanity's representative. Paul envisages this point when he contrasts the penalties of the transgression of the one (death, judgment, bondage to sin) with the blessings of the obedience of the one (justification, eternal life, and freedom from sin) in 5:12–21 and with the argument of 5:17–21.

In 5:17, Paul speaks of Adam's sin by referring to transgression in the singular (παραπτώματι). He states that if death reigns through the transgression of the one, those who receive the gift of righteousness would receive eternal life through the one, namely, Jesus (5:17). Because of διὰ τοῦτο ὥσπερ in 5:12, ἄρα οὖν ὡς, and οὕτως καὶ in 5:18, the latter text continues Paul's initial remarks in 5:12 by inferring from 5:15–17 that the gift of Jesus' obedience and the curse of Adam's disobedience are completely antithetical to one another because one represents universal death for all and the other represents universal life for all. Paul mentions in 5:18 that "condemnation" comes to all as a result of Adam's sin and that "justification" comes to all as a result of Jesus' obedience. Paul reiterates this contrast in 5:19 by stating that Adam's disobedience made many sinners, and Jesus' obedience made many righteous.[16] The disobedience of the one, Adam, brings death to all because he represents all, but the righteous act of the one, Jesus, brings life to the many because both Adam and Jesus represent not only themselves but also others. "Adam represents what man might now have been and by his sin what man is. Jesus represents what man now is and by his obedience what man might become."[17]

Paul makes a similar argument in 1 Cor 15:21–22 as he defends the veracity of a future resurrection (1 Cor 15:1–58). He asserts that Jesus is raised from the dead (1 Cor. 15:20). To defend this, he contrasts Adam with Christ in 15:21–22. Since death entered through a man, then resurrection from the dead enters through a man (1 Cor 15:21). Adam and Jesus are similar in that the actions of both representatively determined for all people

---

convicted person who satisfies the court and justifies the defendant. In his view, the term should not be translated in Rom 5:16 as justification, but as "reparation," which leads to justification. See "Reconsidering *Dikaiōma* in Romans 5:16," 787–92.

16. Paul's rhetorical shift dismisses any possibility that righteousness universally comes to all apart from faith.

17. Dunn, "Paul's Understanding of the Death of Jesus," 125–41, esp. 127.

without distinction the course of history.[18] The contrast is that one man (=Adam) brought death and one man (=Jesus) brought life. Death came as a result of the disobedience of the one man, but life came as a result of the obedience of the other man. Paul spends the rest of 1 Corinthians 15 arguing that although death reigns because of Adam's sin, death is not the final word (15:23-58). Paul explicitly states in 15:22 that the man who brought death was Adam and the man who secured resurrection and life was Christ: "just as in Adam all died, thus also in Christ all will be brought to life."

Finally, Paul concludes the unit of Rom 5:12-21 in 5:20-21 by stating that the law made sin worse; grace abounded over sin through Jesus, and sin abounded in death because of Adam. But grace abounded much more resulting in eternal life through Jesus' obedience. Thus, Adam and Jesus represented humanity. Adam's disobedience cursed the entire creation, and Jesus' obedience reverses the curse away from those who receive his gift of righteousness (5:17).

REPRESENTATION IN ROMANS 6:1-23

In Rom 6:1-23, Paul continues to present Jesus' death as a representation for sinners. This links Jesus' death with the Jewish martyrological narratives. I argue these points by an exegetical analysis of the texts that present Jesus' death as representation in the argument of Rom 6:1-23.

Jesus' Historic Death and Resurrection Represent New Life

The inferential particle (οὖν) in 6:1 links 6:1-23 with 5:12-21 and with Paul's substitutionary presentation of Jesus' death in 5:6-11. Paul's argument in Romans 6 infers from 5:12-21. In the latter unit, Paul presents Adam and Jesus as representatives of Jews and Gentiles by presenting an Adam-Christ antithesis, while arguing that Adam's disobedience introduced sin and death into the world upon everyone and that Jesus' obedience introduced liberation from Adam's transgression for everyone (5:12-19). In 5:20-21, Paul discusses the role of the law in history in light of Adam's sin and Jesus'

---

18. All without distinction places the emphasis on Paul's Jew-Gentile universalism. In 5:12-21, he has not forgotten his universal indictment of Jews and Gentiles in 1:18—3:20 or his words in 3:21—4:25 that God justifies all Jews and Gentiles who believe by faith in Christ. In 5:12—8:11, Paul argues that Adam's transgression universally cursed all Jews and Gentiles, and Jesus' obedience universally reverses the curse away from believing Jews and Gentiles. The Jew-Gentile problem and the Jew-Gentile solution is at the heart of Paul's argument and his gospel throughout the entire letter.

obedience. He states that the "law entered so that transgression would increase" (5:20). That is, the law entered into history to make the spiritual predicament worse for those under Torah. However, when the power of sin increased through the entrance of the law, the power of grace increased more through Jesus Christ and conquered the power of sin. As a result, just as sin reign through death because of Adam's disobedience, the first representative, "so also grace reigned through righteousness resulting in eternal life through Jesus Christ, our Lord," the second representative (5:20b–21). Thus, Paul anticipates the inference that one should continue to be subdued under sin's power so that the power of grace would continue to increase (6:1).

Paul argues that believers died to the power of sin (6:1–23). This death to sin was visualized when believers were baptized into the death of Christ through water-baptism so that they would live in new resurrection-life (6:2–5).[19] Paul makes Jesus' historical death and resurrection the foundation of the believer's new life in Christ, and he makes Jesus' historical death and resurrection representative of the believer's new life in Christ (6:2–5). Paul supports this with his remarks that believers were baptized into the death of Christ (6:3), that believers "were buried with him through baptism" so that they would walk in newness of life, just as Jesus was raised from the dead and now experiences a fresh new life (6:4), and that believers will certainly participate in the resurrection since they have become partakers in the likeness of his death (6:5).

The explanatory γὰρ in 6:5 links the verse with his previous comments about the believer's death with Christ through water-baptism in 6:3–4. His argument appears to be that believers died to sin and should no longer live under its power (6:2). Their water-baptism proves that they participate in the death of Jesus and experience a spiritual death to the power of sin (6:3). Therefore, Paul concludes, that believers have been buried with Jesus through their participation in water-baptism, a baptism that identifies them with the death of Jesus (their representative [5:12–21]) and thereby kills the power of sin in their lives, so that they would live with Jesus in the resurrection just as Jesus presently lives in the power of his physical resurrection (6:4). Believers who died to the power of sin by being baptized into Jesus' death will certainly (ἀλλὰ καὶ) participate in a physical resurrection just as Jesus died and resurrected, because those who died to the power of sin (just as Jesus died= τῷ ὁμοιώματι τοῦ θανάτου αὐτοῦ) will participate in a future resurrection (just as Jesus has already been resurrected) (6:5).

---

19. For a detailed investigation of baptism in Romans 6 and its background, see Agersnap, *Baptism and the New Life*.

In 6:6–7, Paul identifies the believer's new life in Christ, symbolized through water-baptism, as co-crucifixion with Christ (ὁ παλαιὸς ἡμῶν ἄνθρωπος συνεσταυρώθη). In 6:6, he states that "our old man was crucified together with Christ." The "old man" refers to the believer's former identity in Adam before faith in Christ because the "therefore" in 6:1 connects the current argument in 6:1–23 with the previous argument in 5:12–21 and because Paul describes Adam in the latter text as the one man, representing Jews and Gentiles, who introduced sin and death into the world, and he presents Jesus as the one man, representing many Jews and Gentiles, who brought grace and eternal life and righteousness to the many (5:18–21).[20] Sin

20. Paul's use of the phrase "old man" in contrast to the "new man" in Eph 4:22 and Col 3:9 further supports the claim that Paul conceived of the "old man" as a reference to the believer's faithless identity in Adam before faith-identity in/with Christ. He urges the Ephesians to put on the "new man" and to put aside the "old man" by giving them several exhortations throughout the letter. He grounds these exhortations in the great work of God through Jesus Christ. He begins Ephesians by praising God for the great spiritual blessings that they have in Jesus (Eph 1:3–14); he prays that they would better understand these spiritual blessings that God has bestowed upon them (Eph 1:15–22; 3:14–19); he expresses that they were once dead in trespasses and sins until God saved them by his grace through faith and seated them in the heavenly places with Jesus Christ (Eph 2:1–10); he encourages them to remember that they were formerly alienated from God's salvation-historical promises to the Jewish people before they came to faith in Jesus since they were Gentiles, but in Christ Jesus God has incorporated them into both the family and people of God with other believing Jews and Gentiles (Eph 2:11–22). Finally, he urges them to live in a manner that is consistent with their new life in Jesus Christ (Eph. 4:1—6:20). He commands them to live no longer as they did as Gentiles "in the futility of their mind when they were darkened in ignorance" (Eph 4:17). Paul similarly states in Rom 7:23, a verse whose unit possibly points back to Rom 5:12–21, that the mind of the Jew in Adam under Torah apart from Christ was captive to the power of sin. In Eph 4:18, he states that the Ephesians were also formerly separated from eternal life from God because of their ignorance and hardened heart, whose spiritual ignorance enabled them to give themselves over to practice all forms of impurity (Eph 4:19), whereas in Rom 5:17 he asserts that those who received grace and the gift of righteousness will reign in life through Jesus Christ. Paul furthermore urges the Ephesians to put off the "old man," which he describes as "corruptible corresponding to the lusts of deception," to renew their mind, and to put on the "new man" who was created in accordance with God in righteousness and holiness of the truth (Eph 4:22–24). That the "old man" in this text refers to the believer's identity in Adam before faith in Christ seems to be a plausible reading, for Paul associates the "old man" with the Ephesians' "former conduct" (Eph 4:21); he suggests that this "old man" enabled them to pursue an immoral lifestyle marked by ungodliness instead of being marked by the Spirit (Eph 4:18–20), and he contrasts the "old man" with the "new man" and associates the latter with Jesus Christ (Eph 4:20–21, 24). Unlike the "old man," the "new man" was created for righteousness and holiness (Eph 4:24). Similarly, in Rom 5:12–21, Paul speaks of Adam as the one who brought sin, transgression, and death into the world and as the one whose sin resulted in universal condemnation for all, whereas Jesus introduced life and righteousness into the world for all who believe and as the one whose obedience resulted in the gift of righteousness and eternal life

and death entered the world through "one man," and the entrance of sin and death into the world consequently results in the universal condemnation of "all men" (5:12–21). The one representative man, Jesus Christ, brought grace and a free gift to the many (5:15–21), but the other representative man, who sinned, introduced the universal reign of sin and death to the many (5:15–21).

When Paul asserts that the old man was crucified, he simply means that the old man died with Christ at baptism, because he has already argued

---

for all who believe. In a similar text in Col 3:9, Paul urges Gentile Christians to put off the old man and to put on the new man, because they died with Christ. The Colossian Christians were evidently in potential danger of being duped by false teaching (Col 2:4, 8; 3:16–19). Paul reminds them that they had received Christ and had benefited from his redemptive work, for God through Christ placed them into the kingdom of his Son whom he loves (Col 1:3–4, 13–14), and Paul thanks God for the Colossians' steadfast faith in Christ (Col 1:3–4; 2:5). He, then, urges them to live in accordance with the new man since they received Christ (Col 2:6—4:1). Just as in Rom 6:2–4, Paul asserts that they died with Christ in water-baptism and were raised to walk in a new resurrection-life when they were previously dead in trespasses and sins, for God made them alive with Christ (Col 2:12–13). Paul further urges that since they have died with Christ (Col 3:1, 3), they should pursue obedience, because their lives were in fact hidden in Christ (Col 3:3). Paul restates the positive command from Col 3:1–4, to set their mind on the things above, in Col 3:5–17 by telling the Colossians how to set their mind on the things above. He states that they should put to death earthly things such as "sexual sin," "impurity," "sinful passion," "evil desire," and "covetousness" (Col 3:5). He further notes that they should put aside "wrath," "fury," "blasphemy" and "obscene speech" (Col 3:9), and he contends that they should not lie to one another," because they "put off the old man with its deeds and they put on the new man" (Col 3:9–10). The new man is associated with Jesus Christ and is marked by holiness (Col 3:1–10, 12–17), and this new man is the Colossians' current identity in Christ (Col 3:1). The old man represents who they were before they died with Christ and before they were hidden in him (Col 2:12; 3:1–4), for the old man is characterized by disobedience and sin. That this old man was the Colossians' identity in Adam before faith in Christ is certain because Paul here, as in Romans 6, speaks of dying to the old man in Christian baptism and he contrasts the old man with new life in Jesus Christ. Based on this contrast, he urges the Colossians (as the Ephesians) to live in a way consistent with the new man, just as he does in Rom 6:1–23 after he finishes discussing the universal impact of Adam's transgression and the digression of humanity's spiritual predicament after Torah's entrance into salvation-history (Rom 5:12–21). The parallels between the "old man" and Adam and the "new man" and Christ in Rom 5:12–21, Eph 4:24, and Col 3:9 support my interpretation of the "old man" in Romans 6. Identity in Adam/old man is characterized by sin and disobedience (Rom 5:12, 14, 15, 16, 17, 18, 19; Eph 4:17–19; Col 3:5–9a), and identity in Jesus/new man is characterized by obedience, righteousness, and eternal life (Rom 5:15–21; Eph 4:24; Col 2:12–13, 20; 3:1–4). Thus, when Paul affirms that "our old man" was crucified with Christ in Rom 6:6, he refers to the old identity in Adam before faith in Christ since the first man (Adam) was the old man and the one who brought about humanity's curse, but the new man, Jesus, reverses the curse (cf. Rom 5:14) and incorporates those who believe into a new community of the redeemed through faith in his death and resurrection (Rom 6:9).

in 6:2–4 that Christians died with Christ (6:2), were baptized into his death (6:3), and were buried with him through baptism (6:4) and because crucifixion was a popular mode of execution/death in the ancient world.[21] Paul states that the old man was crucified with Christ "so that the body of sin would be abolished and so that we would no longer serve sin" (6:6b). The second clause in 6:6b (ἵνα καταργηθῇ τὸ σῶμα τῆς ἁμαρτίας, τοῦ μηκέτι δουλεύειν ἡμᾶς τῇ ἁμαρτίᾳ) is epexegetical to 6:6a at least because both clauses adverbially modify συνεσταυρώθη. To say that the old man participated in co-crucifixion with Jesus is another way of saying that believers died to sin and participate in new resurrection life with Jesus, for Paul asserts in 6:1–5 and in 6:8 that those who participate in co-crucifixion with Christ will likewise participate in the resurrection (just like Jesus). Evidence of this future hope has invaded the current age in that all who die with Christ are now liberated from sin's tyranny (6:7–23).

Paul's reference to the τὸ σῶμα τῆς ἁμαρτίας in 6:6 speaks to the believer's old man/old identity in the representative man, Adam, before faith in Christ in contrast to the other representative man, Jesus, who reversed Adam's curse, because 5:12–21 contrasts the curse of Adam's transgression with the righteousness and blessing of the obedience of Christ and because Paul parallels ὁ παλαιὸς ἡμῶν ἄνθρωπος in 6:6a with τὸ σῶμα τῆς ἁμαρτίας in 6:6b. Paul speaks of the "sinful body" (6:6), the "mortal body" (6:12), and being "in the flesh" (6:5; 7:18, 25) while making the argument that one should not continue to be subdued to the power of sin (6:1, 15).

The following three arguments further highlight the representative function of Jesus' death and resurrection in 6:6. First, Paul has not yet abandoned his discussion in 5:12–21 about the effects of Adam's (the representative man's) transgression upon all. Second, Adam's transgression introduced a universal curse of sin and death upon the entire creation (5:12). Third, Paul continues to discuss in 6:6, and in the following verses, that believers in Christ have died to the power of sin since they died with Christ (6:6–11). Paul states that the "old man was crucified" (6:6a), the "body of sin would be abolished" (6:6b), and "if we died with Christ" (6:8), "we will live with Christ" (6:8), just as Christ died and was raised (6:9–10). Thus, references to the "old man" and the "body of sin" in 6:6 representatively refer to the old man/previous identity in Adam, and the abolishment of the "body of sin" refers to the believer's new identity in the representative new man, Christ,

---

21. E.g., Matt 27:32–44; Mark 15:21–32; Luke 23:26–43; John 19:17–27; Philo, *Flacc.* 6:36–39; 10:75; Seutonius, *Dom* 11; Josephus. *J.W* 2:14.9; *Ant.* 6.5.3.302–4.

an identity that Jesus' historic death and resurrection representatively personify.[22]

The old man was crucified in order to destroy sin (6:6), because the one who died to sin is liberated from its power (6:7). The clause ὁ ἀποθανὼν δεδικαίωται ἀπὸ τῆς ἁμαρτίας could refer to Jesus, for Paul states in 6:10 that "Jesus died to sin once and for all." However, 6:7 most likely refers to the believer who has died to sin by becoming united to Christ in water-baptism, because Paul states that believers "died to sin" (6:2), that they "were baptized into his death" (6:3), that they were "buried with him through baptism" (6:4), that they "have become united in the likeness of Jesus' death," (6:5), that their old man was crucified and abolished because they participated in co-crucifixion with Christ through baptism (6:5–6), that they "died with Christ," (6:8), that they will live with him (6:5), and because 6:11 commands believers to consider themselves to be dead to sin in Christ, since Christ died to sin once and for all and since he was raised from the dead (6:9–11). Death with Christ results in a liberated resurrection life with Christ for believers (6:7–10, 18), because Jesus' historic death and resurrection represent the spiritual death and spiritual life that believers in Christ experience when they died with him in water-baptism, the moment when they expressed participation in his death and resurrection. Furthermore, Jesus' death and resurrection represent and model the new liberated life of which those who participated in co-crucifixion with Jesus should partake. For example, those who participated in co-crucifixion with Christ through baptism died to sin (6:1, 6), were liberated from sin (6:7, 17–18, 22), should present themselves as dead to sin but alive to God (6:11, 13, 15–16, 19–21), and should not let sin reign over their mortal bodies (6:12, 14).

By presenting Jesus' death as a substitution in Rom 3:21—4:25, 5:6–11, 8:1–4, and 8:31–34 and as a representation in 5:12—6:23, Paul reveals another connection with the Jewish martyrological narratives. In chapter 3, I argued in great detail in favor of the substitutionary narratives of the Jewish martyrs with an analysis of texts in LXX Daniel 3, 2 Macc 7:32–38, 4 Macc 6:28–29, and 17:21–22. The representative function of the martyrs' deaths is likewise evident in their guilt by association with the non-Torah-observant nation and by their death for it. There are numerous statements in 2 Maccabees regarding the representative function of the martyrs deaths and regarding the suffering of the Jewish people as a result of the sins of some within the nation (2 Macc 5:17–18; 6:14–15; 7:18, 32; 8:5; 10:45). 2 Maccabees 5:17 states that God's wrath fell upon the nation because of the sins

---

22. For examples of καταργέω as abolishment in the NT, see Rom 3:3, 31; 4:14; 7:2, 6; 1 Cor 1:28; 2:6; 6:13; 13:8, 10, 11; 15:24, 26; 2 Cor 3:7, 11, 13, 14; Gal 3:17; 5:4, 11; Eph 2:15; 2 Thess 2:8; 2 Tim 1:10; Heb 2:14.

of some within the city, and the seventh son states in 2 Macc 7:32 that the martyrs suffered the wrath of the Almighty because of *their* own sins (7:32; see also 2:17). Yet, 2 Maccabees states nowhere that the martyrs actually violated Torah. Instead, the book presents them as being faithful to it even until death.

The representative function of the martyrs is further evident in 4 Macc 6:28–29 by Eleazar's request that God would be merciful to the nation through his death for the nation and that their judgment for the nation would satisfy him. However, nowhere in 4 Maccabees do the authors affirm that the martyrs violated Torah; indeed, their absolute devotion to Torah is evident by their willingness to die for the sake of God's laws. Their faithfulness to Torah is the impetus behind the author's premise that religious reason masters the passions. Similarly, Paul presents Jesus' historic death and resurrection as representative for the new life that believers experience when they transfer from being in Adam to being in Christ. His presentation of Jesus' death as a representative of Jews and Gentiles in conjunction with his substitutionary presentation of Jesus' death in Romans provides a link with the Jewish martyrological traditions.

CONCLUSION

In this chapter, I have argued that Paul presents Jesus' death as a representation of sinners and that the combination of substitution and representation provide an additional link with Jesus' death and the Jewish martyrological narratives in Romans. I argued this by means of a concise comparative and exegetical analysis of the Jewish martyrological narratives and Rom 5:12—6:23.

7

Conclusion

In this chapter, I develop some general conclusions from the analysis in chapters 2–6. The conclusions serve to clarify the impact of reading Paul's presentation of Jesus' death in Romans in front of a Jewish martyrological background.

PAUL'S USE OF MULTIVALENT JEWISH TRADITIONS IN ROMANS FOR HIS THEOLOGICAL PURPOSES

I have argued throughout the monograph that Paul presents Jesus' death as both a representative of and a substitute for Jews and Gentiles and that the Jewish martyrological narratives are a background behind Paul's presentation of Jesus' death in the texts that I have investigated. My thesis, however, does not claim that Paul *only* used the Jewish martyrological narratives. Instead, I have contended that Paul appropriates Hebrew cultic traditions and Isaiah 53 to Jesus through the interpretive lens of a Jewish martyrolgoical reading of those texts and that he reconstructed the Jewish martyrological traditions' reading of Hebrew cultic traditions and Isaiah 53 to fit his theological purposes in Romans. In other words, he contextualizes both the Hebrew Scriptures and the Jewish martyrological traditions for his own social setting.

The above suggestion does not intend to reduce the Hebrew Scriptures to a secondary importance in Romans. Paul believed that the Hebrew Scriptures had a unique authority within the Jewish and Jewish Christian communities. He believed the Hebrew Scriptures were both inspired and authoritative. However, similar to all Bible readers, Paul read the Hebrew Scriptures in light of his own social situation. However, different from Bible readers before and after him, Paul also read the Bible through the lens of a fresh vision of the crucified, resurrected, and exalted Lord Jesus Christ. He would have naturally reached for those Jewish traditions inside of and outside of the Hebrew Bible in which Levitical cultic language and Isaianic language were applied to Torah-observant Jews who died for the sins of non-Torah-observant sinners. Although the Hebrew Scriptures were foundational to Paul's understanding of God's soteriological plan for Jews and Gentiles, the Jewish martyrological traditions, as well as other Jewish traditions, helped Paul understand and communicate the kind of death that Jesus (a Torah-observant Jew) died for non-Torah-observant sinners better than the Levitical cultic traditions by themselves, since they emphasize *animal* sacrifice. Both the Jewish martyrological narratives and Paul read the Hebrew cultic traditions and Isaiah 53 in a fresh way, the former because of exile and the persecution of Antiochus Epiphanes IV and Paul because of his encounter with the crucified, resurrected, and exalted Lord Jesus Christ on the Damascus Road. Thus, Paul's understanding and presentation of Jesus' death is thoroughly Jewish-Christian and not pagan.

THE IMPORTANCE OF BOTH SUBSTITUTION AND REPRESENTATION FOR PAUL'S SOTERIOLOGY IN ROMANS

Paul presents Jesus' death as both a substitution for and a representation of Jews and Gentiles in Romans. Although one could argue for a central model of Jesus' death in Romans, this monograph has not explicitly attempted to do so. This work has neither attempted to argue that one model of Jesus' death in Romans nor attempted to argue that one model of Jesus' death is more important than another in Romans. Instead, I have simply argued a modest thesis: that Paul presents Jesus' death as *both* a substitution for *and* a representation of Jewish and Gentiles sinners in Romans and that the Jewish martyrological narratives provide a background in front of which Paul's presentation of Jesus' death should be read in Romans. My thesis also acknowledges that Paul at times mentions only substitution (Rom 5:6–10), only representation (Rom 5:12–21), or both in the same text (Rom 8:3), alongside Jewish martyrological vocabulary or concepts or Levitical cultic vocabulary or concepts.

The most striking thing to me as a result of my investigation is that Paul especially seems to present Jesus' death as a substitution when he discusses the soteriological benefits achieved by his death for sinners. For example, with the exception of Rom 5:18, Paul's discussions of justification by faith (Rom 3:21–26; 5:6–10), reconciliation (Rom 5:9–10), and deliverance from God's eschatological wrath (Rom 5:9) only occur in contexts where he seems to emphasize Jesus' death as a substitute for sinners. Even if representation is present in these texts, it is overshadowed by substitution. This observation could support the claim that Paul believed that substitution provides a very important reason why Jesus' death achieves soteriological benefits for Jewish and Gentile sinners. A purely representative death does not benefit those for whom the death was experienced. Rather, representation alone suggests that the one who dies becomes one of those with whom he dies and that he becomes as one of those for whom he dies. However, substitution suggests that the one who dies becomes like the ones for whom he dies *in order* to function like one of those for whom he dies so that the latter group would experience soteriological benefits. In Romans, Paul suggests that Jesus, a Torah-observant Jew, innocently died for non-Torah-observant Jewish and Gentile sinners so that they would experience soteriological benefits, both as a result of his death for them and as a result of their identification with him by faith.

WHY JEWISH MARTYROLOGICAL NARRATIVES IN ROMANS INSTEAD OF SCRIPTURE AND SCRIPTURE ALONE?

Why would Paul borrow from a Jewish martyrological tradition instead of directly borrow from the Levitical cultic traditions and Isaiah 53 since the former traditions (martyrological) borrowed from the latter (Levitical cultic and Isaiah 53) to formulate a Jewish martyrology? I think Paul appropriated a Jewish martyrological understanding of these texts to the death of Jesus because these narratives came to him already fixed with substitutionary, representative, Levitical cultic, and Isaianic language, having already been applied to Torah-observant Jews who died for the soteriological benefit of non-Torah-observant sinners. It is certainly possible, though unlikely, that Paul independently read the Levitical cult and Isaiah 53 apart from a Jewish martyrological background or apart from any antecedent or contemporary interpretive influences upon his reading of the Hebrew Scriptures. Even if one could prove this with certainty, I would argue that once Paul applied Levitical cultic traditions and Isaiah 53 to the death of Jesus, his application of the Hebrew cultic traditions to Jesus' death became a Jewish martyrological appropriation of these texts, so that Paul ends up appropriating these texts in a way similar to the Jewish martyrological appropriation of them. When one compares Paul's presentation of Jesus' death in Romans with the animal sacrifices in the Hebrew cult, one can see that the kind of death that Jesus died was a death more like the Jewish martyrs, to whom the authors of the Jewish martyrological traditions applied Hebrew cultic traditions and Isaiah 53, than a death like animals, because Jesus (like the martyrs) was a Torah-observant Jew who died as a substitute for and as a representative of non-Torah-observant sinners.

PAUL'S JEWISH-CHRISTIAN THEOLOGICAL RECONSTRUCTION OF THE JEWISH MARTYROLOGICAL NARRATIVES IN ROMANS

Paul was not a systematic theologian. He was a missionary. However, he was a biblical and theological missionary, who seems to have thought deeply about how to understand the Jewish Scriptures and other Jewish traditions in light of his encounter with the crucified, resurrected, and exalted Lord Jesus Christ on the Damascus road. Consequently, his worldview after his encounter with Christ was grounded in his Damascus-road vision of the resurrected and exalted Christ. Regarding the Jewish Scriptures, Paul states in no uncertain terms that Christ is the end/goal of the law resulting in righteousness for everyone who believes (Rom 10:5). Since Christ was the goal of the Jewish Scriptures, Paul therefore theologically applied and theologically appropriated both the Jewish Scriptures and the Jewish martyrological narratives to fit his sociological and theological context. Again, this simply means that Paul contextualized every Jewish text. According to him, Jesus was not merely a martyr, but he died a death similar to the Jewish martyrs and yet his death was far superior to theirs because he believed it was God's provision to achieve soteriological benefits for Jewish and Gentile sinners and because he believed his death was how God universally reversed Adam's curse (Rom 5:6–21). Paul's use of the Jewish martyrological traditions in Romans was an intentional missiological move on his part to contextualize the death of Jesus for Jewish and Gentile sinners to highlight the efficacious nature of Jesus' death for them.

REPRESENTATION AND SUBSTITUTION WITHOUT THE JEWISH MARTYROLOGICAL NARRATIVES IN ROMANS?

The Jewish martyrological narratives were a background behind Paul's presentation of representation and substitution in Romans. My thesis is not that without the Jewish martyrological narratives, substitution and representation would be absent from Romans. Instead, I have argued that this background, along with the Levitical cultic traditions and Isaiah 53, provides an insight into Jesus' representative and substitutionary death for sinners. Their deaths were not equal or even the same, but similar. But Jesus' death was far superior in nature and scope according to Paul because he was God's offering for Jewish and Gentile salvation and because his death dealt once and for all with the universal power and problem of sin that began with Adam's transgression (Rom 3:21—6:23). Both the Jewish martyrs and Jesus were Torah-observant Jews who died for the soteriological benefits of non-Torah-observant sinners. A strong and successful case for substitution and representation in Romans can be made without any appeal to a Jewish martyrological background.[1] However, the Jewish martyrological background provides the earliest place in Second Temple Judaism that a Torah-observant Jew died both as a substitution for and as a representative of non-Torah-observant sinners. Apart from Isaiah 53, there is no OT text that explicitly refers to the death of a Torah-observant Jew for the soteriological benefits of non-Torah observant Jewish and Gentile sinners. Thus, since Paul presents Jesus as the Torah-observant Jewish Lord and Christ who died for the soteriological benefit of non-Torah-observant Jewish and Gentile sinners, Paul uses the ideas in the Jewish martyrological narratives as a means to communicate to his audience in Rome that Jesus' death has definitively dealt with the sins of both Jewish and Gentile sinners and achieved by faith universal soteriological benefits for them. While the Jewish martyrological narratives present Torah-observant Jews exclusively dying as substitutes for and as representatives of Jewish sinners, Paul uses the Jewish martyrological narratives to present Jesus, a Torah-observant Jew, as dying inclusively for Jewish *and Gentile* sinners who believe. According to Paul, Israel's God is the God of Jews and Gentiles (Rom 3:29–30), because "while we were yet sinners, Christ died for our sins" (Rom 5:8).

---

1. See, for example, Gathercole, *Defending Substitution*.

Bibliography

Agersnap, Søren. *Baptism and the New Life: A Study of Romans 6:1-14*. Aarhus: Aarhus University Press, 1999.
Bailey, Daniel P. "'Concepts of Stellvertretung in the Interpretation of Isaiah 53.'" In *Jesus and the Suffering Servant: Isaiah 53 and Christian Origins*, edited by William H. Bellinger, Jr. and William R. Farmer, 223-50. Harrisburg, PA: Trinity, 1998.
———. "Jesus as the Mercy Seat: The Semantics and Theology of Pauls's Use of *Hilasterion* in Romans 3:25." PhD diss., University of Cambridge, 1999.
Barnett, Paul. *The Second Epistle to the Corinthians*. Grand Rapids: Eerdmans, 1997.
Barrett, C. K. *A Commentary on the Epistle to the Romans*. Peabody, MA: Hendrickson, 1987.
Barth, Gerhard. *Der Tod Jesu Christi im Verständnis des Neuen Testaments*. Neukirchen-Vluyn: Neukirchener, 1992.
Barth, Karl. *The Epistle to the Romans*. Translated by Edwyn C. Hoskyns. 6th ed. New York: Oxford University Press, 1968.
Bassler, Jouette M. "Divine Impartiality in Paul's Letter to the Romans." *NovT* 26 (1984) 43-58.
Bassler, Jouette M. *Divine Impartiality: Paul and a Theological Axiom*. Dissertation Series (Society of Biblical Literature) 59. Chico, CA: Scholars, 1982.
Baumeister, Theofried. *Die Anfänge Der Theologie Des Martyriums*. Münster: Aschendorff, 1980.
Baumgarten, Albert I. "Setting the Outer Limits: Temple Policy in the Centuries Prior to Destruction." In *Redefining First-Century Jewish and Christian Identities: Essays in Honor of Ed Parish Sanders*, edited by Fabian E. Udoh, Susannah Heschel, Mark A. Chancey, and Gregory Tatum, 90-92. Notre Dame, IN: University of Notre Dame Press, 2008.
Beale, Greg. "The Old Testament Background of Reconciliation in 2 Corinthians 5-7 and Its Bearing on the Literary Problem of 2 Corinthians 6.14—7.1." *NTS* 35 (1989) 550-81.
Becker, Jürgen. *Paul: Apostle to the Gentiles*. Louisville, KY: Westminster John Knox, 1993.
Bell, Richard H. *Deliver Us from Evil: Interpreting the Redemption from the Power of Satan in New Testament Theology*. WUNT 216. Tübingen: Mohr Siebeck, 2007.
———. *No One Seeks for God: An Exegetical and Theological Study of Romans 1.18-3.20*. WUNT 106. Tübingen: Mohr Siebeck, 1998.
———. "Sacrifice and Christology in Paul." *JTS* 53 (2002) 1-27.

Bellinger, W. H., William Reuben Farmer, et al., eds. *Jesus and the Suffering Servant: Isaiah 53 and Christian Origins*. Harrisburg, PA: Trinity, 1998.

Bird, Michael F., and Preston M. Sprinkle, eds. *The Faith of Jesus Christ: The Pistis Christou Debate: Exegetical, Biblical, and Theological Studies*. Milton Keynes, UK: Paternoster, 2010.

Boyarin, Daniel. *Dying for God: Martyrdom and the Making of Christianity and Judaism*. Stanford, CA: Stanford University Press, 1999.

Branick, Vincent P. "The Sinful Flesh of the Son of God (Rom 8:3): A Key Image of Pauline Theology." *CBQ* 47 (1985) 246–62.

Breytenbach, Cilliers. "'Christus Starb für Uns': Zur Tradition und Paulinischen Rezeption der Sogenannten 'Sterbeformeln.'" *NTS* 49 (2003) 447–75.

———. *Grace, Reconciliation, Concord: The Death of Christ in Graeco-Roman Metaphors*. NovTSup 135. Leiden: Brill, 2010.

———. "Salvation of the Reconciled (with a Note on the Background of Paul's Metaphor of Reconciliation)." In *Salvation in the New Testament*, 271–86. Leiden: Brill, 2005.

———. "The Septuagint Version of Isaiah 53 and the Early Christian Formula 'He Was Delivered for Our Trespasses.'" *NovT* 51 (2009) 339–51.

———. *Versöhnung: eine Studie zur paulinischen Soteriologie*. Neukirchen-Vluyn: Neukirchener Verlag, 1989.

———. "Versöhnung, Stellvertretung und Sühne: Semantische und Traditionsgeschichtliche Bemerkungen Am Beispiel der Paulinischen Briefe." *NTS* 39 (1993) 59–79.

Brown, Alexandra R. *The Cross and Human Transformation: Paul's Apocalyptic Word in 1 Corinthians*. Minneapolis: Fortress, 1995.

Brown, William H. "From Holy War to Holy Martyrdom." In *The Quest for the Kingdom of God: Studies in Honor of George E. Mendenhall*, edited by Herbert B. Huffmon, Frank A. Spina, and Alberto R. W. Green, 281–92. Winona Lake, IN: Eisenbrauns, 1983.

Bruce, Frederick Fyvie. *Romans*. Tyndale New Testament Commentaries. Rev. ed. Leicester, UK: IVP, 1985.

Bruno, Christopher R. *"God Is One": The Function of Eis Ho Theos as a Ground for Gentile Inclusion in Paul's Letters*. LNTS 497. London: T. & T. Clark, 2013.

Bultmann, Rudolf Karl. "Adam and Christ according to Romans 5." In *Current Issues in New Testament Interpretation*, 143–65. New York: Harper, 1962.

Byrne, Brendan. *Romans*. SP 6. Collegeville, MN: Glazier, 2007.

Calvin, Jean. *The Epistles of Paul the Apostle to the Romans and to the Thessalonians*. Edited by David W. Torrance and Thomas F. Torrance. Translated by Ross Mackenzie. Grand Rapids: Eerdmans, 1960.

Cambier, Jules. "Péchés Des Hommes et Péché d'Adam En Rom 5:12." *NTS* 11 (1965) 217–55.

Campbell, Douglas A. *The Deliverance of God: An Apocalyptic Rereading of Justification in Paul*. Grand Rapids: Eerdmans, 2009.

Carroll, John T., and Joel B. Green. *The Death of Jesus in Early Christianity*. Grand Rapids: Baker Academic, 2007.

Cohen, Shaye J. D. *From the Maccabees to the Mishnah*. Louisville: Westminster John Knox, 2006.

Constantineanu, Corneliu. *The Social Significance of Reconciliation in Paul's Theology: Narrative Readings in Romans*. LNTS. London: T. & T. Clark, 2010.

Cousar, Charles B. *A Theology of the Cross: The Death of Jesus in the Pauline Letters.* OBT 24. Minneapolis: Fortress, 1990.
Cranfield, C. E. B. *The Epistle to the Romans 1–8.* 11th ed. London: T. & T. Clark, 2004.
Cummins, Stephen Anthony. *Paul and the Crucified Christ in Antioch: Maccabean Martyrdom and Galatians 1 and 2.* SNTSM 114. Cambridge: Cambridge University Press, 2001.
Dahl, Nils Alstrup. "The Atonement—An Adequate Reward for the *Aqedah*." In *The Crucified Messiah, and Other Essays*, 146–60. Minneapolis: Augsburg, 1974.
Danker, Frederick W. "Romans 5:12: Sin under Law." *NTS* 14 (1968) 424–39.
Das, A. Andrew. *Paul and the Jews.* Peabody: Hendrickson, 2003.
———. *Paul, the Law, and the Covenant.* Peabody: Hendrickson, 2001.
———. "Paul and Works of Obedience in Second Temple Judaism: Romans 4:4–5 as a 'New Perspective' Case Study." *CBQ* 71 (2009) 795–812.
Davis, Basil S. *Christ as Devotio: The Argument of Galatians 3:1–14.* Lanham, MD: University Press of America, 2002.
Davis, Christopher A. *The Structure of Paul's Theology: "The Truth Which Is the Gospel."* Lewiston, NY: Mellen, 1995.
Davis, Joshua, and Douglas Karel Harink, eds. *Apocalyptic and the Future of Theology: With and beyond J. Louis Martyn.* Eugene, OR: Cascade, 2012.
Deissmann, Adolf, and Lionel R. M. Strachan. *Light from the Ancient East: The New Testament Illustrated by Recently Discovered Texts of the Graeco-Roman World.* New York: Harper, 1927.
DeSilva, David Arthur. *4 Maccabees: Introduction and Commentary on the Greek Text in Codex Sinaiticus.* Leiden: Brill, 2006.
Dodd, C. H. *The Bible and the Greeks.* London: Hodder & Stoughton, 1954.
———. *The Epistle of Paul to the Romans.* London: Hodder & Stoughton, 1932.
Downing, John. "Jesus and Martyrdom." *JTS* 14 (1963) 279–93.
Dunn, James D. G. "Paul's Understanding of the Death of Jesus." In *Reconciliation and Hope*, 125–41. Grand Rapids: Eerdmans, 1974.
———. "Paul's Understanding of the Death of Jesus as Sacrifice." In *Sacrifice and Redemption*, 35–56. New York: Cambridge University Press, 1991.
———. *Romans 1–8.* Nashville: Thomas Nelson, 1988.
———. *The Theology of Paul the Apostle.* Grand Rapids: Eerdmans, 1998.
Dupont, Jacques. *La réconciliation dans la théologie de saint Paul.* Paris: Publications universitaires de Louvain, 1953.
Eschner, Christina. *Gestorben und hingegeben "für" die Sünder: die griechische Konzeption des Unheil abwendenden Sterbens und deren paulinische Aufnahme für die Deutung des Todes Jesu Christi.* WMANT 122. Neukirchen-Vluyn: Neukirchener Verlag, 2010.
Falk, Daniel K. "Festivals and Holy Days." In *The Eerdmans Dictionary of Early Judaism*, edited by John J. Collins and Daniel C. Harlow, 636–45. Grand Rapids: Eerdmans, 2010.
Feldman, Louis H., James L. Kugel, and Lawrence H. Schiffman. *Outside the Bible: Ancient Jewish Writings Related to Scripture.* Philadelphia: Jewish Publication Society, 2013.
Finlan, Stephen. *The Background and Content of Paul's Cultic Atonement Metaphors.* Atlanta: Society of Biblical Literature, 2004.

Fitzmyer, Joseph A. "Reconciliation in Pauline Theology." In *No Famine in the Land*, 155–77. Missoula, MT: Scholars, 1975.

———. *Romans: A New Translation with Introduction and Commentary*. New York: Doubleday, 1993.

Fryer, Nico S L. "The Meaning and Translation of *Hilastērion* in Romans 3:25." *EvQ* 59 (1987) 99–116.

Gane, Roy E. "Privative Preposition in MN in Purification Offering Pericopes and the Changing Face of 'Dorian Gray.'" *JBL* 127 (2008) 209–22.

Gaster, T. H. "Sacrifices and Offerings, OT." In *IDB*, edited by George Buttrick, 4:148–53.

Gathercole, Simon, Craig Evans, and Lee McDonald. *Defending Substitution: An Essay on Atonement in Paul*. Grand Rapids: Baker Academic, 2015.

Gaventa, Beverly Roberts. *Apocalyptic Paul: Cosmos and Anthropos in Romans 5–8*. Waco, TX: Baylor University Press, 2013.

Gese, Hartmut. "Atonement." In *Essays on Biblical Theology*, 93–116. Minneapolis: Augsburg, 1981.

Gibson, Jeffrey B. "Paul's 'Dying Formula': Prolegomena to an Understanding of Its Import and Significance." In *Celebrating Romans*, edited by Sheila McGinn, 20–41. Grand Rapids: Eerdmans, 2004.

Gnilka, Joachim. "Martyriumsparänese und Sühnetod in Synoptischen und Jüdischen Traditionen." In *Kirche Des Anfangs*, 223–46. Leipzig: St Benno-Verlag, 1977.

Goldstein, Jonathan A. *II Maccabees*. Garden City, NY: Doubleday, 1983.

Gorman, Michael J. *Cruciformity: Paul's Narrative Spirituality of the Cross*. Grand Rapids: Eerdmans., 2001.

———. *Inhabiting the Cruciform God: Kenosis, Justification, and Theosis in Paul's Narrative Soteriology*. Grand Rapids: Eerdmans, 2009.

Gray, George Buchanan. *Sacrifice in the Old Testament: Its Theory and Practice*. New York: Ktav, 1971.

Grayston, Kenneth. "Atonement and Martyrdom." In *Early Christian Thought in Its Jewish Context*, edited by John Barclay and John Sweet, 250–63. Cambridge: Cambridge University Press, 1996.

Hägglund, Fredrik. *Isaiah 53 in the Light of Homecoming after Exile*. FAT 31. Tübingen: Mohr Siebeck, 2008.

Hartley, John E. *Leviticus*. WBC. Dallas: Word, 1992.

Hastings, Rashdall. *The Idea of Atonement in Christian Theology*. London: MacMillan, 1925.

Heard, Warren Joel. "Maccabean Martyr Theology: Its Genesis, Antecedents, and Significance for the Earliest Soteriological Interpretation of the Death of Jesus." PhD diss., University of Aberdeen, 1987.

Hengel, Martin. *The Atonement: The Origins of the Doctrine in the New Testament*. London: SCM, 1981.

Henten, Jan W van. *The Maccabean Martyrs as Saviours of the Jewish People: A Study of 2 and 4 Maccabees*. JSJSup. Leiden: Brill, 1997.

———. "The Tradition-Historical Background of Rom 3:25: A Search for Pagan and Jewish Parallels." In *From Jesus to John*, edited by Martinus C. de Boer, 101–28. Sheffield, UK: JSOT, 1993.

Henze, Matthias. "Additions to Daniel." In *Outside the Bible: Ancient Jewish Writings Related to Scripture*, edited by Louis H. Feldman, James L. Kugel, and Lawrence H. Schiffman, 122–39. Philadelphia: Jewish Publication Society, 2013.

Hieke, Thomas, and Tobias Nicklas, eds. *The Day of Atonement: Its Interpretations in Early Jewish and Christian Traditions*. Leiden: Brill, 2012.

Hill, David. *Greek Words and Hebrew Meanings: Studies in the Semantics of Soteriological Terms*. SNTSM 5. Cambridge: Cambridge University Press, 1967.

Hofius, Otfried. "Erwägungen Zur Gestalt und Herkunft des Paulinischen Versöhnungsgedankens." In *Paulusstudien*, 1–14. WUNT 51. Tübingen: Mohr Siebeck, 1989.

———. *Paulusstudien*. WUNT 51. Tübingen: Mohr, 1989.

Holland, Tom. *Contours of Pauline Theology*. Fearn, UK: Mentor, 2004.

Hooker, Morna D. *From Adam to Christ: Essays on Paul*. Cambridge: Cambridge University Press, 1990.

———. "Interchange in Christ." In *From Adam to Christ: Essays on Paul*, edited by ?, 13–25. Cambridge: Cambridge University Press, 1990.

———. *Not Ashamed of the Gospel: New Testament Interpretations of the Death of Christ*. Didsbury Lectures. Reprint. Eugene, OR: Wipf & Stock, 2004.

———. "On Becoming the Righteousness of God: Another Look at 2 Cor 5:21." *NovT* 50 (2008) 358–75.

Hultgren, Arland J. *Paul's Gospel and Mission: The Outlook from His Letter to the Romans*. Philadelphia: Augsburg Fortress, 1985.

———. *Paul's Letter to the Romans: A Commentary*. Grand Rapids: Eerdmans, 2011.

Janowski, Bernd. "Er Tug Unsere Sünden: Jesaja 53 und die Dramatik der Stellvertretung." In *Der Leidende Gottesknecht: Jesaja 53 und Seine Wirkungsgeschichte: Mit Einer Bibliographie Zu Isa 53*, edited by Janowski, Bernd and Peter Stuhlmacher, 67–70. FAT 14. Tübingen: Mohr Siebeck, 1996.

———. *Sühne Als Heilsgeschehen: Studien Zur Sühnetheologie der Priesterschrift und Zur Wurzel KPR im Alten Orient und im Alten Testament*. WMANT 55. Neukirchen-Vluyn: Neukirchener Verlag, 1982.

Janowski, Bernd, and Peter Stuhlmacher, eds. *The Suffering Servant: Isaiah 53 in Jewish and Christian Sources*. Translated by Daniel P. Bailey. Grand Rapids: Eerdmans, 2004.

Janzen, David. *The Social Meanings of Sacrifice in the Hebrew Bible: A Study of Four Writings*. BZAW 334. New York: de Gruyter, 2004.

Jeffery, S., Michael Ovey, and Andrew Sach. *Pierced for Our Transgressions: Rediscovering the Glory of Penal Substitution*. Wheaton, IL: Crossway, 2007.

Jewett, Robert, and Roy D. Kotansky. *Romans: A Commentary*. Edited by Eldon Jay Epp. 2nd ed. Minneapolis: Fortress, 2006.

Jonge, Marinus de. *Christology in Context: The Earliest Christian Response to Jesus*. Philadelphia: Westminster, 1988.

———. *God's Final Envoy: Early Christology and Jesus' Own View of His Mission*. Studying the Historical Jesus. Grand Rapids: Eerdmans, 1998.

———. "Jesus' Death for Others and the Death of the Maccabean Martyrs." In *Text and Testimony*, 142–51. Kampen, Netherlands: Kok, 1988.

———. *Jewish Eschatology: Early Christian Christology and the Testaments of the Twelve Patriarchs*. NovTSup 63. Leiden: Brill, 1991.

Käsemann, Ernst. *Commentary on Romans*. Grand Rapids: Eerdmans, 1980.

Keener, Craig S. *Romans: A New Covenant Commentary*. Eugene, OR: Cascade, 2009.
Kellermann, Ulrich. *Auferstanden in den Himmel: 2 Makkabäer 7 und die Auferstehung der Märtyrer*. Stuttgart: Verlag Katholisches Bibelwerk, 1979.
———. "Zum Traditionsgeschichtlichen Problem des Stellvertretenden Sühnetodes in 2Makk 7,37f." *BN* 13 (1980) 63–83.
Kim, Kyoung-Shik. *God Will Judge Each One according to Works: Judgment according to Works and Psalm 62 in Early Judaism and the New Testament*. BZNW, 178. Berlin: de Gruyter, 2011.
Kim, Seyoon. "2 Cor 5:11–21 and the Origin of Paul's Concept of 'Reconciliation.'" *NovT* 39 (1997) 360–84.
———. *Paul and the New Perspective: Second Thoughts on the Origin of Paul's Gospel*. Tübingen: Mohr-Siebeck, 2002.
Kirk, J. R. Daniel. "Reconsidering *Dikaiōma* in Romans 5:16." *JBL* 126 (2007) 787–92.
Kiuchi, N. *The Purification Offering in the Priestly Literature: Its Meaning and Function*. JSTOTSup 56. Sheffield, UK: JSOT, 1987.
Klauck, Hans-Josef. *4. Makkabäerbuch*. Gütersloh: Mohn, 1989.
Klawans, Jonathan. *Purity, Sacrifice, and the Temple: Symbolism and Supersessionism in the Study of Ancient Judaism*. New York: Oxford University Press, 2006.
Knöppler, Thomas. *Sühne Im Neuen Testament: Studien Zum Urchristlichen Verständnis Der Heilsbedeutung Des Todes Jesu*. WMANT, 88. Bd. Neukirchen: Neukirchener, 2001.
Kraus, Wolfgang. *Der Tod Jesu Als Heiligtumsweihe: Eine Untersuchung Zum Umfeld Der Sühnevorstellung in Römer 3, 25–26a*. WMANT 66. Neukirchen-Vluyn: Neukirchener Verlag, 1991.
Kurtz, J. H. *Offerings, Sacrifices and Worship in the Old Testament*. Translated by James Martin. Peabody, MA: Hendrickson, 1998.
Lee, Jae Hyun. *Paul's Gospel in Romans: A Discourse Analysis of Rom 1:16—8:39*. Linguistic Biblical Studies. Leiden: Brill, 2010.
Leithart, Peter J. "Adam, Moses, and Jesus: A Reading of Romans 5:12–14." *CTJ* 43 (2008) 257–73.
Levine, Baruch A. *In the Presence of the Lord: A Study of Cult and Some Cultic Terms in Ancient Israel*. SJLA 5. Leiden: Brill, 1974.
Lohse, Eduard. *Märtyrer und Gottesknecht: Untersuchungen Zur Urchristlichen Verkündigung vom Sühntod Jesu Christi*. FRLANT 64. Göttingen: Vandenhoeck & Ruprecht, 1955.
Lohse, Eduard. *Der Brief an Die Römer*. Meyers Kritisch-Exegetischer Kommentar Über Das Neue Testament. Göttingen: Vandenhoeck and Ruprecht, 2003.
Longenecker, Richard N. *Introducing Romans: Critical Issues in Paul's Most Famous Letter*. Grand Rapids: Eerdmans, 2011.
Marshall, I. Howard. "The Development of the Concept of Redemption." In *Reconciliation and Hope: New Testament Essays on Atonement and Eschatology Presented to L. L. Morris on His 60th Birthday*, edited by Robert J. Banks, 153–68. Exeter: Paternoster, 1974.
———. "The Meaning of 'Reconciliation.'" In *Unity and Diversity in New Testament Theology*, edited by Robert J. Banks, 117–32. Grand Rapids: Eerdmans, 1978.
Martin, Ralph P. *Reconciliation: A Study of Paul's Theology*. Rev. ed. Grand Rapids: Zondervan, 1989.

Martyn, J. Louis. *Galatians: A New Translation with Introduction and Commentary.* New York: Doubleday, 1997.
McFadden, Kevin W. *Judgment according to Works in Romans: The Meaning and Function of Divine Judgment in Paul's Most Important Letter.* Minneapolis: Fortress, 2013.
McFadden, Kevin W. "The Fulfillment of the Law's *Dikaiōma*: Another Look at Romans 8:1–4." *JETS* 52 (2009) 483–97.
McLean, Bradley Hudson. "The Absence of an Atoning Sacrifice in Paul's Soteriology." *NTS* 38 (1992) 531–53.
———. "Christ as a *Pharmakos* in Pauline Soteriology." *SBLSP* 30 (1991) 187–206.
———. *The Cursed Christ: Mediterranean Expulsion Rituals and Pauline Soteriology.* JSNTSupp. Sheffield, UK: Sheffield, 1996.
Meyer, Ben F. "The Pre-Pauline Formula in Rom 3:25–26a." *NTS* 29 (1983) 198–208.
Milgrom, Jacob. *Cult and Conscience: The Asham and the Priestly Doctrine of Repentance.* SJLA 18. Leiden: Brill, 1976.
———. *Leviticus 1–16: A New Translation with Introduction and Commentary.* New Haven, CT: Yale University Press, 2009.
———. *Studies in Cultic Theology and Terminology.* SJLA 36. Leiden: Brill, 1983.
Modéus, Martin. *Sacrifice and Symbol: Biblical Šĕlāmîm in a Ritual Perspective.* ConBOT 52. Stockholm: Almqvist & Wiksell, 2005.
Moo, Douglas J. *The Epistle to the Romans.* 12th ed. Grand Rapids: Eerdmans, 1996.
Mørkholm, Otto. "Antiochus IV." In *The Cambridge History of Judaism*, edited by W. D Davies and Louis Finkelstein, 2:278–91. Cambridge: Cambridge University Press, 1984.
Morris, Leon. *The Apostolic Preaching of the Cross.* 3rd ed. Grand Rapids: Eerdmans, 1965.
———. *The Cross in the New Testament.* Grand Rapids: Eerdmans, 1965.
———. "Meaning of *Hilastērion* in Romans 3:25." *NTS* 2 (1955) 33–43.
———. "Redemption" In *Dictionary of Paul and His Letters*, edited by Gerald F. Hawthorne, Ralph P. Martin, and Daniel G. Reid. 784–86. Downers Grove, IL: IVP Academic, 1993.
Newton, Michael. *The Concept of Purity at Qumran and in the Letters of Paul.* Cambridge: Cambridge University Press, 2005.
Nygren, Anders. *Commentary on Romans.* 5th ed. Philadelphia: Muhlenberg, 1949.
O'Hagan, Angelo P. "The Martyr in the Fouth Book of Maccabees." *LASBF* 24 (1974) 94–120.
Origen. *Commentary on the Epistle to the Romans. Books 1–5.* Translated by Thomas P. Scheck. Washington, DC: Catholic University of America Press, 2001.
Oswalt, John N. *The Book of Isaiah.* NICOT. Grand Rapids: Eerdmans, 1998.
Otto Mørkholm. "Antiochus IV." In *The Cambridge History of Judaism.* Vol. 2, *The Hellenistic Age*, edited by Louis Finkelstein, W. D. Davies, and John Sturdy, 2:278–91 Cambridge: Cambridge University Press, 1989.
Owen, Paul. "The 'Works of the Law' in Romans and Galatians: A New Defense of the Subjective Genitive." *JBL* 126 (2007) 553–77.
Pobee, J. S. *Persecution and Martyrdom in the Theology of Paul.* JSNTSup. Cordoba: Ediciones el Almendro, 1994.
Porter, Stanley E. *Καταλλασσω in Ancient Greek Literature with Reference to the Pauline Writings.* Cordoba: Ediciones El Almendro, 1994.

———. "The Pauline Concept of Original Sin, in Light of Rabbinic Background." *TynBul* 41 (1990) 3–30.
Powers, Daniel G. *Salvation through Participation: An Examination of the Notion of the Believers' Corporate Unity with Christ in Early Christian Soteriology.* Contributions to Biblical Exegesis and Theology 29. Leuven: Peeters, 2001.
Rainbow, Paul. *The Way of Salvation: The Role of Christian Obedience in Justification.* Carlisle, UK: Paternoster, 2005.
Räisänen, Heikki. *Paul and the Law.* Philadelphia: Fortress, 1986.
Rajak, Tessa. *The Jewish Dialogue with Greece and Rome: Studies in Cultural and Social Interaction.* AGJU 48. Leiden: Brill, 2001.
Robertson, A. T. *A Grammar of the Greek New Testament in the Light of Historical Research.* Nashville: Broadman, 1934.
Rodriguez, Angel M. "Substitution in the Hebrew Cultus and in Cultic-Related Texts." *AUSS* 19 (1982) 247–48.
Sanday, W., and Arthur C. Headlam. *A Critical and Exegetical Commentary on the Epistle to the Romans.* New York: Scribner, 1896.
Sanders, E. P. *Judaism: Practice and Belief, 63 BCE–66 CE.* London: SCM, 1992.
———. *Paul and Palestinian Judaism: A Comparison of Patterns of Religion.* Philadelphia: Fortress, 1977.
Sapp, David A. "The LXX, 1QIsa, and MT Versions of Isaiah 53 and the Christian Doctrine of Atonement." In *Jesus and the Suffering Servant: Isaiah 53 and Christian Origins*, edited by William H. Bellinger, Jr. and William R. Farmer, 170–92. Harrisburg, PA: Trinity, 1998.
Schiffman, Lawrence H. *Texts and Traditions: A Source Reader for the Study of Second Temple and Rabbinic Judaism.* Hoboken, NJ: Ktav, 1998.
Schlatter, Adolf. *Romans: The Righteousness of God.* Translated by Siegfried Sschatzmann. Peabody, MA: Hendrickson, 1995.
———. *The Theology of the Apostles: The Development of New Testament Theology.* Translated by Andreas Köstenberger. Grand Rapids: Baker, 1998.
Schreiner, Thomas R. *Romans.* Grand Rapids: Baker Academic, 1998.
Schwartz, Daniel R. *2 Maccabees.* New York: de Gruyter, 2008.
Seeley, David. *The Noble Death: Graeco-Roman Martyrology and Paul's Concept of Salvation.* JSNTSup 28. Sheffield, UK: JSOT, 1990.
Seifrid, Mark. "Romans." In *Commentary on the New Testament Use of the Old Testament*, edited by G. K. Beale and D. A. Carson, 607–94. Grand Rapids: Baker Academic, 2007.
Smyth, Herbert Weir, and Gordon M. Messing. *Greek Grammar.* Cambridge: Harvard University Press, 2002.
Snodgrass, Klyne. "Justification by Grace—to the Doers: An Analysis of the Place of Romans 2 in the Theology of Paul." *NTS* 32.1 (1986) 72–93.
Sprinkle, Preston. *Paul & Judaism Revisited: A Study of Divine and Human Agency in Salvation.* Downers Grove, IL: IVP Academic, 2013.
Stanislas, Lyonnet. "Expiation et Intercession." *Bib* 41 (1960) 158–67.
Stanislas, Lyonnet, and Leopold Sabourin. *Sin, Redemption, and Sacrifice: A Biblical and Patristic Study.* Rome: Biblical Institute Press, 1970.
Stauffer, Ethelbert. *New Testament Theology.* London: SCM, 1955.

Stökl Ben Ezra, Daniel. *The Impact of Yom Kippur on Early Christianity: The Day of Atonement from Second Temple Judaism to the Fifth Century*. WUNT 163. Tübingen: Mohr Siebeck, 2003.

Stowers, Stanley Kent. *A Rereading of Romans: Justice, Jews, and Gentiles*. New Haven, CT: Yale University Press, 1994.

Stuhlmacher, Peter. *Der Brief an Die Römer*. Neue Testament Deutsch. Gottingen: Vandenhoeck & Ruprecht, 1989.

———. *Paul's Letter to the Romans: A Commentary*. 1st ed. Louisville: Westminster John Knox, 1994.

Surkau, Hans-Werner. *Martyrien in jüdischer und frühchristlicher Zeit*. FRLANT 36. Göttingen: Vandenhoeck & Ruprecht, 1938.

Swain, C. William. "'For Our Sins': The Image of Sacrifice in the Thought of the Apostle Paul." *Int* 17.2 (1963) 131–39.

Swallow, Fredrick R. "Redemption in St. Paul." *Sacrament* 10 (1958) 21–27.

Talbert, Charles H. *Romans*. Macon, GA: Smyth & Helwys, 2002.

Thielman, Frank. *From Plight to Solution: A Jewish Framework to Understanding Paul's View of the Law in Galatians and Romans*. New York: Brill Academic, 1989.

Thrall, Margaret E. *A Critical and Exegetical Commentary on the Second Epistle to the Corinthians*. ICC 34. Edinburgh: T. & T. Clark, 1994.

Tiwald, Markus. "Christ as *HILASTERION* (Rom 3:25): Pauline Theology on the Day of Atonement in the Mirror of Early Jewish Thought." In *The Day of Atonement: Its Interpretations in Early Jewish and Christian Traditions*, edited by Thomas Hieke and Tobias Nicklas, 189–209. Leiden: Brill, 2012.

Travis, Stephen. *Christ and the Judgement of God: The Limits of Divine Retribution in New Testament Thought*. 2nd ed. Milton Keynes, UK: Paternoster, 2009.

Turner, D. L. "Adam, Christ, and US: The Pauline Teaching of Solidarity in Romans 5:12–21." PhD diss., Grace Theological Seminary, 1982.

van Henten, Jan Willem. "Jewish Martyrdom and Jesus' Death." In *Deutungen Des Todes Jesu im Neuen Testament*, edited by Jorg Frey and Jens Schroter, 139–68. Tübingen: Mohr Siebeck, 2005.

VanLandingham, Chris. *Judgment & Justification in Early Judaism and the Apostle Paul*. Peabody, MA: Hendrickson, 2006.

Versnel, Henk S. "Making Sense of Jesus' Death: The Pagan Contribution." In *Deutungen des Todes Jesu im Neuen Testament*, edited by Jorg Frey and Jens Schroter, 213–94. WUNT 181. Tubigen: Mohr Siebeck, 2005.

Vickers, Brian. "Grammar and Theology in the Interpretation of Rom 5:12." *TrinJ* 27 (2006) 271–88.

Wallace, Daniel B. *Greek Grammar beyond the Basics: An Exegetical Syntax of the New Testament*. Grand Rapids: Zondervan, 1996.

Warfield, Benjamin Breckinridge. "The New Testament Terminology of Redemption." In *The Works of Benjamin B. Warfield*, edited by Ethelbert Dudley Warfield and William Park Armstrong, Vol. 2, 327–98. Grand Rapids: Baker, 2003.

Watson, Francis. *Paul, Judaism, and the Gentiles: A Sociological Approach*. SNTSMS 56. Cambridge: Cambridge University Press, 1986.

———. *Paul, Judaism, and the Gentiles: Beyond the New Perspective*. Grand Rapids: Eerdmans, 2007.

Watts, James W. *Ritual and Rhetoric in Leviticus: From Sacrifice to Scripture*. New York: Cambridge University Press, 2007.

Wengst, Klaus. *Christologische Formeln und Lieder des Urchristentums*. SNT 7. Gütersloh: Gütersloher, 1973.

Whybray, R. N. *Thanksgiving for a Liberated Prophet: An Interpretation of Isaiah Chapter 53*. JSOTSup 4. Sheffield, UK: Sheffield University Press, 1978.

Wilckens, Ulrich. *Der Brief an den Römer*. EKKNT 6. Zürich: Neukrichener Verlag, 1978.

Williams, David John. *Paul's Metaphors: Their Context and Character*. Peabody, MA: Hendrickson, 1999.

Williams, Jarvis J. *For Whom Did Christ Die? The Extent of the Atonement in Paul's Theology*. Eugene, OR: Wipf & Stock, 2012.

———. *Maccabean Martyr Traditions in Paul's Theology of Atonement: Did Martyr Theology Shape Paul's Conception of Jesus's Death?*. Eugene, OR: Wipf & Stock, 2010.

———. "Martyr Theology in Hellenistic Judaism." In *Christian Origins and Hellenistic Judaism: Social and Literary Contexts for the New Testament*, edited by Stanley E. Porter and Andrew W. Pitts, 493–521. Texts and Editions for New Testament Study. Leiden: Brill, 2013.

———. *One New Man: The Cross and Racial Reconciliation in Pauline Theology*. Nashville: B. & H. Academic, 2010.

———. "Violent Atonement in Romans: The Foundation of Paul's Soteriology." *JETS* 53 (2010) 579–99.

Williams, Sam K. *Jesus' Death as Saving Event: The Background and Origin of a Concept*. HDR 2. Missoula, MT: Scholars, 1975.

Witherington, Ben. *The Problem with Evangelical Theology: Testing the Exegetical Foundations of Calvinism, Dispensationalism, and Wesleyanism*. Waco, TX: Baylor University Press, 2005.

Wright, David P. "The Gesture of Hand Placement in the Hebrew Bible and in Hittite Literature." *JAOS* 106 (1986) 433–46.

Wright, N. T. *The Climax of the Covenant: Christ and the Law in Pauline Theology*. Minneapolis: Fortress, 1993.

———. *Pauline Perspectives: Essays on Paul, 1978–2013*. London: SPCK, 2013.

———. "Romans." In *The New Interpreter's Bible*, Vol. 10. Nashville: Abingdon, 1994.

———. *The New Testament and the People of God*. London: SPCK, 1992.

———. *The Resurrection of the Son of God*. 1st ed. London: SPCK, 2003.

Kinger, Kent. *Paul, Judaism, and Judgment according to Deeds*. SNTSMS 105. Cambridge: Cambridge University Press, 1999.

Zohar, No'am. "Repentance and Purification: The Significance and Semantics of *Ḥṭ't* in the Pentateuch." *JBL* 107 (1988) 609–18.

Ancient Document Index

OLD TESTAMENT

Genesis

1–3	174
1–2	173
2–3	173
2:17	163, 173
3	174
3:14–21	173
3:14	173
3:16	173
3:17–19	173
3:17	173
4:5	39
9:4	62
12:17	55n63
14:14	55n63
15:6	131, 138
17:1–14	111
17:23	55n63
17:27	55n63
18:19	55n63
19:3	55n63
22	16, 32
22:1–24	138
24:2	55n63
29:13	55n63
32:21	39, 39n18
35:2	55n63
36:6	55n63
38:1	118
39:4	55n63
39:16	55n63
43:16	55n63
44:1	55n63
44:16	168n96
44:4	55n63
45:8	55n63
50:7	55n63

Exodus

6:6	118n45
7:23	55n63
9:16	133
12	82
12:4	55n63
12:13	18
12:25–26	82
12:48	111
13:5	82
14–15	120
15:13, 16	117
21:1	118
21:8	117
21:10	96n68
22:8	168n96
23:7	69n111, 168n96
24	115
24:4–8	18
25:17–20	100, 122
25:17	125
25:18–22	101, 121n57
25:22	101, 121n57, 122
29:1	37
29:10–14	51n56
29:18	37, 37n10

Exodus (continued)

29:36–37	51n56
29:36	43, 45, 98
29:41	37, 37n10
30	37
30:9–10	37
30:10	45, 45n35, 48, 98, 101n80, 122n58
31:7	121n57, 122
31:17	101
32	108n9
32:12	97n70
32:14	101n80, 122n58
32:33	97n70
32:30–34	20
32:30	162
33:12—34:9	100n78
35:12	101, 121n57, 122
37:6–8	121n, 122
37:6	100

Leviticus

1—16	37, 70
1—7	37
1:1—7:6	104
1—6	78, 84
1:1	39
1:2–3	40
1:3	39, 40
1:4	38, 39, 39n19, 40, 58n78, 60n82, 101n80, 122n58
1:5	40
1:9	40, 78n13
1:10	39
1:13	40, 78n13
1:14	39
1:17	40, 78n13
2:1–2	78n13
2:5–7	78n13
2:11	78n13
2:15	78n13
3:1–4	70
3:1	78n13
3:2	60n82
3:7–8	39
3:8	60n82
3:12	39n21
3:13	60n82
3:14	39n21
4–5	48
4:1—5:13	49, 51n56, 60
4:1–35	163
4	49, 56
4:1–3	45
4:2	45, 49
4:3	45, 70, 162
4:4	48, 60n82
4:6–7	48
4:8–10	45
4:10	70
4:12	45, 46
4:13–22	47
4:13–14	46
4:14	46, 162
4:15	46, 48
4:16–17	46
4:17–18	48
4:18–22	46
4:20–22	46, 47
4:20	38n17, 46, 47n35, 101n80, 122n58
4:21	46
4:23	70
4:24	48, 60n82
4:26	38n17, 46, 47n35, 48, 101n80, 122n58, 163
4:27	49
4:28–35	48
4:28	70
4:31	38n17, 46, 47n35, 48, 101n80, 122n58, 60n82
4:33	60n82
4:35	38n17, 47n35, 70, 101n80, 122n58, 163
5:1–13	48, 56
5:1–8	49
5:1–7	48
5:1	49n44, 52, 52n56, 53
5:5	56, 56n68
5:6–13	56
5:6–11	162
5:6–7	48
5:6	38n17, 47n35, 101n80, 122n58
5:7–8	162
5:8	48, 52

Ancient Document Index   201

5:9	162, 163	10:17	39n19, 49, 67, 68, 70
5:10	38n17, 39, 47n35, 48, 56, 69, 122n58	11:1–47	78
		12–15	49
5:13	38n17, 78n13, 101n80, 122n58	12	38
		12:1–6	44
5:15–17	52	12:3	111
5:15–16	52	12:4	44
5:15	52	12:6	52n56, 162
5:16	48, 101n80, 122n58	12:7–8	38n17, 47n35
5:17–19	52	12:7	44
5:17	49n44, 53	12:8	43, 44, 52n56, 162
5:18–19	52	13:7	72
5:18	38n17, 47n35, 52, 101n80, 122n58	13:59	70
		14:3–4	46
5:19	52, 70	14:13	162
5:26	38n17, 47n35, 48, 101n80, 122n58	14:18–20	38n17, 47n35
		14:19	52n56
6:2	78n13, 79	14:21–22	40
6:4	46	14:21	38n17, 39n19, 39n20, 40, 52, 69, 70
6:16	78n13		
6:18	162	14:22	40, 52n56, 162
6:20	66n101, 70	14:23	40, 72
6:23	39n19, 45, 101n80, 122n58, 162	14:24–29	40
		14:29	39n19
6:25	162	14:30–31	40
7:5	69, 70	14:31	38n17, 40, 47n35, 52n56, 162
7:7	48n42, 52, 101n80, 122n58, 162		
		14:32	98
7:37	70, 162	14:34	40
8:1–14	48	14:53	47n35
8:14–17	51n56	15:1–15	40
8:15	39n19, 43, 44, 48, 49	15:8	49
8:18–21	104	15:13	98
8:21	40	15:15	38n17, 40, 41, 47n35, 162
8:34	39n19	15:28	39n20
9:1—16:34	97	15:30	38n17, 40, 47n35, 162
9:1—16:30	104	16–17	61, 99, 100, 102, 123
9:1—10:2	93	16	18, 52n56, 53, 58, 61, 67, 78, 84, 86n44, 90, 97, 99, 119, 120, 128, 129, 143
9:2–3	51n56, 162		
9:7–15	51n56		
9:7	38n17, 47n35	16:1–34	41, 143
9:15	48	16:1–30	104
10:1–5	46	16:2–34	83
10:1–3	45, 54	16:3–34	53, 84
10:2	54	16:3–28	53, 84
10:4–5	46	16:3–24	104
10:1	41	16:1–7	59
10:16–20	51n56	16:1–2	45, 54

Leviticus (continued)

16:1	41, 55
16:2	55, 56n68, 101, 101n80, 121n57, 122, 122n58, 125n69
16:3	54, 95, 162
16:5–34	99
16:5–20	99
16:5–9	55
16:5–6	54, 55
16:5	44, 54, 55, 58, 95, 162
16:6	38n17, 47n35, 54, 55n63, 58, 95, 163
16:7	58
16:8	54, 58, 59
16:9	58, 58n78, 95, 162
16:10	39n19, 54, 57, 58, 59, 59n81, 60, 61
16:11–19	59
16:11	38n17, 47n35, 54, 55n63, 163
16:13–15	101n80, 122n58, 125n69
16:13	78n13
16:14–15	100, 101, 121, 121n57, 122
16:14	66n101, 70
16:15–26	59
16:15	163
16:16–18	38n17, 47n35
16:16	97, 104
16:17	39n19, 55n63, 61
16:20–21	59
16:20	57
16:21–22	59n81
16:21	57, 59n80, 60n82, 95
16:22	57, 67
16:24	38n17, 40, 47n35, 54
16:26–27	57
16:26	54
16:27	39n19, 44, 45, 46, 61, 163
16:29–32	102
16:29–30	53, 82
16:29	82, 101n80, 122n58
16:30	48n42, 60, 72, 93, 95, 97, 104
16:32–33	38n17, 47n35
16:33	48n42, 55, 60
16:34	39n19, 57, 60, 61, 95
17	60, 61
17:1–4	61
17:1	62
17:5	61
17:6	61
17:7–9	61
17:8–12	41
17:10–11	61
17:10	25, 61
17:11	24, 25, 39n19, 48n42, 61, 62, 62n85, 98, 99
17:12	99
17:13	62
17:14	62
17:16	53, 62
17:21–22	97, 99
18:5	78
19:21	52, 69, 70
19:22	38n17, 47n35, 60, 162
20:20	66
22:9	66
22:11	55n63
23:19	52n56, 162
23:27–32	84n34
24:15–16	41
24:15	66
23:28	39n19
24:10–14	46
24:14	46, 60n82
24:23	46
25:9–10	84n34
25:23–34	118
25:45–55	118
25:47–52	118
26:25	96
26:40	56n68
27:14–15	55n63
27:15–33	118

Numbers

5:1–4	46
5:3	46n34
5:6	41n24
5:7–8	52
5:7	53
5:8	48n42, 101n80, 122n58
6:11	38n17, 43, 47n35, 52n56, 101n80, 122n58

6:14	39n21, 48n39
7	52n56
7:89	101, 121n57, 122, 125n69
8:7–8	52n56
8:12	39n19, 40, 41n22, 52n56, 101n80, 122n58
8:19	101n80, 122n58
8:21	101n80, 122n58
9:13	66
14	97n70
14:1–37	50, 51
14:18	98
15:1–36	50
15:3	40
15:22–29	52n56
15:25	38n17, 47n35, 101n80, 122n58
15:27	49n44
15:28	38n17, 39n19, 39n20, 47n35, 101n80, 122n58
15:32–36	46, 51
16:1–50	50
16:1–35	51
17:11	38n17, 47n35, 101n80, 122n58
17:12	101n80, 122n58
18:1	49, 68
18:22	66
18:32	66
19	50, 51
19:1–2	50
19:2	40
19:3	46, 50
19:4	50
19:5–6	50
19:7	50
19:8–9	50
19:9	51, 51n55, 52n56
19:10–32	50
19:17	52n56
20:1–29	50
20:10–13	51
21:1–35	50
21:4–6	51
22:18	55n63
24:4	113n29
24:13	55n63
25	20, 108n9
25:1–18	51
25:1–9	5089n51
28:22	39n19, 48, 48n39, 101n80, 122n58
28:30	39n19, 101n80, 122n58
29:2	40
29:5	39n19, 48n39, 101n80, 122n58
29:7–11	84n34
29:8	40
29:11	48n40, 101n80, 122n58
29:13	40
29:36	40
31:1–42	50
31:50	39n19, 101n80, 122n58

Deuteronomy

4:15–18	160n71
4:23	160n71
4:25–28	78
4:25	160n71
5:1—27:26	45
5:8	160n71
5:32–33	78
6	108n9, 109, 110
6:22	55n63
7:8	118
8:1	78
9:26	118
11:8–9	78
11:18–25	78
11:28	78
15:12–18	118
15:15	118
21:1–81	97n70
21:22–23	65
24:10	55n63
24:18	118
25:1	69n111, 168n96
25:6	118
27–28	89
27:1—28:62	xii
27:9–26	65
28:1–6 8	89
28:1–14	78, 89
28:15–68	65, 78, 89, 109n15
30:15–16	78
30:16	109n11, 111

Deuteronomy (continued)

30:17–20	78
32	51, 88, 89
32:41	96n68
32:43	38n17, 47n35, 98n68
32:36	88

Joshua

5:2	111

Judges

11:29–40	118
13	41
13:1	41
13:2–14	41
13:15	41
13:16	41
13:20	41
13:22	41

Ruth

3:10—4:12	118
4:1–6	118

1 Samuel

1:21	55n63
2:11	55n63
3:12–13	55n63
7:17	55n63
15:34	55n63
19:5	49n44
24:23	55n63
25:17	55n63

2 Samuel

6:11	55n63
6:20–21	55n63
7:25	55n63
9:9	55n63
11:9–10	55n63
11:13	55n63
11:27	55n63
12:15	55n63
12:17	55n63
12:20	55n63
14:24	55n63

15:4	69n111
15:16	55n63
17:23	55n63
19:12	55n63
19:31	55n63
19:42	55n63
20:3	55n63
21:4	55n63

1 Kings

3:1	55n63
3:14	101n80, 122n58
4:7	55n63
6:5	160n71
7:1	55n63
8:32	69n111, 168n96
9:15	55n63
16:3	55n63
16:7	55n63
20:43	55n63
21:4	55n63
21:29	55n63

2 Kings

2:13	101n80, 122n58
5:1–9	42
5:10	42
5:11–12	42
5:14	42
5:15	42
5:16	42
5:17–18	42
5:17	42
5:18	42
16	43
17:22–23	78
21:3	101n80, 122n57
21:18	55n63
23:26—25:11	78

1 Chronicles

6:34	101n80, 122n58
16:43	55n63
17:23	55n63
23:28	98
28:13	82

2 Chronicles

6:23	69n11
6:25–27	97n69
6:39	97n79
7:14	97n79
8:1	55n63
19:1	55n63
29:15	72
29:24	101n80, 122n58
30:18	101n80, 122n58
33:20	55n63
34:3	72
34:8	72
36:19–20	78

Nehemiah

3:10	55n63
3:23	55n63
3:28–29	55n63
7:3	55n63

Job

1:10	55n63
5:24	49n44
8:5	55n63
20:28	55n63
27:18	55n63
38:20	55n63
38:29	47n35
39:6	55n63

Psalms

5:9	114n36
10:7	114n36
11:7	113n29
14:1–3	114n36
17:31	113n29
36:1	114n36
39:7	162
49:17	55n63
50:6	113, 132
51	84n36
51:9	44
53:1–3	114n36
68:32	96
78:38	48n42
79:9	38n17, 47n35
104:19	113n29
105:20	160n71
105:30	101n80, 122n58
106:11	113n29
106:16–23	20
115:2	113, 132
118:11	113n29
140:3	114n36
142:2	115, 115n39

Proverbs

1:16	114n36
6:31	55n63
7:20	55n63
11:25	55n63
15:27	55n63
16:14	101n80, 122n58
19:5	168n96

Ecclesiates

7:20	114n36

Song of Solomon

8:7	55n63

Isaiah

1:1–26	89n51
1:2	63
1:4	63
1:5–6	65
1:7	168n96
1:10	63
1:11–15	63
1:21	63
2:1–5	63
2:6–22	63
3:1–26	63
3:17	161n73
4:2–6	63
5:1–30	63
5:23	168n96
6:4	66
6:9–13	63n88
7:14	63
8:1–10	63n88
8:11–22	63n89
9:1–7	63

Isaiah (continued)

9:4	152n46
9:8—10:19	63n88
10:10–17	84n86
10:20–4	63n89
11:1–16	63, 63n89
12:1–6	63n89
13:1–22	63n88
13:6–16	109n11
14:1–2	63n89
14:24—21:16	63n88
23:1—25:12	63n88
26:1—27:13	63n89
28:1–13	63n88
28:13	113n29
28:18	47n35
29:1–24	63n88
30:18–33	63n89
31:1–9	63n88
32:1–8	63
32:9–20	63n88
33:1–24	63n89
33:24	53n59
34:1–17	63n88
34:8	109n11
35:1–10	63n89
36:1–22	63n88
40—66	62, 63, 64
40:1—66:24	63n89
40—55	18, 128
40:1—52:12	64n93
40:1–11	63
40:1–5	63
40:1–2	63
40:2	63
40:3	63
40:4	63
40:9	63
40:10	63
40:11	63
41:8–9	64
41:14	63
42:6–7	110, 115n39
43:1	63, 118n45
43:3–4	63
43:8	110n22
43:9	168n96
43:14	63
44:1–2	64
44:1	70
44:21	63, 64
44:22	118n45
44:25	63
45:1–13	63n88
45:4	64
47:1–15	63n88
49:1ff	64
49:6	64, 110, 115n39
49:8–10	64
52:5	111
52:13—53:12	64, 137
52:14	66
52:15	70
53–54	65
53	xi, 33, 35, 36, 62, 64, 64n90, 66, 67, 70–74, 87, 91, 103, 119, 135–37, 139, 184–88
53:1–12	70
53:3	63, 65, 66
53:4–12	53, 66, 69, 70, 120
53:4–6	70, 87
53:4	53n59, 65, 70, 71
53:5	66, 66n102, 67, 68, 71
53:6	67, 68, 70, 72, 137n99
53:7	68, 72
53:8	68, 70, 72, 87
53:9	72
53:10–12	87
53:10	13, 53, 69, 72, 138
53:11–12	69, 70
53:11	68, 69, 73
53:12	53n59, 66, 67, 68, 70, 71, 73, 136–39, 139n105
54:5–6	63
56:1–8	64
56:10	110n22
59:7–8	114n36
59:9–10	110n22
61:1—66:26	64
63:1–6	63n88
63:9	118n45
65:1–16	63n88
65:17–25	70

Jeremiah

5:1	97n70
6:7	65
7:21–23	85n36
10:19–21	65
10:19	65
14	43
18:4	96
22:13	55n63
23:34	55n63
31:31–34	112
32:6–15	118

Lamentations

1:12	65
1:18	65

Ezekiel

14:13	49n44
23:49	66
28:18	66
36–37	112
36:20	111
43	43
43:14–20	101, 101n80, 121n57, 122, 122n58
43:14	125n69
43:17	125n69
43:20	125n69
43:20	101n80
43:22	44, 48, 101n80
43:25–26	48n39
43:26	44
43:27	43
45:15	39n19
45:17	39n19, 101n80
45:25–26	48

Daniel

1–6	75
1:1—2:49	77
1:4	77
1:8–19	77
1:12–19	77
3	75, 75n3, 78, 189
3:1–90 [LXX]	1, 33, 66, 70, 74, 103
3:23	76
3:24–97	75
3:24–90	75, 86, 89n51
3:24–40	75
3:27–40	169
3:24–25	76
3:27–28	77
3:27	76
3:28–90	83
3:28–37	76, 159
3:28–29	87
3:28	76, 77, 79, 150
3:29	76, 150
3:30–31	76
3:32	76, 77
3:33–36	77
3:34–35	77
3:36–37	77
3:36	77
3:37	77, 87
3:38–40	20, 78, 79, 97n71
3:38	78
3:39	79
3:40	79
3:44	133n91
4:2	96
4:34	118
6	75
7:9–11	109n11
11:35 [LXX]	72
11:35	18, 128
12:1–12	18, 128

Hosea

6:6	84n36

Joel

2	112
2:1–2	109n11
2:32 [LXX]	112n28

Amos

5:21–22	84n36
7:2	97
9:1	125n69

Micah

6:4	118n45
6:6–8	84n36
7:6	55n63
7:9	96n68
7:18	53n59

Zephaniah

1:14—2:3	109n11
1:17	110n22
3:8	109n11

Haggai

1–2	83n25

Malachi

4:1	109n11

APOCRYPHA

Tobit

1:3	109n15
1:4	86
1:5–18	109n15
4:10–11	86, 109n12
12:9	86

Judith

14:10	111

Wisdom of Solomon

1:1	103n89
1:8	96n68
2:11	103n89
2:12–16	103n89
2:17–20	103n89
2:19	103n89
2:20	103n89
3:1–6	89n51
3:1	103n89
3:2–3	103n89
3:6	103n89
4:16	163n81, 168n96
11:1—16:1	107, 108n9
12:12	168n96
12:17	133n91
14:16	103n89
14:31	96n68
15:2–3	110
16:24	103n89
18:4	110, 115n39
18:11	96n68

Sirach

1:22	168n96
3:3	101n80, 122n58
3:30	101n80, 122n58
5:6	101n80, 122n58
7:3	168n96
9:12	168n96
10:29	168n96
11:26	109n15
13:22	168n96
17:11	110
17:23	109n15
20:28	101n80, 122n58
23:11	168n96
24:27	110, 115n39
26:29	168n96
28:5	101n80, 122n58
31:5	168n96
33:1	117
34:3	160n71
34:19	101n80, 122n58
34:18	78n13
35:5	78n13
38:30	72
42:2	168n96
45:5	110, 115n40
45:16	78n13, 101n80, 122n58
46:19	168n96
46:23	101n80, 122n58
50:13	78n13
50:17–19	54n61, 85

Baruch

3:36	110
4:1–4	110n21
4:1–2	109n15
4:4	108n9, 110, 115

2 Esdras

3:7–8	173
20:34	101n80

Letter of Jeremiah

1:25	133n91

Song of the Three Young Men

See LXX Daniel 3:24–90

Susanna

1:41	163n81, 168n96
1:48	163n81, 168n96
1:53	163n81, 168n96

1 Maccabees

1–2	82, 88
1	80, 89, 108n9
1:1–64	81, 96, 104
1:1–3	110n19
1:1	80n17
1:2	88
1:10–64	82
1:11–15	78, 80, 84n33, 88
1:16–19	80
1:20–24	80
1:25–28	81
1:29–50	80
1:29–32	81
1:33–50	81
1:36—2:13	81n19
1:41–64	81, 98
1:41–59	86, 104
1:41–47	82
1:41–45	78, 84n33
1:41–42	80
1:41	80
1:43	82n19
1:44	80
1:45–47	80
1:48–49	80
1:48	111
1:50	80
1:51	82
1:52	80
1:54–61	80
1:60–61	111
1:60	96
1:62—2:28	80
1:64	93n64
2:19–22	82
2:20–22	82
2:22	82
2:46	111
3:8	93n64
3:58–59	78, 84n33
4:36–59	85
4:36–58	83, 86
4:36	72
4:41–59	83
4:54–60	78, 84n33
5:32	96n68

2 Maccabees

1:1—8:5	163
1:5	17, 81, 87, 88, 92–94, 98, 151, 157, 158
1:7–8	92
1:8	135
1:10—2:18	85
1:18	98
1:26	96n68
1:28	92
2:8	135
2:16	98
2:17–18	92, 152, 157
2:17	182
2:18	93, 94
2:19—15:37	92
2:19–22	92, 157
2:19	82n19, 98
2:22	82n19
2:23	92
3:12	135
3:22	135
3:32	96
4:1—6:31	96
4:11	7, 8n26, 152, 153n50
4:16–17	96
5:1—8:5	88, 89, 92–95, 156
5:1—7:38	89
5:1–11	93
5:4	81, 95, 98
5:8	168n96
5:11–16	81

Ancient Document Index 209

2 Maccabees (continued)

5:11–14	93
5:15–20	78, 84n33
5:15–16	89
5:17–18	93, 97, 182
5:17	7, 87, 152, 182
5:18	88
5:20—8:5	94
5:20—7:32	88, 100n78
5:20	92–94, 151, 157
5:21—6:11	93
5:27—6:6	89
5:35	81, 95, 98
6	16, 32, 86, 88, 126
6:1–5	81
6:4–6	83, 86
6:6	81
6:10	111
6:12—7:38	104, 158
6:12–17	89, 93, 96, 158
6:12–16	88, 94
6:13–16	93
6:14–15	182
6:15	97
6:18—8:2	93
6:18—7:42	93, 94, 157
6:18	95, 98
6:24–31	91
6:28	91
6:29	97
6:31	91
7	16, 88, 126
7:1	86
7:2–41	87
7:3–6	151, 169
7:6	88
7:7—8:3	169
7:7	151, 169
7:9	139, 151, 169
7:16	89
7:18	87, 87n48, 104, 150, 182
7:23	151, 169
7:28–29	87, 159
7:29	92, 151, 169
7:30–38	13
7:30–32	89
7:30	89
7:31	89
7:32—8:5	157, 161
7:32–38	14, 20, 66, 70, 87n45, 88, 90, 90n54, 94, 95, 98, 104, 108n9, 132, 135, 139, 158, 159, 159n67, 163, 164, 169, 182
7:32–33	6, 9, 139, 153, 154
7:32	87, 87n46, 89, 90, 95–97, 104, 150, 151, 169, 182, 183
7:33	6, 83, 87, 88, 93, 151, 153, 156, 157, 158, 169
7:37–38	87, 90, 169
7:37	90, 94, 95, 151, 169
7:38	89, 90–92, 92n62, 95, 152, 156
8	94
8:1–5	91, 92
8:1–4	94
8:2–3	94
8:3	135
8:4–5	92n62
8:4	94
8:5–7	93
8:5	93, 104, 182
8:11	96, 135n95
8:13	96, 135n95
8:17	7
8:29	17, 87, 88, 151, 157, 158
9:8	133n91
10:4	87n46
10:5	98
10:45	182
12:16	135
12:39–42	104
12:42	96
14:18	135
14:45	135
15:11	92
15:32–37	93, 157
15:37	93, 94

3 Maccabees

4:14	82

4 Maccabees

1:1—6:29	163
1:2	135

1:4	135
1:6	135
1:11	81n19, 97n71
2:6	135
4:7	135
4:13	96, 135
4:21	96, 135
4:19–20	96
4:20	81
4:21	96, 104, 135
4:23	81, 96
5:1—6:30	81
5:4—6:40	96
5:4	98, 98n74
5:6	95
5:19	97
5:24	135
5:35	98, 98n74
6	88, 89, 95
6:1–8	95
6:6	95, 135
6:18–21	91
6:18	98
6:27–29	13, 15
6:28–29	18, 66, 70, 96, 98, 99, 100n78, 102–4, 108n9, 119, 120, 123, 132, 135, 139, 151, 157, 159, 161, 163, 164, 169, 182, 183
6:28	90, 95, 96, 97n70,
6:29	95, 96, 98, 99, 119, 120
7:6	98
7:8	100n78, 104, 135
7:19	135
8:14	96, 97n70, 135
8:22	96, 135
9:9	96
9:15	96
9:20	135
9:22	92
9:23	91
9:24	97n70
9:32	96
10:3	91
10:8	135
10:16	91
11:3	96, 135
11:15	91
12:4–16	97
12:12	96, 135
12:16	91
12:17	97
13:8–18	91
13:13	151, 170
13:20	135
16:15	92
17	129
17:10	100
17:19–20	100
17:20–21	98
17:20	102
17:21–22	3, 15, 17, 19, 70, 94–97, 99, 100, 101n80, 103, 104, 108n9, 120, 122n58, 123, 132, 135, 139, 151, 157, 159, 161, 163, 164, 169, 170, 182
17:21	97–99, 100n78, 119, 120
17:22	4, 5, 13, 81n19, 96, 99, 100, 100n79, 101, 102, 119, 120, 122–24, 125, 128, 152
18:3–5	151, 170
18:4	100n78
18:22	96, 135

PSEUDEPIGRAPHA

2 Baruch (Syriac Apocalypse)

14:12	109n12
44:2–15	110
48:22–24	110
54:15	175
54:19	175

1 Enoch

90:20–27	109n11
105:1	110

4 Ezra

3:21	173
6:5	109n12
6:7—9:25	109n15
7:22–24	114

4 Ezra (continued)

7:77	109n12
8:33	109n12

Jubilees

3:17–32	174
5:10–16	109n11
5:17–18	83n29
14:10	115
15:1–34	111, 115m39
22:15–23	115n39
22:16–23	107, 108n9, 109, 110
22:16–18	78, 83, 84, 104
30:21–22	109n15
34:18–19	53n61, 83n29, 85

Liber Antiquitatum Biblicarum

13:6	83n29

Letter of Aristeas

139	83, 84, 115n39, 115n40
142	83, 108n9, 115n39, 115n40
152–53	78n11, 84, 104, 108n9

Psalms of Solomon

2:2	78n11, 84n33, 104
3:8	83n29
4:2	163n81
8:1–34	113
8:26	168n96
9:1–11	113
9:3–5	109n12
14:2–3	109n15
14:2	115n40
14:10	109n15
15:4	109n15
15:8	109n11
15:16	109n15
17:1	110
17:22	72
18:5	72

Sibylline Oracles

3.194–95	110
3.195	115n39
3.595–606	107

Testament of the Twelve Patriarchs

Testament of Asher

2:1–10	109
6:1–5	109

Testament of Dan

5:1	109

Testament of Joseph

11:1	109

Testament of Judah

13:1–5	109
26:1	109

Testament of Issachar

5:1–2	109

Testament of Levi

14:1–8	111
14:3–8	110
14:4	108n9
14:5–6	108n9
14:6	108n9
14:7	108n9
14:8	108n9

Testament of Naphtali

3:3	108n9
4:1–2	108n9

NEW TESTAMENT

Matthew

12:41–42	168n96
12:41	163
13:13	172n6
20:18	163, 168n96
23	108n9
24:4	172n6
27:3	163, 168n96
27:32–44	181n21

Ancient Document Index   213

Mark

1:44	98
10:33	163, 168n96
12:24	172
14:64	163, 168n96
15:21–32	181

Luke

2:22	98
5:14	98
11:31	163, 168n96
21:28	117n42
23:26-43	181n21

John

2:6	98
3:25	98
5:16	172n6
5:18	172n6
8:47	172n6
10:17	172n6
12:18	172n6
12:39	172n6
19:17–27	181n21

Acts

7:8	174n8
7:33	175n11
7:53—8:3	xiii
7:58—8:4	xii
9:1–19	xiii
9:1–2	xii
13:38–39	168n96
19:38	168n96
19:40	168n96
21:27–30	86
21:27	78n11, 83, 84n33, 104
23:28–29	168n96
26:2	168n96
26:7	168n96
27:44	174n8

Romans

1–4	107n5
1:1–17	107, 158
1:5	133
1:10–11	106
1:13	120n53
1:15	105
1:16—8:39	119
1:16—4:25	158
1:16-17	115, 134, 158
1:16	106, 133
1:17	106, 133
1:18—15:13	134
1:18—11:36	132
1:18—7:25	165
1:18—4:25	158
1:18—3:31	123
1:18—3:26	121, 128, 134
1:18—3:20	105, 106, 114, 115, 115n38, 116, 131, 134, 147, 149, 177
1:18—3:8	114
1:18–32	107, 113, 114
1:18–31	110
1:18–20	106
1:18	106, 106n2, 149, 150
1:19–32	106
1:20	107
1:21–23	106
1:21	106
1:23	160, 160n71
1:24–32	107
1:24–31	107, 108n9
1:24	106, 106n3, 108n9, 166
1:25	106n3
1:26–31	108n9
1:26–27	108n9
1:26	106, 106n3, 108n9, 166, 172
1:27	106n3
1:28	106, 106n3, 166
1:29–31	106n3, 108n9
1:29–30	108n9
1:29	108n9
1:32	106n3, 108n9, 112n28
2:1—3:20	107, 113
2:1—3:8	107, 109, 113
2:1—3:4	113
2:1–29	114
2:1–16	108n10
2:1–10	107, 108
2:1–3	107
2:1	107, 108n9, 163, 168n96

Romans *(continued)*

2:2	108
2:3	108
2:4	108
2:5—3:20	109
2:5–16	106n2
2:5–10	147
2:5	109
2:6–16	107
2:6–10	109n15, 165
2:6	115
2:7–10	149, 150
2:7	109n15
2:8–9	109n15
2:9–10	107, 109
2:10	108, 109n15
2:11	108, 109
2:12–19	109
2:12–16	110, 132
2:13–15	110
2:13	109, 109n15, 115, 132, 148, 168n96
2:16	110
2:17–18	107, 107n5
2:17	110
2:18	110
2:19	110
2:20	110
2:21–24	110
2:21–23	111
2:23	111
2:24	111
2:25–29	111, 112n28
2:26	111, 112n28
2:27	112, 112n28
2:28–29	112
2:28	115n39
2:29	112, 112n8
3–4	16
3:1–30	130
3:1–18	114
3:1–8	113
3:1–4	132
3:1–2	107, 107n5
3:1	113, 113n32, 131
3:2	113, 131
3:3–6	132, 134
3:3	113
3:4–17	132
3:4–8	113
3:4	113, 131, 132, 168n96
3:5	106n2, 133
3:7	133
3:8	113n32
3:9–20	107, 113
3:9–18	107n5
3:9	107, 107n5, 113, 113n32, 114
3:10–18	113, 114
3:10–12	114n36
3:13	114n36
3:14	114n36
3:15–17	114n36
3:18	114n36
3:19–20	114, 115
3:19	114n37, 115
3:20–31	131
3:20–24	135
3:20–22	134
3:20–21	132
3:20	115, 116, 130, 132, 148, 158, 165, 168n96
3:21—6:23	188
3:21—4:25	33, 105, 114, 130, 136, 140, 158, 177n18, 182
3:21–30	116
3:21–26	15, 16, 32, 33, 116, 126–129, 132, 135, 147n36, 186
3:21–25	116
3:21–24	133
3:21–22	116, 121, 130, 133, 134, 150n43
3:22	130, 135
3:23–25	120, 121
3:23–24	116
3:23	165, 174, 175
3:24–26	116
3:24–25	116, 118–21, 159
3:24	116, 117, 119–21, 121n54, 121n55, 148, 150n43, 168n96
3:25–26	3, 15, 116, 124, 127–129, 132, 133, 135, 164
3:25	ix, xiiin12, 3, 3n9, 4, 4n10, 5, 13, 14n62,

Ancient Document Index 215

	16–21, 32, 100–102, 116–18, 119, 119n49, 120, 121, 121n54, 122–28, 128n85, 129, 130, 132, 133, 134, 135	5:6	142, 145, 145n24, 146, 147, 148, 149, 151, 157
		5:7	145, 146, 147, 150
		5:8–11	147, 150, 156
		5:8–10	22, 142, 143, 144n22, 148
3:26–31	130	5:8–9	149
3:26	116, 124, 130, 133, 134, 168n96	5:8	22, 142, 144, 145, 146, 147, 148, 151, 157, 188
3:27–31	135, 135n93	5:9–11	6, 147, 148, 153, 158, 159
3:27	116, 130	5:9–10	146, 148, 148n38, 149, 150–52, 155, 186
3:28–30	116		
3:28	130, 168n96	5:9	106n2, 132, 142, 144, 148, 149, 150, 152, 157, 168n96
3:29–30	118, 188		
3:30–31	130		
3:30	168n96	5:10–11	8, 9, 144, 153, 155, 157, 158
4:1–25	130, 132		
4:1–2	131	5:10	142, 151, 157
4:2–25	131	5:11	151
4:2	168n96	5:11–21	155
4:3	131	5:12—8:11	177
4:5	131, 168n96	5:12—8:4	161, 165
4:13–17	131	5:12—8:3	161
4:15	106n2, 115, 165	5:12—6:23	33, 171, 182, 183
4:18–19	131	5:12–21	146n30, 161, 164, 165, 171–73, 175, 176, 177, 177n18, 179n20, 180, 180n20, 181, 185
4:20	131		
4:23–24	131		
4:24–25	135–39		
4:24	136	5:12–20	173
4:25	18, 71, 136, 137, 137n100, 138, 138n104, 139, 148, 169	5:12–19	177
		5:12–16	176
		5:12	172–76, 180n20
5:1—15:21	158	5:13–17	172
5:1—11:36	134	5:13–14	115, 175
5:1–11	172	5:13	160n71
5:1–10	149	5:14	160, 173, 180n20
5:1–5	141	5:15–21	180n20
5:1	132, 144, 148, 150n43, 152, 157, 168n96	5:15–17	176
		5:15–16	173
5:5–6	21	5:15	173, 175, 180n20
5:5	141	5:16–21	175
5:6–21	187	5:16	173, 175, 176, 176n15, 180n20
5:6–11	33, 96n68, 138n104, 141, 145, 146, 146n30, 150n43, 151, 156, 159, 170, 177, 182		
		5:17–21	176
		5:17	173, 175, 177, 179n20, 180n20
5:6–10	185, 186	5:18–21	172, 179
5:6–8	27, 28, 144	5:18–19	173
5:6–7	146n30	5:18	173, 180n20, 186

Romans *(continued)*

5:19	173, 176, 180n20
5:20–21	177, 178
5:20	178
6	180n20
6:1—8:11	118
6:1–23	177, 178, 179, 180n20
6:1	178, 181
6:2–5	178
6:2–4	180n20, 181
6:2	181, 182
6:3	178, 181, 182
6:4	181, 182
6:5	160, 160n71, 178, 181, 182
6:6	31, 180n20, 181, 182
6:7–23	181
6:7–10	182
6:7	182
6:8	182
6:9–11	182
6:9–10	31
6:9	180n20
6:11	182
6:12	181, 182
6:13	182
6:14	182
6:15–16	182
6:15	181
6:17–18	182
6:18	182
6:19–21	182
6:22	182
7:1—8:11	159
7:1—8:10	161
7:1—8:4	164
7:1—8:3	168
7	162
7:1–25	159
7:1–24	160
7:1–23	165
7:6	112n28
7:7—8:3	151
7:7–25	165
7:7–23	115
7:18	181
7:23	179n20
7:25—8:3	160
7:25	181
7:33	158
8:1–4	112, 112n28, 141, 159, 170, 182
8:1–3	164, 166
8:1	159, 159n69, 163
8:2–3	112n28, 166
8:2	159
8:3	33, 159, 160, 161, 161n75, 162, 163, 164–66, 168, 169, 171n1, 185
8:4	112n28, 114, 165
8:12–25	166
8:23	117n42
8:28–34	168
8:28–30	166
8:29–30	166
8:29	158
8:30	168n96
8:31–34	33, 141, 166–70, 182
8:31	167, 168
8:32	96n68, 138, 167–69
8:33–34	167, 168, 169
8:33	168, 168n96
8:34	163, 167, 168, 168n96
9–11	112n28, 113
9:1—11:36	113, 114
9:30—10:3	112n28
10:3	112n28
10:4–5	132
10:4	113
10:5–13	112n28
10:5	187
10:8–9	112n28
10:13	112n28
10:14—11:36	112n28
11:15	152
11:26	174n8
12:1—15:21	148n38
12:1—15:13	134
13:6	172
14:9	31
14:23	163, 168n96
15:2	133
15:22–24	158
15:24	106
15:28	158

1 Corinthians

1:13	29, 96n68
1:17	29
1:18	23, 28, 143
1:23	29
1:28	182n22
1:30	117n42
2:2	29
2:6	182n22
2:8	28
4:4	168n96
5:7	18
5:8	156n64
6:9	108n9
6:10	108n9
6:13	182n22
6:19	31
6:20	117n42
7:11	151
7:23	117n42
10:1–22	108n9
11:23	18
11:24	96n68
11:28	174n8
11:32	163
13:8	182n22
13:10	182n22
13:11	182n22
14:25	174n8
15	177
15:1–58	176
15:3	8n28, 18, 28, 96n68, 153n52
15:11	174n8
15:20	176
15:21–22	176
15:21	176
15:23–58	177
15:24	182n22
15:26	182n22

2 Corinthians

3:7	182n22
5:4	175
5:11–21	9, 155
5:11	151
5:14–15	25, 31, 96
5:14	8, 26, 153n52
5:15	26, 31
5:18–21	6, 14, 142, 153, 156
5:18–20	7–10, 22, 142, 151, 152, 155, 156, 159n67
5:18–19	152
5:18	10, 23, 143
5:19	10, 23, 26, 143
5:20	8, 10, 144n22, 153, 155
5:21	23n106, 27, 31, 96, 161
8:9	31
8:24	133, 133n90

Galatians

1:4	31, 96n68
2:11–14	18
2:11–12	18
2:16–17	168n96
2:16	30
2:20	24, 145n22
3:6—4:5	30
3:8	168n96
3:10–14	24, 145n22
3:10–13	5
3:10	30
3:11	168n96
3:13	4, 5, 10, 10n40, 11, 30, 117n42
3:17	182n22
3:19	165
3:22	30
3:24	168n96
4:3	30
4:5–6	161
5:2–4	111
5:4	168n96, 182n22
5:11	182n22
6:2	174n8

Ephesians

1:3–14	179n20
1:7	117n42, 120
1:15–22	179n20
2:1–10	179n20
2:3	106n2
2:11–22	179n20
2:11–12	112
2:15	182n22
4:1—6:20	179n20

Ephesians *(continued)*

4:17—5:8	108n9
4:17–19	180n20
4:17	179n20
4:18–20	179n20
4:18	179n20
4:19	179n20
4:20–21	179n20
4:21	179n20
4:22–24	179n20
4:22	179n20
4:24	179n20, 180n20
5:6	106n2
6:13	172n6

Philippians

2:5–9	161
2:7	160, 161
3:12	175
4:10	175

Colossians

1:3–4	180n20
1:13–14	180n20
1:14	117n42
2:4	180n20
2:5	180n20
2:6—4:1	180n20
2:8	180n20
2:12–13	180n20
2:12	180n20
2:20	180n20
3:1–10	180n20
3:1–4	180n20
3:1	180n20
3:3	180n20
3:5–17	180n20
3:5–9	180n20
3:5	108n9, 180n20
3:6	106n2
3:9–10	180n20
3:9	179n20, 180n20
3:12–17	180n20
3:16–19	180n20
4:5	117n42

1 Thessalonians

1:10	106n2
2:13	172n6
2:16	106n2
3:7–8	172n6
4:7	174n8
5:9–10	23, 31, 144n22
5:9	106n2
5:10	96n68

2 Thessalonians

2:8	182n22
2:11	172n6

2 Timothy

1:10	182n22

Titus

2:14	117n42
3:7	168n96

Philemon

15	172n6

Hebrews

2:1	172n6
2:14	182n22
6:15	174n8
9:5	17, 117n42, 172n6
11:7	163, 168n96
11:35	117n42

James

2:12	174n8
2:21	168n96
2:25	168n96

2 Peter

1:9	98
2:6	163, 163n96

1 John

3:1	172n6

Revelation

9:17   174n8

DEAD SEA SCROLLS

Cario Genizah copy of *Damascus Document*

4:20	78n11, 84n33
5:6–9	78n11, 84n33
5:13–17	114
20	113

Thanksgiving Hymns

2:9	110, 115n39
7	113
9	113
9:14–16	115n39
14	113

War Scroll

1:1	110
1:7	110
1:11	110
1:13–15	110

Pesher Habbakuk

7:4–5	110

Rule of the Community

1–3	98
1:6–11	89
1:9	110
2:16	110
3:4	53
3:13	110, 115n39
3:24–25	110
10	98

JOSEPHUS

Jewish Antiquities

1.129	161n73
1.324	161n73
5.137	158n67
6.143	158n67
6.353	158n67
6.5.3.302–4	181n21
7.184	158n67
8.195	161n73
9.240	134
11.195	158n67
11.236	134
12.27	118n48
12.316–26	85
13.257–58	111
14.278	158n67
15.136	7, 152
15.5.417	78n11, 84n33
16.182	122, 185

Against Apion

2.24.193	83n26, 86
2.291–95	110
2.293	115n39

Jewish War

2.14.9	181n21

PHILO

De Abrahamo

98	110, 115n39

De cherubim

1:25	123, 125

De decalogo

1:87	158n67

Quod deterius potiori insidari soleat

1:168	134

De ebrietate

1:208	157n67

In Flaccum

6:36–39	181n21

In Flaccum (continued)
10:75   181n21

De fuga et inventione
1:100   123, 125
1:101   123, 125

Quis rerum divinarum heres sit
1:166   123, 125

Legum Allegoriae III
3:134   158n67

Legatio ad Gaium
306   83n29, 85
308   86

De migratione Abrahami
1:48–49   161

De vita Mosis
1:149   110, 115n39
2:23–24   83n29
2:24   85
2:95   123, 125
2:97   123, 125

De mutatione nominum
1:233   43

De opificio mundi
1:120   161n73

De praemiis et poenis
1:143   134
1:145   134

De somniis
1:216–217   85

De specialibus legibus
1:11.67–69   81, 83n25, 86
1:186   85n39

1:193–203   83n29
2:193–94   82
2:196–99   85
2:196   54n61, 85
2:203   85n39
7:431   85n39

GRECO-ROMAN WRITINGS

Aelius Aristidies
Orataions
3.344   8, 152

Dionysius of Halicarnassus
Atiquitates romanae
2.45.6   7, 8n26, 152, 153n50
3.9.3.   7, 8n26, 152, 153n50
3.50.4   7, 8n26, 152, 153n50
5.21.1   7, 8n26, 152, 153n50
5.31.1–2   7, 8n26, 152, 153n50
5.62.1   7, 8n26, 152, 153n50
6.67.2   7, 8n26, 152, 153n50
6.88.2   7, 8n26, 152, 153n50

Euripidies
Alcestis
1–36   147n34

Heraclidae
501–50   147n34

Hecuba
38–41   147n34
367–78   147n34
484–582   147n34

Iphegenia aulidensis
1553–56   147n34

Iphegenia taurica
3–24   147n34

Phoenissae
968–75   147n34

Horace

Carmina

3.19.2   147n34

Livy

History of Rome

8.9.9–10   147n34
8.9.13–14   147n34
10.28.18   147n34

Plato

Menexenus

237a   147n34

Symposium

179b   147n34

Plutarch

Pelopidas

26.2   8

Moralia

156f   8, 152

Seutonius

Domitianus

11   181n21

Papyri

P.Giss

17.13–14   8, 152

P.Mich

8.502.7–8   8, 152

www.ingramcontent.com/pod-product-compliance
Lightning Source LLC
Chambersburg PA
CBHW051055230426
43667CB00013B/2311